Springer Series in Design and

Volume 13

Editor-in-Chief

Francesca Tosi, University of Florence, Florence, Italy

Series Editors

Claudio Germak, Politecnico di Torino, Turin, Italy

Francesco Zurlo, Politecnico di Milano, Milan, Italy

Zhi Jinyi, Southwest Jiaotong University, Chengdu, China

Marilaine Pozzatti Amadori, Universidade Federal de Santa Maria, Santa Maria, Rio Grande do Sul, Brazil

Maurizio Caon, University of Applied Sciences and Arts, Fribourg, Switzerland

Springer Series in Design and Innovation (SSDI) publishes books on innovation and the latest developments in the fields of Product Design, Interior Design and Communication Design, with particular emphasis on technological and formal innovation, and on the application of digital technologies and new materials. The series explores all aspects of design, e.g. Human-Centered Design/User Experience, Service Design, and Design Thinking, which provide transversal and innovative approaches oriented on the involvement of people throughout the design development process. In addition, it covers emerging areas of research that may represent essential opportunities for economic and social development.

In fields ranging from the humanities to engineering and architecture, design is increasingly being recognized as a key means of bringing ideas to the market by transforming them into user-friendly and appealing products or services. Moreover, it provides a variety of methodologies, tools and techniques that can be used at different stages of the innovation process to enhance the value of new products and services.

The series' scope includes monographs, professional books, advanced textbooks, selected contributions from specialized conferences and workshops, and outstanding Ph.D. theses.

Keywords: Product and System Innovation; Product design; Interior design; Communication Design; Human-Centered Design/User Experience; Service Design; Design Thinking; Digital Innovation; Innovation of Materials.

How to submit proposals

Proposals must include: title, keywords, presentation (max 10,000 characters), table of contents, chapter abstracts, editors'/authors' CV.

In case of proceedings, chairmen/editors are requested to submit the link to conference website (incl. relevant information such as committee members, topics, key dates, keynote speakers, information about the reviewing process, etc.), and approx. number of papers.

Proposals must be sent to: series editor Prof. Francesca Tosi (francesca.tosi@unifi.it) and/or publishing editor Mr. Pierpaolo Riva (pierpaolo.riva@springer.com).

More information about this series at http://www.springer.com/series/16270

Özge Cordan · Demet Arslan Dinçay ·
Çağıl Yurdakul Toker · Elif Belkıs Öksüz ·
Sena Semizoğlu
Editors

Game + Design Education

Proceedings of PUDCAD 2020

Springer

Editors
Özge Cordan
Department of Interior Architecture
Istanbul Technical University
Istanbul, Turkey

Demet Arslan Dinçay
Department of Interior Architecture
Istanbul Technical University
Istanbul, Turkey

Çağıl Yurdakul Toker
Department of Interior Design
Raffles College of Higher Education
Singapore, Singapore

Elif Belkıs Öksüz
Department of Interior Architecture
and Environmental Design
Nişantaşı University
Istanbul, Turkey

Sena Semizoğlu
Department of Industrial Design
Istanbul Technical University
Istanbul, Turkey

ISSN 2661-8184   ISSN 2661-8192 (electronic)
Springer Series in Design and Innovation
ISBN 978-3-030-65062-9   ISBN 978-3-030-65060-5 (eBook)
https://doi.org/10.1007/978-3-030-65060-5

© The Editor(s) (if applicable) and The Author(s), under exclusive license to Springer Nature Switzerland AG 2021
This work is subject to copyright. All rights are solely and exclusively licensed by the Publisher, whether the whole or part of the material is concerned, specifically the rights of translation, reprinting, reuse of illustrations, recitation, broadcasting, reproduction on microfilms or in any other physical way, and transmission or information storage and retrieval, electronic adaptation, computer software, or by similar or dissimilar methodology now known or hereafter developed.
The use of general descriptive names, registered names, trademarks, service marks, etc. in this publication does not imply, even in the absence of a specific statement, that such names are exempt from the relevant protective laws and regulations and therefore free for general use.
The publisher, the authors and the editors are safe to assume that the advice and information in this book are believed to be true and accurate at the date of publication. Neither the publisher nor the authors or the editors give a warranty, expressed or implied, with respect to the material contained herein or for any errors or omissions that may have been made. The publisher remains neutral with regard to jurisdictional claims in published maps and institutional affiliations.

This Springer imprint is published by the registered company Springer Nature Switzerland AG
The registered company address is: Gewerbestrasse 11, 6330 Cham, Switzerland

Preface

Project PUDCAD stands for *Practicing Universal Design Principles in Design Education through a Cad-Based Game*, and it is representing one of the foremost priorities of European commission: applying the inclusion and efficient accessibility for people with disabilities into everyday life.

The project was designed to work towards a major purpose through a minor addition in design education between September 2017 and 2020. PUDCAD deals with undergraduate design education to trigger the awareness of accessibility and let future designers and architects to develop accessible and innovative design ideas. It involves a design game on a CAD-based platform, allowing students to learn about basic and advanced universal design principles and train them with an entertaining context.

Istanbul Technical University proudly coordinated this project for 3 years. We developed this project with our partner universities and NGOs; Bahçeşehir University, İstanbul, Turkey; Institute of Design and Fine Arts, Lahti, Finland; Politecnico di Milano, Milano, Italy; University of Florence, Florence, Italy; University of Applied Science and Arts, Detmolder, Germany; The Association for Well-being of Children with Cerebral Palsy, Ankara, Turkey; and The Occupational Therapy Association of Turkey, Ankara, Turkey. In this term, we made lots of collaborations such as international and local workshops and conferences with our project partners to develop the main outputs of the project. We would like to thank to all of our partners for their valuable contributions. We would like to extend our thanks to the Rectorate of ITU and EU National Agency for their support in the administering works of the project and also special thanks to Efe Can Arslan. He and his friends, as brilliant young people with cerebral palsy, became the muses of this project.

As part of PUDCAD Project, the "PUDCAD Universal Design Practice Conference: Game + Design Education" international conference (E5) was organized by ITU-PUDCAD Team between 24 and 26 June 2020. Due to the global pandemic of COVID-19, the conference was held online through zoom. The conference, which was focused on the dissemination and promotion of the developed game and pre-launching of E-learning courses of the PUDCAD Project, aimed to open up to discussions the studies regarding the conference topics as "Universal Design", "Game and Design Studies" and "E-Learning in Design Studies".

Under these three main topics, the 33 papers under nine sessions were presented in three days. We would like to thank Hülya Kayıhan, Gonca Bumin, Güven Çatak, Birgül Çolakoğlu, Çetin Tüker, Barbaros Bostan, Çakır Aker, Veli-Pekka Räty and Aslıhan Ünlü Tavil for chairing the sessions in the specified order; "Universal Design and Education", "Universal Design and User Experience", "Games for Change", "Game Design Experiment", "Virtual Reality Experiment I", "Virtual Reality Experiment II", "Playful Experience Design", "Playful Spaces and Interfaces" and "Gamification and E-Learning in Design".

Besides, we hosted five keynote speakers from different disciplines and from a different expertise in each day. In the first day, Fiemmetta Costa from PUDCAD Partner University POLIMI spoke about "The Principles of Universal Design in PUDCAD Project Development" and Güven Çatak and Çetin Tüker from PUDCAD Partner University BAU introduced the PUDCAD Game in their speech about "Developing a CAD-Enriched Empathy Experience for Universal Design Principles: Journey of the PUDCAD Game". In the second day, Christopher Holmgård, who is co-owner of Die Gute Fabrik, spoke about "AI (eyay) Personas for Designing, Testing, and Optimizing Games" and Dylan Yamada Rice, from Royal College of Art, gave her speech about "Children and VR" sequentially. In the third day, Francesca Tossi as PUDCAD Partner University, UNIFI, gave her speech about "Asking Users: Questionnaires and Interviews as Indirect Observation Tools in Human-Centred Design Approach".

We believed that the "PUDCAD Universal Design Practice Conference: Game + Design Education Conference" has contributed to the creation of a discussion platform for academicians, students, relevant stakeholders and professionals from different areas of expertise for future research inquiries and relationships. Furthermore, we hope that the 32 studies presented at the conference and included in the proceedings book contribute to widen our perspectives in all senses.

Istanbul, Turkey	Özge Cordan
Istanbul, Turkey	Demet Arslan Dinçay
Singapore, Singapore	Çağıl Yurdakul Toker
Istanbul, Turkey	Elif Belkıs Öksüz
Istanbul, Turkey	Sena Semizoğlu

Contents

Asking Users. Questionnaires as Indirect Observation Tools in Human-Centred Design Approach. Application Cases 1
Francesca Tosi, Antonella Serra, Alessia Brischetto, and Giovanna Nichilò

Universal Design and Education

An Educational Path on Universal Design. Video Games as Learning Tools 21
Giorgio Buratti, Fiammetta Costa, and Michela Rossi

Evaluation of Playgrounds in Terms of Universal Design: İzmir, Karşıyaka Coast After İzmir Deniz Project 35
Eda Paykoç, Gülnur Ballice, and Gizem Güler

Effects of Educational Policies on Design of Inclusive Schools: SERÇEV Case 53
Simge Gülbahar and Özge Cordan

A Transdisciplinary Approach to Accessibility for Novice Designers' Education of Inclusive Design 65
Elif Belkıs Öksüz, Demet Arslan Dinçay, Özge Cordan, Çağıl Yurdakul Toker, and Sena Semizoğlu

Universal Design and User Experience

Handicap as a Design Catalyst 77
Ulrich Nether and Johanna Julia Dorf

Relationship Between Quality of Life with Physical Fitness and Home Environmental Factor Among Elderly Individuals 91
Gökçen Akyürek, Esra Alan Öztürk, and Gonca Bumin

Investigation of the Relationship Between Activity Performance in the School Settings and Occupational Performance of High School Students with Cerebral Palsy 101
Gökçen Akyürek, Gonca Bumin, Meral Huri, Hülya Kayıhan, and Süheyla Gürkan

Heuristics in Design for Sustainable Behavior Change 109
Mirja Kalviainen

Games for Change

Improving Awareness and Empathy with Video Games: A Qualitative Analysis Study of PUDCAD Game 121
Cetin Tuker and Güven Çatak

Using Board Games as a Method for Improving Awareness and Empathy in Inclusive Design: PUDCAD Game Case Study 133
Poyraz Özer and Güven Çatak

Raising Awareness Through Games: The Influence of a Trolling Game on Perception of Toxic Behavior 143
Gökçe Komaç and Kürşat Çağıltay

Game Design Experiment

Using Mathematical Models in Game Design: A Survival Mechanics Case 157
Kutay Tinç and Reyhan Eren

The Impact of Human-Centered Design of Game Mechanics on Feelings of Belonging 167
Gina Al Halabi, Kutay Tinç, and Ertuğrul Süngü

Virtual Reality Experiment

Design Process of a VR Sports Games Trilogy for Paraplegic Players: VR4Inclusion Case Study 181
Semih Bertuğ Benim, Mehmet İlker Berkman, and Güven Çatak

Use of Virtual Reality in Participatory Urban Design 193
Zeynep Burcu Kaya Alpan and Güven Çatak

Virtual Reality Application for Relieving the Pain of Child Dental Patients 205
Fatma Betül Güreş and Gökhan İnce

Audio Centered Game Development in Mobile VR 217
Ece Naz Sefercioğlu and Hatice Köse

Contents

VR and AR in Teaching 3D Environment Design for Video Games 233
Çağlayan Karagözler and Didem Dönmez Karagözler

A New Environment: Augmented Reality 241
Hakan Anay, Ülkü Özten, and Merve Ünal

A Novel Approach in High School Design Education Using Virtual Reality 255
Tuğba Çelikten and Gökhan İnce

Smartphone as a Paired Game Input Device: An Application on HoloLens Head Mounted Augmented Reality System 265
Mehmet Sonat Karan, Mehmet İlker Berkman, and Güven Çatak

Playful Experience Design

Mapping Current Trends on Gamification of Cultural Heritage 281
Sevde Karahan and Leman Figen Gül

Exploring the Future of Spatial Typography in Immersive Design Applications 295
Barış Atiker

A Critical Review of Video Game Controller Designs 311
Serefraz Akyaman and Ekrem Cem Alppay

Proposal and Requirements for a Platform that Assists Teaching–Learning in the Problematization of Design Projects 325
Luiza Grazziotin Selau, Julio Carlos de Souza van der Linden,
Carlos Alberto Miranda Duarte, and Teemu Leinonen

Playful Spaces and Interfaces

An Exploration of Interactivity and Tangibles in Blended Play Environments 341
İpek Kay and Mine Özkar

A New Data Collection Interface for Dynamic Sign Language Recognition with Leap Motion Sensor 353
Burçak Demircioğlu Kam and Hatice Köse

Gamification and e-Learning in Design

A User-Centered Design Research for Gamification Applications 365
Duygu Koca and Ebru Yücesan

Asset-Based Extended Reality Model for Distance Learning 375
Barış Atiker, Ertuğrul Süngü, Kutay Tinç, and A. Burçin Gürbüz

Exploring Success Criteria of Instructional Video Design in Online Learning Platforms 393
Atakan Coşkun, Elif Büyükkeçeci, and Gülşen Töre-Yargın

Challenges in Synchronous e-Learning in Architectural Education 409
Meriç Altıntaş Kaptan, Ecem Edis, and Aslıhan Ünlü

Asking Users. Questionnaires as Indirect Observation Tools in Human-Centred Design Approach. Application Cases

Francesca Tosi, Antonella Serra, Alessia Brischetto, and Giovanna Nichilò

Abstract Human-Centred Design (HCD) investigation and assessment methods record the user's needs and satisfaction level and are widely used to evaluate usability and orientate design decision making.Questionnaires are among the most useful and popular observation tools to study users' opinions using quantifiable and comparable data. Their drafting needs requirements and evaluations in order to use them efficiently. Therefore, this paper intends to provide designers and researchers with useful tips for designing these tools. For this reason, it describes features of method and systematizes instructions from the literature. It also shows application cases to exemplify the relationship between method and type of data collected and to explore impacts of using different types of questionnaires in design processes.

Keywords Human-Centred Design · Questionnaire · Indirect observation · Usability · Tools

1 Introduction

Usability is defined as "extent to which a system, product or service can be used by specified users to achieve specified goals with effectiveness, efficiency and satisfaction in a specified context of use" [8]. Usability evaluation involves user participation and uses Human-Centred Design (HCD) investigation and assessment methods [9] that record the user's needs and satisfaction level. This design approach aimed at the

---

F. Tosi (✉) · A. Serra · A. Brischetto
Department of Architecture, University of Florence, 50122 Florence, Italy
e-mail: francesca.tosi@unifi.it

A. Serra
e-mail: antonella.serra@unifi.it

A. Brischetto
e-mail: alessia.brischetto@unifi.it

G. Nichilò
School of Doctorate Studies, Università Iuav di Venezia, 30135 Venice, Italy
e-mail: gnichilo@iuav.it

© The Author(s), under exclusive license to Springer Nature Switzerland AG 2021
Ö. Cordan et al. (eds.), *Game + Design Education*, Springer Series in Design and Innovation 13, https://doi.org/10.1007/978-3-030-65060-5_1

SEMANTIC DIFFERENTIAL SCALE

good ○ ○ ○ ○ ○ bad

LIKERT SCALE

1	2	3	4	5
strongly agree	agree	uncertain	disagree	strongly disagree

Fig. 1 Semantic differential scale and Likert scale

quality of interaction between people and physical or virtual systems with which they relate. It is based on data and information collection and processing to understand people's needs and expectations in the relationships they establish with a system, product or service which they interact [18].

Therefore, collecting and processing information derived from the user is a fundamental step in orienting design choices and evaluating the usability of systems.

For this reason questionnaires are among the most useful and popular tools to achieve this goal. These tools are defined as indirect observation methods since they not study the system itself but the users' opinions about it [10].

This paper describes features of method and explores impacts of the use of different kinds of questionnaires in design processes for: (a) the definition of system/product requirements, (b) the validation of design solutions.

The paper also intends to systematize instructions from the literature that are useful for drafting these tools for designers and researchers; it also shows application cases—from research activities of the Laboratory of Ergonomics and Design (LED)[1] of the University of Florence—to exemplify the relationship between method and data type collected.

2 Questionnaires. Features and Uses

A questionnaire is a structured set of questions that are submitted by an evaluator or researcher to the user to record his/her opinion on a product or system.

The choice of a specific type of question must be carefully evaluated by the evaluator/researcher depending on the data he wants to get from the user.

Usually questionnaires consist of closed questions, by which the user provides univocal data, identified on a scale or in a list of options. This type of question generates quantitative and comparable data.

In contrast to this type, open-ended questions—even if they allow the user to express opinions in a personal way that may be relevant for the researcher—generate data that cannot be quantified and not directly comparable and also, as stated by Nielsen [10], can produce answers that are difficult to interpret or "non-answers".

Especially useful for usability studies are questionnaires that use the Likert scale and semantic differential scales (Fig. 1):

---

[1] https://www.ergonomicsdesignlab.com.

(a) Likert scale offers the user the choice of the answer with respect to a range of pre-formulated statements;
(b) Semantic differential scales use evaluation scales that identify the answer as an intermediate value between a pair of opposite attitudes or adjectives.

Both are particularly effective for usability studies and are the most used because they getting people to make a judgement about the analyzed system (e.g. how easy, how usable etc.) and later to compare the interviewees' data [11, p. 401].

2.1 Likert Scale

Likert scale is the most frequently used for products evaluation. Generally, for each questions/affirmations, answers as numerical or word marks are possible. A scale of values is associated with these where the user can identify himself and express a state ranging from "strongly dis-agree" to "strongly agree".

The process for making a Likert scale proposed by Guidicini [7, p. 76] is interesting. He explains that the construction of scale depends on the number of options in which you want, and it is possible, to break down a concept; to do this it is necessary to carefully identify all the sub-sets in which you can break down the concept that generates scale, reduce them to a reasonably low number and isolate the most significant ones. These concepts determine the number and type (numerical, textual, etc.) values used in the scale.

Most questionnaires use 7- or 5-point scales, but there are also examples of more compact (3-point) or larger scales. It is clear that a more large scale allows to pick more shades in the user evaluation, while a more compact scale focuses the data collection on a smaller number of items: therefore, the most fitting scale is the one that best responds to the goal defined at the beginning of the data collection and to its application.

A scale of odd numbers gives the user the possibility to indicate a neutral position with respect to two endpoints, instead, an even number forces interviewees to make a decision and indicate a value that expresses a stronger proximity to an opposite concept.

The **Quebec User Evaluation of Satisfaction with Assistive Technology**—QUEST (Fig. 2) is an example of 5-point scale. It is an assistive technology (AT) user satisfaction assessment tool used both for clinical field—as it allows clinicians to document the real benefits of AT and to validate the need for these devices—and as a research tool because it compares satisfaction data with other outcome measures such as clinical outcomes, quality of life, functional status, cost factors and comfort [5, p. 102].

QUEST includes 12 questions related to product features and divided into two section:

a. 8 questions that evaluate the Satisfaction Level of "Assistive Device";
b. 4 questions that evaluate the Satisfaction Level of "Services".

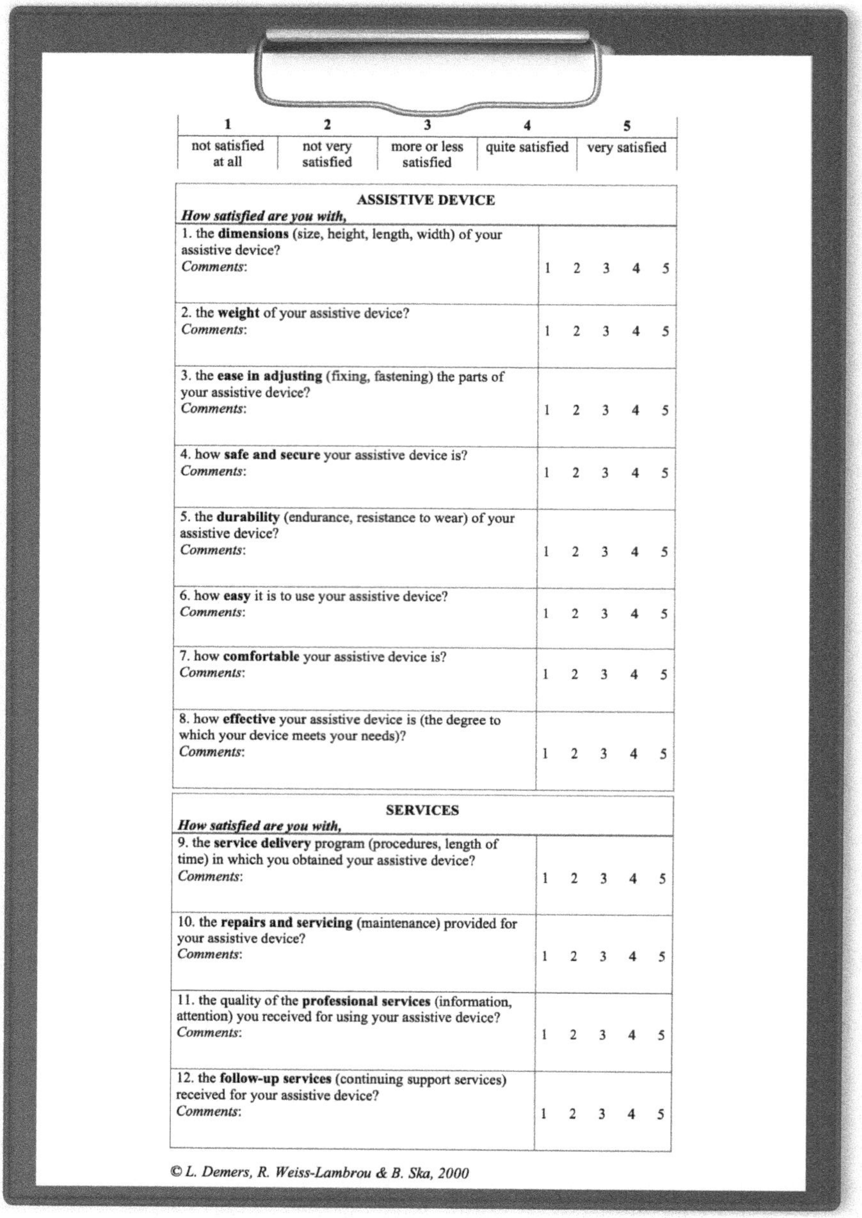

Fig. 2 QUEST—Quebec. *Source* Demers et al. [4]

Each question is associated with a "comments" area where the user has the possibility to record further opinions and input in a more free format.

At the end of the questions, the user is asked to indicate the three aspects/services of the device that he personally considers most important. In this way, the interviewer obtains both an analytical evaluation of each item and the user's priorities about the device.

Even if it is a synthetic questionnaire, the articulation in sections is important because it allows users to be more oriented when formulating the evaluation, making a distinction between what impressions, expectations, values are associated with each item analyzed, and reducing overlaps and interferences.

This structure is correctly understood by users when the sections are clearly distinct, not only in terms of content, but also through graphic and compositional elements that consolidate the user's perception of the responses' subdivision (see Fig. 2).

Another important QUEST feature is its versatility. In fact it is structured to be compiled in autonomy by users but, if this way is not suitable, also to be supplied in interview format or using 12 satisfaction cards—made by modifying the layout, printing and cutting out the 12 items—by which the user can express orally, or just indicate, his opinion. Variability of the support and the administration format allows to involve a wider number of users, including users with motor, cognitive or sensory disabilities.

To follow some application cases developed at the Laboratory of Ergonomics and Design (LED) of the University of Florence.

The first one concerns the UX Skillrow Evaluation,[2] conducted in collaboration with Technogym s.p.a. [17], which aimed to define usability and user experience levels of a new company product—"Skillrow" rowing machine—and its user interfaces.[3]

Users were involved in a four-day program of activities, during which different HCD methodologies were applied in synergy:

(a) during the first two days, users' opinions on critical issues and/or benefits found during UX were recorded, using both direct and indirect observation methods: thinking aloud and post-use questionnaire on the first day; focus group on the second day;
(b) the following days were dedicated to their representation and visualization by methodologies such as Task Analysis, Personas and Scenarios (days 3–4).

Overall the data obtained derives from an integrated use of different HCD methodologies, each of which is characterized by a different way of collecting and processing data.

---

[2]SKILLROW Team: Francesca Tosi (Scientific Coordinator), Alessia Brischetto, Mattia Pistolesi, Ester Iacono, in collaboration with Technogym Research Center.
[3]See Brischetto [2].

The post-use questionnaire of this research was structured in three blocks: (1) Personal Data (5 questions); (2) User Experience (10 questions); (3) Understanding (21 questions). Each one is characterized by different types of questions:

- *Personal Data Questionnaire* is aimed to define the user profile and uses closed-choice questions with a predefined number of answer options set by the interviewer;
- *Understanding Questionnaire* is aimed to record the difficulties in the use of the machine and the interface and the understanding of the commands and instructions by the user. It uses questions with only two alternative answers, of the yes/no type;
- *UX Questionnaire* quantifies the different aspects of the user experience through a 10-points Likert scale. By this questionnaire the user evaluates 5 issues both Machine and Interface: (1) Level of Frustration, (2) Mental Request; (3) Physical Request; (4) Effort; (5) Performance.

Each questionnaire used a different type of questions depending on the data to be processed, outlining user profiles (Personal Data Questionnaire) and providing qualitative data on the actual usability levels of the product, its components and the graphical user interface (Understanding and UX Questionnaire) (Fig. 3).

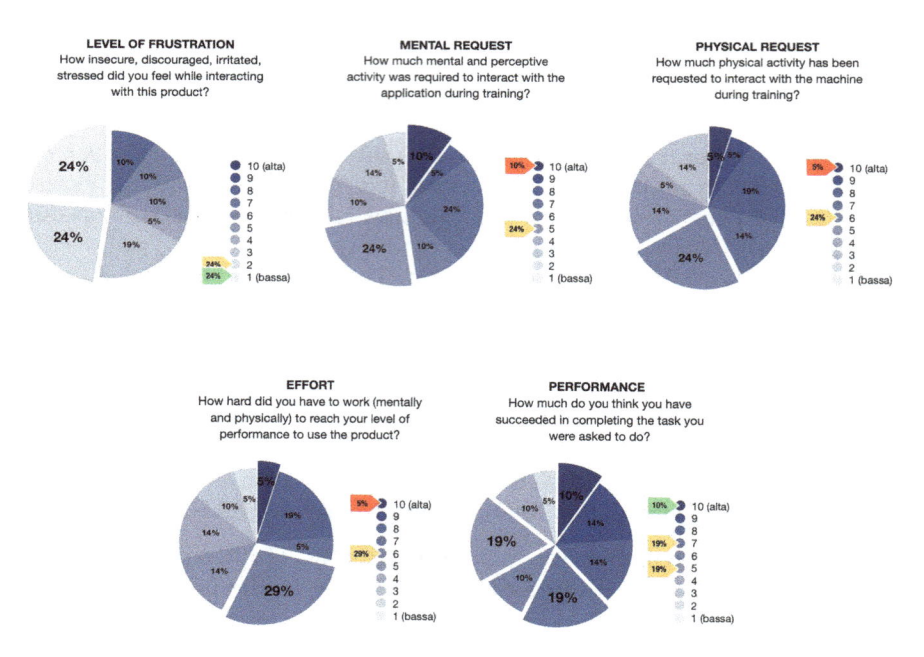

Fig. 3 UX Skillrow evaluation. Results of experience of use questionnaires—interaction with machine [2]

The second application case concerns the PUDCAD[4] research project, a three-year Strategic Partnership project financed by European Erasmus + programme.

PUDCAD involves an Educational Game [12] design to introduce Design Students to Universal Design and the design, together with the game, of a dedicated website including a Game tutorial and an e-learning course for learning Universal Design.

During the three years of activity more than one hundred students from the six partner universities have been involved by four international workshops. Their involvement both as designers and end users has created a particularly intense and authentic Human Centred Design (HCD) teaching and design experience, given the correspondence of the two profiles [16].

Following are some examples of questions from the questionnaire submitted to a sample of 12 students in the preliminary design phase of the Game Tutorial.

Purpose of the questionnaire was to evaluate effectiveness of information offered to users by a tutorial external to the game, which can be consulted before the game session, without compromising motivation to play the game, maybe feed it.

Example 1 Users were asked to evaluate how much the tutorial content they were shown caused: (a) Curiosity; (b) Interest; (c) Challenge; (d) Empathy—dimension through which the motivation is expressed.

Users expressed their evaluation by a 5-point Likert scale, according to which a numerical score of 0–4 corresponded respectively to evaluations between "strongly disagree"—"strongly agree". Figure 4 shows question/answer formulation (3a) and processing of collected data (3b).

The question formulated in this way allowed to clearly deduce that having introduced the use of the PUDCAD Game by an external Tutorial—a solution increasingly less common among videogames—did not decrease the motivation to play the game by the sample of students interviewed, which on the contrary showed a high motivation.

Example 2 Users were asked to evaluate the tutorial contents submitted to them on a 7-point semantic differential scale. Each of the eight components evaluated—(a) Contents, (b) Example, (c) Language, (d) Wording, (e) Information sequence, (f) Graphical representation, (g) Text, (h) Keywords—is combined with a pair of adjectives that aim to record a user evaluation of clarity, effectiveness, completeness and readability of information. Figure 5 shows the structure of the question and the results obtained from data processing.

Question 5 results indicate mostly positive values (5, 6, 7) for all investigated items, but highlight areas where the user shows less satisfaction or uncertainty.

These data, combined with those obtained from short interviews following the questionnaire, have provided new input for a review of the design elements.

---

[4]PUDCAD Team: Francesca Tosi (Scientific Coordinator), Antonella Serra, Alessia Brischetto, Ester Iacono.

3. The information you've received makes you feel about the game:

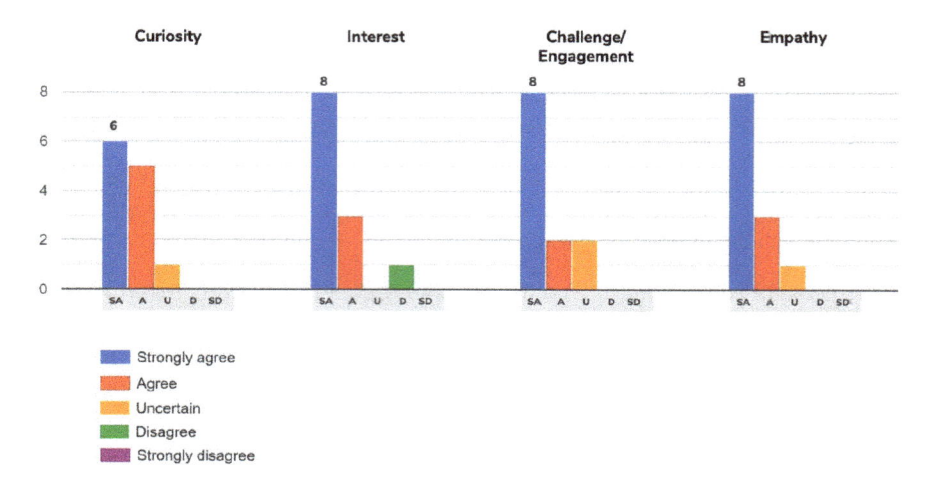

	Strongly agree	Agree	Uncertain	Disagree	Strongly disagree
	4	3	2	1	0
Curiosity					
Interest					
Challenge					
Empathy					

Fig. 4 Tutorial questionnaire 1, Question 3: Formulation of question (3a) and results processing (3b)—[16]

2.2 Semantic Differential Scale

Using semantic differential scales, users base their evaluation expressing a status of semantic proximity in a range of two bipolar concepts. Each pair is represented by two opposing adjectives and the user is asked to express his position with respect to the two poles to indicate how much he agrees with the formulated concept.

The User Experience Questionnaire—UEQ [19] is an internationally accepted example of semantic differential scale application. It is a questionnaire dedicated to User Experience evaluation of interactive products (Fig. 6).

The current questionnaire version contains 26 items related to 6 scales: Attractiveness—Perspicuity—Efficiency—Dependability—Simulation—Novelty—about which Schrepp et al. [15] explain: "Attractiveness is a pure valence dimension. Perspicuity, Efficiency and Dependability are pragmatic quality aspects

5. How do you evaluate the following *(indicate a value)*:

		1	2	3	4	5	6	7	
Contents	Poor								Exhaustive
Examples	Effective								Ineffective
Language	Complicated								Simple
Wording	Clear								Confused
Information sequence	Ineffective								Effective
Symbols, icons, other graphical representation	Intuitive								Unintuitive
Text	Readable								Not readable
Keyword	Effective								Ineffective

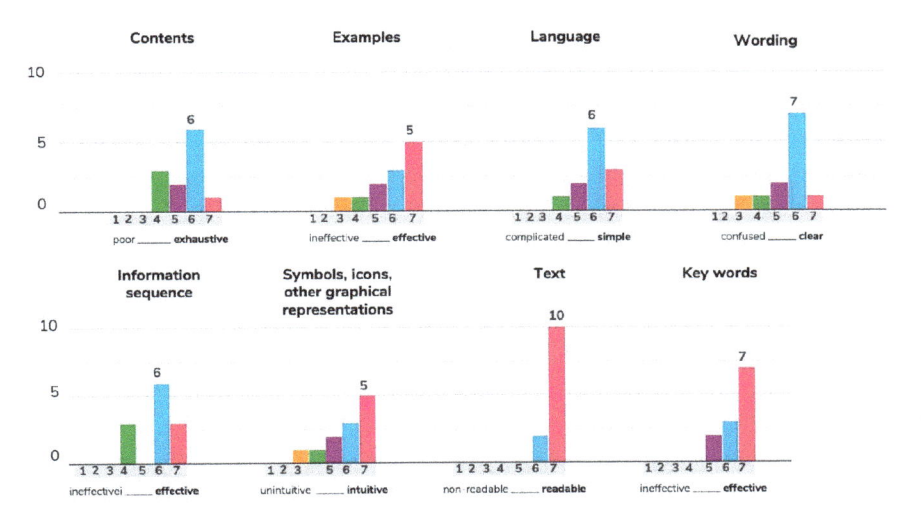

Fig. 5 Tutorial questionnaire, Question 5: Formulation of question (5a) and results processing (5b)—[16]

(goal-directed), while Stimulation and Novelty are hedonic quality aspects (not goal-directed)".

Users express their opinion by a 7-point semantic differential scale. Both the order of the items and the disposition on the right or left of the terms that make up the pair is randomized.

For semantic differentials it is especially important that participants have access to appropriate content for the user target group and in their natural language. For this reason the UEQ is available in various languages and there is also a version for children and teenager in German that uses a simplified language (Table 1).

A second internationally accepted example of a questionnaire with a semantic differential scale is the Questionnaire for User Interaction Satisfaction—QUIS [3].

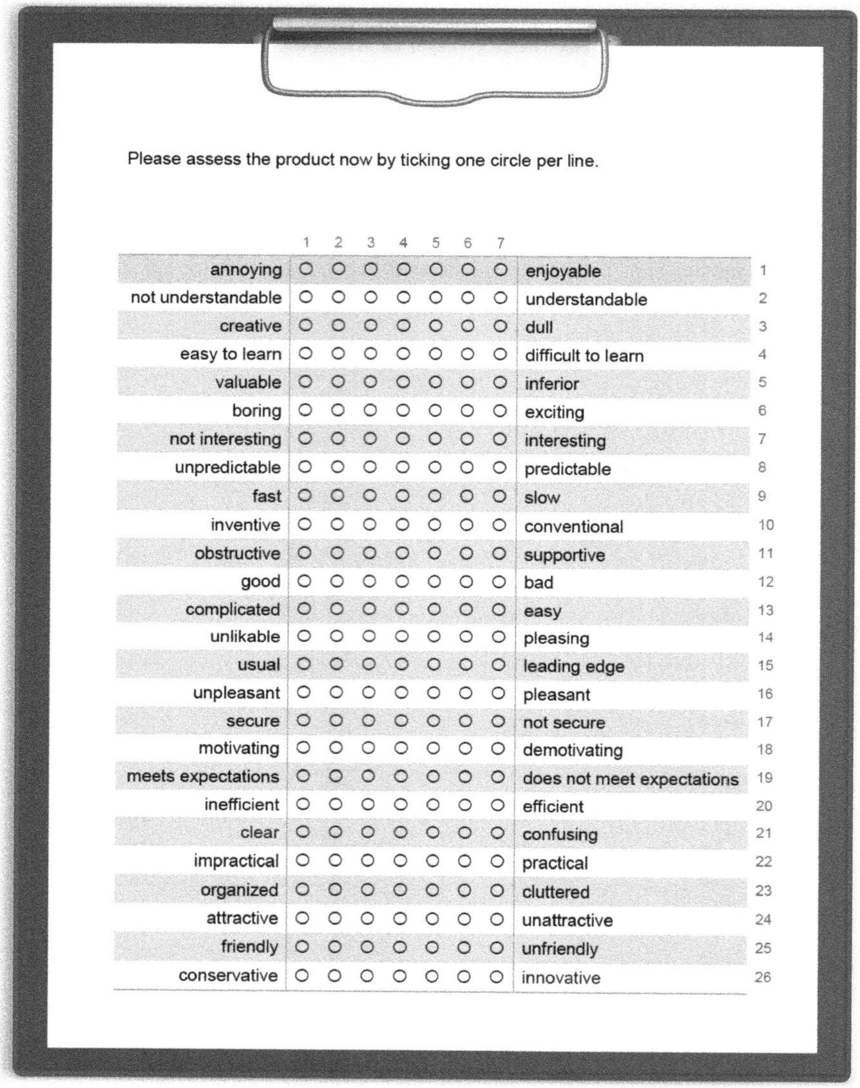

Please assess the product now by ticking one circle per line.

	1	2	3	4	5	6	7		
annoying	○	○	○	○	○	○	○	enjoyable	1
not understandable	○	○	○	○	○	○	○	understandable	2
creative	○	○	○	○	○	○	○	dull	3
easy to learn	○	○	○	○	○	○	○	difficult to learn	4
valuable	○	○	○	○	○	○	○	inferior	5
boring	○	○	○	○	○	○	○	exciting	6
not interesting	○	○	○	○	○	○	○	interesting	7
unpredictable	○	○	○	○	○	○	○	predictable	8
fast	○	○	○	○	○	○	○	slow	9
inventive	○	○	○	○	○	○	○	conventional	10
obstructive	○	○	○	○	○	○	○	supportive	11
good	○	○	○	○	○	○	○	bad	12
complicated	○	○	○	○	○	○	○	easy	13
unlikable	○	○	○	○	○	○	○	pleasing	14
usual	○	○	○	○	○	○	○	leading edge	15
unpleasant	○	○	○	○	○	○	○	pleasant	16
secure	○	○	○	○	○	○	○	not secure	17
motivating	○	○	○	○	○	○	○	demotivating	18
meets expectations	○	○	○	○	○	○	○	does not meet expectations	19
inefficient	○	○	○	○	○	○	○	efficient	20
clear	○	○	○	○	○	○	○	confusing	21
impractical	○	○	○	○	○	○	○	practical	22
organized	○	○	○	○	○	○	○	cluttered	23
attractive	○	○	○	○	○	○	○	unattractive	24
friendly	○	○	○	○	○	○	○	unfriendly	25
conservative	○	○	○	○	○	○	○	innovative	26

Fig. 6 UEQ—user. *Source* UEQ website

This questionnaire is one of the most commonly used and was designed to evaluate user satisfaction in human–machine interfaces use and is one of most used. It uses a 9-point scale, and because it is a general questionnaire that will be used with a wide variety of products it also includes NA (not applicable) as a category (Fig. 7).

It consists of 12 parts that can be used in total or in parts: (1) System experience, (2) Past experience, (3) Overall user reaction, (4) Screen design, (5) Terminology

Table 1 User experience questionnaire—UEQ: scales and items [14]

Scales	Items
Attractiveness Do users like or dislike the product? This scale is a pure valence dimension	Annoying/enjoyable Good/bad Unlikable/pleasing Unpleasant/pleasant Attractive/unattractive Friendly/unfriendly
Efficiency Is it possible to use the product fast and efficient? Does the user interface looks organized?	Fast/slow Inefficient/efficient Impractical/practical Organized/cluttered
Perspicuity Is it easy to understand how to use the product? Is it easy to get familiar with the product?	Not understandable/understandable Easy to learn/difficult to learn Complicated/easy Clear/confusing
Dependability Does the user feel in control of the interaction? Is the interaction with the product secure and predicable?	Unpredictable/predictable Obstructive/supportive Secure/not secure Meets expectations/does not meet expectations
Simulation Is it interesting and exciting to use the product? Does the user feel motivated to further use the product?	Valuable/inferior Boring/exiting Not interesting/interesting Motivating/demotivating
Novelty Is the design of the product innovative and creative? Does the product grab users attention?	Creative/dull Inventive/conventional Usual/leading edge Conservative/innovative

Reworked from Rauschenberger et al. [14, p. 40]

and system information, (6) Learning, (7) System capabilities, (8) Technical manuals and online help, (9) Online tutorials, (10) Multimedia, (11) Teleconferencing, (12) Software installation [11, p. 402].

3 Questionnaires: How to Do

Nielsen [10] says that "a questionnaire is a user interface in its own right". Therefore, in order for users to interpret it correctly and carry it completely, it must meet the usability requirements; for this reason "is therefore essential that all questionnaires be subjected to pilot testing and iterative design before they are distributed to the users in large numbers".

Guidicini [7] highlights instead the importance of language accuracy in the formulation of the questionnaire: the choice of adjectives, words, symbols or expressions that feature the question promotes the assumptions of a correct reading by the user.

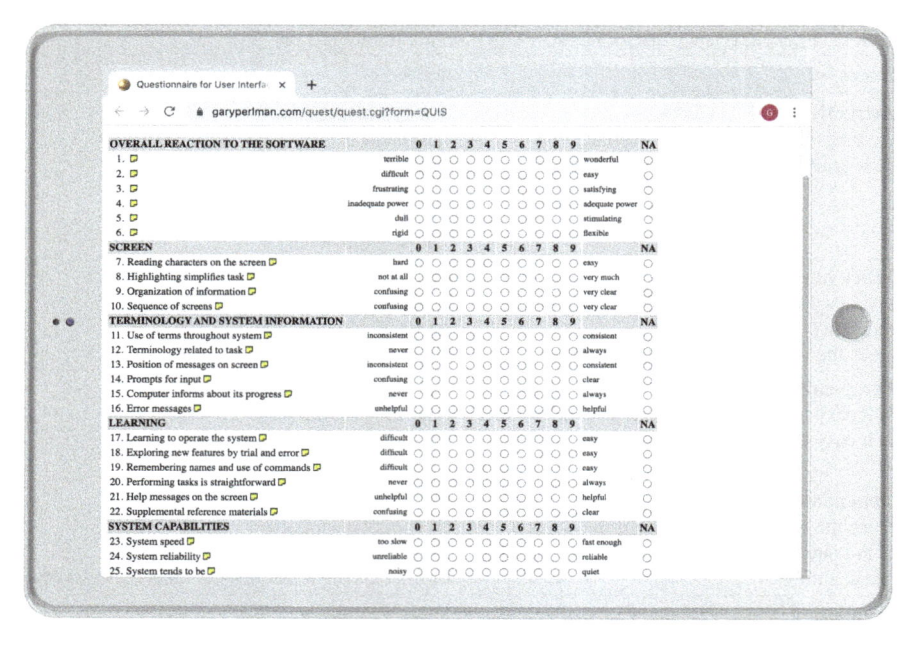

Fig. 7 QUIS—questionnaire. *Source* Perlman [13]

At its base, moreover, there must also be a deep knowledge of the language used by a certain culture and a certain social group.

Guidicini identifies 8 types of questions to be included in a questionnaire and for everyone it indicates the recommended formulation (see Table 2). In fact, the author affirms that it is the choice of the most appropriate type that allows users to answer.

Therefore, the evaluator/researcher has the possibility, from time to time, to structure and formulate the questionnaire according to its purpose, the target users and the way the data are collected and processed.

An important and already mentioned aspect to keep in mind when structuring a questionnaire is the division in question blocks, generally coinciding with topic groups and arranged in an order from general to particular. Following example shows the block subdivision designed for questionnaire of the XAll project.[5]

The project focuses on the museum field and aims to make the visit experience inclusive and performing for all target groups, including people with special needs: sensory, motor and cognitive disabilities and/or socio-cultural.

XAll Questionnaire (Fig. 8) is a tool for evaluating museum accessibility and developed according to a Design for All approach. It includes three types of questions: (a) open-choice questions, permitting multiple answer options; (b) closed-choice questions, with only one answer option; (c) questions with only two choice

---

[5] XAll Team: Francesca Tosi (Scientific Coordinator), Antonella Serra, Alessia Brischetto, Giovanna Nichilò; project funded by Fondazione TIM [6].

Table 2 Types of questions

Types	Features	Setting
1st Type **Targeted** questions about individual	Overview on condition, background, gender, education, status, job etc.	Predetermined number of questions
2nd Type **Open-choice** questions	Include above type questions and specific topic questions	Variable range of choice
3rd Type **Closed-choice** questions	On all topics!	Predetermined range of choice
4th Type Questions with **only two** **choices**	Choices of juxtaposed judgment are offered	Yes/No, True/False, Agreement/Disagreement
5th Type **Scalar choices** questions	More predetermined judgments are offered and placed on a scale of insensitivity	Increasing intensity of judgement (positive or negative)
6th Type **Open topic** questions	The interviewee is called to propose his opinion with a more or less extensive speech on a focused topic	Free opinions without restriction
7th Type **Multiple variables** questions	A judgement is asked on multiple answers, in several directions, from a given topic	Options on all expected directions
8th Type questions with **sentence completion**	One or more sentences are presented with missing elements to complete it	Adding adjectives, sentence completing

Reworked from Guidicini [7], p. 19

alternatives, YES/NO type. This combination makes it possible to obtain both quantitative and qualitative data, by which it will be possible to measure the level of accessibility of every museum area to which it is applied.

The second peculiarity of the questionnaire is that it is structured to be compiled by researchers/evaluators and professionals during inspection of museums and therefore blocks represent the museum spaces while the sequence corresponds to the itinerary inside spaces.

The sub-blocks (shown in grey in Fig. 8) will be used/not used depending on if that type of space or feature is present or not in museum to which they are applied.

Table 3, summarizes some of the most important tips identified in the literature and coming from Preece [11, p. 400], Guidicini [7, pp. 19–20] and Bradburn [1, pp. 283–285] that aim at a good questionnaire usability by the interviewees.

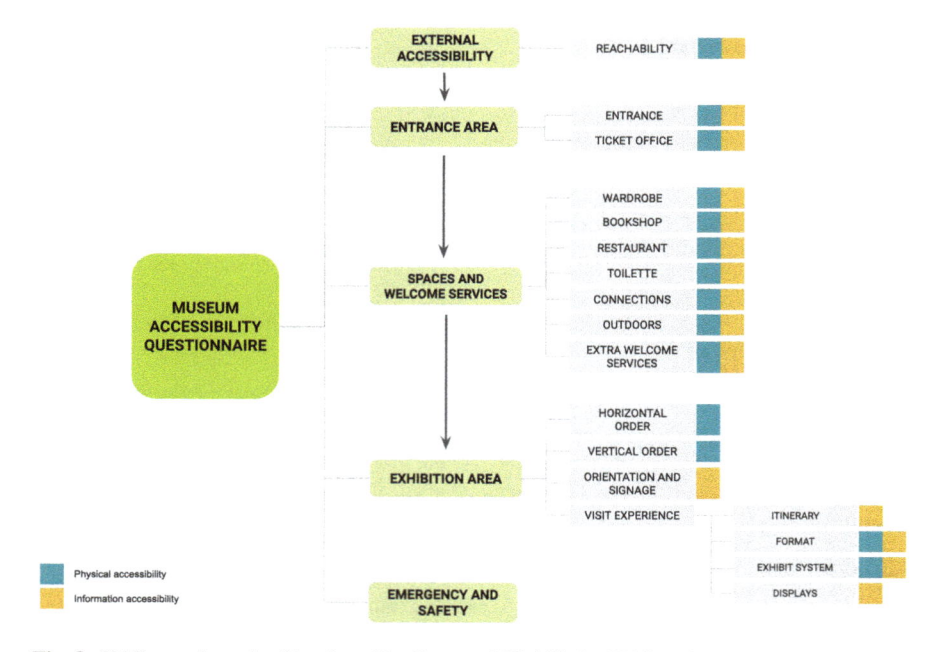

Fig. 8 XAll questionnaire (developed by Serra and Nichilò for XAll project)

Table 3 Instructions for structuring a questionnaire

1—General structure
• Give an appropriate order to the questions and number them because the impact of a question can be influenced by their order [11]
• Numbering questions can alert either the respondent or the interviewer that a question has been skipped and will suggest to respondents how long the task will take [1]
• Organize questionnaire in blocks of questions, each one oriented to develop a different topic [7]
2—Question formulation
• Make questions clear and specific; when possible, ask closed questions [11]
• Minimize number of questions that may encourage uncertain answers [7]
3—Answers formulation
• Find a formulation able to involve the respondents in each answer option/In order to obtain meaningful answers [7]
• "Consider including a "no-opinion" option/for questions that seek opinions" [11]; this helps not to create false results if the user does not recognize himself/herself with the given categories
4—Evaluation scales
• Make sure the range scale is appropriate, intuitive and does not overlap
• Use numbers consistent with the evaluation you are asked to express: for example, it is more intuitive in a scale of 1–5 for 1 to indicate low agreement and 5 to indicate high agreement [11]

(continued)

Table 3 (continued)

5—*Language*
• Use a language appropriate to the target group, as it favours a correct reading of contents [7]
6—*Instructions*
• Provide clear instructions on how to complete the questionnaire [11], put theme at the point where they will be used [1].
7—*Layout*
• Design a layout that help graphically to make the questionnaire clearer and more readable but keeping it as compact as possible [11] • Avoid split a question, including all its answer categories, between two pages or screens [1] • Avoid having two or more columns of questions or put two or more answer categories on the same line to make the questionnaire appear shorter because it interferes with standard reading patterns [1] • Use a typeface sufficiently large and clear as to cause no strain in rapid reading for all potential respondents [1]

4 Conclusion

The results of research conducted by LED Laboratory—on numerous projects concerning: (a) product usability evaluations; (b) innovative and/or inclusive products/systems/services design; (c) product comparison; (d) drafting of guidelines—confirm that questionnaires are the most appropriate methodology for collecting user evaluation by means of quantifiable and comparable data.

The tool has also demonstrated to be functional to data integration when it is used to support other survey methodologies or in synergy with them.

The quality and relevance of the data obtained proved to be directly proportional to the correct design or the correct use of the questionnaire by the researcher/interviewer.

References

1. Bradburn NM, Sudman S, Wansink B (2004) Asking questions: the definitive guide to questionnaire design—for market research, political polls, and social and health questionnaires, Rev. Sons, New York
2. Brischetto A, Pistolesi M, Fedele G, Tosi F (2018) UX evaluation of a new rowing ergometer: the case study of the Technogym "SkillRow". In: International conference on applied human factors and ergonomics. Springer, Cham, pp 233–243
3. Chin JP, Diehl VA, Norman KL (1988) Development of an instrument measuring user satisfaction of the human-computer interface. In: Proceedings of the SIGCHI conference on human factors in computing systems, pp 213–218
4. Demers L, Weiss-Lambrou R, Ska B (2000) Quebec user evaluation of satisfaction with assistive technology QUEST (Version 2.0). Text available at https://www.midss.org/sites/default/files/questeng.scoring_sheetpdf_0.pdf
5. Demers L, Weiss-Lambrou R, Ska B (2002) The quebec user evaluation of satisfaction with assistive technology (QUEST 2.0): an overview and recent progress. Technol Disab 14(3):101–105

6. FONDAZIONE TIM XAll project page. https://www.fondazionetim.it/progetti/patrimonio-storico-artistico/xall-tutta-unaltra-guida, last accessed 2020/06/22
7. Guidicini P (1995) Questionari, interviste, storie di vita: come costruire gli strumenti, raccogliere le informazioni ed elaborare i dati. FrancoAngeli, Milano
8. ISO 9241-2019 Ergonomics of human-system interaction, Part 210: Human-centred design for interactive systems
9. Maguire M (2001) Methods to support human-centred design. Int J Hum Comput Stud 55(4):587–634
10. Nielsen J (1994) Usability engineering. Morgan Kaufmann, Burlington
11. Preece JR, Rogers YY, Sharp H (2002) Interaction design: beyond human-computer interaction. Wiley, New York
12. PUDCAD GAME Homepage. https://www.pudcadgame.com/, last accessed 2020/06/22
13. GARY PERLMAN QUIS page. https://garyperlman.com/quest/quest.cgi?form=QUIS, last accessed 2020/06/22
14. Rauschenberger M, Schrepp M, Pérez Cota M, Olschner S, Thomaschewski J (2013) Efficient measurement of the user experience of interactive products. How to use the user experience questionnaire (UEQ). Example: Spanish language version. Int J Artif Intell Inter Multimedia 2(1):39–45
15. Schrepp M, Hinderks A, Thomaschewski J Applying the user experience questionnaire (UEQ) in different evaluation scenarios. In: Marcus A (eds) Design, user experience, and usability. Theories, methods, and tools for designing the user experience. DUXU 2014. Lecture Notes in Computer Science, vol 8517. Springer, Cham, pp 383–392
16. Serra A (2020) Teaching universal design. Human-centred process and methodologies. In the PUDCAD Project. In: Tosi F, Serra A, Brischetto A, Iacono E (eds) Design for inclusion, gamification and learning experience. FrancoAngeli, Milano, pp 255–272
17. Technogym SPA (2020) Homepage. https://www.technogym.com/it/, last accessed 2020/06/22
18. Tosi F, Brischetto A, Pistolesi M (2019/2020) Human-centred design—user experience: tools and intervention methods. In: Tosi F (ed) Design for Ergonomics. Springer Series in Design and Innovation, pp 111–128. https://doi.org/10.1007/978-3-030-33562-5_6
19. UEQ user experience questionnaire. https://www.ueq-online.org/, last accessed 2020/06/22

Francesca Tosi Full Professor of Industrial Design at Department of Architecture - DIDA, University of Florence. Scientific Director of LED, Ergonomics & Design Laboratory, she develops her research and didactic activities in the fields of Product and Interior Design, Ergonomics in Design, Inclusive Design. She is Past national President of SIE, Italian Society of Ergonomics and human factors and, currently, President of CUID, Italian Design Academic Conference – francesca.tosi@unifi.it.

Antonella Serra PhD in Design, she is Research Fellow at the Department of Architecture DIDA, University of Florence. She focused her research on HCD and Universal Design/DfA approaches in the sector of the Cultural Heritage and Education. She is also an architect, journalist and design educator. Adjunct Professor at the University of Florence (2005-14) and at the University of Rome "La Sapienza" (2012–13), she has written for "Il Sole24 Ore" (2007–10) and "Opere" (2011–14) and performed editorial activities for several architecture magazines (2003–06) – antonella.serra@unifi.it.

Alessia Brischetto PhD in Design, is a fixed-term Researcher at the Department of Architecture, University of Florence. Since 2010 she works mainly on the fields of Ergonomics for Design, usability of industrial products and design for inclusion, supporting the use of ICTs in learning environments. She has also taken part in several national and international research projects and collaborated with public administrations and important companies. She is also author of several peer-review papers, conference proceedings and books – alessia.brischetto@unifi.it.

Giovanna Nichilò Master's Degree in Architecture at the University of Campania Luigi Vanvitelli; Postgraduate specialisation in Fair Architecture and Exhibit Spaces. Research fellow in Industry 4.0 strategies for product marketing at Iuav University of Venice; Grant Research in Inclusive Museum Design at Laboratory of Ergonomics & Design at the University of Florence. Her professional experience includes work in Exhibit Design, Creative Industry, Digital Fabrication and Design of teaching activities for STEAM matters – giovanna.nichilo@unifi.it.

Universal Design and Education

An Educational Path on Universal Design. Video Games as Learning Tools

Giorgio Buratti[ID], Fiammetta Costa[ID], and Michela Rossi[ID]

Abstract PUDCAD (Practicing Universal Design Principles In Design Education Through A Cad-Based Game) is a project founded by the European Erasmus + program for innovation and sharing of good practices in education. It provides, at systemic level, the modernization and activation of educational paths through cooperation with partners from different countries through participatory approaches based on ICT. The aim of PUDCAD is the creation of a playful computer assisted drawing application that allows interior architecture and design students to learn and use Universal design principles. This paper explains the different stages of research implementation. The first step was a workshop focused on a survey method developed to verify the compliance of educational environments with the principles of Universal Design (Checklist). Together with simulated direct experience (Empathy trial), it led the students involved to the creation of scenarios for school integration. In the second workshop the application of ad hoc parameter of universal design for spaces of learning led to the definition of Game Maps, where environments and characters of the game were identified. In the third, building on the second step material, table games able of sensitizing the user and supporting her/him in the design of inclusive environments were developed. In the fourth workshop the students developed and tested the videogame's Alpha version providing feedback and ideas for the ultimate version presented in the fifth workshop. Reviewing the process applied to build the application, the article explores educational experimentation and pedagogical aspects, emphasizing how the videogame, beyond entertainment, can support and promote new learning paths complementary to canonical teaching methods.

Keywords Ergonomics · Universal design · Gamification · Inclusion · Participation · Design education

G. Buratti · F. Costa (✉) · M. Rossi
Politecnico Di Milano, Milano, Italy
e-mail: fiammetta.costa@polimi.it

© The Author(s), under exclusive license to Springer Nature Switzerland AG 2021
Ö. Cordan et al. (eds.), *Game + Design Education*, Springer Series in Design and Innovation 13, https://doi.org/10.1007/978-3-030-65060-5_2

1 Introduction

PUDCAD (Practicing Universal Design Principles in Design Education Through A Cad-Based Game) is a project founded by the European Erasmus + program for innovation and sharing of good practices in education. It promotes, at systemic level, the modernization and activation of educational paths through cooperation with partners from different countries through participatory approaches based on ICT. The project is related to one of the foremost priorities of the European Commission: to provide the inclusion and efficient accessibility of people with disability in everyday life. Regarding the European Universal Design Standards and the current state of universal design education in international networks, the aim of PUDCAD is the creation of a playful computer assisted drawing application that allows interior architecture and design undergraduate students to learn and apply Universal design principles through an empathic approach.

Universal Design [1] means a design method that provides for environments fruition and products use regardless of age, physical abilities and/or user social condition. This approach refers to Ergonomics, an essential discipline for the implementation of the social inclusion and non-discrimination targets set by the EU, but often not taught enough or considered a fringe element in future designers' training. The accessibility issue is not limited to just "compliance with the rules", but rather to the best avail-able solutions. An inclusive project goes beyond the concept of "Barriers free design", replacing the use of equipment dedicated to individual user profiles (disability aids, elderly furniture etc.), by efficient solutions suitable to the widest possible range of population.

The project partners are: Faculty of Architecture, Istanbul Technical University, Turkey (leading institute); Bahcesehir University of Istanbul, Turkey; Institute of Design and Fine Arts, Lahti University of Applied Sciences, Finland; Detmold School of Architecture and Interior Architecture, Technische Hochschule Ostwestfalen-Lippe, Germany; Dipartimento di Architettura, Università degli Studi di Firenze, Italy; Dipartimento di Design, Politecnico di Milano, Italy; Association for Wellbeing of Children with Cerebral Palsy, Turkey; Occupational Therapy Association of Turkey.

2 Method

The project has been developed through the coordination of an international research group thanks to a transactional meeting program based on interdisciplinary conferences and workshops involving students from the five participating universities.

The first step was a workshop held in Politecnico di Milano, where the students applied a survey method developed by the project partners adapting the Americans with Disabilities Act (ADA) Checklist (Fig. 1) to verify the compliance of high school educational environments with the principles of Universal Design.

Together with a simulated experience (Fig. 2), aimed at improving the direct perception of universal design problems, it was expected to lead the involved students to the creation of scenarios for school integration and proposals of innovative interior design concepts for school environments.

The proposals were scored according to the 7 basic principles developed by the Center for Universal Design North Carolina State University, weighted as:

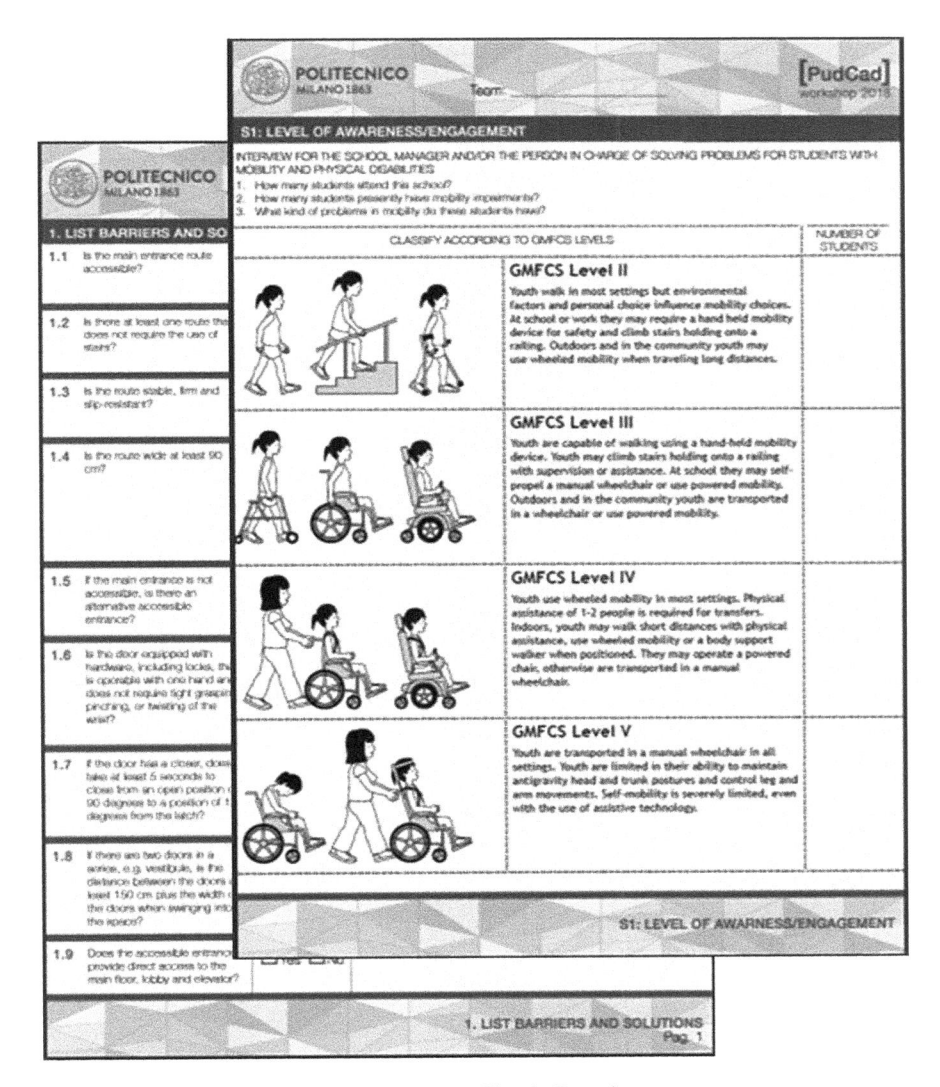

Fig. 1 Checklist for High school survey. *Source* Giorgio Buratti

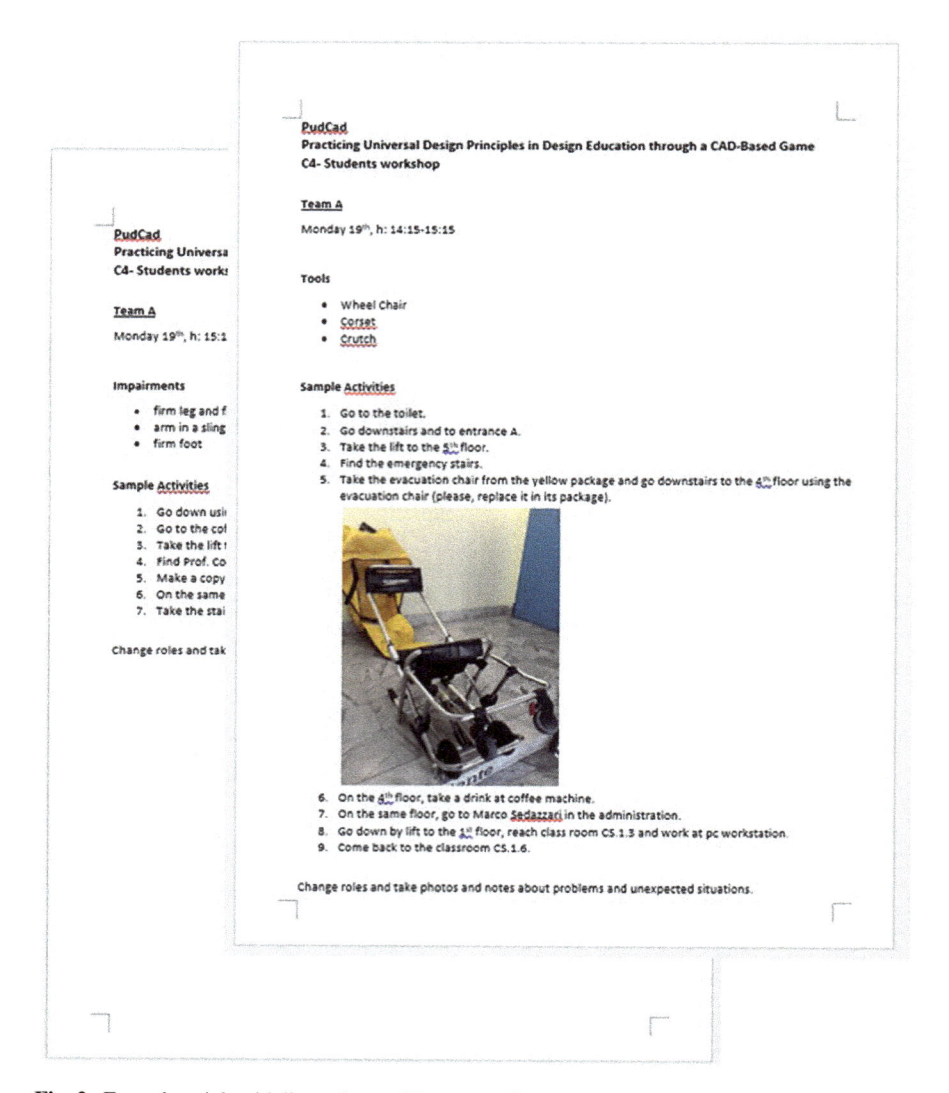

Fig. 2 Empathy trial guidelines. *Source* Fiammetta Costa

- Equitable use (15 points)
- Flexibility in use (15 points)
- Simple and intuitive use (10 points)
- Perceptible information (10 points)
- Tolerance for error (10 points)
- Low physical effort (20 points)
- Size and space for approach and use (20 points).

A second workshop, titled Universal Playground, took place at the University of Applied Science and Arts Ostwestfalen-Lippe. The application of ad hoc parameters of universal design for spaces of learning was planned in order to define Game Maps where environments and characters of the game should be identified.

The proposed Parameters of Universal Design for Spaces of Learning are:

1. Well-being
2. Organisation
3. Communication
4. Transformation
5. Creativity and Collectiveness
6. Action
7. Diversity.

The third workshop, titled Game Jam, was hosted by University of Florence, students were asked to develop board games starting with the creation of characters, whose disability profiles and skills will affect the game design and mechanisms. Game themes and names were identified with the support of Bahçeşehir University Game Lab to face Universal Design principles in the games.

Game themes (and names):

- Escape From the Campus (Theme: Quake!)
- Match (Theme: What If?)
- Fire Alarm (Theme: Fire Alarm)
- A Short Daydream (Theme: Daydream)
- Tsialidybi (Theme: Alien Invasion)
- Campus Challenge (Theme: First Day)
- Crazy Granny (Theme: Holiday).

The decision to focus on brainstorming and paper prototyping was intended to let all the participants contribute in the short time, since most of them were not expert in digital game design. Focusing on the digital game itself would shift the emphasis from thinking on the design parameters to the tools. Whereupon the game design was finalized translating the findings to a first-person perspective digital game and he video-game's Alpha version was experimented in the fourth workshop, Designing and testing a game-based environment (Fig. 3), which was held at Lahti University of Applied Sciences.

A Beta version of the game was then released and refined through partner's collaboration in order to present and promote the digital game in June 2020 at the final PUDCAD conference.

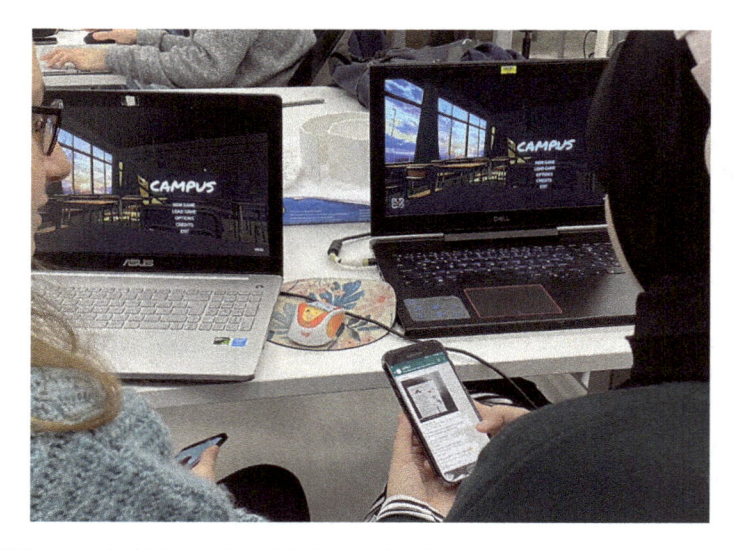

Fig. 3 Video-game's Alpha version trial. *Source* Ester Iacono

3 Results

3.1 Universal School Environments

The five groups, composed by a student of each partner school, developed scenarios and designed an innovative school environment, namely the entrance and exhibition hall, a classroom, a laboratory, an auditorium and a library [2].

Each environment concept takes into account Universal Design principles and the library, conceived with modular furnishing elements that can be used by both able-bodied and disabled people (Fig. 4), obtained the highest Universal Design score.

3.2 Universal Playground

Applying the Parameter of Universal Design for Spaces of Learning as a starting point for the design process the students searched for corresponding locations and next included specific interactions and activities.

As a sample of profound results a group developed five design criteria for action: freedom, companionship, flexibility, fun and subtlety. The criteria were applied by the students in the outside space of the campus extended through Augmented Reality (AR) as "culturaction" (Fig. 5). "The object they designed was to give the opportunity to be a meeting and orientation point and a space for spontaneous lectures. By

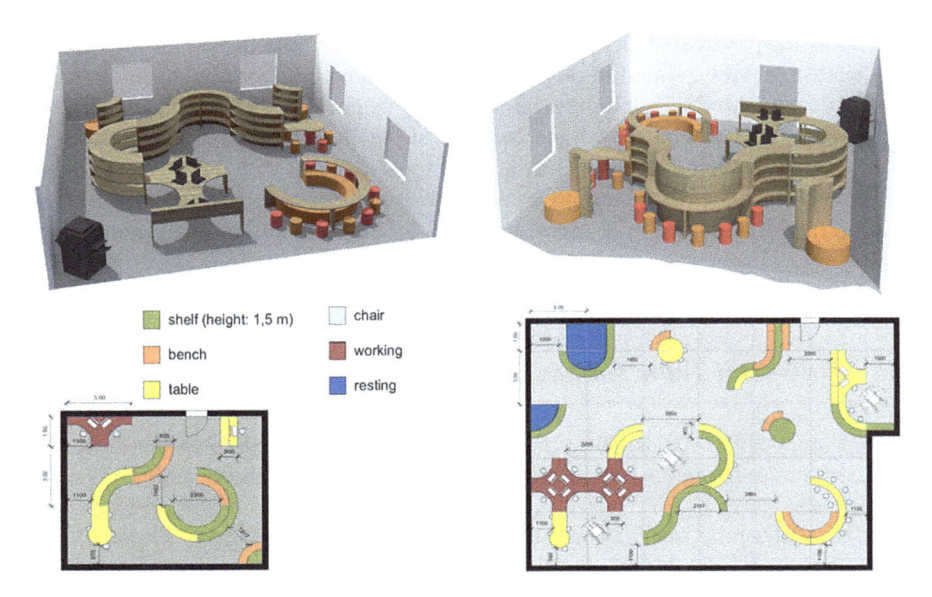

An Educational Path on Universal Design. Video Games … 27

Fig. 4 Library environment designed by Andrea Zito, Anita Deckers, Rojda Edebali, Sabina Elena Quocchini, Mirka Pellikka

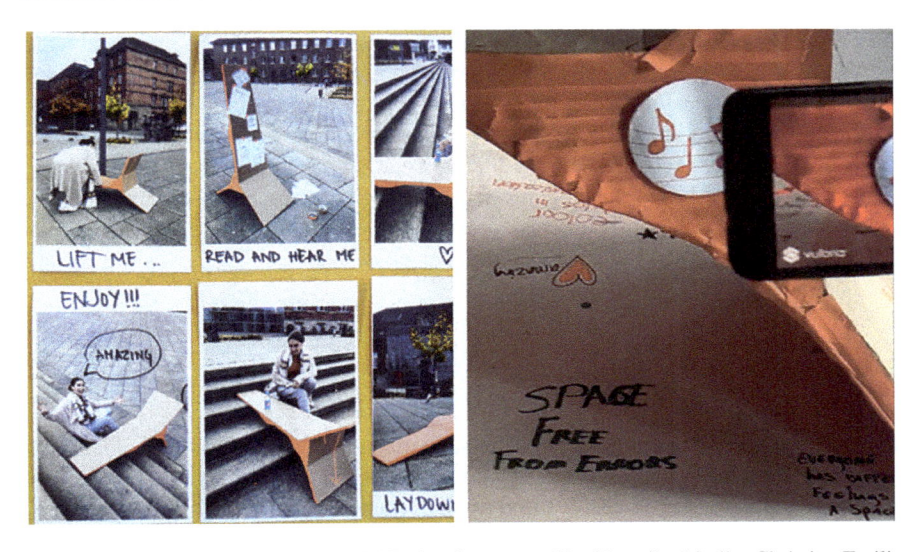

Fig. 5 Culturaction: storyboard **a** and AR-App **b** proposed by Veronika Merlin, Christina Emilia Fager, Federica Ferrini, Michele Corna, Annabelle Brons

extending the physical object with a digital layer that can be activated through an AR application, a public sound library for teaching and an outdoor cinema and a place for music were implemented. Interesting about this process was that the exploration of the Parameter extended with the analysis of the chosen location helped them to even add to it in their way. The term "action" was enhanced with the social character of "culture". This guided them to come up with a distinct design language in their build object that enables the users' potential to create inclusive environments for multisensory experiences and social interaction" [3].

3.3 Universal Table Games

Table games able of sensitizing the user and supporting her/him in the design of inclusive environments were developed with the support of Bahçeşehir University Game Lab.

"Six of the proposed games are based on ad hoc boards (grids or paths), the seventh is a card game. Many of them involve dices and tiles representing rooms, architectonic elements or pieces of furniture (doors, stairs, shelves …). Characters are defined considering perceptive impairments (blindness, mono-chromatism …), specific anthropometric features (i.e. small person), physical temporary or permanent disabilities, specific characteristics like old age or skin disease" [4].

As a whole they can offer useful contributes in terms of game mechanism, win conditions and inclusion strategies for the digital game development. The Escape From the Campus game (Fig. 6) for instance has a high potential by its replayability, cooperation mechanics and the idea of creating design solutions to preventing disaster. It's a grid based board game where two characters try to escape from the school campus that just had an earthquake. The two has to cooperate due to their differences in disability and speed as quick as possible.

3.4 Universal Digital Game

The game development targets a first-person perspective game run on a digital platform, based on the previous workshop delivered board games playable by multiple players. Feedbacks and ideas for the refinement where provided by students experimenting the Alpha version. The students advised to consider different disabilities for the characters comprehending also temporary and situational ones, other paths and environments inside the play field, further tasks to be accomplished also in interaction between players, alternative commands to move around and interfaces to choose between design solution, rewarding response for players.

In particular interesting hints were given by a group suggesting 6 distinguished characters with their features, the problems they should face and the possible solutions. Related to their characteristics (dwarfism, age, blindness, color blindness,

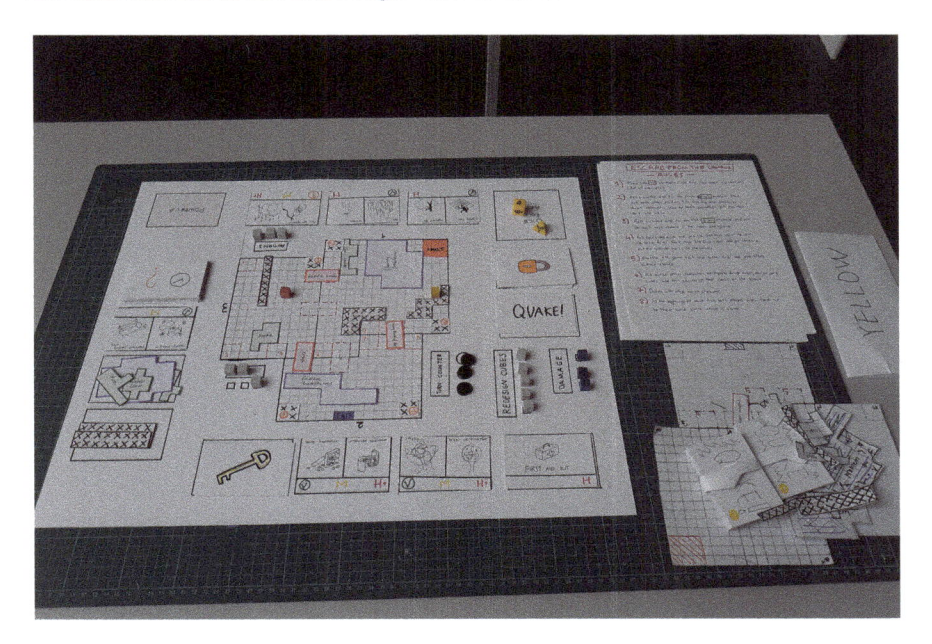

Fig. 6 Escape from the Campus table game by table Xin Xin, Saba Eraslan Sevin, Nikita Jelisejeff, Poyraz Ozer

broken arm, paralysis) the students proposed different mouse and keyboard use mode, new paths and additional tasks, for example in the cafeteria or to reach the bus stop. Storyboards are used to exemplify the play scenarios and the shift from a the dark gloomy mood at the beginning of the game to colorful inspiring mood towards the end is planned to encourage the player progress (Fig. 7).

Bahçeşehir University Game Lab team enriched the digital prototype (Fig. 8) by CAD features and implemented several cases discussed and studied in the workshop, other, as the proposal to include blindness or visual impairments go beyond the project boundaries, but are promising ideas for future developments.

4 Discussion

Participants in the project had widely varied backgrounds (e.g., different nationalities, cultures, skills) and role (researchers, teachers and students). That made the interaction sometimes complex, but in the meanwhile has been a chance to share knowledge and experiences between partners and students, making it possible to produce a wide range of proposals all useful to build empathy and awareness on Universal Design principles and practice.

Fig. 7 Feedbacks and ideas for the game development by development by Anne Backus, Irene Bacherotti, Sinem Biçer

The game development part of the project started by an empathy trial and a field survey and arrived to a first-person perspective digital game through paper prototyped board games playable by 4–5 players. "Thinking of the game experience and presence perceived by the gamer, designing a board game for 4–5 players and translating the findings to a first-person perspective digital game for next step may cause some loss because not every game mechanic and case, even the feeling of the overall game,

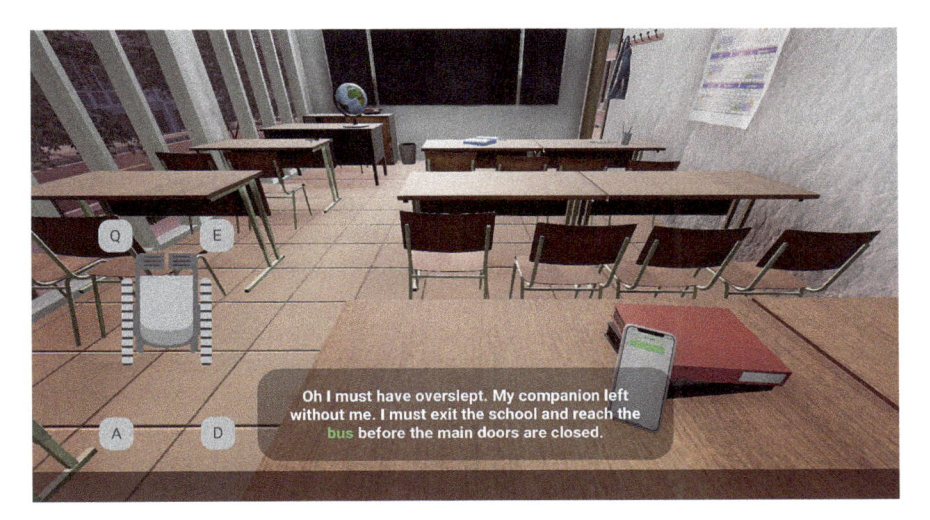

Fig. 8 Beta version startup screen. *Source* www.pudcadgame.com

designed for the board game will work in the digital game" [4]. This kind of loss can be considered as a limitation, nevertheless it is compensated along the iterative design development process [5] through the contribution of students and experts experimenting and improving the Alpha and Beta versions of the digital game.

More in general the relationship between experimental learning [6] and gamification [7] opens up practices where learning is not based on the capability to remember and apply information, but on the ability to find information, evaluate and use it coherently. Through PUDCAD game teachers have the possibility to incorporate Universal Design principles in a narrative context, start the learning process by providing accessibility problems and solutions, beginning from an elementary level to achieve progressively more difficult tasks and finally evaluate the expected results.

Talking about video games in education and training today no longer arouses attitudes of mistrust or alert as a decade ago. Research and publications in various sectors [3, 8–10], underline how this media manages to synchronously stimulate different brain functions, improving those cognitive pathways that allow learning. The proliferation of new definitions such as *Gamefication, Serius Game, Applied Games, Edutainment*, to name a few, denote a consolidated research approach that goes beyond the function of pure entertainment and investigates the pedagogical and educational potential. The PudCAD research project, now at its final stage, confirms the qualification potential of the educational experience inherent in video games, inducing several critical reflections.

4.1 Designing a Serious Game

The need to develop a digital application led students to confront a computational process, developing a logical reasoning in developing systems and processes capable of solving a problem. The study of programming leads to the development of logic, through a path that uses analysis, the breakdown of problems, the verification of results and the organization of thought. This usually occurs in any design path, but the fact of creating a computer application leads to thinking in terms of sequence and rules that can be effectively performed by a processing agent, bringing the student from a "passive" user of technology to be a conscious subject, endowed with critical autonomy. The technology must be known, to be used effectively, and the only way to know it is to study it. Fluency with digital modeling software, together with the presence multimedia design students, who shared their knowledge with the rest of the working group, certainly facilitated the task.

4.2 Learning with a Serious Game

Interactive applications are rapidly leading from the distribution of content, to the construction of the same in a context shared by several individuals and which simultaneously involves different expressive codes. The immersion and interactivity components expand the learning experience, through *"immersion in a world simulated and regulated by technical laws in which the actions of the active user are theologically oriented"* [11].

The video game is in fact a playful activity that does not require prior knowledge of rules. The user discovers what he has to do by trial and error then, as the simulation progresses, he comes to understand the goal and decode the rules of the game. The space of the game is investigated and the information code creates the constraints, guiding the user who learns, studying, what the game allows you to do and how it responds to the inputs. This explains the link between learning and technology. Digitization offers the advantage of collecting data starting from the actions performed within the game, measuring user behaviour and allowing profiling and categorization. The outcome is a more efficient active participation, because it is personalized and because through the implementation of dynamic behaviours the meanings are connected to an action favouring experiential learning. This allows us to understand the effects of the particular case and anticipate its consequences, thus generalizing a principle. The user is engaged in an empirical process that leads to *"learning by doing"* [12].

The gamification processes therefore promote the direct experimentation of ideas followed by immediate feedback, capable of evolving into innovative practices and theories. The ability to immerse yourself in correct consolidation activities through the simulation of real projects, while avoiding errors that in reality could have disastrous effects in economic and construction terms, provides the user with the freedom to experiment and conceive innovative approaches.

4.3 Empathy and Universal Design

In the case of PudCAD, the didactic value of simulations lies not only in the manipulation of variables and in the evaluation of the consequences, but in a building knowledge process, which is expressed in the possibility of "putting oneself in someone else's shoes". The possibility of observation by immersive experience opens up to otherwise precluded realities, capable of assisting the formation of aspects of empathy, here understood as the assumption of the point of view of others regardless of a personal bond. The Empathy concept—from the ancient Greek "εμ παθεία" (empatéia, composed of en-, "inside", and pathos, "suffering or feeling" - is used to indicate the participation emotional relationship that linked the author-singer to his audience.

Already at the end of the nineteenth century the aesthetic theory of *Einfühlung* [13] theorized a mental simulation spatial process by which we project ourselves into another person. The etymological root (*ein*-inside, and *fühlen*-subjective sensory or emotional experience) suggests a dynamic interaction between the simultaneous experiences of one's own body and the other's body. More recent studies on mirror neurons [14] that are activated when an action is performed, when it is seen to be performed, but also when the action is only seen depicted, confirm the theory. It is therefore possible for the gamer to abandon the egocentric perspective to adopt an allocentric perspective. By avatar observation, the mirror neurons translate the shape into a motor program, allowing us to grasp the needs of different users in relation to space. Predicting the spatial prefiguration of a body, develops the functional capacity of representation and manipulation of space, it is a fundamental skill for ergonomically orienting designers.

According to Universal Design principles, designing must combine the different needs declining them in a real context of products, environments and viability based on the observation of anthropometric diversity, evolving needs and changes occurring in the course of a life. Exploring the space via avatar, the designer can infer the different human characteristics, using them consciously in the relationship between the user and the built environment and verifying them in terms of compatibility.

Acknowledgements Authors of this paper wish to thank Istanbul Technical University, Faculty of Architecture team that led the project and all the participants from Bahcesehir University of Istanbul; Lahti University of Applied Sciences, Institute of Design and Fine Arts; Università degli Studi di Firenze, Architecture Department; Technische Hochschule Ostwestfalen-Lippe, Detmolder School of Architecture and Interior Architecture; Politecnico di Milano, Department of Design; SERÇEV, Association for Well-being of Children with Cerebral Palsy; Occupational Therapy Association of Turkey.

References

1. Mace RL, Hardie GJ, Place JP (1996) Accessible environments: toward universal design. AUED 9(96) (1996)
2. Buratti G, Amoruso G, Costa F, Pillan M, Rossi M, Cordan O, Arslan Dincay D (2019) PUDCAD project. Towards a CAD-based game for the implementation of universal design principles in design education. In: Luigini A (ed) Proceedings of the 1st international and interdisciplinary conference on digital environments for education, arts and heritage. Springer, Cham (2019)
3. Nether U, Ley JP, Dorf JJ, Herrmann K (2020) Parameter of inclusive design for spaces of learning: new methods in design education. In: Tosi F, Serra A, Brischetto A, Iacono E (eds) Design for inclusion, gamification and learning experience. FrancoAngeli, Milan
4. Costa F, Buratti G, Serra A, Brischetto A, Francesca Tosi F, Catak G, Tukerg C, Bostan B (2019) A cad-based game for inclusive design. In Bisson MM (eds) Proceedings (reviewed papers) of the 3rd international conference on environmental design. New Digital Frontiers (2019)
5. Norman DA, Draper S (1986) User centered system design: new perspectives on human-computer
6. Kolb A (1984) Experiential learning: experience as the source of learning and development. Prentice Hall, Englewood Cliffs
7. Desmet A, van Ryckeghem D, Compernolle S, Baranowski T, Thompson D, Crombez G, Poels K, van Lippevelde W, Bastiaensens S, van Cleemput K, Vandebosch H, De Bourdeaudhuij I, Hospital G, Street T, Gard T, Hoge EA, Kerr C (2014) A meta-analysis of serious digital games. Prev Med (Baltim) 69:95–107
8. Bertolo M, Mariani I (2014) Game design: gioco e giocare tra teoria e progetto. Pearson, Milano
9. Bittanti M (2002) Per una cultura dei videogames: Teorie e prassi del video giocare. Edizioni Unicopli, Milano
10. Amann TL (2003) Creating space for somatic ways of knowing within transformative learning theory. Mount St. Mary"s Colleger
11. Accordi Rickards M (2014) Storia del videogioco: Dagli anni Cinquanta a oggi. Carocci Editori, Roma
12. Papert S (1996) The connected family: bridging the digital generation gap. Longstreet Press, Atlanta
13. Husserl E (1973) Experience and judgment: investigations in a genealogy of logic. Northwestern University Press, Evaston
14. Rizzolatti G, Craighero L (2004) The mirror-neuron system. Ann. Rev Neurosci 27:169–192

Evaluation of Playgrounds in Terms of Universal Design: İzmir, Karşıyaka Coast After İzmir Deniz Project

Eda Paykoç, Gülnur Ballice, and Gizem Güler

Abstract Playgrounds are the areas that are specifically designed for children to play which are actually the places enable them to take part in the everyday life. In addition to taking place, the quality of this participation is also important. For analysing the quality of these areas, evaluating them in terms of Universal Design principles is one of the effective methods through seven parameters that enable to evaluate from the perspective of all different user profiles like children, elderly, disabled, playgrounds can be analysed like their dimensions, material usages, whether they are meeting the needs of children from different ages or with different abilities, and other design qualities specific to open public areas. As a case study, the playgrounds located in İzmir, Karşıyaka coast which was re-designed and re-arranged with İzmir Deniz Project were analysed. As a part of this project, some playgrounds are re-generated whereas some of them are added. As a method of this study, observations which will also be proved with photograph taking and analysis were used. It can be concluded that although the playgrounds in the area are just considered, they cannot fulfil the needs of children completely, especially with the focus of the universal design.

Keywords Universal design · Playground · Children · İzmir · İzmir deniz project

1 Introduction

A playground is the place where children can spend their enjoyment time freely. The idea of the playground was first originated in Germany as a platform for teaching children correct ways to play [1]. During the first decades of the twentieth century, several pioneering persons emerged as influential promoters of play and recreation. Joseph Lee, Luther Halsey Gulick, and Jane Addams were the most effective ones who had critical roles [2] (Table 1).

After 1965 until now, the types of playgrounds used in some research include traditional, designer or contemporary, adventure, and creative or adapted playground

E. Paykoç (✉) · G. Ballice · G. Güler
Yaşar University, İzmir 35100, Turkey
e-mail: eda.paykoc@yasar.edu.tr

Table 1 History of playgrounds

Year	Playground history
1848	The first sketched concept of a playground by Henry Barnard
1859	The first playground was built in Manchester, England
1885	The Boston Sand Gardens: the first supervised playground for children, built by the Boston Women's Club[1]
1887	The first public access playground was opened at Golden Gate Park in San Francisco: swings, slides, and a carousel. Most popular, though, was the Roman temple carousel, complete with Doric columns. This was replaced in 1912 with another wooden carousel. It was so popular that it even did a turn at the 1939 World's Fair in New York[2]
1890	New York Society for Parks and Playgrounds was established by Walter Vrooman[3]
1898	Playgrounds to Save Souls. Do-gooders with a passion for improving the plight of the urban poor latched onto playgrounds as a progressive ideal[4]
1903	The first government-funded playground was installed. New York City installed Seward Park, complete with a slide and sand box
1907	Playgrounds were properly introduced to the United States by President Roosevelt[5]
1912	The Safety Backlash Begins. New York banned climbing structures, citing them as too dangerous[6]
1931	Adventure Playgrounds a creation of architect C. Th. Sørensen
1943	The first adventure playground opened in Emdrup, Denmark, during World War II (https://adventureplaygrounds.hampshire.edu/history.html)
1953	Introduction of 'junk playgrounds' in the period following World War II in London, by Lady Allen of Hurtwood. She changed the name to 'Adventure Playground' in 1953; creating the National Playing Fields Association (now Fields in Trust)
1960s	The McDonaldsification of Playgrounds
1965	The Demise of the Visionary Playground
1980s	Lawsuits and Government Guidelines
2005	The "No Running" Playground. Schools in Broward County, Florida, famously posted "No Running" signs in their playgrounds, prompting reflections about whether a playground could be "too safe"
Later of the 2000s	Emergence of "pop-up playgrounds," in which the city closes one or more streets to serve as a forum for games and athletic coaching

[1] https://www.prm.nau.edu/prm346-old/sand_garden.htm, Boston Sand Gardens, Written Spring 1998 by: Olivia Rogers, Lydia Sheppard, Sarah Burch
[2] Further information on: https://www.bloomberg.com/news/articles/2012-03-14/the-politics-of-playgrounds-a-history
[3] McLean and Hurd [2]
[4] https://www.bloomberg.com/news/articles/2012-03-14/the-politics-of-playgrounds-a-history
[5] Matt Heap, The History of Playgrounds—Past, Present and Future, Posted Oct 10, 2012, https://www.espplay.co.uk/the-history-of-playgrounds/, accessed 16.06.2020
[6] https://www.bloomberg.com/news/articles/2012-03-14/the-politics-of-playgrounds-a-history
Source Designed by Authors

[3]. *The traditional playground* is a flat, barren area equipped with steel structures, such as swings, slides, seesaw, climbers, and merry-go-rounds, fixed in concrete and arranged in a row. The equipment is designed for exercise play exclusively and is primarily single or limited function. *The designer or contemporary playground* includes equipment designed with wood, metal, and/or plastic manufactured equipment, with plastic, concrete, or wood timbers to retain safety surfacing. The emphasis is on modular, linked equipment with a variety of heights and a range of motor challenges in aesthetically pleasing arrangements. *The adventure playground* is a highly informal playground within a fenced area, stocked with scrap building materials, tools, and provision for animals and cooking. This playground is characterized by children's construction using loose parts and scrap materials. The success of this environment requires the guidance of a skilled adult playleader [4–6]. Within its boundary's children can play freely, in their own way, in their own time and they can build and shape the environment according to their own creative vision [7].

Although there are several types of playgrounds, their common characteristics can be listed as following: **successful and creative landscaping** for natural environment, **surfacing** for natural engagement, **intelligent mounding** for having increased sense of fun, **usage of stone elements** for promoting creative skills, active play and experiencing risk, **various plantations, types of trees and foliage** for creating interaction with nature, **use of wooden elements** for creating an impression of open environment [1].

Playgrounds support young children for exploring and stretching their imaginations. Playground equipment must support physical and cognitive development while providing a safe play environment. *Active play, imaginative play and sensory learning* are the basic components of effective early childhood playground equipment [8].

As the children's one of the main areas for being a part of everyday life, playgrounds have important role for them. Frost (1986) and colleagues found that primary school children exhibited more fantasy play on adventure playgrounds and more functional play on traditional playgrounds. On the other hand, some researchers' findings have significant variations and show that children act very differently on different types on playscapes [9]. On the other hand, children behaviors on playgrounds are also influenced by socioeconomic and personality variables as they built in different residential areas [9]. Playgrounds have essential because they have health benefits, support development, promote imagination, show kids the value of community, introduce learning opportunity by recess, teach kids about nature and life skills. Advantages of playing children outdoors can be summarized as follows: learning, creativity, health, social skills, well-being, independence and explore.

İzmir Karşıyaka Coast region, which has been re-designed and re-arranged with the İzmir Deniz Project has been selected as a case study for evaluating the playgrounds (Fig. 2). Within this paper, the analysis and evaluation are based on selected six playgrounds (Fig. 3). Especially the playgrounds located in the coast region between Alaybey and Karşıyaka regions is discussed in this study. Literature review, on-site observation, photography shooting, analysis, and evaluation are among the methods of this study.

2 Universal Design

As it was cited by Ronald Mace in 1998 [10], the term *Universal Design (UD)* refers to "the design of products and environments to be able to usable by all people, to the greatest extent possible, without the need for adaptation or specialized design". After Mace, the most current definition of UD was made in Disability Act which was designed to advance and underpin the participation of people with disabilities in society by supporting the provision of disability specific services and improving access to mainstream public services [11]. According to Disability Act, UD can be described as below [11]:

- The design and composition of an environment so that it may be accessed, understood and used,
- To the greatest possible extent,
- In the most independent and natural manner possible,
- In the widest possible range of situations,
- Without the need for adaptation, modification, assistive devices or specialized solutions, by any persons of any age or size or having any particular physical, sensory, mental health or intellectual ability or disability, and
- Means, in relation to electronic systems, any electronics-based process of creating products, services or systems so that they may be used by any person.

When the history of the UD concept is searched, it is seen that the roots of UD are in the field of architecture. In the 1950s, the UD concept evolution started in Japan, the United States, and Europe with the idea of "barrier-free design". As its first emergence, the barrier-free design aimed to remove obstacles for people with disabilities (especially World War II veterans) which needed to adapt the buildings and also a change in the methodology for upcoming designs. In the 1970s, the term barrier-free design was replaced by the new term "accessible design" which is actually a result of an attempt to integrate people with disabilities in the community and public life especially in Europe and the United States. In the 1980s, several factors (including World Design Congress in 1987), came together to the first emergence of the concept "universal design" [10]. In 1989; Ronald Mace (who was an architect, product designer, and educator) established the Center for Universal Design at North Carolina State University. 8 years later than the establishment of the center, in 1997; The Principles of UD was introduced by a team of 10 advocates (architects, product engineers, engineers, and environmental design researchers) with aiming three different targets [12]. The first aim of UD is to guide the design of environments, products, and communications [13]. The second aim is to maximize the usability by individuals with a wide variety of characteristics [14]. The third aim is to evaluate existing designs, guiding the design process, and educate both designers and consumers about the characteristics of more usable products and environment [15]. Referring to these three aims, seven principles were developed with their specific guidelines and questions to each principle to control either they are applied or not [16]. The principles are as following:

- ***Principle 1: Equitable Use***—The design is useful and marketable to people with diverse abilities.
- ***Principle 2: Flexibility in Use***—The design accommodates a wide range of individual preferences and abilities.
- ***Principle 3:Simple and Intuitive Use***—Use of the design is easy to understand, regardless of the users' experience, knowledge, language skills or current concentration level.
- ***Principle 4: Perceptible Information***—The design communicates necessary information effectively to the user, regardless of ambient conditions or the users' sensory abilities.
- ***Principle 5: Tolerance for Error***—The design minimizes hazards and the adverse consequences of accidental or unintended actions.
- ***Principle 6: Low Physical Effort***—The design can be used efficiently and comfortably and with a minimum of fatigue.
- ***Principle 7: Size and Space for Approach and Use***—Appropriate size and space is provided for approach, reach, manipulation and use regardless of users' body size, posture or mobility.

According to Maisel and Ranahan [17], the seven principles of UD has seven different goals to achieve:

- *Body Fit*: Accommodating a wide range of body sizes and abilities
- *Comfort*: Keeping demands within desirable limits of body function
- *Awareness*: Ensuring that critical information for use is easily perceived
- *Understanding*: Making methods of operation and use intuitive, clear and unambiguous
- *Wellness*: Contributing to health promotion, avoidance of disease and prevention of injury
- *Social Integration*: Treating all groups with dignity and respect
- *Personalization*: Incorporating opportunities for choice and the expression of individual preferences

3 Universal Design in Playgrounds

When the playgrounds are analyzed upon seven UD principles specifically, user-oriented playgrounds with universal design principles which can be entitled as "Inclusive Playgrounds" should fulfill the below criteria [18]:

- *Equitable use*: Allowing children with different abilities and disabilities can play with the same playground equipment at the same time.
- *Flexible use*: Allowing children to try and succeed by themselves, and to make the users feel safe.

- *Simple and intuitive use*: Eliminating unnecessary complexity which can be understood by children from different age groups and with different abilities easily and intuitively.
- *Perceptible information*: Enabling children to process information via visual, sensory or experimental means.
- *Tolerance of error*: Minimizing the risks and allowing children to make minor errors while they are exploring and challenging their surroundings.
- *Low physical effort*: Design does not require children to spend extraordinary effort during play.
- *Size and space for approach and use*: Facilitating the design process by ensuring designs that are appropriate for children with different body dimensions, postures, activity and motor skills.

However, rather than using UD principles directly, different criteria or guidelines for universally designed playgrounds are developed and put forward. Although UD principles are certain and it is sure that playgrounds should meet the needs of children with several different types of abilities and disabilities, there are still more than one principle proposal for universally designed/inclusive playgrounds [19, 20].

Even though there are different principles, guidelines and paths are proposed, the well-accepted playground principles were made by the Disability Rights Commission [20] with six principles as below:

(1) **Variety and Difference** (Being aware of that disabled individuals are not the same group. There are also children who have different abilities due to their different disabilities.)
(2) **Easy Use** (Easy use includes the material selection, the direction and the location of the playground equipment.)
(3) **Freedom of Choice and Accessibility to Main Functions/Activities** (Access to equipment and services should be free as well as the help should be provided who needed to sustain the unity of different users.)
(4) **Being Qualified** (The main characteristic of design should be that it meets the needs of individuals with disabilities which will provide equality.)
(5) **Readability and Predictability** (There should be plans with figures and direction tools. They should be put where needed in maximum numbers with including all children like having Braille Alphabet.)
(6) **Being safe** (Playground areas should both include accident or risk and safety at the same time. For safe areas, enough lighting especially for visually impaired children, surfaces, materials and tones can be used.)

In addition to the principles that are related to holistic design approach of playgrounds, there is also some equipment listed to be included in universally design playgrounds which will meet the needs of children with different abilities and disabilities as below [21]:

- *Sandpit*: Through the interaction with sand, the creativity of children is developed. It is one of the most inclusive materials which enables children with different disabilities to play together.

- **Labirent / Maze**: Mazes with railings enables both healthy and disabled children to play. These railings both let disabled children continue without getting any help and protect children against the risk of accident and falling.
- **Dual Flying Fox**: This equipment can be used by a variety of users at the same time without putting so much effort.
- **Carousels**: With their huge size and chance to be used by wheelchair users and children who are using ancillary equipment, it increases the chance of being used by a huge number of children.
- **Nest Swing and Liberty Swing**: It enables healthy and disabled children to swing. It also has a place for families or friends of disabled children to swing with them.
- **Musical Instrument**: Equipment designed in the height of wheelchairs; musical instruments provide a chance for children to play with their hands.
- **Water Play**: It is one of the much-preferred elements in the playgrounds especially in the summer or hot times. Although it is thought that water can be unsafe if it is transferred on elevated surfaces or there are surfaces designed on water elements; it enables disabled children to interact with it directly and safely.

4 Method and Case Study

The İzmir Deniz Project was shaped after the decisions taken as a result of the İzmir Culture Workshop held in 2009 and the İzmir Design Forums convened in 2011 and later on. The main purpose of this project is to strengthen the relationship of the people of İzmir with the sea in daily life, to improve the quality of life of the society, and to contribute to the urban identity of İzmir. It was a comprehensive project with the participation of many designers on different topics.

This project design has three main issues:

1 Transforming the use of the bay and designing it as a performance area.
2 Making the ten coastal areas from Mavişehir to İnciraltı more useful with new regulations.
3 Creation of city terraces or balconies on the slopes of the city.

The main themes that the designers focused on during the design process of this project were sea use, coast use, transportation, festivity, and landscape. The regions to be designed were determined by İzmir Metropolitan Municipality. 11 coastal areas where the study is carried out (Fig. 1) [22].

Within the scope of this paper, the 1st (Between Mavişehir- Bostanlı Pier) and 2nd (Between Bostanlı Pier—Alaybey Shipyard) Regions (Fig. 2) with six playgrounds (Fig. 3) that were renewed with the İzmir Deniz Project were discussed. While residential use is intense in both regions, there are recreation areas, children's playgrounds, cafes and restaurants, entertainment facilities, and private health facilities in the 1st Region. The 2nd Region contains uses such as Karşıyaka Market, Karşıyaka Ferry Port and Karşıyaka Marriage Office [22].

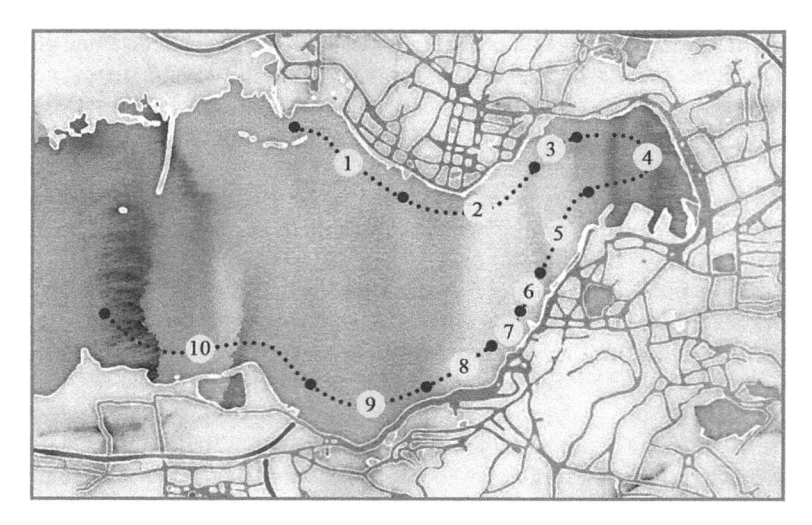

Fig. 1 İzmir Deniz Project, Project Area. *Source* İzmir Deniz Project Design Strategy Report, designed by Authors

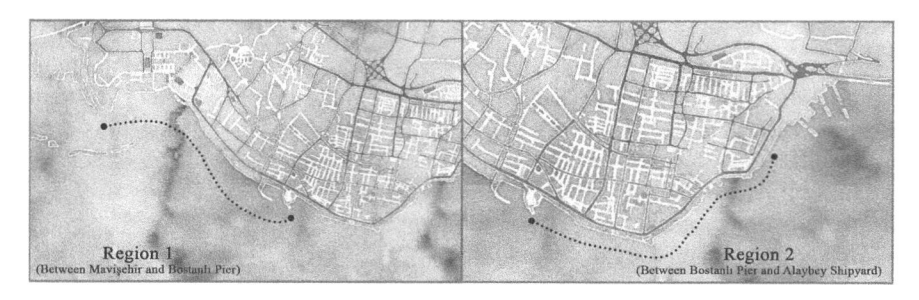

Fig. 2 Project Region 1 between Mavişehir and Bostanlı Pier and Project Region 2 between Bostanlı Pier and Alaybey Shipyard. *Source* İzmir Deniz Project Design Strategy Report, designed by Authors

Six selected playgrounds (Figs. 4, 5, 6, 7, 8 and 9) were analyzed through Universal Design principles. This analysis brings a comprehensive perspective to the design strategy and characteristics of playgrounds. Also, the evolution and change of playgrounds are observed with the analysis of selected case studies.

5 Analysis and Concluding Remarks

In conclusion, when Tables 2 and 3 are analysed from the perspective of seven principles of UD, the following can be put forward. The playgrounds are not proper for ***equitable use***, especially for wheelchair users due to floor material usage. When other

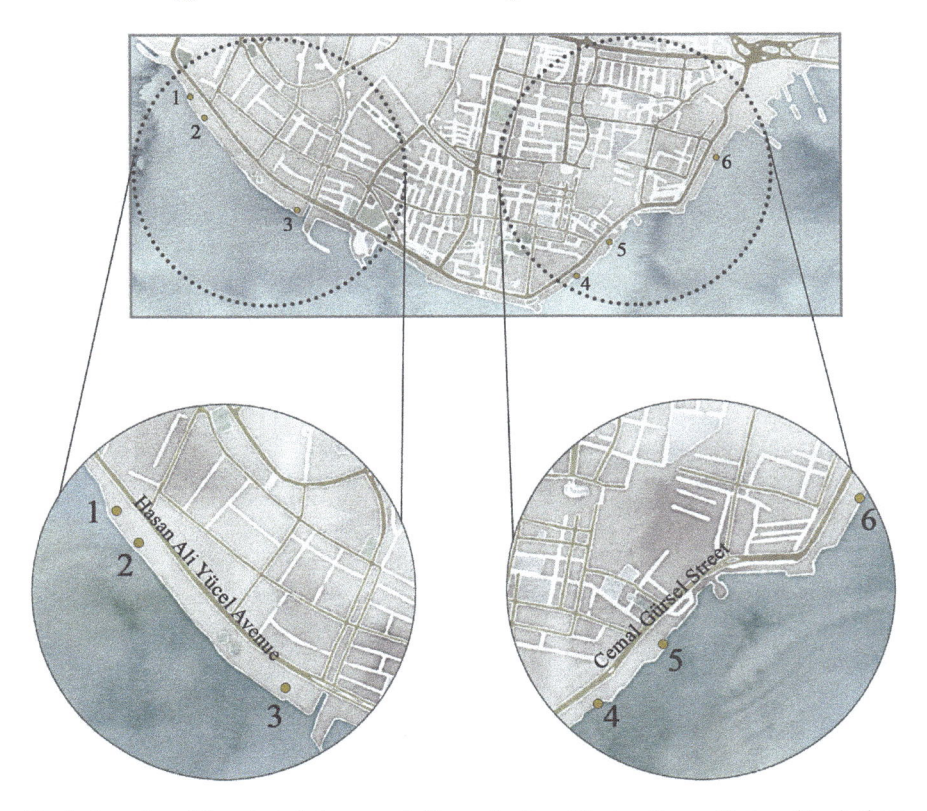

Evaluation of Playgrounds in Terms of Universal Design... 43

Fig. 3 Location of the selected playgrounds Karşıyaka Coast Region. *Source* Designed by Authors

Fig. 4 Playground 1 collage work. *Source* Designed by Authors

Fig. 5 Playground 2 collage work. *Source* Designed by Authors

Fig. 6 Playground 3 collage work. *Source* Designed by Authors

disabilities are considered like vision impairment, there are no Braille Alphabets, audio-recorded elements, and colour contrast. Also, plans with figures and direction tools are not included. One of the most common equipment in the playgrounds, mounding is not proper for wheelchair users which is good for other children. So that, alternatives to this equipment can be considered. In terms of *flexibility in use*, no equipment that enables users with different characteristics in a single element or more than one user in single equipment like family swings and space for caregivers, peers, and family members although spaces for them are defined with shelters like in

Evaluation of Playgrounds in Terms of Universal Design... 45

Fig. 7 Playground 4 collage work. *Source* Designed by Authors

Fig. 8 Playground 5 collage work. *Source* Designed by Authors

Playground 4. In addition to these, none of the equipment is with adaptable heights or levels. When *simple and intuitive use* is considered, it can be said that the design language of all equipment gives a direct message to all types of users with their basic characteristics. In *perceptible information*, there are no perceptible surfaces, touching maps, and pictograms which will aid the orientation of visually disabled. Also, there is no direct interaction or access to natural elements (water, sand, sea, green texture, etc.) which are good for the perceptible qualities of the playgrounds. From the perspective of *tolerance for error*, the common materials that are used

Fig. 9 Playground 6 collage work. *Source* Designed by Authors

in the selected playgrounds (rubber mat, pea gravel, sand, and wood) decrease the level of risk of injury. Although, the other materials used in surfaces like grass, soil, and cobblestone are not safe and acceptable due to weather conditions which will be resulted in falling risk. In terms of ***low physical effort***, the playgrounds analyzed can be described as good quality because there is no need to put that much effort during play. Due to the dimensions both in the plan and in the equipment, the material of the floor (pea gravel) and not having a proper access route, ***size and space for approach and use*** cannot be achieved in the playgrounds and the equipment.

Evaluation of Playgrounds in Terms of Universal Design... 47

Table 2 Analysis of Selected Playgrounds according to Universal Design (PE: Playground Equipment)

Playground #	Variety and difference	Easy use (in terms of physical accessibility)	Freedom of choice and accessibility to main functions /activities	Being qualified	Readability and predictability	Being safe
Playground 1	– Variety of PE is not enough – No suitable for different ages: only for 6 + ages – Not suitable for children with different abilities	– Accessible route – Wheelchair users can access – Possible to use PE in different angles	– Free access to equipment and – Physical assistant and social support are not provided	– Enough space between the equipment – Natural elements: glass and trees surrounded by seating (P2, P3) – Missing perceptible qualities with touching – Shading elements support the comfort environment (P4)	– No plans with figures and direction tools – No information panels (Only P4 have information panel for fitness – No alternatives for communication (braille, audio-record, touching maps and pictograms, etc.) – Perceptible surfaces are not included	– PE and ground joint details are not safe (P1) – Only street lighting is used on the periphery of the playground – Non- slippery surfaces – Structural safety
Play ground 2	– Different kinds of PE – Not suitable for different ages: only for 2–6 ages – Suitable for children with different abilities					

(continued)

Table 2 (continued)

Playground #	Variety and difference	Easy use (in terms of physical accessibility)	Freedom of choice and accessibility to main functions/activities	Being qualified	Readability and predictability	Being safe
Playground 3	– Different kinds of PE – Suitable for different ages – Suitable for children with different abilities	– Not accessible route – Wheelchair users cannot access – Not possible to use PE in different angles				
Playground 4						
Playground 5	– Variety of PE is not enough – Not suitable for different ages: only for 6 + ages – Not suitable for children with different abilities	– Accessible route – Wheelchair users cannot access – Possible to use PF. in different angles				
Playground 6	– Different kinds of PF – Suitable for different ages – Suitable for children with different abilities	– Not accessible route – Wheelchair users cannot access – Not possible to use PE in different angles				

Source Designed by Authors

Table 3 Analysis of selected playgrounds in terms of materials and PE (PE: Playground Equipment)

Playground #	Material	Variety of playground equipment
Playground 1	Rubber mats on the playground area (safe and suitable for UDP)/Cobblestone on the access route (not suitable for UDP)/PE is made of plastic material	**4 different types of PE**: Liberty swing, dandle board, multiuser rope swing (not suitable for UDP)/Climbing equipment (apart from net unit, not suitable for UDP)
Playground 2	Rubber mats on the playground area (safe and suitable for UDP)/Wooden deck surface on the access route (safe and suitable for UDP)/PE is made of plastic, metal and wooden material	**5 different types of PE**: Liberty and nest swings, cave formed adventure PE, sandpit surrounded by seating elements (suitable for UDP)/House-like equipment with metal slide and net climbing (not suitable for UDP)
Playground 3	Rubber mats on the PE (safe and suitable for UDP)/Pea gravel on the playground area (safe and suitable for UDP)/Grass floor (unsafe and suitable for UDP)/PE is made of plastic material	**10 different types of PE**: Multiuser rope swing, rectangular climbing equipment (not suitable for UDP)/slides built into a mound, spider web climbing equipment, bouncing zone, plastic swings, dandle board, horizontal bars, circular swing unit (suitable for UDP)
Playground 4	Rubber mats on the playground area (safe and suitable for UDP)/Pea gravel on the fitness area (safe and suitable for UDP)/PE is made of plastic and metal material	**11 different types of PE**: Dandle board, metal slides built into a mound (not suitable for UDP)/Seating elements in flower form, spring PE, concrete table tennis table, different types of swings integrated with metal sun shading elements, different types of rotating PEs, sandpit surrounded by seating elements, fitness equipment, skateboard area, gradual playing platforms and hopscotch zone (suitable for UDP)
Playground 5	Pea gravel on the playground area (safe and suitable for UDP)/PE is made of plastic and metal material	**Single type of PE**: Polyhedron shaped multipurpose PE (metal tunnel slide, net climbing, tunnel walking, metal tubes for sliding) (not suitable for UDP)
Playground 6	Pea gravel on the playground area (safe and suitable for UDP)/PE is made of wooden material	**8 different types of PE**: Wooden swing, elevated wooden walking platform, tree house with slider and stairs and climbing nets, bollard like wooden elements, horizontal bar, angled wooden sticks, climbing net (suitable for UDP)/Cable line (not suitable for UDP)

Source Designed by Authors

References

1. Henderson Recreation (2018) What are the general characteristics of natural playgrounds? https://www.quora.com/profile/Henderson-Recreation. Last Access 16 June 2020
2. McLean DD, Hurd AR (2012) Recreation and leisure, 9th edn. Recreation and Leisure in Modern Society, Jones and Bartlett Learning, p 65
3. Saracho ON, Spodek B (1998) Multiple perspectives on play in early childhood education: divine accommodation in Jewish and Christian Thought. SUNY Press
4. Frost JL (1979) Children's play and play environments. Allyn and Bacon, Boston
5. Dempsey JD, Frost JL (1993) Play environments in early childhood education. In: Spodek B (ed) Handbook of research on the education of young children. Macmillan, New York, pp 306–321
6. Hartle L, Johnson JE (1993) Historical and contemporary influences of outdoor environments. In: Hart CH (ed) Children on playgrounds. State University of New York Press, Albany, pp 14–42
7. Shier H (1984) Adventure playgrounds: an introduction. National Playing Fields Association, London
8. AAA State of Play, Characteristics of Early Childhood Playground Equipment, Kim Hart, https://www.aaastateofplay.com/characteristics-of-early-childhood-playground-equipment/. Last Access 16 June 2020
9. Pellegrini AD (1995) School recess and playground behaviour: educational and developmental roles. SUNY Press
10. Case BJ (2003) Policy Report: Universal Design, https://images.pearsonassessments.com/images/tmrs/tmrs_rg/UniversalDesign.pdf. Last Access 16 June 2020
11. Department of Justice, Equality and Law Reform (2005) Guide to the Disability Act 2005. https://www.justice.ie/en/JELR/DisabilityAct05Guide.pdf/Files/DisabilityAct05Guide.pdf. Last Access 16 June 2020
12. About the Center (2008) Center history, the center for universal design—environments and products for all people. https://projects.ncsu.edu/ncsu/design/cud/about_us/ushistory.htm. Last Access 16 June 2020
13. What Is Universal Design (2020) The seven principles, centre for excellence in universal design. https://universaldesign.ie/What-is-Universal-Design/The-7-Principles/The-7-Principles.html. Last Access 16 June 2020
14. University at Buffalo (2020) Accessibility at UB, Universal design principles. https://www.buffalo.edu/access/help-and-support/topic3/universaldesignprinciples.html#:~:text=The%20goal%20of%20Universal%20Design,to%20maximize%20access%20by%20everyone. Last Access 16 June 2020
15. NC State University and The Center for Universal Design (2020) The principles of universal design. https://projects.ncsu.edu/ncsu/design/cud/about_ud/udprinciplestext.htm. Last Access 16 June 2020
16. Story MF, Mueller JL, Mace RL (1998) The universal design file: designing for people of all ages and abilities. https://www.certec.lth.se/fileadmin/certec/Kirre/102-154-1-PB.pdf. Last Access 16 June 2020
17. Maisel JL. Ranahan M (2017) Beyond Accessibility to Universal Design. Whole Building Design Guide, https://www.wbdg.org/design-objectives/accessible/beyond-accessibility-universal-design. Last Access 16 June 2020
18. Ayataç H, Pola İ (2016) No "Obstacles" in Playgrounds that are Not Only Accessible but Also Inclusive. In: ICONARP Int J Architect Plann 4(2):1–14. https://doi.org/https://doi.org/10.15320/iconarp.2016120233. Last Access 16 June 2020
19. Yılmaz Z (2019) Özel Gereksinimli Çocuğu Olan Ebeveynlerin Açık Hava Oyun Parklarına İlişkin Görüşlerinin İncelenmesi (Unpublished Master Thesis). Pamukkale University, Turkey
20. Günay N (2016) Fiziksel Çevrelerin Çocuk Üzerindeki Etkisi Bağlamında 'Kapsayıcı Oyun Alanları' (Unpublished Master Thesis). Yıldız Technical University, Turkey

21. Pola İ (2015) Çocuk Oyun Alanlarına Kapsayıcı Yaklaşımlar: İstanbul için bir Değerlendirme (Unpublished Master Thesis). İstanbul Technical University, Turkey
22. İzmir Büyükşehir Belediyesi (İzmir Metropolitan Municipality), Tasarım Stratejisi Raporu İzmirlilerin Denizle İlişkisini Güçlendirme Projesi (Design Strategy Report–Project Reinforcing the Relation of Citizens with the Sea) (2012) Available at: https://www.izmeda.org/Upload_Files/FckFiles/file/kiyi_tasarim_tasarim_stratejisi.pdf. Last Accessed 7 July 2020

Effects of Educational Policies on Design of Inclusive Schools: SERÇEV Case

Simge Gülbahar and Özge Cordan

Abstract Universal design and inclusive education aroused as paradigms based on egalitarianism in the twentieth century. The countries are responsible to update the approaches on their own education policy including inclusive education. Updates on education policy become a problem to articulate spatial requirements of inclusive schools according to them. In this sense, universal design gives an opportunity to find effective and practical spatial solutions for problems of inclusive education environment through creating an interdisciplinary ground in design process. The aim of the study is to find out the effects of the inclusive educational policy of Turkey on the design of inclusive school environments under the umbrella of both universal design and inclusive education. In this scope, the laws, regulations, legislations, regarding the inclusive education in Turkey within the international discourse are reviewed. SERÇEV (Children with Cerebral Palsy Association) inclusive schools, which are Gökkuşağı Primary School and SERÇEV Accessible Vocational and Technical Anatolian High School, are examined in the scope of universal design. These inclusive schools are chosen as the case studies to examine the spatial reflection of the current policies in inclusive school environment. The methodology of the study includes commentary of on-site observations on spatial requirements regarding universal design approach and interviews from site visits. The study contributes to determine the design approaches of inclusive school environment in the case of SERÇEV inclusive schools in Turkey.

Keywords Inclusive school · Universal design · Education policy · SERCEV · Turkey

---

S. Gülbahar (✉)
School of Architecture and Design, FMV Işık University, Şile, İstanbul, Turkey
e-mail: gulbaharsimge@gmail.com

Ö. Cordan
School of Architecture, Istanbul Technical University, Taksim, İstanbul, Turkey
e-mail: cordanozge@gmail.com

1 Introduction

Human rights movements promote inclusive politics in design against discrimination of people with disabilities in society. Human diversities in the societies were realized as a requirement that should consider in design approaches which were conceived after 1950s. Considering differences in human abilities, universal design (UD) emerged to enhance equality in built-environment, and inclusive education (IE) emerged to create equal access for education. Both approaches avoid to discrimination of people with disabilities in terms of environmental and social dimensions.

UD was defined by Ron Mace that the product and environment are independently usable by all people, to the greatest extent possible without the need for adaptation or specialized design [1]. While this development was happening in design paradigm, IE was referred by 'Salamanca Statement' in 1994 as a shift of integration to inclusivity within a child-centered pedagogy in education [2]. These developments in educational policies for equality between all people, which bring new approaches and additional methods using in education, influence the physical environments in the schools. This opens a discussion on how effective use of space sustains in inclusive school regarding regulations on educational policies. Existing or newly constructed inclusive school buildings have to ensure physical and functional requirements by spatial adaptations according to spatial reflections of updated educational policies for providing equal use for all participants of inclusive school. Study aims to find out the effects of educational policies on design of inclusive schools under the umbrella of both UD and IE.

In the scope of the study, UD and IE are discussed by means of literature review. The laws, regulations, legislations regarding the inclusive education in Turkey, in international discourse, are reviewed by literature commentary. SERÇEV (Children with Cerebral Palsy Association) inclusive schools, which are Gökkuşağı Primary School and SERCEV Accessible Vocational and Technical Anatolian High School, are examined to explore the spatial reflection of the current policies in inclusive school environment regarding literature review and on-site observation and interviews within the universal design approach. The result of the study will help to determine design approaches for all stakeholders of IE.

2 Relation between Universal Design and Inclusive Education

Disability is a considerable issue in both IE and UD approaches. It conceptualizes as an interaction which happens between person and its individual and material environment [3–5]. Disability firstly was described by WHO (The World Health Organization) in two models which are called the medical model and the social model. The medical model is used for disabled people who cannot provide freely their mobility due to their bodily systems, and social model is used for disabled people who are excluded by societal obstacles such as architectural and other barriers [6, 7]. Later on, WHO (2001) [5] proposed bio-psychosocial model which was based on the synthesis of both medical and social model. This model provides a coherent view of different perspectives of health such as biological, individual and social [5]. This definition gives an individualized consideration that indicates the equality rights among societies about disability issue. Disability reasoned by manifold individual experiences recognizes as a reflection of human plurality in this subject. In short, the definition of disability finalizes beyond a health problem, and it is a mismatch between people and the environment around them [8]. UD is a concept which WHO suggested to apply for the socially inclusive solutions of disability problems [9].

UD came out for responding accessibility problems of the disabled people in built environment at the beginning. Later on, user structure of issues in UD was based on not only ergonomic but also social inclusion regarding the ventures such as ADA (American Disabilities Act) in 1990, DDA (Disability Discrimination Act) in 1995 [1, 10]. For this reason, it starts to address to increase the participations of majority in society by using UD's perspective. Participation problems in the society are solved by minimizing non-available issues in built environment. Thus, human interaction with environment is increased, and contributes the social inclusion. UD represents seven principles to make a framework of the environment and the products (Table 1). Lid [3] claims that UD is an interdisciplinary field of knowledge using by the disciplines such as architects, spatial planners, politicians, rehabilitation professionals etc. in order to promote non-discriminated environment for citizens.

Table 1 Principles of universal design, Copyright © 1997 NC State University, The Center for Universal Design [11]

Principle	Description
Equitable use	The design is useful and marketable to people with diverse abilities
Flexibility in use	The design accommodates a wide range of individual preferences and abilities
Simple and intuitive use	Use of the design is easy to understand, regardless of the user's experience, knowledge, language skills, or current concentration level
Perceptible information	The design communicates necessary information effectively to the user, regardless of ambient conditions or the user's sensory abilities
Tolerance for error	The design minimizes hazards and the adverse consequences of accidental or unintended actions
Low physical effort	The design can be used efficiently and comfortably and with a minimum of fatigue
Size and space for approach and use	Appropriate size and space is provided for approach, reach, manipulation, and use, regardless of user's body size, posture, or mobility

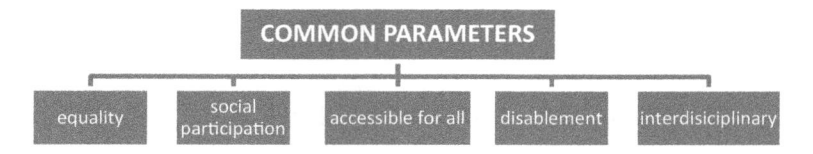

Fig. 1 Common parameters of both UD and IE (produced by authors)

Equality promotions for disabled citizens in education bring the discussion of special educational needs and equal opportunities in education. Education for All (EFA) report in 1990 points to eliminate discrimination problems in education with *"universalizing access to education for all children, youth and adults, and promoting equity"* [12]. For this reason, IE was offered as a special education method. Within this perspective, IE aims social inclusion and universalization that are common purposes with respect to the conceptualization of the UD. IE promotes against the segregated methods in the special education while responding to the practical problems presented by the differences of students [13, 14]. It is enhanced by providing extra resources. Different professionals who have broaden specializes are participated because of necessity of extra resource in inclusion [14]. IE drives its participants into an interdisciplinary practice which serves a common ground with UD.

There are common parameters that both approaches take into consideration (Fig. 1). Both approaches aim equality among citizens in order to promote social participation providing accessibility within an interdisciplinary practice. UD and IE have been a voice for the individualized disablements in their area of study. For this reason, inclusive school environment is supported by concept of universal design to reach IE goals [15]. Thus, UD principles help to make a framework for creating effective inclusive schools.

3 Inclusive School Environment from the View of Educational Developments in Turkey

There is apparently a strong relationship, which is proven by literature review, between UD and IE to criticize interior design concerns in inclusive school environment. UD is a leading concept that takes into attention to design inclusive school environment [16]. Countries are responsible to develop their own policy about IE, so they are responsible to design their own criteria for inclusive school environment. Development of special education in Turkey has its roots to late 1950s considering educational right of children and disabled individuals (Table 2). In this chapter, legal dimensions about IE and guidelines for school environments which have been published by MEB (Republic of Turkey Ministry of National Education) are discussed to explore spatial requirements for inclusive school environment in Turkish case.

Table 2 Legal dimensions on educational rights of people with special needs in Turkey, p. 30 [17]

Year/issue	Policy
1949/5387	Law on Children in Need of Protection
1961/222	Law on Primary Education and Basic Education
1962 and 1968	Regulation on Children in Special Need
1983/2916	Law on Children in Special Need
1983/2828	Law on Social Services Child Protection
1986/3308	Law on Apprenticeship and Vocational Education
1991	First Special Education Council
1992	Regulation On Educational Practices For Mentally Retarded Children
1997/571	Degree of Law on Organization and Duties of the Presidency of the Administration for Disabled People
1997/573	Decree of Law on Special Education
2000	Regulation on Special Education Services
2005/5378	Law on People with Disabilities
2006/26,184	Regulation on Special Education Services (updated)
2018/30,471	Regulation on Special Education Services (updated)

'Regulation on Special Education Services' published in 2018 is the latest version that is considered today [18]. The regulation identifies how special education methods practice in Turkish inclusive schools. 'Regulation on Special Education Services' defines the stakeholders of special education method, and explains the application methods of IE. IEP (individualized education program), resource room, supportive services, and collaboration with family and communities are the essentials of IE according to 'Regulation on Special Education Services'. There are three type of IE, which are full time, part time and reversed inclusion for students with SEN (special education need) in Turkey [19, 20]. This separation in application of IE affects the classroom layout regarding the spatial requirements.

There is 'Minimum Design Standards for Educational Buildings' published by MEB in 2015 as a reference source considered firstly in the design of school buildings. In the beginning of this guideline, information about construction, site and infrastructure of mainstream school building are given. Spatial concerns about design criteria of school environment are titled while stressing that the inclusive school environments which are flexible and sustainable should be student centered in the school's design process [21]. In this guideline, building components are explained under separate titles to give a general framework regarding the materials selection and their applications. Some rules are not in an order in terms of technical or visual concerns of interiors in the guideline. For example, the rules under floor covering title explain how the floor covering in the school environments should be considered; however, they indicate different aspects of design such as,

- *The materials used for the flooring should be in accordance with the needs of the place and compatible with the floor coverings in other places.*
- *The wooden flooring must be polished with non-toxic hardening and non-slip materials.*
- *Floor covering of tribunes of sport hall should be epoxy coated.*
- *Materials to be used in kitchens should be resistant to instant heat shocks (pp. 47–48)* [21].

According to the rules listed above, the first rule is about visual, aesthetic and functional aspects, the second rule is more detailed technical aspect in general, and the third and the forth rules are regarding technical aspects for a particular space in the school. Spaces in mainstream schools are separately identified in terms of their purpose, location, area, building components in the end of this guideline. Nevertheless, there is not any helpful information regarding the design parameters of the special education environment or inclusive school environment.

Special educational needs in inclusive school are another issue that points physical abilities of student with SEN. Regarding this issue, the title of the 'Design Standards for the Disabled' in the 'Minimum Design Standards for Educational Buildings' can be assumed for the actions that can take for disability issues in design. In addition, there are some requirements mentioned under different titles in this guideline regarding the phenomenon of the disability in educational building construction. These requirements are not recognizable in terms of responding the aspects of design and user demands, because they are listed under different title. These types of definitions regarding the inclusive or special education school's design become a challenge for designers and design practitioners to take into account what kind of impairments they have to find out a solution within interior design context.

The guideline, which was published by MEB in 2011 with the title of 'Why How What for Mainstreaming Education at Our Schools: A Guide Book for School Principals, Teachers, Parents', explains all dimension of IE. In this guideline, arrangements for physical environment are explained in 14 rules which are general or detailed descriptions that examples of three of them are listed below;

- *Special ramps must be provided in the building entrances; entrance doors must be the normal type and not the revolving or swing types.*
- *Boards must be 70 cm high from the floor; part of the coat racks and hooks must be at such a height as within reach for the disabled pupils as their need may be.*
- *Physical environment must be designed according to the needs of the disabled (pp. 34–35)* [20].

Another guideline of MEB titled as 'Special Education Schools Standard Equipment Guideline' [22], gives some information about the furnishing instructions for each places in special schools which limit the ergonomics of furniture or equipment. Description of furniture includes name of the furniture and its features such as color, amount, form and sizes. However, spaces where this equipment and furniture are placed in the school are not defined in terms of their qualifications.

The guidelines and regulations suggested by MEB include piecemeal definitions which Erkılıç and Durak [15] stated same assumption for previous versions of them. Spatial expectations about inclusive school environments are defined inefficiently for meeting the purposes of IE successfully [15] and it is still hard to define them for any step of design process [17]. IE has a student-centered provision; however users are not in the center of recommendations in the guidelines. Spatial organization of a particular educational method was not indicated exceptionally in the guidelines discussed in this chapter. For this reason, guidelines are also hard to follow for the designers or other participant of the design process of inclusive schools in terms of defining user needs, type of use, and spatial requirements in inclusive school environments. Guidelines of MEB do not suggest UD or any other approaches as a design concept for education environment contrary to international policy.

4 Spatial Assessments of Inclusive Schools

In this chapter, the two inclusive schools of SERCEV are investigated to examine the spatial reflection of the current policies in inclusive school environment with the help of UD approach regarding their current situation. The case study includes commentary of site visits and face to face interviews in both schools.

These schools belong to reversed inclusion type in education both the students with SEN and the students with the 'Cerebral Palsy (CP)'. CP is an umbrella term that defines brain damages in birth or early development of human being cause motor impairments. Children with CP have difficulties such as diverse level muscle related physical disabilities, attention, concentration [16]. For this reason, disability concerns in design process of both schools need to have comprehensive solutions to provide the requirements of medical model of disability definitions.

Gökkuşağı Primary School is the first inclusive school, which was designed according to IE model in Turkey [17]. The building is U-shaped and has two storeys. On ground floor, there are general classrooms on one side of the building, and on the other arm of the building belongs to special education classrooms and supportive services. Dining hall, canteen, teachers' room and counseling service are also on ground floor. All rooms on ground floor have access directly to outside.

On the first floor, there are special education kindergarten, sports hall, multi-purpose hall, family room, library, and administration rooms. The investigations on Gökkuşağı Primary School demonstrate that some spatial adaptations in the building which are different from the first establishment. Therapy space and the counseling service placed one of the niches on the special education corridor. Counseling service is placed on the niche opposite corridor. During the use of building, new functions are added in the building program considering the necessities that occurred in time. Life center unit is one of the new functions in the school. These changes demonstrate that the spatial organization needs adaptable arrangements for future demands in inclusive schools.

First noticeable necessity from the visits in 2015 was a parking area for assistive equipment which was parking on corridors (Fig. 2a). Hygiene room was adapted later to building; however the room failed to recover some fulfillment of spatial requirements (Fig. 2b). Privacy controls are not trustable, and the users' demands are ignored about furniture decisions ergonomically. A storage space is needed for cleaning supplies as well. There is not any specific order about arrangement of desks in classrooms, so flexibility is needed for arrangements (Fig. 2c). Alternatives for spatial organization should be developed to provide appropriate circulation and perception in classroom. Therapy spaces are placed without considering any acoustic and lighting issue into niches on corridor (Fig. 2d). Boundaries of therapy space are provided by a fence that privacy concerns are controversial. Flooring in therapy space that is different than flooring in corridor demonstrates that material chose need to be changed according to the functions in the school building.

User type of inclusive school includes also family members who accompany student with SEN all day in the school building. User needs must be reconsidered about design of this room since accompanies of student with SEN are also permanent users of the inclusive school environment. Contrary to mainstream schools, family room is one of the essential places in inclusive education environment (Fig. 3a). This place is defined by MEB [21] for nursery level in the mainstream school buildings in Turkey. In addition, life center unit which is placed in the building as a new form of

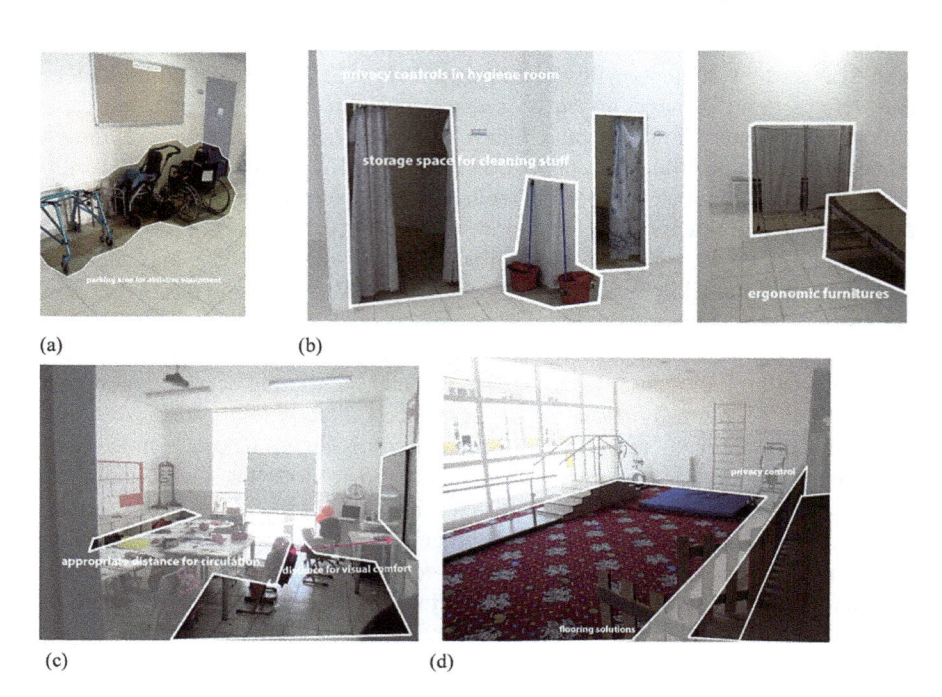

Fig. 2 Some spatial failures in Gökkuşağı Primary School in 2015. *Source* S.Gülbahar

Effects of Educational Policies on Design of Inclusive … 61

(a)

(b)

Fig. 3 Family room and life center unit in Gökkuşağı Primary School in 2015. *Source* S.Gülbahar

supportive educational services is not mentioned in any guide in terms of its purpose and design parameters (Fig. 3b).

The second example is the SERÇEV Accessible Vocational and Technical Anatolian High School. The building scheme is similar to Gökkuşağı Primary School. This building has two storeys; however the building has entrance on both floors. The building program is generated considering Gökkuşağı Primary School. Some of the inadequacies found out by the report[1] at the project phase of the building about design decisions and accessibility problems were;

- Length of main corridors is 70 m that is too long for a disabled person to walk.
- Slope of ramps (%9) are more than appropriate amount though it is defined as maximum %6.
- Rehabilitation area is not determined.
- Dining hall is not appropriate size considering the amount of users in the school.
- Wet spaces should be revised considering accessibility distances.
- Spatial organization should be revised in terms of the relation of spaces with each other.

---

[1]This unpublished report was an evaluation of the SERÇEV Accessible Vocational and Technical Anatolian High School building to find out the spatial and functional inadequacies during the construction process of TOKI. This report was produced by Assoc. Prof. Dr. Özge Cordan as tutor and Dr. Demet Dinçay and Dr. Çağıl Yurdakul as advisors as a part of Interior Architecture Project III of IMIAD Master programme in ITU in 2015–2016 fall semester within the thesis project's study of Simge Gülbahar and, Ali Shoar.

There are some spaces such as life center unit, roof garden that are not explained in 'Regulation on Special Education' or the guidelines investigated in this study within a spatial or architectural context. Studies also demonstrate that the students with SEN have ergonomic problems in terms of using equipment of school, especially in wet spaces and classrooms besides accessing to recreational or activity areas [23].

5 Evaluation and Conclusion

Assessments of the two inclusive schools of SERCEV in Turkey demonstrate that they need modifications even after they are constructed. The general rules discussing in the educational policies of MEB are partially applied in these projects. Ergonomic solutions are needed, because users are not the center of the issue for taking design decisions. Information for easing design process is still needed for an effective use regarding the condition of investigated inclusive schools. There is not any direct guide or source that is published by MEB indicating the possible problems and approaches for the spatial obstacles in inclusive schools.

Shortly to say that disability is a social inclusion problem in a built environment and UD is internationally a suggested concept to design inclusive settings for disability models both Turkey and the World. UD principles are the key strategies integrating human needs and factors into design process. Spatial requirements in inclusive schools must be fulfilled by responding UD principles holistically instead of piecemeal design specifications in policies. In this sense, a unique understanding of spatial requirements in guidelines and policies which is structured considering UD principles can create a common ground for all collaborators of design process of inclusive school environment.

Acknowledgements This study was funded by Istanbul Technical University with the project number of 39791.

References

1. Imrie R (2012) Universalism, universal design and equitable access to the built environment. Disabil Rehabil 34(10):873–882
2. Peters SJ (2007) Education for All?: A Historical analysis of international inclusive education policy and individuals with disabilities. J Disabil Policy Stud 18(2):98–108
3. Lid IM (2014) Universal Design and disability: an interdisciplinary perspective. Disabil Rehabil 36(16):1344–1349
4. Erlandson RF (2008) Universal and accessible design for products, services, and processes. CRC Press
5. WHO (2001) International classification of functioning, disability and health. World Health Organization, Geneva
6. Goldsmith S (1997) Designing for the disabled: the new paradigm. Taylor and Francis

7. Erkılıç M (2011) Conceptual challenges between universal design and disability in relation to the body, impairment, and the environment, where does the issue of disability stand in the philosophy of UD? METU J Fac Archit 28(2):181–203
8. Walls A, Price M (2018) Diversity as a source of innovation: the case for inclusive design. Available from: https://medium.com/ixda/diversity-as-a-source-of-innovation-the-case-forinclusive-design-e300537ad5e4. Last Accessed 24 Mar 2020
9. WHO (2011) World report on disability. World Health Organization, Malta
10. D'souza N (2004) Is universal design a critical theory? In: Keates S et al (ed) Designing a more inclusive world. Springer, London. pp 3–9
11. The Center for Universal Design (1997) The principles of universal design, version 2.0. North Carolina State University, Raleigh, NC. Available from: https://projects.ncsu.edu/design/cud/about_ud/udprinciples.htm. Last Accessed 24 Mar 2020
12. UNESCO (2009) Policy guidelines on inclusion in education. UNESCO, France
13. Riddell S (2007) A sociology of special education. In The SAGE handbook of special education. pp 34–45
14. Tomlinson S (2015) Is a sociology of special and inclusive education possible? Edu Rev 67(3):273–281
15. Erkılıç M, Durak S (2013) Tolerable and inclusive learning spaces: an evaluation of policies and specifications for physical environments that promote inclusion in Turkish Primary Schools. Int J Inclusive Edu 17(5):462–479
16. UNESCO (2009) Teaching children with disabilities in inclusive settings. Bangkok. Available from: https://sid.usal.es/idocs/F8/FDO23186/teaching_children_disabilities.pdf. Last Accessed 27 July 2020
17. Gülbahar S (2017) An investigation on life center unit's design criteria in inclusive education environments: a case study on Serçev accessible vocational high school, Unpublished Master's thesis. İstanbul, İTÜ SBE
18. MEB (2018) Regulation on special education services, Available from: https://www.resmigazete.gov.tr/eskiler/2018/07/20180707-8.htm. Last Accessed 27 July 2020
19. MEB (2013) Inclusive education. Ankara. Available from: www.megep.meb.gov.tr/mte_program_modul/moduller_pdf/Kayna%C5%9Ft%C4%B1rma%20E%C4%9Fitimi.pdf. Last Accessed 27 July 2020
20. MEB (2011) Why how what for mainstreaming education at our schools: a guide book for school principals, teachers, parents. General directorate of special education guidance and counseling services. Ankara. Available from: https://orgm.meb.gov.tr/alt_sayfalar/yayimlar/kaynastirma/kaynastirma_EN.pdf. Last Accessed 27 July 2020
21. MEB (2015) Minimum Design Standards for Educational Buildings. Available from: iedb.meb.gov.tr/meb_iys_dosyalar/2015_08/17032245_2015asgaritasarmklavuzu.pdf. Last Accessed 27 July 2020
22. MEB (2020) Special education schools standard equipment guideline. General directorate of special education guidance and counseling services. Available from: https://orgm.meb.gov.tr/meb_iys_dosyalar/2020_03/11163313_OZEL_EYYTYM_OKULLARI_STANDART_DONATIM_KLAVUZU.pdf. Last Accessed 27 July 2020
23. Bumin G, Kars S, Huri M, Kayıhan H (2019) Is it really accessibility: a qualitative study about school accessibility. Ergoterapi Ve Rehabilitasyon Dergisi 7(3):129–134

A Transdisciplinary Approach to Accessibility for Novice Designers' Education of Inclusive Design

Elif Belkıs Öksüz, Demet Arslan Dinçay, Özge Cordan, Çağıl Yurdakul Toker, and Sena Semizoğlu

Abstract Whether for a unique in-door experience or virtual assistance, the interactive use of mobile devices has brought up new perspectives for designers across fields. The design and development of mobile applications that offer interactive spatial experiences for their users have brought new responsibilities for the twenty-first century designers. When it comes to design of these assistive technologies for the physically impaired, designers are expected to be more empathetic to their end-users and cautious about the values of the physical space. Hence, it has become essential for novice designers to develop a deeper and broader understanding of the concept of accessibility in their design education. And without a doubt, this progress needs new frameworks that empower educators to facilitate the concept of accessibility for their design students. For that, we share the impacts of encouraging a transdisciplinary approach to accessibility in design education within the outcomes of our design workshop. Last year, we organized a design workshop for an inclusive indoor navigation app design for smartphones to discuss the concept of accessibility over different fields of design. With this workshop, we wanted to grab and raise students' attention to accessibility issues in universal design by following a transdisciplinary approach. We aimed to design a learning experience and create a theme for students from different departments to develop an understanding of accessibility in design over different disciplines. The workshop was held with the participation of 55 novice designers from interior architecture and game design departments. Based on our experience with the workshop outlined in this paper, we identify that encouraging accessibility with a transdisciplinary approach has provided an improvement in the designer's understanding of inclusive design.

E. B. Öksüz (✉)
Department of Interior Architecture and Environmental Design, Nisantasi University, Istanbul, Turkey
e-mail: eeoksuzz@gmail.com

D. Arslan Dinçay · Ö. Cordan · S. Semizoğlu
Faculty of Interior Architecture, Istanbul Technical University, 34437 Istanbul, Turkey

Ç. Yurdakul Toker
Department of Interior Design, Raffles College of Higher Education, Singapore, Singapore

© The Author(s), under exclusive license to Springer Nature Switzerland AG 2021
Ö. Cordan et al. (eds.), *Game + Design Education*, Springer Series in Design and Innovation 13, https://doi.org/10.1007/978-3-030-65060-5_5

Keywords Transdisciplinary approach · Accessibility · Inclusive design education · User experience/interaction · In-door navigation

1 Introduction

The interactive use of mobile devices within the implementation of (Augmented Reality) AR, (Virtual Reality) VR, and (Mixed Reality) MR solutions has brought up new perspectives for the designers across fields. Whether for a unique in-door experience or virtual assistance, these technological advances are now on high demand in various ways. Following that, the design and development of mobile applications that offer interactive spatial experiences for their users have brought new responsibilities for the twenty-first century designers. When it comes to the design of these assistive technologies for the physically impaired, designers should be more empathetic to their end-users and prudent about the values of the physical space. Therefore, the merging concepts of technological and societal developments for inclusive design require us to rethink the concept of accessibility at all scales. As the technological capabilities of these devices continue to extend, it has become essential for designers to have a broader understanding of the universal accessibility in design. And without a doubt, this extension requires new frameworks that empower design educators to facilitate the concept of universal accessibility for their design students. Whether for physical or digital accessibility, all design-related fields are in need to find effective ways to encourage inclusive design for the benefit to their learners. As technological capabilities are used to solve real-life problems in physical space and provide user accessibility solutions, we're likely to see transdisciplinary or multidisciplinary approaches in different design fields.

In this regard, this paper presents the impacts of encouraging accessibility with a transdisciplinary approach in the case of an in-door mobile navigation application design workshop. Last year, we organized a design workshop for an inclusive indoor navigation app design for smartphones to discuss the concept of accessibility over different fields of design. With this workshop, we wanted to grab and raise students' attention to accessibility issues in inclusive design by following a transdisciplinary approach. The workshop was held with the participation of 55 novice designers from interior architecture and game design departments.

2 Background

The concept of accessibility remains as one of the trending topics in design studies. Design for inclusivity has its origins in the 1960s when a small number of designers, engineers and scientists began to grapple with the implications of a global society [1]. It was only two decades ago that concrete steps were taken towards the establishment of universal guidelines for the design of accessible spaces [2]. Additionally, its integration to design education is relatively new. The early reflections of inclusive design in education policies can be seen within the suggestions of the United States Department of Education [3] and the Committee of the Rehabilitation and Integration of People with Disabilities [4]. However, much progress has been made for the integration of inclusive design education to design related disciplines in recent years. So today, the concept of accessibility is usually introduced to novice designers under the principles of universal design. On the other hand, considerable progress has also been made in the technology development for inclusive design.

Many problems that occur due to the user–environment incompatibility can now be solved using mobile devices as virtual assistive technologies. Various tools, techniques and resources have become available to support and facilitate user-experiences in different ways (e.g., [5–8]). And yet, this progress has moved the concept of accessibility to a whole new level for novice designers. Design students are expected to be more cautious about technological capabilities, think towards disciplines, and work in collaboration for developing effective design solutions. As Altay et al. claim [9], "the problems that occur due to user–environment incompatibility can be solved if designers can relate to and understand all potential users' needs. This approach calls for an inclusive outlook that encompasses an empathic understanding of the user group, and establishes its foundations in education."

Thus, new frameworks that could provide students not only the tools to understand the universal design principles but also to confront the diverse needs of people around them are required in inclusive design education. Regarding how AR, VR, and MR solutions are re-shaping and enhancing our in-door experiences, the twenty-first century designers are expected to be cautious of the user experience and skilled at designing with these technological advances. Novice designers need to learn how a physical space can be presented in inclusive ways, how technology helps to experience physical space. Therefore, creating learning experiences towards accessibility guidelines with a transdisciplinary approach would be a good start for future designers' education.

Transdisciplinarity holds great potential to make contributions to a sustainable change in inclusive design education. As a strategy, it has evolved from the earlier research fields of multidisciplinarity and interdisciplinarity; and it involves what is between disciplines, across disciplines and beyond disciplines [10]. Therefore, transdisciplinary approaches are highly recognized in the fields of education and research. Additionally, since technological advances pursue designers to adopt new skills from other disciplines, transdisciplinary approaches in designers' education become inevitable. Regarding that, we wanted to use the beneficiary role of transdisciplinarity for widening the novice designers' understanding of accessibility in inclusive design; and we conducted a design workshop that requires merging the accessibility guidelines for physical and digital spaces.

3 The Novice Designers' Transdisciplinary Approach to Accessibility in Inclusive Design

With our design workshop, we wanted to grab and raise students' attention to accessibility issues in inclusive design by encouraging a transdisciplinary approach. We aimed at designing a learning experience for students from different departments and widening their perspectives for the accessibility at different scales. Within the contribution of five workshop instructors from interior architecture and game design fields, we managed to accomplish our half-day design workshop with students.

3.1 Task Description

Since we wanted students to interpret accessibility at different scales, we have looked for a design theme that requires the attention of students for user experience in digital and physical spaces. For that, we considered the navigability issue in complex buildings and the use of indoor navigation applications for the people with diverse needs. However, regarding the complex design and development procedure behind these types of navigation applications, we narrowed down the students' design task into the paper-prototyping of in in-door navigation application for our campus building. In this regard, we defined a persona spectrum for seven user profiles with diverse needs/physical impairments for the design task. We want the design students to consider these profiles as their app users and design an indoor navigation application by addressing solutions to their accessibility issues in physical and digital spaces.

As instructors, we wanted students to consider the five W strategy for their app design. According to Jonathan et al. [11] the five W's strategy starts by considering who will use the tool and how they will use it; so these W words can be considered as who, what, where, when and why. Regarding Jonathan et al. [11] strategy, we requested from designers to consider the five W's for their app design. Followingly, we determined our evaluation criteria for the same W's. Therefore, for a workshop outcome, our expectation was limited to the graphic interface design of the app and its demonstration for five screenshots. We allowed designers to show some of the perceivable features of the mobile devices (cam, mic, sound, vibration) as visuals in their design presentations.

As a design outcome, all student groups were expected to present and promote their app designs in 5 screenshots, with 150 word-length descriptive information (Fig. 1). Along with the use of analog design tools in the ideation and paper prototyping processes, the students were allowed to use various visualization tools and software for their design presentations.

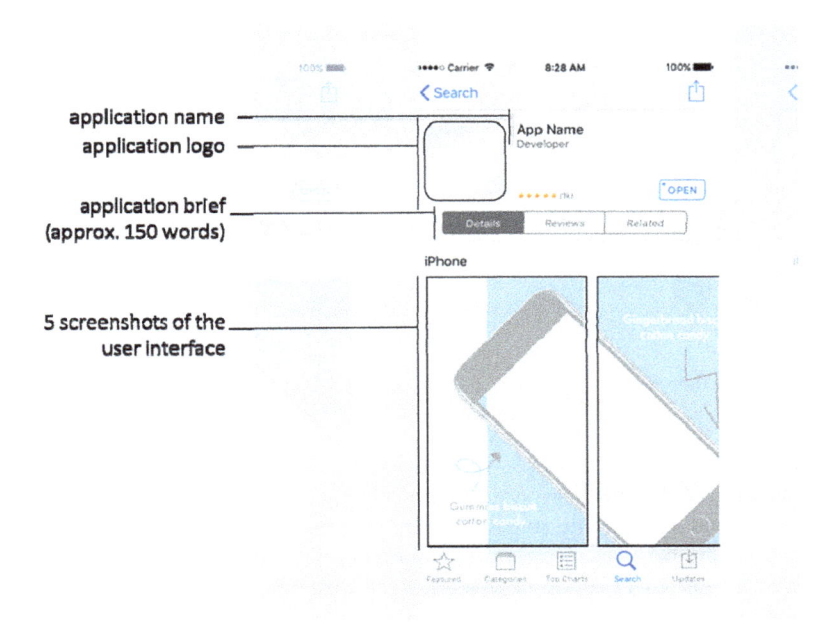

Fig. 1 Requested visuals and descriptions for the students' designs

3.2 Participants

For the workshop, we looked for the participants, who have developed their spatial design and representation skills by practicing either in physical spaces or digital spaces. In this regard, the participants were selected among sophomore design students from interior architecture and game design departments; and the workshop was conducted with the same content for these two designer groups.

3.3 The Process

In order to see how our transdisciplinary approach works to endorse accessibility in inclusive design, we organized the workshop in two sessions with two novice designer groups. While the first session was held with 35 interior architecture students' participation, the second session was held with 25 game design students. The same format was applied in each session, which took four hours approximately (Fig. 2).

For both groups, we started the workshop with an informative introduction about the principles of universal design and the implications of accessibility guidelines on mobile applications. Later, we introduced the workshop theme by opening a discussion on the way-finding in complex buildings and the role of in-door navigation

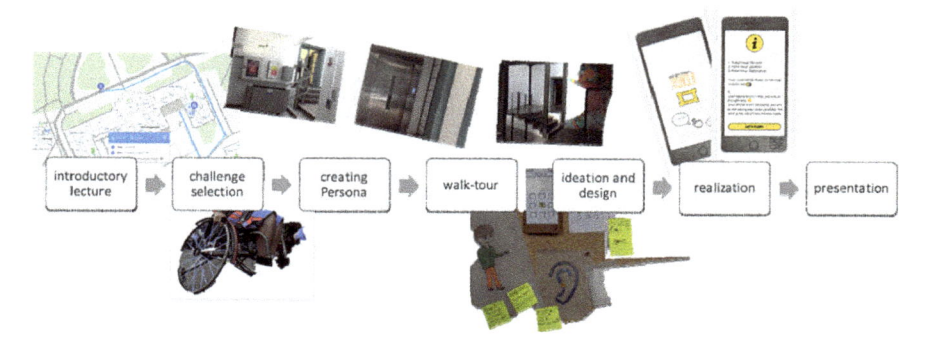

Fig. 2 The workshop format

(assistive) technologies for people with diverse needs. After the discussion session, we divided the students into groups of five.

In the second session, the student groups were assigned to pick one of the user profiles from the persona spectrum we defined earlier. Inspired by the Microsoft's Inclusive Design Kit [12]; we described seven different user profiles with certain physical impairments/diverse needs, such as a person on a wheelchair, a person with a hearing problem, or a person carrying a heavy object for their design task. After picking their user profiles, the groups started researching the accessibility guidelines for their app users and acknowledge their diverse needs for the third session.

In the fourth session, we sent the groups for a walk-tour in the campus building. For the walk-tour, we shared the floor plans of the building with students. We asked them to draw a route inside the building and use that route to demonstrate their navigation application. Considering the three criteria that determine the navigability of space [13], we asked the students to empathize with their user-profiles and be the navigators. We wanted them to draw the shortest path for their user profile by.

- discovering or infer their present location in the building;
- finding a route to the destination; and
- accumulating their way-finding experience in the space.

During the walk-tour, the groups were allowed to take photos, notes to use afterward in their design. They were warned to be cautious about the accessibility adjustments in the building. Once their walk-tour ended, the groups went back to the studio to continue their work. The ideation, brain-storming, design, and realization processes were completed with the guidance of the workshop instructors (Fig. 3). For the final, the groups presented their work with the screenshots and demonstrations they've prepared.

A Transdisciplinary Approach to Accessibility for Novice ... 71

Fig. 3 A photograph of the design board from one of the groups

4 Results and Discussion

The outcomes of both workshops were evaluated and compared under the five W's we described in the beginning. As workshop instructors, we referred to their notes from the groups' presentations for evaluation. By looking at their design outcomes, we saw that all student groups successfully finished their design tasks. All groups managed to address the diverse needs of the user profiles they picked and offer possible accessibility solutions with their interface designs. Hence, despite the differences in the forms of their presentations, we can say that the groups from both departments have reflected their knowledge of accessibility guidelines and gained new insights for the accessibility concept in inclusive design. However, when we compared the design solutions of both designer groups, we recognized a highly unexpected result.

While the solutions of interior architecture designers were mostly fixated with user experience in digital space, the game design students were quite the opposite (Figs. 4 and 5).

We noticed that almost every group of interior architecture focused heavily on the perceptual experiences of their users and provided design solutions based on the user's physical interaction with mobile devices. None of them offered to use any AR or MR technologies that require interaction with a physical space. As opposed to that, the game design students were less concerned about the perceptual experience

Fig. 4 The screenshots of one of the interior architecture groups' design

Fig. 5 The screenshots of one of the game design groups' design

of the users and more concerned about the user's interaction with the physical space. They prefer to use architectural elements of the building to alert their user.

5 Conclusion

We issued the accessibility concept in design with a transdisciplinary approach by bringing design students from different departments together for an indoor navigation application design. By looking at the workshop outcomes, it is possible to say that the transdisciplinary approach has contributed to the workshop participants' understanding of inclusive design. The interpretation of physical and digital spaces for users with diverse needs provided students discussing the concept of accessibility from a broader perspective. Based on our experience with the workshop outlined in this paper, we identify that encouraging accessibility with a transdisciplinary approach has provided an improvement in the designer's understanding of inclusive design.

References

1. Coleman R, Clarkson J, Cassim J (2016) Design for inclusivity: a practical guide to accessible, innovative and user-centred design. CRC Press, Boca Raton
2. The Center for Universal Design (1997) The principles of universal design, version 2.0. raleigh: North Carolina State University. https://www.ncsu.edu/www/ncsu/design/sod5/cud/about_ud/udprinciplestext.htm. Accessed 14 Jan 2011
3. United States Department of Education (2013) Accessibility and universal design. Office of vocational and adult education. https://www2.ed.gov/about/offices/list/ovae/pi/AdultEd/disaccess.html#3. Accessed 24 Feb 2013
4. Committee on the Rehabilitation and Integration of People with Disabilities (2001) Resolution ResAP (2001)1 on the introduction of the principles of universal design into the curricula of all occupations working on the built environment. Council of Europe, Strasbourg. https://www.coe.int/t/e/social_cohesion/soc-sp/ResAP%282001%29E%20.pdf. Accessed 14 Dec 2014
5. Damaceno RJP, Braga JC, Mena-Chalco JP (2018) Mobile device accessibility for the visually impaired: problems mapping and recommendations. Univers Access Inf Soc 17(2):421–435
6. Ko E, Kim EY (2017) A vision-based wayfinding system for visually impaired people using situation awareness and activity-based instructions. Sensors 17(8):1882
7. Serra A, Carboni D, Marotto V (2010) Indoor pedestrian navigation system using a modern smartphone. In: Proceedings of the 12th international conference on human computer interaction with mobile devices and services, pp 397–398
8. Shin BJ, Lee KW, Choi SH, Kim JY, Lee WJ, Kim HS (2010) Indoor WiFi positioning system for Android-based smartphone. In: the 2010 international conference on information and communication technology convergence (ICTC), 17–19 Nov 2010, pp 319–320
9. Altay B, Ballice G, Bengisu E, Alkan-Korkmaz S, Paykoç E (2016) Embracing student experience in inclusive design education through learnercentred instruction. Int J Inclusive Educ 20(11):1123–1141. https://doi.org/10.1080/13603116.2016.1155662
10. Nicolescu B (2014) Multidisciplinarity, interdisciplinarity, indisciplinarity, and transdisciplinarity: similarities and differences. RCC Perspect 2:19–26. From https://www.jstor.org/stable/26241230. Retrieved 4 Sep 2020
11. Roberts JC, Headleand CJ, Ritsos PD (2017) Five design-sheets: creative design and sketching for computing and visualisation. Springer, Cham
12. https://www.microsoft.com/design/inclusive/. Accessed 23 June 2020
13. Foltz MA (1998) Designing navigable information spaces (Master's thesis, Massachusetts Institute of Technology, Department of Electrical Engineering and Computer Science)

Universal Design and User Experience

Handicap as a Design Catalyst

Ulrich Nether and Johanna Julia Dorf

Abstract The UN Convention on the Rights of Persons with Disabilities (UNCRPD) of 2006 is signed by 163 nations worldwide including all European countries. The agreement doesn't imply just the will to give people with disabilities access and the opportunity of participation but demands society to develop actively towards inclusion and diversity (https://www.un.org/development/desa/disabilities/convention-on-the-rights-of-persons-with-disabilities/convention-on-the-rights-of-persons-with-disabilities-2.html, [1]). From this, the need deduces to develop strategies for a *design for the real world* as a new standard in architecture and design (Victor Papanek in Design for the Real World, Pantheon Books, New York, 1971, [2]). Therefore the aim is to develop design strategies which understand handicap as design catalyst, i.e. inventing and testing new methods which open up designers' minds towards inclusion by giving them tools for more diversity through human handicaps. As a first step, a comparing case study was carried out with two groups of each 150 design students. The results show in which way handicaps as design catalysts could be integrated into the design education successfully and facilitate students to understand them as a design opportunity.

Keywords Design education · Design ergonomics · Universal design · Interior architecture · Inclusion

1 Introduction

In Germany, the claims of the UNCRPD led to a program of measures which is fixed in the National Action Plan (NAP 2.0) of the Federal Government (https://www.bmas.de/DE/Schwerpunkte/Inklusion/nationaler-aktionsplan-2-0.html [3]). In this plan, inclusion is not only required as an important social goal, but activities are also designated for an implementation of an inclusive design of environments that enables participation and diversity.

U. Nether (✉) · J. J. Dorf
TH Ostwestfalen-Lippe, 32756 Detmold, Germany
e-mail: ulrich.nether@th-owl.de

This concerns first schools and school buildings: in the federal German school system, action plans are already underway since 2009, programmes have had to put into practise inclusion nationwide. In accompanying studies from educational sciences perspective like Space and Inclusion is shown how inclusion in the context of learning environments can only work if it is part of a holistic concept including architecture [4].

Furthermore, Germany is currently the country with the third-highest average age in the world; in 2020 19% of the population is over 67 years old, a total of 16.2 million people. In 2000 it was 11.8 million people, 14% of the population, in 2040 there will probably be 16.2 million 67+ age, 26% of the total population [5]. With this change in the age structure and the age-related physical and mental demands, the challenges of an inclusive environment and architecture are changing fundamentally. These challenges must be met by society.

Education in general is a key to establish ideas of humanity in society. Architecture as discipline develops spaces that support or hinder possibilities of living, which are inclusive or exclusive. Due to this architecture has the potential to plan and produce the surroundings which enable inclusion. Universal Design, Design for All, and Human Centered Design are methodical approaches of designing spatial environments, buildings, and objects towards inclusion. However, in architect's minds they are still understood only as an integrative planning option and not as a requirement. And if so, they are understood merely as rules and obstacles which make planning more complicated and lead to limited solutions.

The proposal is to change this mindset by new methods in design that understand ergonomics human factors and universal design not just as rules and normative settings determining and influencing design decisions but as creative tools leading to a strategy which is widening and sharpening the process of finding human centered solutions.

The objective is to develop and test methods to achieve this in architectural design education as the first step of further development of a planning tool.

2 Methods

2.1 Methodical Background

The authors conduct the ergonomics human factors obligative course as 6 ECTS part of the Bachelor of Interior Architecture program which is absolved each year by about 150–160 students in their second semester. The case studies reported here were carried out in the courses of 2018 and 2019. As they were integrative part of the content of the course this is described briefly in the following as far as it has an impact on the derivation, direction, and design of the study:

The objective of the course is first to get the students familiar with the contents of ergonomics as far as this is significant for their aimed practical work as designers of spatial solutions of interiors.

As well the physical human factors, anatomy, anthropometry, physiology, and biomechanics are imparted through lectures and deepening research focused exercises as the sensorial factors due to environmental influences of light, sound, climate, vibrations, vapor, etc. and the cognitive, affective and conative psychological factors of interaction with the environment, space, and objects. Through all these parts the understanding of ergonomics as a system is emphasized according to the definition of the International Ergonomics Association, IAE, Council, 2000: "Ergonomics (or human factors) is the scientific discipline concerned with the understanding of interactions among humans and other elements of a system, and the profession that applies theory, principles, data, and other methods to design in order to optimize human well-being and overall system performance" [6].

In addition knowledge about human factors from other disciplines like philosophy, sociology, communication science, architectural and design theory is included in the course content, so the students learn about themes like orientation, acceptance, use and usability, proxemics, affordance, appropriation of space, gestures, spatial behavior and production of space through use.

As more than ninety percent of the students will work as practicing architects later all contents are brought into correlation to the design process through application-oriented exercises, too.

These links are essentially established in two larger projects over several weeks each. In the second project, the students summarize the findings from the module towards the end of the course and design an exemplary spatial environment with focused reference to human factors.

In this task "MachOrt" (German for MakingPlace/Place for Making), in addition to the explicit thematisation of the human-object-space relationship, the design process is practised in a special way as a methodical procedure and documented in all sub-steps. Thus, this project is extraordinarily suitable for conducting studies on how changes in the design process by adding or removing partial requirements or reformulating individual work steps also result in changes in the results of the project and in the students' reflections.

Based on this, a comparative case study was carried out in June/July of the years 2018 and 2019 by slightly modifying the tasks, with the corresponding two independent groups of each year classes, which had a size of 150–160 interior architecture students each. The students worked together in teams of three as a rule, so that there were about 50 project results per group.

Before the case study and its results are described in detail, the didactic and design methodological backgrounds will be briefly explained for classification.

Didactically, the Ergonomics Human Factors module as a whole and the exercises included are designed in a manner that as many different learning types and types of intelligence as possible can be reached, involve and develop themselves. According to this base participation and profit are made possible in parallel visually, audibly, cognitively through reading- writing, and bodily-kinesthetically.

A programme in interior architecture centrally aims to enable the students to learn designing spaces independently and consciously which are experienced by their users physically and with their senses. Thereby all skills are required, but always with a view to transforming theoretical and abstract content, ideas, and concepts based on analysis into concrete materiality. This can be achieved through projects in experiental learning. Different individual ways of thinking and behaviour are worked out and used by working together in small teams and in the group, so that students learn to recognise and appreciate the abilities of others and to integrate these into their work, because, depending on the phase, architecture and design projects always require divergent thinking and acting as well as converging, assimilating or accommodating [7].

The structure of the case study follows constructivist didactics according to Kersten Reich [8], the qualities reconstructing/discovering world, constructing/inventing world and criticizing world are depicted in the typical design phases, which are followed by this process: analysing, elaborating criteria, concept, and design, prototyping, testing, and reflecting. In the combination of experimental learning with a complex user-related design including a 1:1 implementation and its physical examination and intellectual reflection in a coordinated work, depending on the subtask either individual, in a team or a group work with intensive supervision, the didactic process itself is an inclusive one, with which all students identify physically and mentally, as evaluations of the didactic approach show [9].

The basis of the task utilised for the case study was developed methodologically from the known iterative process, also to impart and consolidate design fundamentals in a systematic form in the second semester of the course. Human factors are taken as a starting point and guideline and as a goal as well. Thus, the contents of ergonomics are applied in a focused manner in a project to make the potential of design comprehensible from a human point of view. Thereby other factors such as choice of material and construction have been levelled and subordinated.

In order to enhance this possible quality, accentuation and design of the sub-steps are based on methods described in the Design Thinking process: In the beginning, the phase of analysis is systematically broad and deep, and explicit space is given to understanding the problem and observing it closely. Students must emphazise, i.e. engage intensively with the topic, the use, and the location, to define their design criteria and parameters and to develop their concepts and design approaches.

These are directly prototyped: creating, inventing iteratively, selecting, and developing takes place on a 1:1 model, so that actual testing and concrete reflection is possible via physical involvement, which leads to the documentation. Throughout the entire process, a structured, guided examination of one's own design aspirations takes place in team discussions, group presentations, and expert rounds to evoke and train an understanding of the qualities of intra- and interpersonal development of solutions according to goals and phases.

2.2 Case Study Methods

Overview As the students' task usually is a basic and integral component of the ergonomics human factors course it was adapted in a special way to carry out the case study finding indications how methods in design education could be developed which understand ergonomics human factors and universal design not just as rules and normative settings determining and influencing design decisions but as creative tools leading to a strategy widening and sharpening the process of finding human centered solutions.

In the experiment the two groups of students got the same specific task to design an object that made a place they chose useable in the way of their desire, taking human properties, needs, and planned activities as design parameters. The design process up to prototyping and testing was documented and reflected by each team and observed by the supervisors. Both groups were introduced into Universal Design. Both groups embodied their designs. When starting into the prototype phase, one of the groups was challenged to consider and embody three specific exaggerated handicaps additionally to their state of design so far.

Implementation In the beginning, the students were given a structured written problem definition that was identical for both groups. The aim of the exercise was briefly formulated in this way in the overhead:

> MakingPlace/MachOrt: Create a place where something can be done. Specifications: We want to virally alter the campus. Your task is to intervene in a way that creates places where you can do something.

This task was specified by a few basic conditions: The students could choose any activity they were interested in, but the chosen usage should have not to be found elsewhere on campus and it had to meet a need and/or desire that had to be developed especially. A further entry condition was that the intended activities should have to be carried out, demonstrated, and practiced at the location.

Any place on the Detmold campus of TH OWL could be chosen as a location, inside the buildings or in the outside area, under the conditions not to endanger security and not to disturb other events.

Activity (Mach) and place (Ort) should correlate, it was demanded not to develop mobile objects, but individual extensions for a certain place generated from the intentions of use.

Accordingly, the criteria were formulated as follows:

> The central requirement is a well working usability of the result. For this purpose, man, activity, tools, equipment, and environment must be coordinated as optimally as possible. Following your Ergonomics Human Factors knowledge, take into account stresses and possible strains, both physical and psychological. Also note that objects and environments are suitable for use if they first, fulfil the intended function, second, open up possibilities without forcing and third, can be appropriated easily, i.e. that they show which activities t they might enable and how they do it through their design language (affordance). Symbolic and formal aesthetic aspects also play a role, they contribute to interest and acceptance.

Finally, only certain sturdy cardboard (corrugated cardboard) was allowed as a building material for the prototypes, of which each group was provided with a maximum of 6 m^2; joints and finishes should correspond to the material.

In total, the duration from introduction to completion and testing of the prototypes was planned for four weeks, divided into four steps of one week each, corresponding to the weekly seminar times of the module. The entire process was accompanied by four tutors in parallel and alternately. Subsequently, the students had two more weeks to finish their documentation of the results without consultation.

All specifications were identical for both groups up to step 4.

In step 1, the first week, the students received worksheets in which they were given intensive analytical access to the two central aspects of the task Mach und Ort through step-by-step instructions. During this phase, they should work explicitly individually—not in teams of three and without exchange. The students first examined a place that interested them on campus and carved out its qualities, for whatever reason—independent of any activities which might be possible at the place. (Fig. 1, steps 1a). Then, regardless of the location, they chose three activities that they wanted to provoke and formulated superordinate concepts and exact parameters for this purpose, too, to get a clear idea of what they wanted. They deepened these by looking for examples of implementation in architecture (Fig. 1, steps 1b-1c).

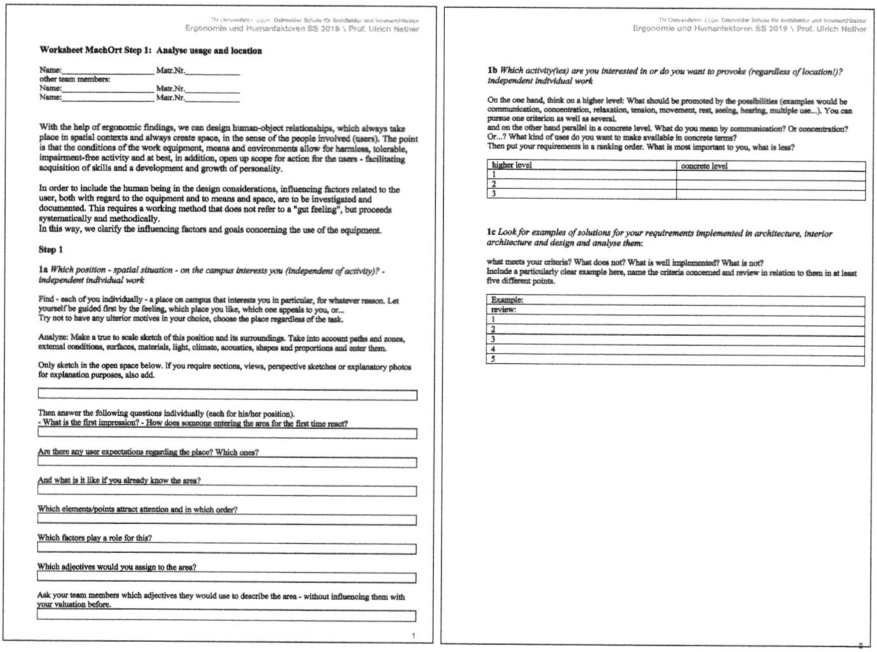

Fig. 1 Worksheets steps 1a and 1b,c: analysis location and usage. © Ulrich Nether

Handicap as a Design Catalyst

Then they searched for activities and defined some which might fit the location on campus examined under 1a, defined them as in 1b, and justified their decision. (Fig. 2, step 1d), Finally, they looked for a location on campus suitable for the activities from 1b, analyzed them as in 1a, and again gave reasons for their decision (Fig. 2, step 1e).

The results were uploaded to the university's online platform so that they could not be post-processed.

In step 2, the second week, the students went into a discussion with the results from the first step in their initially defined teams of three. In the teams, they now had to decide for the location and activities. Again, the students received worksheets to follow. First, they selected at least two possible variants in a team, based on the findings from step 1, i.e. six different usage scenarios and six different locations, which they compared with each other (Fig. 3), by answering wh-questions about the intended use, by working out the expected stresses and stimuli at the respective location through the intended human-object-space interaction, and by naming possible disturbing and supporting factors. Subsequently, they named defined desired usage requirements of the planned object based on the above findings. Thereby they had to consider the functional use as well as the aspirations for the perception of the planned object and its impact. Out of the usage requirements, the intended activities, and the properties of the location they were asked to define exact human-centred criteria for

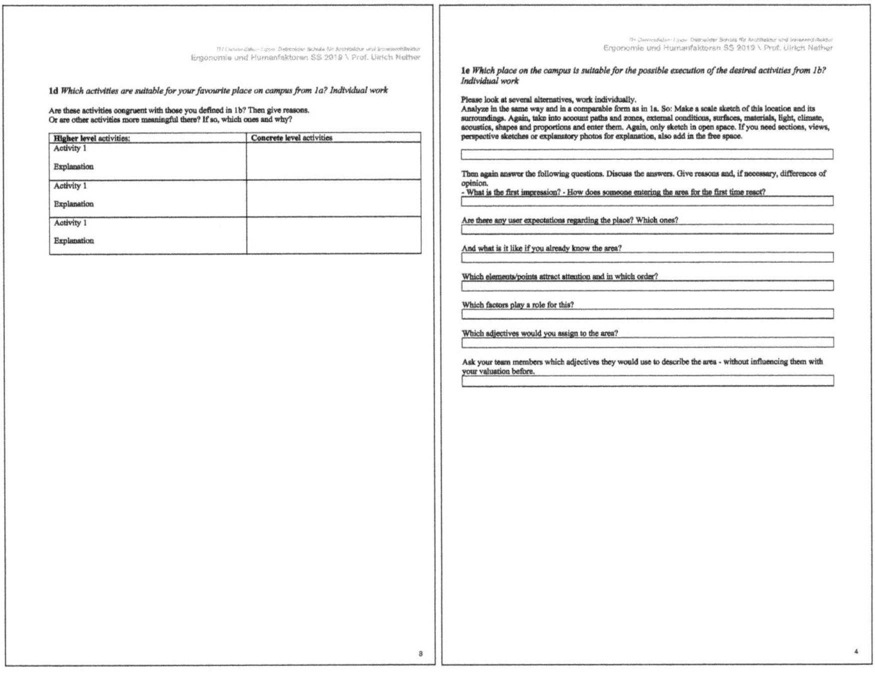

Fig. 2 Worksheets steps **d** and **e**: synthesis location and usage. © Ulrich Nether

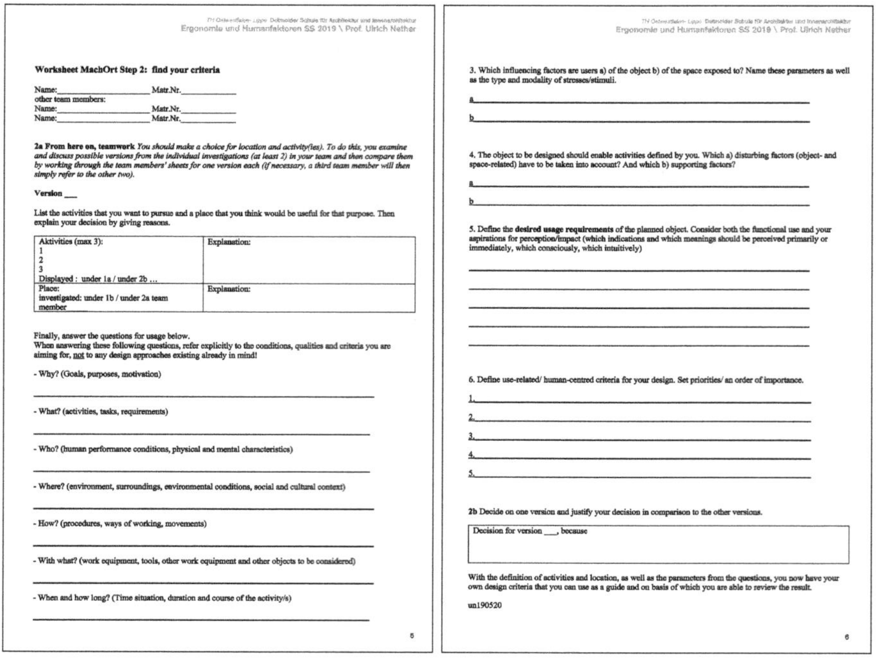

Fig. 3 Worksheets steps 2a and 2b: Criteria finding, © Ulrich Nether

their design arranging them in an order of importance. Finally, they had to decide on one variant comparing with the others and to write down reasons. The results were again uploaded to the university's online platform.

Through the definition of activities, location, and the parameters they worked out in the questionnaires, the students had developed their own design criteria, which they could use to orientate themselves and evaluate the results themselves.

In step 3, the third week, the students were asked to develop alternative concepts and design approaches, as sketches or scale models, and to discuss these in their teams, then to document all sub-steps and to present their results reflecting on the criteria to the group and the tutors. The documentation of the step was also uploaded in parallel to the university's online platform.

Step 4, the fourth week, started with a lecture on the topic of accessibility/Universal Design/Design for All, so that the problem of handicaps was present to all students.

In a two-day workshop, the prototypes then were created and build then. The workshop took place on the weekend, which meant the campus was clear of other activities and the groups could work concentrated. During the whole time, the tutors motivated to design, revise, optimize, and pre-test the prototypes, so that they were constantly changing until completion.[1] On the following days, the prototypes were presented and tested in tours with the tutors and groups of about 35–40 students each. The students were instructed to the requirements for the documentation in step 5 before.

Step 5, fifth and sixth week, the students documented their work, this should include *a full explanation of the process of the design finding and implementation, and a vivid presentation of the result, shown both in its formal qualities and as an object in use (i.e. photographic with people). A (self-)reflection of the work should complete it.* There were no guidelines given for the reflection, nor was there any discussion or opportunity to ask questions about it, only the following advice: *Reflect on your self-imposed criteria from step 2. To what extent does the design meet your requirements? Furthermore, the following points will be taken into account in the evaluation: the quality of the documentation in terms of content and form, the proof of the design process in the documentation, the handling of the material, the constructive, and the design quality of the prototypes, the presentation.* By this proceeding, the contents of the reflections were not pre-influenced.

3 Results

First, the groups and their results were observed. The design qualities of the prototypes are irrelevant regarding the research question, therefore they are not reflected upon here, but only the impact on the students by modifying the task.

The alienations of the students' own bodies by the handicaps, which were carried out in the group 2019—with handicaps—are directly visible in the photographic documents of the use and self-testing of the prototypes. It can also be read in these documents that the unusual bodily experience has a formative influence on physical behavior (Fig. 4).

The documents of the 2018 group—without handicaps—cannot show this, because here the own bodies are perceived as usual. Although special attention also had to be paid to use and behavior, this is apparently integrated into the context of perception and movement (Fig. 5).

To determine if there are differences in the understanding of priorities regarding human factors, Universal Design, and design process qualities, the documentations of all teams were evaluated qualitatively.

---

[1]The intervention that made the difference between the two groups was inset after the beginning of the first workshop day of prototype construction: In the 2019 group, unlike in the 2018 group, the task "MachOrtforAll" was put in addition to the identical requirements: people with disabilities should be enabled to use and to participate. Each group was given two "special features" which the students actually added to their bodies. These features were either physically motorics-restrictive, such as overlong arms or legs tied together, or sensory restrictive, such as impaired vision or hearing. These handicaps were deliberately formulated in an experimentally pointed manner to challenge a playful way of dealing with them [10, 11]. Linked to the task was the question of how the objects are changing as a result of the so-called special features.

Fig. 4 With handicaps group: example results, © Ulrich Nether, Johanna Julia Dorf

The analysis of the text documents was carried out following three questions: first, what was the self-chosen focus of reflection in each team, second, which were the key statements of each team and third, which were the key terms of each team. Based on the evaluation categories were formed for the extracts, so that possible differences could be seen.

In the no handicaps group the identified priorities in the reflections can be categorized mostly under the term affordance, and further noteworthy under the term adaptability. In the with handicaps group, the largest number of terms could be sorted under design process handicap interaction, further noteworthy here as a category is affordance.

The key statements of the teams of the no handicaps group can be assigned to the headline's functions, place und recognizability those of the teams of the with handicaps groups to the categories opened design process, universal and inclusive design, enrichment of design through human factors.

The key terms of the teams of the no handicaps group have been in the order of the number of nominations affordance, place, adaption, needs and use; The key terms

Handicap as a Design Catalyst 87

Fig. 5 No handicaps group: example results, © Ulrich Nether, Johanna Julia Dorf

of the teams of the with handicaps group change of view, improvement, affordance, usability, adaption, needs and place.

Hence significant differences can be determined: The teams of the no handicaps group described transforming desired activities into affordances integrating ergonomic aspects and the location as their main experience. The teams of the handicaps group focused on the opening of their mind in the design process through the handicaps as well as on human factors and inclusion.

Finally, four experts, who were not informed about the research question, were asked to select from the documentation as meaningful core sentences as possible that express the students' reflections.

The sentences most frequently mentioned extracted from the documentations of the no handicaps group were:

- Especially in public spaces, it is important that the function of objects is clearly visible.

- Functions should be designed so that everyone can use them.
- Functions must be recognizable without prior knowledge.
- Testing shows what the object really needs and can simplify the shape so that functions become clearer.
- The aspect of a self-explanatory design has the potential for further development.

The most frequently of the with handicaps group were:

- The inclusion of disabilities has enriched the design. There was no reduction in the quality of use.
- By examining how people with a disability can use the object, a reduced and universal design was created.
- By including disabilities, the design was expanded and thus made universally accessible. The attempt to include all people in a design does not have to be connected with great effort.
- The inclusion of disabilities can contribute to the development of a concept and expand the spectrum of ideas.
- The confrontation with the restrictions has led to new ideas and brought the design in new directions.

The expertise on the core statements not only confirms the findings of the text analysis. The experts assessed—as the quoted sentences also indicate—the reflections of the handicaps group as altogether much more elaborated, showing more and deeper understanding of challenges and opportunities in design than those of the no handicaps group.

4 Discussion

The results of the case study have shown that by consciously including handicaps as an additional challenge in the design process, it is possible not only to create a greater awareness of the need for inclusion among students and that this is understood in its determinants, but also that these handicaps are actually used as diversifying factor as a catalyst for design and are seen as added value.

The two comparison groups of the study had been pre-set in exactly the same way in the same sequence of predetermined and structured steps for several weeks, the only minimal intervention led to substantially different reflections. The project results are comparable in terms of quality, which showed that the groups were also comparable in terms of motivation and level of performance, as can be assumed from their study status.

In addition to the result in relation to the evidently answered question that handicap can be used as a diverging design tool, it is interesting to see how differently the students of the two groups interpret and classify their findings—that the learning success can be described much more profoundly in comparison, due to the provocation made regarding design methodology in general as well as the human factors.

5 Conclusion

This study is to be understood as a first step not to make demands for methods for design for limitations and otherness as normal as an almost unsolvable increase of regulations on architecture and products, but as options, as creative tools to develop open and inclusive environments, which in turn lead to greater diversity and participation in society.

It has been shown in this first experiment that the little variation during the four weeks process leads to a significantly deeper understanding not just of Universal Design, but also of human factors in general. Second, a remarkable turn in mind taking human factors, handicaps, and diversity as design catalyst was noticeable. Handicaps as a catalyst works if they are integrated into the process methodically and strategically. Furthermore they can stimulate deeper reflection.

To develop methods from this which can be transferred to other environments than those of the study conducted, further modifying and sharpening experiments are needed. The handicaps were formulated very freely and were very different. In a case study currently being conducted, it will be investigated whether it leads to different results if all participating students receive the same selected two handicaps for their work process, one physically motoric and one sensory, each with a thesis underlying. In addition to the described concrete methods of prototyping and embodiment, digital methods will also be integrated. In the next step, a further study is in preparation, to formulate handicaps right at the beginning of the task and to accompany the processes of the students not only with teachers but also with a team of experts made up of people with disabilities, who will be included in a final extraction of a methodology of consciously using handicaps as a catalyst to open and expand the design of spatial environments through a strategic approach aimed at inclusion.

References

1. https://www.un.org/development/desa/disabilities/convention-on-the-rights-of-persons-with-disabilities/convention-on-the-rights-of-persons-with-disabilities-2.html. Last Accessed 15 June 2020
2. Papanek V (1971) Design for the real world. Pantheon Books, New York
3. Federal Ministry of Labor and Social Affairs (2016) National Action Plan (NAP 2.0) of Germany's Federal Government based on the UN-Convention on the Rights of Persons with Disabilities (UNCRPD) (28 June 2016). (Online). A/HRC/RES/2/11. Accessed 14 Jan 2019. Available at: https://www.bmas.de/DE/Schwerpunkte/Inklusion/nationaler-aktionsplan-2-0.html. Last Accessed 15 June 2020
4. Kricke M, Reich K, Schanz L, Schneider J (2018) Raum und Inklusion. Neue Konzepte im Schulbau, Beltz, Weinheim und Basel

5. https://service.destatis.de/bevoelkerungspyramide/#! Last Accessed 15 June 2020
6. https://iea.cc/what-is-ergonomics/. Last Accessed 15 June 2020
7. Kolb DA (1976) The learning style inventory: technical manual. McBer, Boston
8. Reich K (2012) Konstruktivistische Didaktik. Luchterhand, Neuwied 2012; 5. Auflage: Beltz, Weinheim
9. Reich K (2014) Inklusive Didaktik. Bausteine für eine inklusive Schule, Beltz, Weinheim
10. Lupton E (2014) Beautiful users. Princeton Architectural Press, New York, Cooper Hewitt
11. Carpentier T, The measure(s) of man, in: Lupton, E., loc. cit., pp 32–34

Relationship Between Quality of Life with Physical Fitness and Home Environmental Factor Among Elderly Individuals

Gökçen Akyürek, Esra Alan Öztürk, and Gonca Bumin

Abstract **Objective** Due to the rapid aging of the world population, it is important to determine the factors affecting the quality of life of these individuals and take precautions. The aim of this study is to examine the relationship between the quality of life with physical fitness and home environment features in elderly individuals. Method: This study was included 99 elderly individuals (51.5% female; 71.36 ± 6.50 years) ranging from 65 to 95 years of age. In order to evaluate the quality of life, physical fitness and home environmental characteristics of the participants, the Quality of Life Scale in Older People (CASP-19), Physical Fitness and Exercise Activity Levels of Older Adults Scale (PFES) and the Way of falling, Home Environmental Factor Evaluating Form (WIHFEF) were used. In evaluating data in addition to determining statistics Pearson correlation coefficient and Mann Whitney U test is used. Results: According to the analysis, a statistically significant relationship was found between the quality of life with physical fitness and environmental characteristics of the elderly ($p < 0.001$). Conclusions: The decreased physical fitness of elderly individuals and the increase of the risk of falling home environment characteristics negatively affect their quality of life. According to these results, it is important to evaluate the physical fitness of the elderly individuals and their home environment characteristics before the interventions aimed at increasing the quality of life of elderly individuals.

Keywords Elderly · Falls · Quality of life · Environmental factors · Physical fitness

---

G. Akyürek (✉) · E. A. Öztürk · G. Bumin
Department of Occupational Therapy, Faculty of Health Sciences, Hacettepe University, 06100 Ankara, Turkey
e-mail: gkcnakyrk@gmail.com

E. A. Öztürk
e-mail: esraalan00@gmail.com

G. Bumin
e-mail: gbumin@hacettepe.edu.tr

1 Introduction

According to Turkey Statistical Institute's (TSI) 2018 data, in Turkey 7.163.354 people aged 65 and over, it constitutes 8.7% of entire population [1]. According to population estimates, the rate of elderly population in 2080 is expected to be 25.6% [2]. The increase in number of elderly individuals in total population with aging brings important changes in policies of countries and societies [3]. These policies are especially aimed at solving health and care problems of elderly population, preventing diseases and maintaining functionality for maintaining and increasing health and well-being [3–5]. World Health Organization (WHO) has developed the "Active Ageing" terminology with aim of reducing effects of aging in societies and maintaining lives of individuals actively and independently [3, 6]. WHO states that falls are the most important health problem of old age period [7]. About a third of elderly people falls every year [3]. Risk factors of fall are individual's age, gender, living alone, existing health problems, the characteristics of physical environment [8–14]. The falls cause injuries in elderly [3, 15]. For this reason, hospital or emergency applications of these people are increasing and falling negative changes in attitude of the elderly, his family, and the caregiver [3, 16, 17].

There are many studies examining effect of physical activity on fall of elderly individuals. Hamed et al. showed that physical activity interventions significantly reduced fall rates and risk of falling in healthy elderly people [18]. As a result of 6-week Pilates intervention applied to elderly women with chronic low back pain, fear of falling of participants decreased, as well as improved functional balances, pain notifications also decreased [19]. In another review by Andy et al., they found that physical activity improved flexibility, balance and lower limb muscle strength in older individuals [20]. A review showing the relationship between physical activity and falling in 2016 found that only physical activity intervention prevented falls in the community dwelling elderly [21].

There are many factors that affect quality of life in elderly people. Having a history of falls in last six months, having at least one chronic disease requiring continuous medication, low income status, and being dependent in activities of daily living are main factors that decrease quality of life [22]. Altuntas et al., showed that, doing home modifications and changing behavior to prevent falls improves elderly individuals' quality of life significantly [23]. Kang found that there is a relationship between fear of falling with quality of life and activities of daily living of elderly people [24]. Mishra et al. stated that "fear of falling" is one of the most important factors affecting independence. As a result of their research, they concluded that individuals with "old age depression" and "fear of falling" have decreased quality of life [25]. As a result of compilation study conducted by Hanapi et al., they found that environmental modifications increase sociality and quality of life in elderly people. They also stated that sociality is the most important factor that increases quality of life and reduces risk of falling in elderly people [26]. According to literature, increased physical activity and behavioral changes with environmental changes reduce chronic diseases that require medication and increase their independence in daily life activities in elderly people. In addition, with these changes in individual's life, health expenditures of individual and time spent in hospital will be reduced, thus the increased quality of life will be maintained in long term.

For "life satisfaction" survey results of Turkey General Directorate of Public Health, the proportion of elderly people indicating that "they are happy" was found to be 61.2% [2]. Although this rate is quite high for Turkey, has potential to decrease with growing elderly population. In literature, many studies indicate that quality of life will increase with physical activity and environmental modification, however, sample sizes of them are quite small. Additionally, literature shows relationship between falls, physical activity and quality of life, but it does not provide any information about the activity levels of individuals. Therefore, aim of this study is to examine the relationship between quality of life with physical fitness and home environmental features in elderly individuals.

2 Materials and Methods

2.1 Research Pattern and Sampling

Permission was obtained from Hacettepe University Non-interventional Clinical Research Ethics Board for research regarding that there is no ethical objection in conducting the research.

A cross-sectional study was conducted in Ankara and data were collected in three neighborhoods of Çankaya district randomly selected by interviewing local authority. There were 350 elderly people living in these areas. The size of the study group (n = 135) was calculated by using a sample size formula. Participants in study were selected by using a systematic sampling method. Authors informed participants about details of study. Thirty-six people refused to participate in the study. The mean age of participants (n = 99) was 71.36 ± 6.50 (65–95 years) and 51.5% were women (Table 1).

In this study, in addition to sociodemographic information form, the Quality of Life Scale in Older People (CASP-19), Physical Fitness and Exercise Activity Levels of Older Adults Scale (PFES) and the Evaluation Form of Domestic Environmental Risk Factors of Falling (EFDERF) were used.

2.2 Data Collection Tools

Sociodemographic Form. In addition to age, gender, height and weight information of individuals participating in research, level of education, employment status, marital status, place of residence and if they have any chronic disease were obtained. Individuals were also questioned about risk of falling and a fall history.

Table 1 Sociodemographic information

		n	%
Gender	Female	51	51.5
	Male	48	48.5
Marital status	Married	80	80.8
	Single	19	19.2
Education level	Not a school graduate	28	28.3
	Primary School	35	35.4
	Secondary School	26	26.2
	University	10	10.1
Job Status	Has a job	10	10.1
	Retired	89	89.9
Income	Yes	78	78.8
	No	21	21.2
Chronic disease	Yes	64	64.6
	No	35	35.4
Any risk of falling	Yes	45	45.5
	No	54	54.5
Fall history	Yes	41	41.4
	No	58	58.6

Produced by authors (Gokcen Akyurek, Esra Alan Ozturk and Gonca Bumin)

The Quality of Life Scale in Older People (CASP-19). Hyde et al. developed this in 2003 and Türkoğlu and Adıbelli conducted its Turkish adaptation, validity and reliability study. The scale measures quality of life of elderly individuals. Turkish version of scale consists of 13 items. The answers for each item are "never, occasionally, sometimes and always". Points are "never" 0 points, "always" 3 points, but items 1, 2 and 4 are reversed. The increase in total score indicates that quality of life increases [27, 28].

The Evaluation Form of Domestic Environmental Risk Factors of Falling (EFDERF). Akın and Lök conducted validity and reliability study of evaluation form created according to literature for evaluate properties that may pose a risk to fall in home. Turkish version of scale consists of 43 questions in total: living room 7, kitchen 6, bedroom 7, bathroom/toilet 9, staircase 10, corridor 4. Each question is answered as "Yes (1)", "No (0)" and "No Observation (0)". There is an open-ended question at the end of each section and this question is not included in the scoring. It is understood that the higher score at the end of form, the higher risk of falling [29, 30].

Physical Fitness and Exercise Activity Levels of Older Adults Scale (PFES). In 2017, Yılmaz et al. made Turkish reliability and validity study of scale, which developed in 1997 by Melillo et al. A minimum of 34 and a maximum of 136 points can be obtained on the scale of 34 questions in total. Items that question physical activity in scale are answered as none (1), once a week (2), two–three (3) a week, and every day (4). Other questions are scored as "absolutely agree" 1 point and "absolutely disagree" 4 points [31, 32].

2.3 Statistical Analysis

Statistical analysis of data was done with Statistical Package for the Social Sciences (SPSS) 22.0 analyze program. The normal distributions of all variables were examined with the Kolmogorov–Smirnov test. The relationship of numerical variables was examined with Pearson Correlation Coefficient. Significance level was accepted as 0.05.

3 Results

According to analyses, a significant and negative correlation was found between the mean scores of the CASP-19 scale and the mean scores of the EFDERF scale and the PFES scale in all participants (p and r values are respectively $r = -0,260; p = 0,009$; $r = -0,429; p < 0,001$). A significant and negative correlation was found between the mean score of the CASP-19 scale and the mean scores of the EFDERF scale and the PFES scale in people without a previous fall history (n = 58) (the values of p and r are $r = -0,363; p = 0,005; r = -0,396; p = 0,002$). In people with a history of falling (n = 41), a statistically significant and negative correlation was observed only between the mean score of the CASP-19 scale and the mean scores of the PFES scale ($r = -0.477; p = 0.002$) (Table 2). Analysis showing relationship between scales are given in Table 2.

4 Discussion

The increasing elderly population and factors associated with quality of life of these individuals are among important research topics that keep up to date. There are many factors that affect quality of life in older individuals. However, some questions about the falls are still up to date. The major goal of this study was to examine the relationship between quality of life with physical fitness and home environmental features in elderly individuals. According to results of this study, quality of life and home environment conditions and physical fitness and activity exercise levels were statistically related in these individuals. This relationship also varied according to individual's history of fall.

Table 2 Analysis table showing the relationship between quality of life and physical fitness and exercise activity levels of individuals and their domestic environmental risk factors according to all participants and their falling situations

			EFDERF	PFES
All participants (n = 99)	CASP-19	r	− 0.260*	− 0.429**
		p	0.009*	0.000
	EFDERF	r	1	0.055
		p		0.587
Have you ever fall before? (No) (n = 58)	CASP-19	r	− 0.363*	− 0.396*
		p	0.005	0.002
	EFDERF	r	1	0.108
		p		0.419
Have you ever fall before? (Yes) (n = 41)	CASP-19	r	− 0.137	− 0.477*
		p	0.393	0.002
	EFDERF	r	1	− 0.018
		p		0.910

*$p < 0.05$; **$p < 0.001$. Produced by authors (Gokcen Akyurek, Esra Alan Ozturk and Gonca Bumin)

Altuntas et al., found that quality of life of the elderly people can be improved by protective environmental modifications made in homes where elderly individuals live [23]. Hanapi et al., stated that physical environment is the most important factor in determining quality of life of elderly people and that arrangements to be made in physical environment will make elderly individuals more social and therefore their quality of life will increase [26]. In a study by Kara et al., it was found that indoor area where elderly people have the highest risk of falling is bathroom and quality of life of the elderly is positively affected when domestic security conditions are sufficient [33]. In this study, significant relationship between domestic security conditions and quality of life is compatible with literature.

As a result of exercise program aimed at preventing falls, Kang found that participation of elderly individuals in activities of daily living, their fear of falling decreased and their quality of life increased compared to before program. Also, Kang found that quality of life and participating in activities of daily living are related [24]. Sherrington et al. and Hamed et al. in their review, they found that physical exercise programs reduced fall rates [18, 21]. Göktaş et al., stated that participation in activities and daily routines affects positively quality of life [34]. Kitiş et al., as a result of their research, it has been revealed that quality of life and functional level are related in elderly people. They emphasized that low functional level negatively affects quality of life [35]. This study also supports other researches, and it is seen that there is a significant relationship between physical fitness and activity exercise level and quality of life and this relationship increases even more in elderly individuals with a history of falling.

Özerdoğan et al., has shown a history of falls in last six months as a risk factor that negatively affects quality of life of elderly people [22]. In this study, the quality of life was compared according to whether elderly had a history of falls in the last six months, but no significant difference was found. While quality of life was examined by physical factors in the study of Özerdoğan et al., in this research, questioning of quality of life by psychological factors may be a reason for this contradiction. However, in this study, history of falls is indirectly related to the quality of life. Although history of falls does not directly affect the quality of life, it has negatively affected physical fitness of individual by decreasing in-home mobility and function. Again, it is observed in studies that low physical fitness had a negative impact on quality of life of elderly people [11, 33, 36]. This is an indication that this relationship is indirect.

This research had some limitations. One of these limitations is that participants are limited to three neighborhoods from Çankaya, Ankara. All participants were living in city center, elderly people living in countryside were not included in the study. In future studies, we predict that examining and comparing factors related to the quality of life of individuals living both in the city, in the rural areas, and collectively in the institutions will provide important information to literature.

As a result, quality of life is related to domestic environmental factors and physical activity levels in elderly people. This relationship is preserved in elderly individuals who do not have a history of falls. However, while relationship between quality of life and physical fitness and exercise activity levels of older individuals with history of falls continues to increase, the relationship between domestic environmental factors has disappeared. This shows us that history of falling is related to quality of life of elderly individuals and affect their physical fitness and domestic environmental factors. For this reason, it is thought that it is important to determine practices and interventions to be made considering the changed factors that affect quality of life according to fall history of elderly individuals who are followed in family health centers.

References

1. Nüfus İ (2018) Türkiye İstatistik Kurumu. https://www.tuik.gov.tr/UstMenu.do?metod=temelist. Last Accessed 15 Apr 2020
2. İstatistiklerle Y (2018) Halk Sağlığı Genel Müdürlüğü. https://hsgm.saglik.gov.tr/depo/birimler/kronik-hastaliklar-engelli-db/hastaliklar/Yasli_Sagligi/raporlar_istatistikler/TUIK_Yasli_Istatistik_2018.pdf. Last Accessed 15 Apr 2020
3. Atay E, Akdeniz M (2011) Yaşlılarda düşme, düşme korkusu ve bedensel etkinlik. GeroFam 2(1):11–28
4. Ageing and Health Programme (1998) World Health Organization, Geneva
5. Andrews GR (2001) Promoting health and function in an ageing population. BMJ 322(7288):728–729
6. Yaman H, Akdeniz M (2008) Etkin yaşlanma: Birinci basamak sağlık hizmetlerinde yaşlı sağlığına yeni bir bakış açısı. STED

7. Ageing WHO, Unit LC (2008) WHO global report on falls prevention in older Age. World Health Organization, Geneva
8. Güner SG, Nural N (2016) Yaşlılarda düşmeler ve önlemler. Turkiye Klinikleri Int Med Nurs Spec Top 2(1):30–37
9. Güner SG, Ural N (2017) Yaşlılarda Düşme: Ülkemizde Yapılmış Tez Çalışmaları Kapsamında Durum Saptama. İzmir Katip Çelebi Üniversitesi Sağlık Bilimleri Fakültesi Dergisi 2(3):9–15
10. Irmak HS, Karaaslan T, Arman N, Tarakci E, Akgül A (2019) Düşme Öyküsü Olan Yaşlıların ev Ortamlarının ve Düşme Risklerinin İncelenmesi. Turkiye Klinikleri J Health Sci 4(1):7–15
11. Kılınç Ö, Polat ST, Turla A, Aydın B (2017) Samsun'da Yaşlılık Dönemi Düşmeler: 2010–2015. Adli Tıp Bülteni 22(1):21–26
12. Qader MAA, Amin RM, Shah SA, Isa ZM, Latif KA, Ghazi HF (2013) Psychological risk factors associated with falls among elderly people in Baghdad city Iraq. Open Am J Prev Med 3(07):441
13. Savaş S, Yenal S, Akcicek F (2019) Factors related to falls and the fear of falling among elderly patients admitted to the emergency department. Turk J Geriatr Türk Geriatri Dergisi 22(4)
14. Falls: World Health Organization. https://www.who.int/violence_injury_prevention/other_inj ury/falls/links/en/. Last Accessed 15 Apr 2020
15. Stevens JA, Corso PS, Finkelstein EA, Miller TR (2006) The costs of fatal and non-fatal falls among older adults. Injury Prevent 12(5):290–295
16. Meriç M, Oflaz F (2007) Yaşlı bireylerin düşme yaşantısıyla ilgili algıları ve günlük yaşamlarına etkisi üzerine niteliksel bir çalışma. Türk Geriatri Dergisi 10(1):19–23
17. Rao SS (2005) Prevention of falls in older patients. Am Family Phys J 72(1):81–88
18. Hamed A, Bohm S, Mersmann F, Arampatzis A (2018) Follow-up efficacy of physical exercise interventions on fall incidence and fall risk in healthy older adults: a systematic review and meta-analysis. Sport Med-Open 4(1):56
19. Cruz-Díaz D, Martínez-Amat A, Manuel J, Casuso RA, de Guevara NML, Hita-Contreras F (2015) Effects of a six-week Pilates intervention on balance and fear of falling in women aged over 65 with chronic low-back pain: a randomized controlled trial. Maturitas 82(4):371–376
20. Andy C, Wong TW, Lee PH (2015) Effect of low-intensity exercise on physical and cognitive health in older adults: a systematic review. Sport Med-Open 1(1):37
21. Sherrington C, Michaleff ZA, Fairhall N, Paul SS, Tiedemann A, Whitney J (2017) Exercise to prevent falls in older adults: an updated systematic review and meta-analysis. Br J Sports Med 51(24):1750–1758
22. Özerdoğan Ö, Yüksel B, Çelik M, Oymak S, Bakar C (2018) Associated factors affecting the quality of life of the elderly. Türkiye Halk Sağlığı Dergisi 16(2):90–105
23. Altuntaş O, Kayihan H (2015) The effect of home modifications to the quality of life in elderly people. Türk Fizyoterapi Ve Rehabilitasyon Dergisi/Turk J Physiotherapy Rehabil 1(26):1–13
24. Kang K-S (2016) The effects of the fall prevention exercise program focussed on activity of daily living, fear of fall and quality of life for the senior citizen center elderly. J Korea Acad-Indus Cooperation Soc 17(8):267–272
25. Mishra N, Mishra AK, Bidija M (2017) A study on correlation between depression, fear of fall and quality of life in elderly individuals. Int J Res Med Sci 5:1456–1460
26. Hanapi NL, Ahmad SS, Abd Razak A, Ibrahim N (2019) Contribution of the built environment towards elderlies' quality of life and risk of falling. Environ Behav Proc J 4(12):101–107
27. Hyde M, Wiggins RD, Higgs P, Blane DB (2003) A measure of quality of life in early old age: the theory, development and properties of a needs satisfaction model (CASP-19). Aging Mental Health 7(3):186–194
28. Türkoğlu N, Adıbelli D (2014) Yaşlılarda Yaşam Kalitesi Ölçeğinin (CASP-19) Türk Toplumuna Adaptasyonu. Akad Geriatri 6:98–105
29. Aslan GK (2007) Assessment of environmental risk factors related to falls in rest homes. Turk J Geriatr 10(1):24–36
30. Lök N, Akın B (2013) Domestic environmental risk factors associated with falling in elderly. Iran J Publ Health 42(2):120

31. Melillo KD, Williamson E, Futrell M, Chamberlain C (1997) A self-assessment tool to measure older adults' Perceptions regarding physical fitness and exercise activity. J Adv Nurs 25(6):1220–1226
32. Yilmaz M, Temel A, Yelten G, Böckün E, Karahuseyin A (2017) Reliability and validity of Turkish version of "physical fitness and exercise activity levels of older adults" scale. Official J Ital Soc Gerontol Geriatr 254
33. Kara B, Yıldırım Y, Genç A, Ekizler S (2009) Geriatriklerde ev ortamı ve yaşam memnuniyetinin değerlendirilmesi ve düşme korkusu ile ilişkisinin incelenmesi. Fizyoterapi Rehabilitasyon 20(3):190–200
34. Göktaş A, Kudret H, İrem K, Uyanik M, Varli M (2020) Geriartrik Bireylerin Aktivite-Rol Katılımlarının Yaşam Kalitesi Üzerine Etkisi. Hacettepe Üniversitesi Sağlık Bilimleri Fakültesi Dergisi 7(1):13–31
35. Kitiş A, Ülgen SY, Zencir M, Büker N (2012) Evde yaşayan yaşlılarda kognitif düzey, depresyon durumu, fonksiyonel düzey ve yaşam kalitesi arasındaki ilişkinin incelenmesi. Fizyoterapi Ve Rehabilitasyon Dergisi 23(3):137–143
36. Kawanabe K, Kawashima A, Sashimoto I, Takeda T, Sato Y, Iwamoto J (2007) Effect of whole-body vibration exercise and muscle strengthening, balance, and walking exercises on walking ability in the elderly. Keio J Med 56(1):28–33

Investigation of the Relationship Between Activity Performance in the School Settings and Occupational Performance of High School Students with Cerebral Palsy

Gökçen Akyürek, Gonca Bumin, Meral Huri, Hülya Kayıhan, and Süheyla Gürkan

Abstract Occupational performance, including the performance of both physical and cognitive/behavioral activities, has been to be a strong predictor of school performance and participation. This study was to investigate the relationship between the activity performance in the school settings and occupational performance of high school students with cerebral palsy. A sample of thirty school aged children with cerebral palsy (33.3% girls) and their teachers were recruited in the study. The occupational performance was assessed with the Canadian Occupational Performance Measure (COPM) and the activity performance in school setting was assessed with the School Function Assessment-Turkish version (SFA-T) which divides activity performance into performance of physical activities and cognitive/behavioral activities. Pearson Correlation *coefficient* analysis was used to determine the relation between the COPM and SFA-T. According to the analysis, there is a significant relationship between COPM (performance score) with task support, activity performance and participation subscales of SFA (r = 0.451, $p = 0.021$; r = 0.521; $p = 0.019$; r = 0.442; $p = 0.002$ respectively). In addition, there is no relationship between COPM (satisfaction score) with SFA subtests ($p > 0.05$). The school participation of

---

G. Akyürek (✉) · G. Bumin · M. Huri
Faculty of Health Sciences, Department of Occupational Therapy, Hacettepe University, 06100 Ankara, Turkey
e-mail: gkcnakyrk@gmail.com

G. Bumin
e-mail: gbumin@hacettepe.edu.tr

M. Huri
e-mail: meralhuri@yahoo.com

H. Kayıhan
Faculty of Health Sciences, Department of Occupational Therapy, Biruni Üniversitesi, Istanbul, Turkey
e-mail: hkayihan@biruni.edu.tr

S. Gürkan
SERÇEV, the Association of Children with Cerebral Palsy, Ankara, Turkey
e-mail: suheylagurkan@sercev.org.tr

students with cerebral palsy is significant for inclusive education. There is a significant relationship between occupational performance with activity performance in school settings of students with cerebral palsy. Future studies should be directed towards revealing the environmental factors that enable and restrict full participation of the students with cerebral palsy in various community environments. A better understanding of these patterns is essential for the development of appropriate and effective intervention programs aimed at increasing participation of these students.

Keywords Cerebral palsy · Participation · School setting · Occupational performance

1 Introduction

Cerebral palsy (CP) is a non-progressive permanent movement and posture disorder due to brain damage. In addition to motor disorders, it is a disorder that affects sensory, perception and cognitive development, communication and behavior negatively and causes limitations in occupations and participation [1]. Therefore, understanding the social participation limitations of school-aged children with CP is very important in developing their treatment plans [2].

World Health Organization's International Classification of Functionality, Disability, and Health (WHO ICF) highlighted the concept of participation in daily living activities and roles [3]. Participation which is seen as the highest level of function is the ultimate and long-term goal of the rehabilitation intervention. The individual finds the meaning of life while connecting with others through participation. Therefore, participation is essential for life satisfaction and a sense of competence. School participation is a rather complex concept that is emphasized by rehabilitation specialists [4].

School participation defines participation in a school context that meets individual needs and goals and social expectations of a child, as well as being the basis for understanding and learning the world [5]. Participation in school includes not only participation in academic tasks, but also the efficient use of school tools, meeting their personal needs at school, and independent movement within the school building [5]. The studies concluded that children with disabilities have limitations of occupational performance and problems in participating in school activities compared to their typically developing peers [6, 7].

According to the disability model, the individual's level of participation to the environment is related to the nature and the severity of the individual's disability addition to personal and environmental factors [8]. According to the current policies, the number of students with disabilities in schools is increasing and schools are tried to be structured according to the needs of children with disabilities. It is thought that as the suitability of schools increases, the participation in educational and social activities of children with disabilities will increase in schools.

Occupational therapists work intensively to increase the participation and occupational performance of individuals in all performance (life) areas, including children with CP, with meaningful and purposeful activities [9]. Occupational therapists evaluate the skills that affect the child's participation in daily living activities, the difficulties they face, and the conditions such as the physical and cultural environment [10]. Children with CP are mentioned as one of the most disadvantaged groups in education and social relations [11].

There are limited studies evaluating the occupational performance and participation of children with disabilities in inclusive environments such as schools. Studies generally support the relations between participation level and demographic characteristics, clinical data, and functional measurement results of children with disabilities [4, 8, 12, 13]. In the literature, there is no study focusing on the relationship between functions in school context and participation in occupational performance. Therefore, the purpose of this study is to investigate the relationship between school functions and occupational performance among children with CP.

2 Material and Method

The sample of this study (n = 30; 13–18 years old) was selected randomly among the students who were diagnosed with cerebral palsy at Ankara Karakusunlar İMKB Technical Industrial Vocational High School. Informed Consent Form was signed to the parents of the students who participated in the assessments. Assessments were made face to face with students and teachers at school. It was stated that the name of the questionnaire was not written, the data would only be used within the scope of the research and confidentiality would be ensured. This research was conducted in accordance with Research and Publication ethics. Demographic information form and Canadian Occupational Performance Scale were applied to each participating student and School Function Assessment was answered by their teachers.

2.1 Data Collection Tools

Canadian Occupational Performance Measure (COPM). In the study, Canadian Occupational Performance Measure was used to evaluate students' participation from their own perspectives. COPM is a semi-structured interview that helps identify problems in occupational performance [14]. The validity and reliability study of the measure was done by Torpil [15]. COPM evaluates the occupational performance in self-care, productivity, and recreation domains from the individual's perception of satisfaction from the performance. COPM focuses on the occupations that the individual wants, needs, and expects [16]. The individual first evaluates the satisfaction and participation level in each occupation domain on a 10-point. In the next stage, the individual is asked to choose the most important five occupations and score them separately according to their performance and satisfaction. Total performance and satisfaction points are obtained by summing the performance and satisfaction points obtained separately and dividing by the number of activities that the individual indicates as important.

School Function Assessment (SFA). Students' participation in school activities and activity performances was evaluated with the School Function Assessment test. This scale, developed by Coster et al. [17] and the Turkish version was made by Bumin et al. [18]. It is used to measure the academic and social functional participation of students in school. Unlike many other cultural development tests, SFA has been developed and standardized in a heterogeneous group with motor, cognitive, communication, emotional, behavioral, and sensory impairments. The validity and reliability of SFA has been demonstrated in many studies [19, 20]. The test consists of three parts: participation, task support, and activity performance. In the participation part, the evaluation is made in 6 groups including classroom, playground, school access, bathroom and toilet activities, classroom access, and dining activities. The rating is scored by a scoring system between 1 and 6 scale. 6 points indicate full participation in activities and 1 point indicates limited participation. Task support and activity performance sections are scored by scoring 1–4 points in two sections, cognitive and physical tasks.

3 Statistical Analysis

Descriptive information and other data of the participants were analyzed using the SPSS 23.00 program. Descriptive statistical information was shown as mean ± standard deviation (X ± SS) and frequency (%). Spearman Correlation Analysis was used to examine the relationship between occupational performance and school functions in data that do not fit the normal distribution. Statistical significance level was accepted as $p < 0.05$ [21].

4 Results

The demographic information of the students included in this study is given in Table 1. A total of 30 students with cerebral palsy were included in our study. Twenty students (66.6%) were male; 10 (33.3%) were women. The average age of the students was 15.41 ± 2.00 (n = 30) years. 18 (60.0%) of the students go to inclusive education and 12 (40.0%) to special education (Table 1).

According to the result of the correlation analysis conducted to examine the relationships between the evaluation scales, it was determined that the total scores of the COPM and SFA have positive relationships with each other. Accordingly, there was a statistically significant relationships between the performance score of COPM and the participation ($r = 0.442$; $p = 0.002$), task support ($r = 0.445$; $p = 0.021$)

Table 1 Demographic information of the participants

	n = 30	%	X ± SD
Gender			
Male/female	20/10	66.6/33.3	
Education			
Special education/inclusive education	12/18	40.0/60.0	
Age	30		15.41 ± 2.00

Produces by authors (Gonca Bumin and Gokcen Akyurek)

Table 2 Relationship between students' school functions and occupational performance

SFA's subtests	COPM satisfaction	COPM performance
Participation	0.282	0.442*
	0.115	0.002
Task support	0.271	0.451*
	0.281	0.021
Activity Performance	0.052	0.521*
	0.732	0.019

*$p < 0,05$; spearman correlation analysis; produces by authors (Gonca Bumin and Gokcen Akyurek)

and activity performance (r = 0.521; p = 0.019) scores. In addition, no significant relationships were found between the satisfaction score of the COPM and SFA. The findings obtained are given in Table 2.

5 Discussion

According to our study which examines the relationship between occupational performance and school functions in children with cerebral palsy, a significant relationship was found between all areas of school functions and occupational performance. The results of this study show that the relationship between occupational performance and activity performance and task support is more evident than the relationships between participation are valuable.

According to the literature, it is observed that young people with disabilities have more limited participation than young people without disabilities [22] and young people with cerebral palsy or other neurological problems have more limited participation than young people with disabilities [23]. According to the study of Schenker et al. it has been shown that increased motor disorders and activity limitations in children with CP negatively affect participation and occupational performance [7]. The structure of participation is multidimensional [24], and studies show that personal factors (such as age, gender, cerebral palsy type), physical and social environment (such as family status, culture and living space) can have an impact on children's participation [25–27]. Accordingly, children's participation should be considered in school, home, and community settings. School attendance is also quite complex with different dimensions and it is an important variable that should not be overlooked by rehabilitation professionals [28]. In the study conducted by Coster et al. [29], factors affecting the school participation of children with disabilities and healthy children were examined and 576 families participated in the study. As a result of the research, it has been found that the participation of children with disabilities in school activities affected by physical and social environments as well as limited resources. This study shows us that school participation is a more sensitive subject than social participation and depends on various variables.

The findings of this study show that in children with cerebral palsy, there is a positive correlation between school functions and occupational performance, and especially the correlation is higher between the performance score of the COPM and the school performance scale. Again, according to the correlation results; It is observed that there is a relationship between the performance score of COPM and the task support and activity performance score of SFA, but the relationship is weaker compared to the activity performance subscale. With this relationship, we see that participation in school activities and task support that require cognitive and physical skills are predictive in determining the occupational performance of children with cerebral palsy. These findings are compatible with studies that previously showed the relationship between skills related to school activities and occupational performance [7, 12]. The findings also show that intervention in cognitive and physical skills should be maintained in existing rehabilitation interventions to improve the occupational performance of students with cerebral palsy. Moreover, it is seen that it is important to include the adaptive approaches to the rehabilitation program to increase the occupational performance of these children regarding their activities and duties in their daily life.

This study has some limitations as the limited number of samples, the use of limited variables (e.i., absence of environmental or motivational data), selection of the sample from a single school, and the absence of a control group. For these reasons, the factors affecting the occupational performance of children with cerebral palsy can be examined by reaching samples from larger and different locations (city/rural or schools with different environmental conditions). A good understanding of the occupational performance of these children is necessary for them to develop appropriate and effective rehabilitation programs.

In conclusion, this study explained the relationship between school functions and the occupational performance of children with cerebral palsy. Since cerebral palsy is not a progressive but permanent disease; the physical and cognitive skills, occupational performances, and social participation of these children should be considered in the interventions applied to them. It is thought that developing these areas at the moment will positively affect the vital roles, participation, and quality of life of children with cerebral palsy.

References

1. Richards CL, Malouin F (2013) Cerebral palsy: definition, assessment and rehabilitation. Handbook Clin Neurol 111:18395
2. Pashmdarfard M, Amini M, Mehraban AH (2017) Participation of Iranian cerebral palsy children in life areas: a systematic review article. Iran J Child Neur 11(1):1
3. World Health Organization (2001) ICF: international classification of functioning disability and health. World Health Organization, Geneva
4. Simeonsson RJ, Leonardi M, Lollar D, Bjorch-Akesson E, Hollenweger S, Martinuzzi A (2003) Applying the international classification of functioning, disability and health (ICF) to measure childhood disability. Disabil Rehabil 25:602–610
5. Coster W, Law M, Bedell G, Liljenquist K, Kao YC, Khetani M, Teplicky R (2013) School participation, supports and barriers of students with and without disabilities. Child Care Health Dev 39(4):535–543
6. Imms C (2008) Children with cerebral palsy participate: a review of the literature. Disabil Rehabil 30(24):1867–1884
7. Schenker R, Coster W, Parush S (2005) Participation and activity performance of students with cerebral palsy within the school environment. Disabil Rehabil 27(10):539–552
8. Simeonsson RJ, Carlson D, Huntington GS, McMillan JS, Brent JL (2002) Students with disabilities: a national survey of participation in school activities. Disabil Rehabil 23:49–63
9. Mulligan S (2003) Occupational therapy evaluation for children: a pocket guide. Lippincott Williams & Wilkins
10. Law M, Petrenchic T, Ziviani J, King G (2006) Participation of children in school and community. In: Rodger ve J. Ziviani S (ed)
11. Karagözoğlu A (2014) Serebral Palsili Çocukların Fonksiyonel Durumları ile Aktivite ve Katılım Düzeyleri Arasındaki Ilişkinin Incelenmesi (Master's thesis, Sağlık Bilimleri Enstitüsü)
12. Dudgeon BJ, Massagli TL, Ross BW (1997) Educational participation of children with spinal cord injury. Am J Occup Ther 51:553–561
13. Mancini MC, Coster WJ, Trombly CA, Heeren TC (2000) Predicting primary school participation in children with disabilities. Arch Phys Med Rehabil 81:339–347
14. Law M, Baptiste S, McColl M, Opzoomer A, Polatajko H, Pollock N (1990) The Canadian occupational performance measure: an outcome measure for occupational therapy. Can J Occup Ther 57(2):82–87
15. Torpil B (2017) Multipl Skleroz'lu Bireylerde Kanada Aktivite Performans Ölçümü'nün Türkçe Kültürel Adaptasyonu, Geçerlilik ve Güvenilirliği
16. Law LS, Webb CY (2005) Gait adaptation of children with cerebral palsy compared with control children when stepping over an obstacle. Dev Med Child Neurol 47(5):321–328
17. Coster W, Deeney T, Haltiwanger J, Haley S (1998) School Function Assessment (SFA). Pearson
18. Bumin G, Yaylacı İ, Akyürek G, Ozgur S (2018) School function in children with disabilities: school function assessment' Turkish version, validity and reliability. Dev Med Child Neurol 60(supp2):12
19. Davies PL, Soon PL, Young M, Clausen-Yamaki A (2004) Validity and reliability of the school function assessment in elementary school students with disabilities. Phys Occup Therapy Pediatr 24(3):23–43
20. Egilson ST, Coster WJ (2004) School function assessment: performance of Icelandic students with special needs. Scandin J Occup Therapy 11(4):163–170
21. Buyukozturk S, Çakmak EK, Akgun OE, Karadeniz S, Demirel F (2017) Bilimsel araştırma yontemleri, 23. Baskı. Pegem Yayincilik, Ankara
22. Ehrmann LC, Aeschleman SR, Svanum S (1995) Parental reports of community activity patterns: a comparison between young children with disabilities and their non-disabled peers. Res Dev Disabil 16:331–343

23. Law M, Finkelman S, Hurley P (2004) Participation of children with physical disabilities: relationships with diagnosis, physical function and demographic variables. Scand J Occup Ther 11:156–162
24. King G, Law M, King S, Rosenbaum P, Kertoy MK, Young NL (2003) A conceptual model of the factors affecting the recreation and leisure participation of children with disabilities. Phys Occup Ther Pediatr 23:63–90
25. Hammal D, Jarvis SN, Colver AF (2004) Participation of children with cerebral palsy is influenced by where they live. Dev Med Child Neurol 46(5):292–298
26. Sakzewski L, Boyd R, Ziviani J (2007) Clinimetric properties of participation measures for 5-to 13-year-old children with cerebral palsy: a systematic review. Dev Med Child Neurol 49(3):232–240
27. Engel-Yeger B, Jarus T, Law M (2007) Impact of culture on children's community participation in Israel. Am J Occup Ther 61(4):421–428
28. Law M, King G, Rosenbaum P (2000) The participation of children with physical disabilities. National Institute of Health, Bethesda, MD
29. Coster WJ, Law MC, Bedell GM (2013) School participation, supports and barriers of students with and without disabilities. Child Care Health Dev (Special Issue) 39(4):535–543

Gökçen Akyürek Ph.D., Assoc. Prof. She graduated from Hacettepe University School of Physical Therapy and Rehabilitation in 2004. Received the degree of Master of Science in 2011 and the degree of Doctorate in 2017 from Hacettepe University, Health Sciences Institute. She is currently as an associate professor at the Hacettepe University, Department of Occupational Therapy.

Gonca Bumin Ph.D., Prof. She graduated from Hacettepe University School of Physical Therapy and Rehabilitation in 1992. Received the degree of Master of Science in 1995 and the degree of Doctorate in 1998 from Hacettepe University, Health Sciences Institute. She is currently as a professor at the Hacettepe University, Department of Occupational Therapy.

Meral Huri Ph.D., Assoc. Prof. She graduated from Hacettepe University School of Physical Therapy and Rehabilitation in 2000. Received the degree of Master of Science in 2005 and the degree of Doctorate in 2012 from Hacettepe University, Health Sciences Institute. She is currently as an associated professor at the Hacettepe University, Department of Occupational Therapy.

Hülya Kayıhan Ph.D., Prof. She graduated from Hacettepe University School of Physical Therapy and Rehabilitation in 1979. Received the degree of Master of Science in 1982 and the degree of Doctorate in 1986 from Hacettepe University, Health Sciences Institute. She is currently as a professor at the Biruni University, Department of Occupational Therapy.

Süheyla Gürkan Ankara state theater artist and the Chairman of the Board of the Association of Children with Cerebral Palsy (SERÇEV). She graduated from the Ankara State Conservatory in 1986. She took part in Izmir State Theater. She still continues her works under the Ankara State Theater.

Heuristics in Design for Sustainable Behavior Change

Mirja Kalviainen

Abstract The *design for all* challenge is not only to design accessible and usable solutions but to actually push people to change their behavior to more beneficial ones. The growing interest in design for behavior change is evident especially with sustainability challenges due to the environmental impact from our excess consumption habits. Despite positive attitudes towards an environmentally conscious lifestyle, realized behavior does not follow these attitudes. This attitude–behavior gap includes everyday barriers to action and a lack of drivers for sustainable behavior. This paper presents the results from a design-based, qualitative, user research on sustainable behavior. These results are compared to research-based general models from behavior change psychology and consumption research. The user-research-based findings match the factors in the COM-B model, depicting the simultaneous effects of user capabilities, motivation and contextual opportunities. The practical guidance for the realized nudges exist already in the form of some design tools such as ideation cards. The user research agrees also with the behavior science on the necessity for a process-driven approach to behavior change and matches the SHIFT framework for successful change factors acquired through consumer research meta-analysis. SHIFT describes the factors of social influence, habit formation, identity matching, feelings, cognition, and tangibility. The observations and analysis comparing different approaches to sustainable behavior change confirm that generalizable heuristics in support of design for sustainable behavior change can be found. This form of heuristics could accelerate solution creation for the changes necessary for sustainable lifestyles as a future field of design for us all.

Keywords Sustainable lifestyles · Design heuristics · Behavioral psychology · Behavior change · User research

M. Kalviainen (✉)
LAB University of Applied Sciences, 15210 Lahti, Finland
e-mail: mirja.kalviainen@lab.fi

1 The Behavioral Change Challenge

The *design for all challenge* is not only to design accessible and usable solutions for people to do whatever they please. In many important societal areas, Western lifestyles and activities have become destructive to ourselves and to our planet. It is becoming urgent to push or nudge people into changing their behavior from harmful habits to more beneficial ones. Preventive health and security needs are typical targets for the growing interest in design for behavior change. The urgent need to design for behavioral change is especially evident with sustainability challenges due to the environmental impacts arising from our excessive consumption habits. In Western countries the impact of our daily everyday consumption amounts to around 70% of all the carbon dioxide emissions on the planet [1]. Although production has been the focus of sustainability activities, the root cause for it is our consumption.

Our current consumption habits have led to exceeding various planetary boundaries of safe operations for both humans and nature around us [2]. This has resulted in increased risks to nature and humans due to climate change, loss of biodiversity and the use of biogeochemical flows. Returning to a safe operational zone from a planetary boundaries perspective calls for urgent action to change the current consumption habits especially in developed countries.

There is an abundance of information available on how households can reduce the environmental impacts related to their consumption in the areas of housing, energy and water use, mobility, food, material products, and services through anti-consumption measures or changes in consumption [3]. Despite the available low impact action advice, there has not been a significant shift towards more sustainable consumption practices even though negative impacts are well-known.

Many actions concerning household consumption that could help to reduce the environmental burden may also provide other positive impacts, such as increasing society's resilience in the face of crises. This is because locally resilient systems, such as local-ecological and distributed energy production, locally produced vegetable-based food, and local material cycles can sustain external shocks better than systems that are tightly connected to global systems through transnational value chains. In addition, more sustainable consumption may also provide positive impacts from health or economic perspectives.

2 Consumer-User Perspectives on Sustainable Behavioral Change

The found attitudes towards an environmentally conscious lifestyle are generally positive. Despite this, actual realized consumer behavior does not follow these attitudes in practice. The found attitude–behavior gap includes barriers for action and lack of drivers for sustainable behavior in our current everyday settings [4]. One

Heuristics in Design for Sustainable Behavior Change

evident starting point is to conduct user research to understand the reasons and realities of the attitude–behavior gap from the consumer-user perspective.

The results from design-based, qualitative, user-research-based study on sustainable behavior carried out in Finland in 2014 revealed the reasons for the gap and drivers to support consumers. The drivers presented in Fig. 1 cross the barriers and hindrances of sustainable practices and the fact that sustainable actions seemed not to be interesting enough in the midst of other everyday pressures. Found drivers included areas of interests that worked as scaffolds for the respondents to start exercising sustainable consumption practices such as eating more vegetables, bicycling, saving energy or purchasing recycled products, even if the respondents would not be especially committed to sustainable choices. It was evident, that information about environmental sustainability questions, in addition to sustainable actions and solutions was hard to find and often confusing. The found drivers also propose ways to provide understandable, concrete, and findable information about sustainable solutions. The design for all issues of accessibility and ease of use were vital also in sustainable solutions. Furthermore, social support and normality seemed to be important factors in supporting people in initiating and following sustainable practices [5].

The most interesting finding was that the sustainable solutions need to be presented to the consumer as a service process that blends smoothly into their everyday activities. The initial interest promoting the starting point of the process is crucial, since typically there are low impact solutions available, but they are hard to notice and find. After stoking the interest of the consumer-user, the process should support understandable information communication and moments of diverse activity with

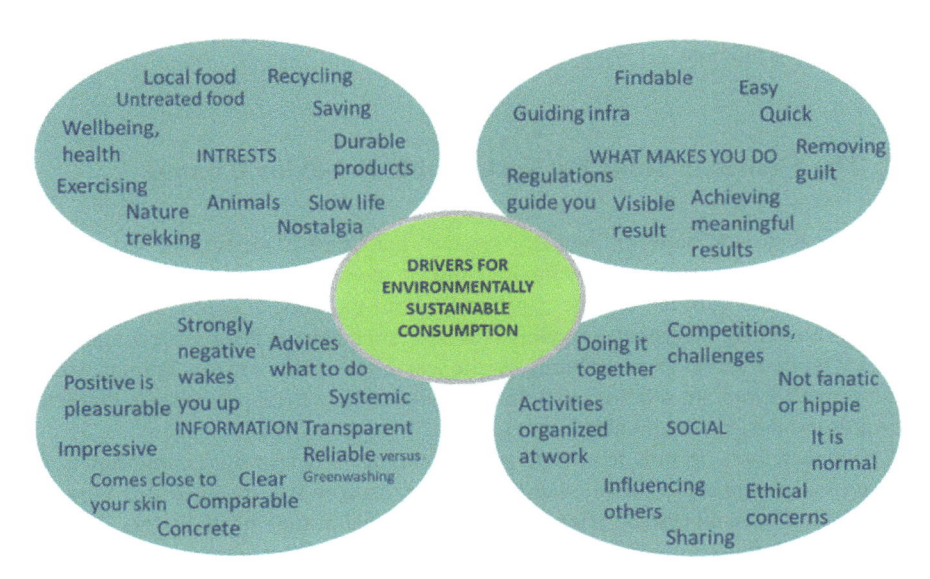

Fig. 1 Drivers for sustainable consumption behavior [5]

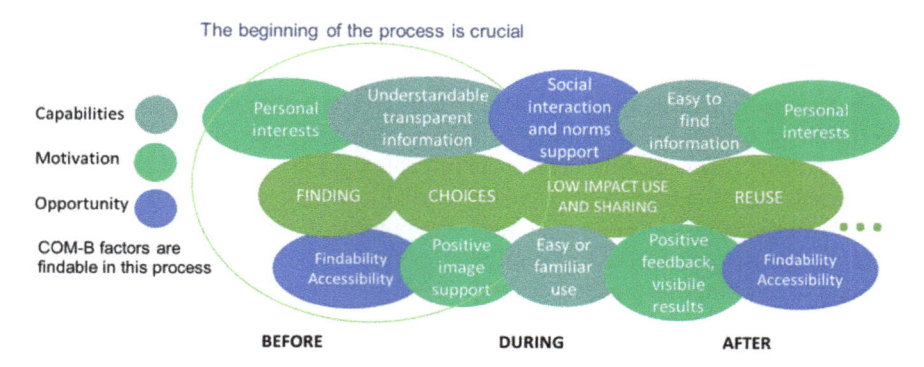

Fig. 2 Service process for sustainable behavior change consists of capability, motivation and opportunity factors for behaviors to take place [5]

supportive touchpoints and necessary interactions throughout the hoped for sustainable behavior [5]. The results concerning the drivers and process requirements can be reflected against research-based theoretical models from behavior change psychology as Fig. 2 shows. The user research-based findings match well with the factors in the COM-B model. The COM-B model assumes that executing a behavior is dependent on the simultaneous effect of user capabilities, motivation, and contextual opportunity and the various ways that these factors are realized in practice [6]. Contextual opportunity points also to the necessity for timely prompts as a psychological requirement for adapting new habits [7]. The environment of the action should offer opportunities, cues, and reminders to take the right action at the decision and action taking moment.

3 The Heuristic Tools for Sustainable Behavior Change

As the comparison between behavior science, the COM-B model, and the service process promoting sustainable behaviour shows, the service process for sustainable behavioural and habitual change can benefit from the understanding and perspectives provided by the general models and heuristics behind behavior change. The service process serves as an umbrella for the service moments and touchpoints where supportive factors are required to help the consumers in their interactions that lead towards the desired sustainable behavior.

Guidance tools on how to change specific human behavior utilize findings from behavioral psychology. As an example, choice research has revealed that humans tend to display a bounded rationality in their decision-making moments through fast, intuitive thinking which is related to experience-based biases, heuristics and emotional influences [8]. Additionally, findings on how to psychologically influence peoples' acts by softly nudging them has been a popular starting point in the field of psychological behavioral change [9]. Various practical factors and heuristics for nudging the consumer exist and are emerging in the forms of behavioral change and sustainability tools. Specific design-based ideation cards have also been produced based on psychological findings concerning behavioral change interventions and how to influence this change.

The user-research-based service process findings match well with the factors in the psychological COM-B model. The COM-B model describes how behavior is dependent on the simultaneous influences of user capabilities, motivation, and contextual opportunity. The model has been extended through a meta-analysis of theories of behaviors and behavioral change and formed into a tool called a behavior change wheel, which provide a wide variety of intervention functions of COM-B-related factors including education, training, persuasion, incentives, coercion, restriction, enablement, environmental restructuring and modeling. These functions can be connected to physical or psychological capabilities, and aspects such as reflective or automatic motivation and social or physical opportunity [10]. In the service process, where touchpoints drive the interaction process forward, the COM-B model provide advice as to what kinds of touchpoints could be constructed for different interaction purposes and for ensuring the necessary factors (capabilities, motivation and opportunity) for the behavior to occur.

Behavioral psychology advises instigating behavioral change using interventions that nudge or otherwise support people to carry out the desired acts or gently prevent them from carrying out the undesired ones [11]. In the Design with Intent card deck the behavioral interactions include insights and patterns from behavioral, cognitive, and environmental psychology. As a result the deck provides design-related suggestions for user interfaces, visual communication, and physical design [12]. The Design with Intent cards were developed in design workshops and they support analyzing existing idea spaces or target behaviors and can be applied also as ideation tools.

The Design with Intent cards are grouped into eight 'lenses' representing different research fields to support behavioral change. The architectural lens contains intervention suggestions through forms or materials, or via hiding things, or through structures of systems. The error proofing lens applies typical usability rules such as confirmation, choice editing, defaults or modifying sizes. The interaction lens applies process feedback, guidance and personification. The ludic lens promotes game-based and playful interactions via challenges, targets, and enjoyable materials. The perceptual lens enhances visibility, guidance, mood, and understanding through meaning building and compositional elements. The influence of heuristics and biases is acknowledged in the cognitive lens, which offers engagement, framing, renaming or social proof type of interventions. The Machiavellian lens even suggests means of manipulative affect and control. The security lens works through countermeasures to undesirable acts [13].

In addition to the service process-based user research findings, the behavioral change models in general, and those for sustainable behavior argue that habit change requires a process type of solution [14]. In the behavior change process there are similar process moments and touchpoints as in the service process, where the touchpoints drive the interaction process forward and barriers or hindrances must be overcome. For a behavior change intervention it is important to find especially suitable

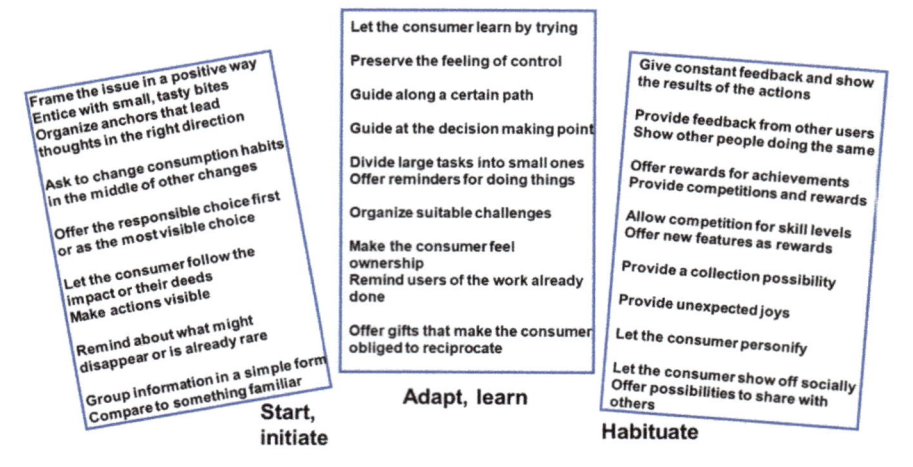

Start, initiate
- Frame the issue in a positive way
- Entice with small, tasty bites
- Organize anchors that lead thoughts in the right direction
- Ask to change consumption habits in the middle of other changes
- Offer the responsible choice first or as the most visible choice
- Let the consumer follow the impact or their deeds
- Make actions visible
- Remind about what might disappear or is already rare
- Group information in a simple form
- Compare to something familiar

Adapt, learn
- Let the consumer learn by trying
- Preserve the feeling of control
- Guide along a certain path
- Guide at the decision making point
- Divide large tasks into small ones
- Offer reminders for doing things
- Organize suitable challenges
- Make the consumer feel ownership
- Remind users of the work already done
- Offer gifts that make the consumer obliged to reciprocate

Habituate
- Give constant feedback and show the results of the actions
- Provide feedback from other users
- Show other people doing the same
- Offer rewards for achievements
- Provide competitions and rewards
- Allow competition for skill levels
- Offer new features as rewards
- Provide a collection possibility
- Provide unexpected joys
- Let the consumer personify
- Let the consumer show off socially
- Offer possibilities to share with others

Fig. 3 Examples of behavioral interventions suitable for the ideation of the different stages of the sustainable behavioral change process (Kälviäinen 2020)

functions for the different stages of the behavior change. As presented in Fig. 3, some interventions would especially support the motivation and activity to start the behavioral change process, while some interventions would support the learning of the new behavior, and others would help to carry on with the habit in the long run.

Social-cultural influence factors from marketing, psychology and economics literature have been analyzed in the SHIFT framework, which is a design tool which provides advice on how to promote sustainable consumer alternatives and encourage ecologically sustainable consumer behavior. The SHIFT framework presents theme-based factors for engaging consumers in ecologically sustainable consumer behavior [15].

Behavior should appear to be **socially approved**, desirable and visible and include socially observable commitments or competitions which would encourage consumers towards sustainable action. **Habit formation** requires breaking down earlier habits during shifts in life contexts or by instigating penalties but supporting new, desired habits by making them cheap, easy to do or offering feedback, prizes and reminders. Effective sustainable behavior is derived from the **individual self**, including personal norms, self-expectations, and self-standards concerning personal obligations and through self-efficacy. Pro-environmental behavior related **feelings and emotions** includes pride in self-efficacy. Guilt should be emphasized only in subtle ways. Fear easily leads to avoidance, so hope should be emphasized as a positive coping resource. **Cognitive factors** include understanding possible types of sustainable consumer behavior and the reasons they have an impact. As ecological consumer behaviors involve putting aside proximal, immediate, and individual benefits, and engaging in distal, future-focused, and other-oriented ones, **tangibility**, highlighting specific outcomes, steps, and future benefits are important. Additionally, the SHIFT framework encourages the use of combinations of factors to achieve desirable impacts [16]. Visual, sensual, identity related and social elements connect also to the emotional feel of activities especially important in the crucial initial phase of the change processes.

For concrete implementation, the SHIFT framework requires indepth contextual information and understanding of the use situation and user behavior. The use of factors should make content-based sense given the behavior and the context, the target and the specific barriers, and the benefits. The presented user research shows both concretizations of the SHIFT-factors and lends support to the idea that the social influence, habit integration into everyday life contexts, individual interests, feelings, cognition, and tangibility are important as drivers for sustainable behavior change.

4 Conclusion: Drafting the Heuristics for Changes Towards Sustainable Behavior

The observations and analysis comparing user research and different approaches to changes towards sustainable behavior confirm that generalizable heuristics to support sustainable behavior change design can be found. One important conclusion is that process-based solutions are vital. The process idea should be applied from two perspectives. For sustainable behavior solutions leading to low environmental impacts consumers need a supportive service process, that blends smoothly into their everyday life, where they may struggle with pressures and lack of time due to many other requirements. Consumers also need a process-based structure to start, learn and become habituated to a new behavior. This requires promoters to instigate the process and suitable interaction touchpoints to support the change from old habits to adapting, learning, and keeping up new ones.

The start of these two types of processes is especially crucial. It is connected to the motivation, desirability, individual interests and understanding of the meaningfulness of initiating the change. It can be supported via offering the change in the frame of consumer interests, through identity and social matching and opportunity-related social approval. The findability, accessibility, and concretization of the information are important factors which help to provide opportunities and capabilities at the outset of the process. The solutions and their touchpoints should be offered so that they blend smoothly into other obligatory activities which are necessary in everyday life.

The capability aspect is emphasized later in the use phase, which should be smooth and easy. Further along in the process, social-cultural factors may support the motivation to stick to the new behavior. Suitable interaction touchpoints with intervention functions in the service and change process ensure that the well begun journey continues to result in real sustainable change.

The understanding of these mechanisms of behavioral change and intervention heuristics provides a powerful tool to accelerate solution creation for the necessary change towards more sustainable lifestyles. However, the general models and heuristics do not work without contextual user understanding and content relating to real users and their environments. With sustainable solutions local variation also counts technologically and biologically. As there is some urgency for sustainable behavioral change, the behavioral change models and heuristics described in this paper can support consumers in making sustainable lifestyle choices. With the urgency of the crisis concerning our planetary boundaries these aspects should become an important future field of design for us all.

References

1. Hertwich EG, Peters GP (2009) Carbon footprint of nations: a global trade-linked analysis. Environ Sci Technol 43:6414–6420
2. Rockström J, Steffen W, Noone KJ, Persson A, Chapin FS, Lambin EF (2009) A safe operating space for humanity. Nature 461:472–475 (2009). https://doi.org/10.1038/461472a. Steffen W, Richardson K, Rockström J, Cornell SE, Fetzer I (2015) Planetary boundaries: guiding human development on a changing planet. Science 347, 623. https://doi.org/10.1126/science.1259855
3. Claudelin A, Uusitalo V, Pekkola S, Leino M, Konsti-Laakso S (2017) The role of consumers in the transition toward low-carbon living. Sustainability 9(6):958. White K, Habib R, Hardisty DJ (2019) How to SHIFT consumer behaviors to be more sustainable: a literature review and guiding framework. J Market 83(3):22–49
4. White K, Habib R (2018) Shift. A review and framework for encouraging sustainable consumer behaviour. Helsinki: Sitra
5. Kälviäinen M (2019) Green design as service design. In: Miettinen S, Sarantou M (eds) Managing complexity and creating innovation through design. Routledge, Abingdon, pp 100–113
6. Michie S, Atkins L, West R (2014) The behaviour change wheel. A guide to designing interventions. Silverback Publishing, London
7. Fogg BJ (2019) Tiny habits. The small changes that change everything. Virgin Books, London
8. Samson A (2014) An introduction behavioural economics. In Samson A (ed) The behavioral economics guide, pp 1–12 [Cited 16 Apr 2019]. Available at http://www.behavioraleconomics.com
9. Thaler RH, Sunstein CR (2008) Nudge: Improving decisions about health, wealth and happiness. Yale University Press, New Haven
10. Michie S, Atkins L, West R (2014) The behaviour change wheel. A guide to designing interventions. Silverback Publishing
11. Artefactgroup (2014) Behavior change strategy cards. [Cited 11.9.2019]. Available at https://www.artefactgroup.com/case-studies/behavior-change-strategy-cards/
12. Lockton D, Harrison D, Stanton NA (2012) Design with intent 101 patterns for influencing behavior through design. Requisite Variety [Cited 11.9.2019]. Available at http://designwithintent.co.uk/docs/designwithintent_cards_1.0_draft_rev_sm.pdf
13. Lockton D (2018) Design, behaviour change and the design with intent toolkit. In: Niedderer K, Clune S, Ludden G (eds) Design for behaviour change. Theories and practices of designing for change, pp 58–73. Abingdon, Routledge
14. Tischner U, Stebbing P (2015) Changing paradigms: designing for a sustainable future. In: Aalto University School of Arts, Design and Architecture, pp 317–327. 1st Cumulus Think Tank Publication, Helsinki

15. White K, Habib R (2018) Shift. A review and framework for encouraging ecologically sustainable consumer behaviour. Sitra, Helsinki
16. White K, Habib R (2018) Shift sustainable consumer behaviour change workbook. Sitra, Helsinki

Games for Change

Improving Awareness and Empathy with Video Games: A Qualitative Analysis Study of PUDCAD Game

Cetin Tuker and Güven Çatak

Abstract This study aims to understand the efficacy of a CAD enhanced video game on improving the awareness and empathy of design students on the issues of people with disabilities. Previous literature shows video games may have an impact on improving awareness and empathy of players. "This War of Mine" is a well-known game which allows players to build empathy towards the civilians who were trying to survive in a war zone. In this study, it was hypothesized that, a video game can be used as an educational tool to raise awareness and empathy of design students on the problems of disabled people. This is a controlled presurvey-postsurvey, quasi-experimental qualitative research. Participants were divided into two groups as experiment and control. Experiment group played the PUDCAD game. Control group played another environmental puzzle game. Data collection instruments were three questionnaires consist of open-ended questions. The presurvey was focused on the participants' emotions, thoughts, and previous experience about the disabled people. Postsurvey, which was applied right after the gameplay was focused on the issues of the usability of the game. Delayed postsurvey which was applied 7–10 after the game play focuses on possible changes in the emotions and thoughts of the participants about disabled people. Qualitative coding methods were used to analyze the responses. Findings show, based on the declarations of the participants, PUDCAD game has a larger impact on the improvement of awareness and empathy of the participants than the control game.

Keywords Educational games · Empathy games · Design for all · Games for change · Awareness games

1 Introduction

During the design process, some parts of the population, like the elderly, physically disabled people, and children can be excluded from the design goals nonintentionally, because neither the client nor the designer considers their existence. PUDCAD project aims to improve awareness and empathy of design students towards these excluded populations by creating a video game. The PUDCAD game can be classified as a "game-for-change" that focuses on rising empathy, awareness or changing behaviors of the players. We can also classify these kinds of games in educational games group as they have the potential to teach something to player by changing a behavior.

Games-for-change is not a popular genre in game industry. Therefore, outstanding examples of this genre developed mostly by indie game developers. As prominent examples of this genre This War of Mine [1], Dys4ia [2], Depression-Quest [3], 3D World Farmer [4], Auti-Sim [5], and Sea Hero quest [6] can be listed.

PUDCAD is an adventure game with first person perspective (Fig. 1). The protagonist is a student with cerebral palsy and uses a wheelchair. Therefore, player see the environment from the character's point of view.

Plot of the game takes place in a school which has a very unfriendly environment for a student using a wheelchair. Main character has overslept in the classroom in the evening and all friends including the caretaker has left the school and they were waiting for the player on the school bus. The player has to reach the school bus before it left the school. To achieve this goal, protagonist has to solve environmental puzzles to advance in the school building. The aim of the puzzles are about improving bad design decisions that are blocking the way to school bus. Player solves puzzles by entering in a CAD like environment, as it was called CAD-Mode in the game, in which it is possible to improve designs by editing the environment (Fig. 2).

Fig. 1 A scene from the PUDCAD game (image created by writers)

Improving Awareness and Empathy with Video Games ... 123

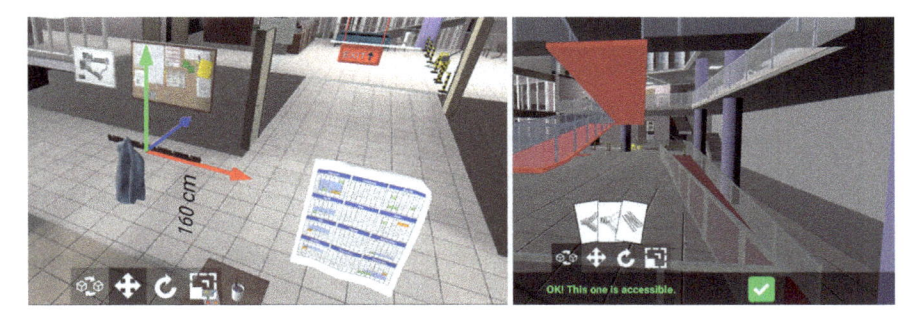

Fig. 2 Two scenes from the CAD-mode (images created by writers)

2 PUDCAD Game

The educational model of the game, which was explained by Tüker and Çatak [7] aims two main achievements: Rising empathy, and rising awareness and design knowledge. To raise empathy, the story line was used. The overall story gives the player the chance of experiencing an ordinary day of a disabled person in an unusable environment, in this case the school building. Player firstly learns to use a wheelchair, which is not very easy. The game environment (the school building) has several design issues designed intentionally to be unusable. Toilets have accessibility problems, corridors are too long, coat hanger is too high, some doors are too tight to be passed through, trench drain in the garden catches the wheel of the chair, you it is not possible to climb up even 1 single step because there were no ramps for vertical circulation. All these designated situations help player to feel like they were really disabled and help them to create empathy with the person on the wheelchair.

To acquire design knowledge repetitive micro learning units were used (Fig. 3). The micro learning pattern has three steps:

First, player bumps into a problem while exploring the building. Game warns the player that this a problem to be fixed and guides the player to the CAD-Mode

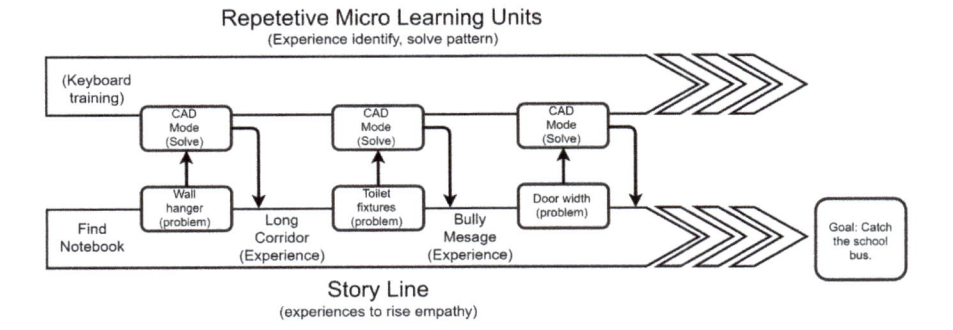

Fig. 3 Educational model of the PUDCAD game (image created by writers)

Table 1 List of design issues

	Location	Object	Problem	Tool/solution
1	Classroom	Notebook	Training for controls	–
2	Classroom	Coat	Wall hanger height	Move
3	Corridor	–	Too long corridor	Mentioned in the game as an experience. No specific solution
4	WC	–	Insufficient design	Choose the correct solution
5	Art Class	Bag	Door too tight	Scale
6	Corridor	–	Insufficient door opening direction	Choose the correct solution
7	Hall	–	Stairs/lack of ramps	Choose the correct solution
8	Garden	–	Trench drain gratings too wide	Choose the correct solution
9 and 10	Garden/center	–	Ramp angle and missing safety balustrade	Scale and choose the correct solution
11	Garden exit	–	Single step/lack of ramps	Choose the correct solution

in which the player can use the tools to manipulate the environment and solve the problem.

Second, in the CAD-Mode, game briefly informs the player that why this is a problem. A hand drawn sketch is used for communicating this information as if these sketches were drawn by the protagonist sometime before the day the story takes place.

Last, player solves the problem by improving design by either selecting better design options from a three-item list or by manipulating the object by using manipulation tools. Additional information on why the manipulations or choices made by the player were correct or wrong were also added during the CAD-Mode process.

After the micro learning pattern has been completed with a satisfactory result, player continues to the journey in the building. A list of all design issues to be solved by the player is listed in Table 1.

3 Method

This is a controlled presurvey-postsurvey, quasi-experimental qualitative research study.

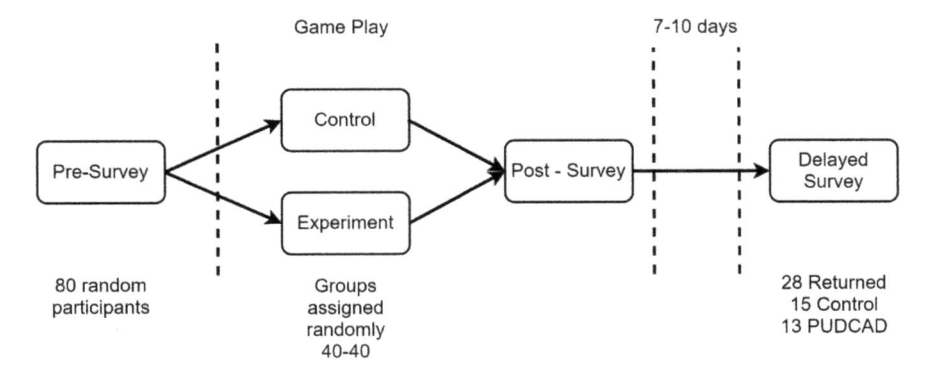

Fig. 4 Schematic diagram of the research study design (image created by writers)

3.1 Participants

Participants applied to our online open call on several social media sites on the internet and research team communicated with them by email. A total of 80 participants applied to be included in the study.

3.2 Procedure

80 participants applied to the open call. Participants were divided into two groups randomly as experiment (n = 40) and control (n = 40). Firstly, both groups filled the same online pre-game survey. In the next step research team emailed them to the internet links of the games both groups must play. Experiment group received the links of the PUDCAD game. Control group received the links of another environmental puzzle called Wyst. Immediately after playing the games both groups filled the same post-game survey, which is mainly focused on usability issues of the games. After 7–10 days, research team emailed the participants the delayed post-game survey. 28 participants replied the delayed post game survey. 13 of them were in experiment group, 15 of them were in control group. While playing games, participants did not know which group they were in. So, they were blind to games (Fig. 4).

3.3 Control Game

To control the effects of playing an environment puzzle on the dependent variables, a neutral environment puzzle game was selected. The game the control group played is named as "Wyst." It is a first-person perspective, online, abstract environment puzzle—adventure game. The game environment of the puzzle is an island like giant rock that floats in the infinity. Players solve environmental puzzles to collect special objects and this helps them to advance in the game storyline. It has no emphasis on education, accessibility, or any design solutions. Therefore, because of this neutral atmosphere research team decided to choose "Wyst" to support the null hypothesis.

3.4 Data Collection

The data was collected by three surveys which consist of open-ended questions. Pregame survey mainly focuses on the background experiences of the players with disabled people and the context of disabilities. This survey aims to check if the experiment and control groups are equally distributed by means of the background knowledge and experience.

Postgame survey is mainly for usability of the current game. Participants gave precious feedback about the story line, keyboard controls, dialogues and glitches and bugs in the game. Research team used these feedbacks to polish the final product.

Delayed survey mainly focuses on follow up questions for comparing the change between pre and postgame survey conditions. Table 2 includes a list of topics covered

Table 2 Topics covered by survey questions

Presurvey	Postsurvey	Delayed Postsurvey
Experience with disability		
Close circle of family and friends		
Personal feelings about disabled		Changes of feelings about disabled people
Personal experience		Possible future experience
Caring experience		
Knowledge about accessibility		
Knowledge about problems with built environment	Knowledge about design problems	Knowledge about problems with built environment
Solution proposal to previous problems		Solution proposal to previous problems
Knowledge about dimensions		Knowledge about dimensions Knowledge of easier use
Awareness—empathy gain		
	Efficacy of game about awareness/empathy	Efficacy of game about awareness/empathy
Game usability		
	Best and worst features and bugs	

by three surveys. Efficacy of the PUDCAD game about awareness, empathy, and knowledge about design problems and their solutions are the main subjects that this paper focuses on.

3.5 Data Analysis

As surveys consists of open-ended questions, qualitative coding methods are used to analyze the answers [8]. Descriptive coding and provisional coding methods mainly used to analyze the surveys. Provisional codes have been predetermined within the context of the open-ended question. After coding, frequencies of the concepts were counted. As an example, predetermined list of codes are any accessibility problems that participants can mention while coding for the question "can you give three examples of accessibility problems?" Some of these problems were included in the PUDCAD game. These were coded as target concepts. Problems that were not included in the game were also coded. The frequencies of how many times and by how many participants these concepts were mentioned counted separately.

4 Findings

Question: Do you have any knowledge about dimensions or/and layout standards of built environment for better accessible design solutions?

For this question, participants mostly answered clearly as "yes" or "no". Only some of them supported their answers with additional concepts. For both group pregame survey levels are almost same, 23–20%. After postgame survey, experiment group gains 69 points and control group gains minus 7 points. So, it can be concluded that based on the declarations of participants, PUDCAD game has a solid positive effect on the knowledge levels of the participants about dimensions or/and layout standards of built environment for better accessible design solutions (Table 3).

Question: Have you learned new knowledge about how to solve accessibility problems of the built environment?

Table 3 Knowledge change about dimension and layout standards

	Experiment (%)		Control (%)	
	Pre	Post	Pre	Post
Yes	23	92	20	13
No	61.5	8	66	60
A few	15.5	0	14	0
Not Sure	0	0	0	27

Table 4 Knowledge change about solving accessibility problems

	Experiment (%)		Control (%)	
	Pre	Post	Pre	Post
No	23	61.5	20	13.3
Yes	61.5	31	66.6	73.3
Difficult to relate	15.5	0	13.4	0
Unrelated Answer	0	7.5	0	13.4

Both groups were almost equal before playing the game. After playing the game experiment group gained 38.8 points and control group gained minus 6.7 points. One thing to mention here, some participants in the experiment group noted that they already know the standards, so they did not gain any new knowledge.

It can be concluded that based on the declarations of participants, PUDCAD game has a solid positive effect on the knowledge levels of the participants about solving accessibility problems of the built environment (Table 4).

Question: Do you think that the game you have just played can give design students awareness of what problems the physically disabled people have regarding the built environment?

This question was coded with descriptive coding methodology. All members of experiment group answered with "positive" sentences and supported their answers with 19 unique concepts. These concepts were mentioned with a total of 55 times in their answers. Only 6 members of control group answered with "positive" sentences and supported their answers with only 2 unique concepts mentioning with a total of 4 times.

It can be concluded that based on the declarations of participants, PUDCAD game has a positive effect on gaining awareness about the problems of the disabled people as compared to the effect of the control game (Table 5).

Question: Do you think this game you played helped you empathize with people with physical disabilities?

For this question, participants preferred to answer shortly as "yes" or "no." All members of experiment group answered as "yes." The answers of the control group

Table 5 Awareness about problems of disabled people

	Experiment	Control
No	0	5
Yes	13	6
Difficult to relate	0	2
Unrelated answer	0	2
Total unique concepts mentioned	19	2
Total concept mentions	55	4
Concept mentions per participant	4.23	0.266

Improving Awareness and Empathy with Video Games ...   129

Table 6 Empathize with people with disabilities

	Experiment	Control
No	0	8
Yes	13	7

mimic a random distribution. Seven participants answered as "yes", and 8 participants answered as "no." It can be concluded that based on the declarations of participants, PUDCAD game has a positive effect on gaining empathy about the problems of the disabled people as compared to the effect of the control game (Table 6).

Question: Give three examples of accessibility problems that physically disabled people experience with the built environment.

With this question the participants mentioned three accessibility problems they know before and after playing the games. We expect the experiment group will mention more problems that exist in the game in the delayed postgame survey then they mentioned in the pregame survey. Before playing the game both groups mentioned almost same numbers of unique concepts, 15–17. Although they did not play the game yet, 5 of these concepts were still in the game. These 5 concepts mentioned 20–18 times. (Multiple mentions by the same participant counted once.) So, we can say both groups were almost equal in pregame survey. After they played the game, experiment group mentioned 7 concepts that exist in the game 26 times and control group mentioned 6 concepts that exist in the game 16 times. It seems experiment group focused on the concepts that exist in the game so we can say the PUDCAD game has more impact on experiment group than the control game (Table 7).

A list of concepts mentioned by the control group and their frequencies are given in table. After playing the control game, "door width" concept, that was mentioned only once, has been dropped from the list. In the postgame survey concept list, participants mentioned 2 more concepts that exist in the PUDCAD game, but they were mentioned only once (Table 8).

Table 7 Examples of accessibility problems that participants can remember

	Experiment		Control	
	Pre	Post	Pre	Post
Total unique concepts mentioned	15	16	17	19
Total concept mentions	44	38	45	41
Concept mentions per participant	3.38	2.93	3	2.73
Total unique target concepts mentioned (out of 10)	5	7	5	6
Total target concept mentions	20	26	18	16
Total concept mentions per participant	1.54	2	1.2	1.06

*Concepts already included in the game

Table 8 Concepts mentioned by control group

Presurvey		Postsurvey	
Concepts	Freq.	Concepts	Freq.
Sidewalk height/quality*	**7**	Rudeness of people	7
Problems of blind people	7	Elevators	7
Ramps*	**6**	**Sidewalk height/quality***	**7**
Access to public transport	5	**Ramps***	**3**
Building entrances	3	Communication problems	2
WC access and usability*	**2**	**WC access and usability***	**2**
Rudeness of people	2	Not suitable designs	2
Staircases*	**2**	**Staircases***	**2**
Door width*	**1**	**Corridor length***	**1**
		Height of hanged objects*	**1**

*Concepts already included in the game

A list of concepts mentioned by the experiment group and their frequencies are given in table. Experiment group started with 5 concepts, mentioning these 20 times. After the game they added 2 more concepts without dropping any of the concepts mentioned in the pregame survey. These concepts were mentioned very frequently. Total number is 26. So, it can be concluded that PUDCAD game has an impact on remembering the concepts related with the problems of the disabled people compared with the control game (Table 9).

5 Conclusion

In this study, it was hypothesized that by manipulating several parameters a video game can be used as an educational tool to raise awareness and empathy of design students on the problems of disabled people on the built environment. A controlled presurvey-postsurvey, quasi-experimental qualitative research study conducted on participants attended randomly. Experiment group played the PUDCAD game and control group played another environmental puzzle game called Wyst.

It can be concluded that, according to the declarations of the participants PUDCAD game has a larger impact than the control game on factors presented here (knowledge, awareness, and empathy gain).

Improving Awareness and Empathy with Video Games ... 131

Table 9 Concepts mentioned by PUDCAD group

Presurvey		Postsurvey	
Concepts	Freq.	Concepts	Freq.
Access to public transport	10	**Staircases***	**10**
Sidewalk height/quality*	**7**	Doors*	4
Ramps*	**5**	Sidewalk height/quality*	4
Staircases*	4	Ramps*	3
Problems of blind people	4	Surface pavement for blind ppl.	2
Height of hanged objects*	**2**	**Height of hanged objects***	**2**
Elevators	2	Access to public transport	2
Rudeness of people	2	Building entrances	2
WC access and usability*	**2**	**WC access and usability***	**2**
		Balustrades*	1

It can also be concluded that PUDCAD game model which was presented in this paper (Fig. 1) is affective for improving awareness, empathy and knowledge for the factors presented here.

Acknowledgements Practicing Universal Design Principles in Design Education through a CAD Based Game (PUDCAD) is an Erasmus + project which was started in 2017 and will be completed in September 2020. The main goal of the project is to raise the empathy of design students with people who have physical disabilities. Istanbul Technical University in Turkey is the applicant organization. Partner universities are Bahçeşehir University from Turkey, Hochschule Ostwestfalen-Lippe from Germany, Lahden Ammattikorkeakoulu Oy from Finland, Universita Degli Studi di Firenze and Politecnico di Milano from Italy. There are two non-profit organizations from Turkey: SERÇEV (Serebral Palsili Çocuklar Derneği/Association of Children with Cerebral Palsy) and Ergoterapi Derneği (Ergotherapy Association).

References

1. This War of Mine [Computer Software] (2014) 11Bit Studios. Retrieved from www.tlo.thiswarofmine.com/. Last accessed 2020/07/15
2. Dys4ia [Computer Software] (2012) Anna anthropy. Retrieved from www.gamesforchange.org/game/dys4ia/. Last accessed 2020/07/15
3. Depression Quest [Computer Software] (2014) The Quinnspiracy. Retrieved from https://store.steampowered.com/app/270170/Depression_Quest/. Last accessed 2020/07/15
4. D World Farmer [Computer Software] (2006) 3D World farmer team. Retrieved from https://3rdworldfarmer.org/. Last accessed 2020/07/15

5. Auti-Sim [Computer Software] (2013) Taylan Kadayifcioglu, Matt Marshall, Krista Howarth Retrieved from www.gamesforchange.org/game/auti-sim/. Last accessed 2020/07/15
6. Sea Hero Quest [Computer Software] (2016) T-Mobile. Retrieved from www.seaheroquest.com/site/en/. Last accessed 2020/07/15
7. Tüker Ç, Çatak G (2020) Designing a CAD-enriched empathy game to raise awareness about universal design principles: a case study. In: Game user experience and player-centered design, pp 327–346. Springer, Cham
8. Saldaña J (2015) The coding manual for qualitative researchers. Sage

Using Board Games as a Method for Improving Awareness and Empathy in Inclusive Design: PUDCAD Game Case Study

Poyraz Özer and Güven Çatak

Abstract The aim of this research is about how inclusive design can be taught to design students by introducing game design principles rather than traditional education methods. This study focuses on a smaller part of the project called PUDCAD (Practicing Universal Design Principles in Design Education through a CAD-Based Game), which aims to increase awareness and empathy of design students about design problems regarding people with disabilities. The project develops through 4 student workshops and three international conferences on Universal Design, Ergonomics, Game, and Education. This paper focuses on the third workshop held in Florence in Design Campus Firenze, specifically on the board game workshop process, excluding the held conferences. In the workshop, Design students were asked to work in groups and given a task to create a board game based on inclusive design principles and elaborate on game mechanics regarding inclusive design. Later they are given an open-ended questionnaire about how they found it and how they would implement the mechanics to an educational video game. Final board game outputs are then taken to a comparison chart to define the mechanics and reveal the similarities and differences. Then the results are compared to develop a video game for PUDCAD for the fourth workshop in the alpha stage for further studies. Questions and the workshop methods are then revised for the next student workshop. This research is hoped to inform game designers and teachers to find the most efficient method to educate and have a better understanding of inclusive design principles.

Keywords Inclusive design · Serious games · Edugames · Board games · Design education

---

P. Özer (✉)
BAU Game Design Graduate Programme, İstanbul, Turkey
e-mail: pyrz.ozer@gmail.com

G. Çatak
BAU Digital Game Design Department, İstanbul, Turkey
e-mail: guven.catak@comm.bau.edu.tr

© The Author(s), under exclusive license to Springer Nature Switzerland AG 2021
Ö. Cordan et al. (eds.), *Game + Design Education*, Springer Series in Design and Innovation 13, https://doi.org/10.1007/978-3-030-65060-5_11

1 Introduction

Inclusive design is an important subject in design education, and its existing knowledge is aimed to adapt to contemporary education methods with the help of innovative ways. This paper focuses on a specific workshop event as a case study inside the PUDCAD project. PUDCAD (Practicing Universal Design Principles in Design Education through a CAD-Based Game), a project is granted by the European Commission for the Erasmus + Program, and it is coordinated by Istanbul Technical University, Department of Interior Architecture. PUDCAD also involves five academic partners: Lahti Institute of Design and Fine Arts, Finland; Detmolder School of Architecture and Interior Architecture, Technische Hochschule Ostwestfalen-Lippe, Germany; Architecture Department, Università degli Studi di Firenze, Italy; Department of Design, Politecnico di Milano, Italy; Bahcesehir University Foundation, Turkey; and the Turkish non-governmental organizations SERÇEV (Association for Well-being of Children with Cerebral Palsy) and Occupational Therapy Association of Turkey (Costa et al. 2019).

PUDCAD aims to widen the awareness of universal design principles and inclusive design to the future designers by exploring and practicing with innovative methods, and it aims to address this awareness problem by developing a digital video game (game for a change) for design students through mechanics involved with empathy and inclusive design principles. The project's development is divided into four student workshops and three international conferences on Universal Design, Ergonomics, Game and Education. This paper focuses on the third workshop, which was held in Università degli Studi di Firenze (May 6–10, 2019), and specifically takes the board game case study rather than the entire workshop's schedule. This game jam workshop has been executed with the participation of 35 design students from partner universities (specialized in interior architecture, architecture and industrial design) well as BAU game design experts.[1] Even though we are looking to find ideas about empathy and how to integrate it into the board game mechanics, our focus is more on the game design side in this workshop because participants and mentors were mainly in the role of game designers, not players.

Using game design as a tool to teach students the concepts of inclusive design may be more efficient than traditional methods. There are several studies regarding applying game design as an education method to teach basic tasks of the topic and have a better cognitive thinking process (Bright et al. 1985). Studies also show that introducing game design to education has also improved students' motivation towards learning the topic (Claypool and Claypool 2005). This workshop is an excellent foundation for testing this method since it will be supported by many presentations about the core concepts of game design.

One of the reasons to choose board games for this workshop is to introduce the game design concept in a better way. Participants were not familiar with the game design concepts, so keeping our focus on learning these principles rather than

---

[1] Barbaros Bostan, Cetin Tuker, Ecehan Akan, Ege Kumlali, Guven Catak, Kutsal Mustafaoglu, Poyraz Ozer, Semih Bertug Benim.

branching out to different points was our concern. If the medium were a video game or another digital media, students might have needed to additionally train themselves on the software before focusing on the game design itself, so there would be a deviation from the main point. Focusing on board game goes similar to another aim: to minimize the risk of losing time with the wrong design decisions by having an analog prototype before the production stage. Board game ideas can be quickly prototyped and have quick results, so students would have more time to focus on the game design part rather than the production of the assets.

Other than having possible positive outcomes for the workshop, card/board games are a good starting point for approaching subjects that are thought traditionally (Drake and Sung 2011). There are numerous studies about board games being used as a serious game such as in health education or Science, Technology, Engineering And Mathematics (STEM) education (Gibson and Douglas 2013; Bochennek et al. 2007; Blakely et al. 2009; Nakao 2019), so choosing board games as a medium in this workshop was an intention to increase the engagement and quality of education.

One of our aims was to systemize and find relationships and interactions about the game design concepts in this workshop and take those data back to developing the video game on the further PUDCAD project. Behavioural studies of board games have a similar approach that we can study because they focus on finding connections between board game mechanics and social interactions. Researchers from the Georgia Institute of Technology had a study about the conversion of board games into augmented reality games. They created a table based on Randall Collins' Interaction Ritual theory about transferring social play elements from board games into the digital realm (Xu et al. 2011). Although they aimed to focus more on the social interaction part, it is a good starting point for us to think about a way to translate the findings to concrete results. Because ultimately, the workshop's findings will aim to have a starting point in developing the video game itself, and finding a suitable framework to adapt the board game idea outputs to other mediums is a crucial element.

In addition to the board game, the format of the workshop is chosen to be a game jam. Kultima defines game jam as "An accelerated opportunistic game creation event where a game is created in a relatively short timeframe exploring given design constraint(s), and end results are shared publically" (Kultima 2015). There are also many studies about implementations of game jams in game-based education (Fowler et al. 2016; Hrehovcsik et al. 2016; Mikami et al. 2016; Fowler et al. 2013), and this model can be applied to ant kind of idea or product if the main objective is creation or presentation of it (Barba-Guaman et al. 2017) the Game jams differ in terms of how long they are, this game jam inside the PUDCAD workshop was five days, which the last day was reserved for the presentation of the final works.

2 Game Design Workshop

The workshop's structure revolves around informing the design students with the basic knowledge of topics such as games for change, universal design principles, game design process, storytelling, and level design in games, fast prototyping; giving a foundation to the students to get familiar with the workshop's concepts. Most of the design students were not familiar with games and game design before, so informing these concepts in conjunction with the board game jam was one of the goals in this workshop program (Fig. 1).

Participants have initially requested outputs such as the name of their team, the name of the game, slogan (if any), and their intro/synopsis of the game. They were expected to describe how they used their selected theme to their ideas and how they turned it into a story; also how they addressed the inclusion issues with levels that they thought of. After the introduction of their ideas, they were requested to create a story/level board to point out their story and their game elements, rule book (which includes the number of players, average playtime, the goal of the game, example game turn description, etc.), short gameplay videos to give a basic idea of the game and introducing the team, documentation photos of the board game, their process and the team, in addition to the board/card game prototype. After the conclusion of their prototype, participants were requested to give their thoughts about how new technologies like virtual reality (VR) and augmented reality (AR) can be implemented into the digital game version of the board/card games.

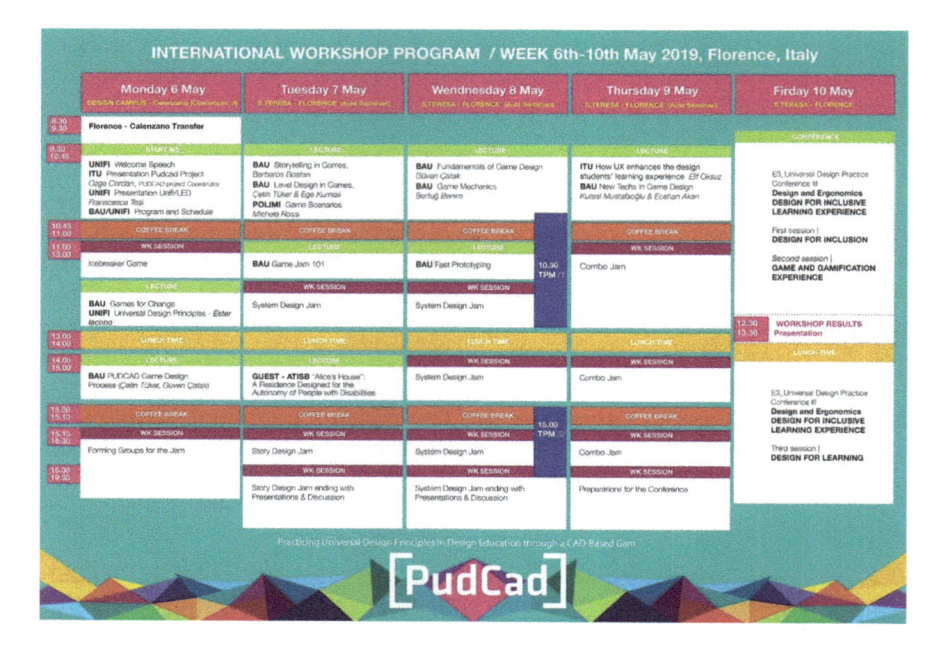

Fig. 1 Game design workshop program

2.1 Workshop Log

Monday: Students were first introduced into an icebreaker game to meet with each other, and they were encouraged to create their teams from different universities to create a more dynamic teamwork environment. Seven teams were assembled, and they were picked themes to start their brainstorming session (Quake!, What if?, Fire Alarm, Daydream, Alien Invasion, First Day, Holiday). After selecting the themes, teams are gathered to brainstorm until the end of the day and expected to make a presentation for Tuesday.

Tuesday: Presentation of the initial ideas and feedback from other students was made, and the workshop has begun with the help of assisting mentors from BAU for each group. Although mentors were occasionally looking at different teams in regular time intervals to share ideas and get feedback, they were assigned mainly to one team. Rather than just working with the team as their leader or just an observer, mentors' aim was to encourage the students to share new ideas and implement them together with the ideas from the other lectures they have learned. Creating a balance between guiding and making the students create solutions was important because the workshop's aim was to have critical thinking about the given problems in addition to the introduction of basic game design principles.

Wednesday: Production of the board games are continued, mentors were encouraging participants to focus on the gameplay mechanics and playtesting before focusing on the visual details or final touches.

Thursday: Production of the board games are continued; all of the initial game mechanic ideas were playtested, and game ideas are finally implemented into the final output.

Friday: The teams presented their board games, explaining their creative process, mechanics, and their approach to the inclusive design. All of the board games are stored and documented for further analysis.

2.2 Board Games

The proposed games (Fig. 2) were developed on the given themes and named as follows:

Escape from the Campus (Theme: Quake!) is a two-player grid-based board game, which is about two characters trying to escape from the school campus that just had an earthquake. The two have to cooperate with each other by trading cards each turn and making a strategy due to their differences in skills and speed as quickly as possible. Its replayability, cooperation mechanics, and the idea of creating design solutions to preventing disaster has a high potential of contributing to the digital game.

Match (Theme: What If?) is a card game that is played with four people. Players choose a card set that about different themes such as animal plants, which are drawn

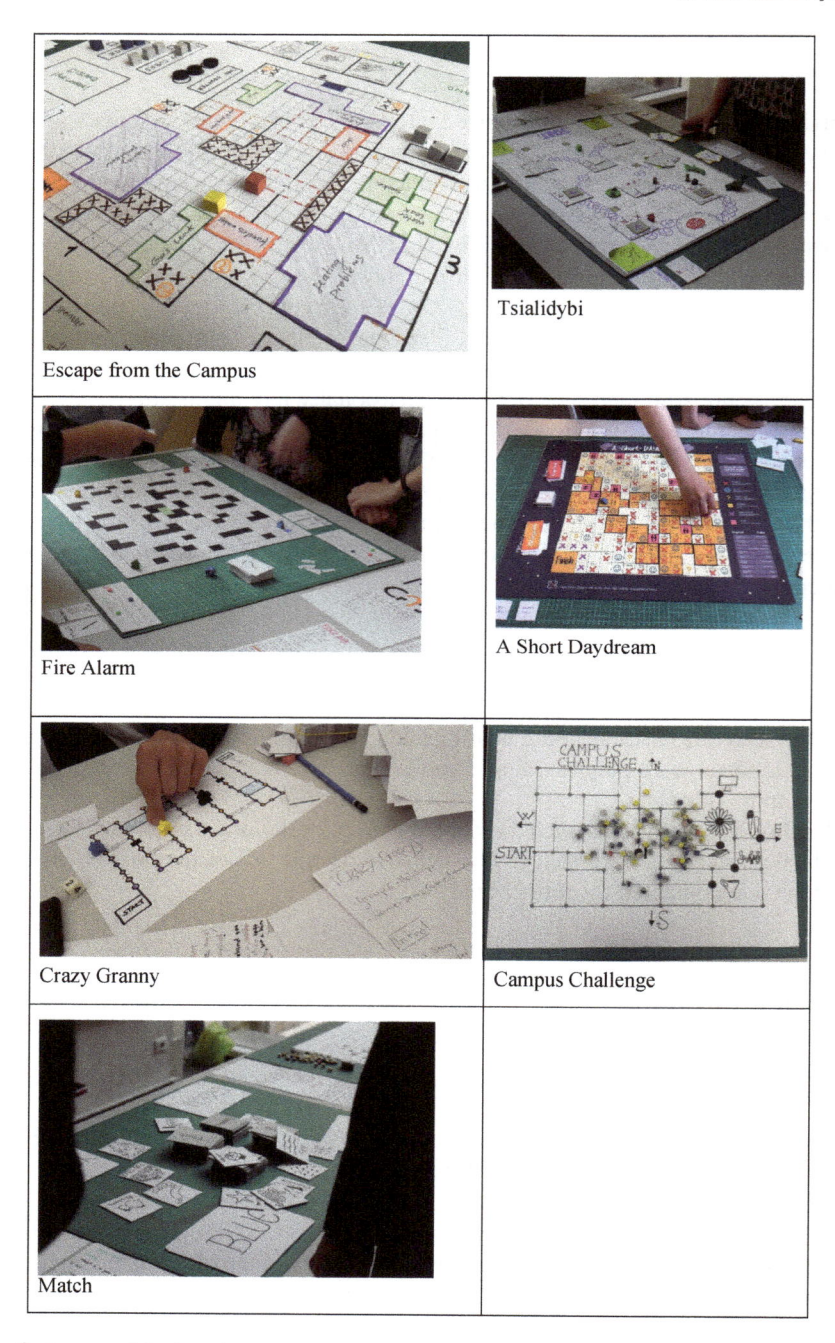

Fig. 2 Images of the board games

black and white, then each player chooses a color. Finally, the cards are put on the board, and the first one who collects six of the cards that are connected with their color wins. Contrast recognition, alternative pictogram ideas, and symbol recognitions for colorblind people can be listed as a contribution to the game.

Fire Alarm (Theme: Fire Alarm) is a four-player competitive game that is about scientists trying to escape from a science lab where an explosion occurred, which caused temporary blindness and fire around them. Players have oxygen and carbon monoxide as their health resource, and they have to maintain a balance between them in order not to get poisoned and eliminated. Each player starts with a perk, and a turn consists of moving and drawing a card if the player has ended their turn on a question mark tile.

A Short Daydream (Theme: Daydream) is a four-player grid-based roll and move type of board game in which players are trying to reach a destination from start to beginning to remove their curse from them. As the story goes, players are used to be bullies at school to a certain person, which turns out to be a witch, and now they are cursed by her. Main mechanics consist of grid-based board game and roll and move.

Tsialidybi (Theme: Alien Invasion) is about four people trying to escape from an alien ship where they are abducted. Players need to cooperate in order to win the game with dice rolling and point to point mechanics. Room unlocking, fantasy atmosphere, asynchronous character cooperation are interesting mechanics that can be adapted to the video game.

Campus Challenge (Theme: First Day) is about students that are on their first day on Campus and who are trying to reach their destination first. Players are started by having different types of disabilities, such as hearing aid, blindness, and walking disability. Players draw an event card, and they can put a certain obstacle on the board to block a player that has a specific disability. PvP ideas such as preventing other players' bad designs and random destination mechanics can be applied to the video game.

Crazy Granny (Theme: Holiday) is about a granny trying to find his husband on cruise travel. Players are traveling in the board game with a start to finish and roll and move mechanics. Players are also encouraged to think like old people while making their turn decisions not only to make empathy but also to create a meaningful strategy. Design problems for old people can be adapted to the video game.

After the conclusion of the workshop, BAU students[2] analyzed the board games to transfer the results to the digital game that is going to be developed. Transferring the ideas from one medium to another may cause a loss of information because some mechanics might not be compatible in another medium (Tuker 2018). With the awareness of this, they created six charts (mechanics, win condition, inclusion, pros, cons, and contribution to the digital game) to compare and find similarities or differences between the results (Table 1). These results are then used to be a foundation of the development of the video game.

---

[2]Poyraz Ozer, Semih Bertug Benim.

Table 1 Comparison of board games (Costa et al. 2019)

Game name	Mechanics	Win condition	Inclusion	Pros	Cons	Contribution to the digital game
Escape from the campus	Grid-based trading dice rolling	Special conditions	Limb disabilities	High replayability	Lack of challenge	Replayability by procedural generation ideas Cooperation mechanics 'Prevent disaster by good design solutions' mechanics
Crazy Granny	Roll and move	First to finish	Being Old	Old people empathy	No movement choice	Design problems for the elderly
Match	Card game Take that	First to finish	Color blindness	Basic, fun for children, teach for inclusion	Ambiguous color cards	Colorblind peoples' symbol recognitions Alternative pictograms Contrast recognitions
Campus Challenge	Point to point Take that	Destination	Language barrier Blindness Wheelchair	Take that mechanic with the "bad design"	Repetitive gameplay Unbalanced card deck	PvP Ideas. Such as prevent other players by bad designs Random destinations mechanics
Fire Alarm	Grid-based trading co-operative play	Special conditions	None	Oxygen management as health	No Inclusion	None
A Short Daydream	Grid-based roll and move	First to finish	Midget	None	The map is too big	None
Tsialidybi	Dice rolling point to point movement Co-operative Play Time track	Special conditions	Skin disease Wheelchair Blindness Amputee	Interesting theme risky shortcuts	Real-time boardgame (10 real minutes to finish the game)	Fantasy atmosphere Asynchronous character cooperations Room unlock mechanics Shortcuts

3 Conclusion and Further Thoughts

Participants of the workshop were happy about the general process; they had varied backgrounds (e.g., different nationalities, cultures, experience). They were not familiar with the game design concept before, implementing their existing knowledge of design principles in combination with the aims of the workshop was satisfying for them. Traditional instructional methods may be less effective in delivering ideas to the learners, whereas introducing gaming adds energy and interest to the learners (Sardone and Devlin-Scherer 2016). Participants also gave positive feedback about teamwork, playtesting, prototyping, and, most importantly, had fun while doing all of the tasks. Having a game design approach to educational topics could be beneficial for student learning and motivation. This outcome can be applied not only for design students but also for general.

The proposed board games and the final results were quite different. The cause of this difference might be due to the iterative design approach by the mentors. This approach consists of cycles of brainstorming ideas and mechanics, prototyping the board game, and playtesting the board game. The difference between the initial proposal and the final product can be considered a good sign because it means prototyping and playtesting was done a lot.

Besides the focus of outcomes for the use of the game design in this workshop, empathy was also an important point. Teams were successful in integrating empathy in the mechanics of their proposed board games. For example, "Escape From the Campus" was about two players who had a different kind of disabilities. This difference in the story and the gameplay was apparent to playtesters as they reported that they created a strong empathy while playing the game. Game mechanics having empathic features was an excellent sign to have the potential of finding impressive results to adapt to the video game. Later that, board games were broken down into their mechanics for a table study.

Table study of the board games was an effective method to point out which mechanics from analog prototypes were suitable to adapt to the digital product. Transferring results and game mechanic ideas might have a loss of information due to the different mediums, some mechanics and ideas can be implemented on one medium, but it might be inconvenient for the other (Fang et al. 2016). Some elements such as 'replayability' and 'cooperation' can be directly used as core ideas, some mechanics such as 'take that' might be more effective if used in a card/board game or some ideas can create a contribution that has not been in the board game before (i.e., Escape from the Campus inspiring the idea of adapting a procedurally generated world in the digital game even though this mechanic was not the main element in the board game). Pros and cons were also a useful analysis to understand and minimize the potential bad design elements regardless of the medium.

Ideas taken from the board game were constructive to create a strong foundation for creating the video game part of the PUDCAD project. All of the concerns, essential points regarding inclusive design, and empathy were taken as a guideline during the development process. The game development part of the PUDCAD project will be about a first-person perspective serious game that will run on a digital platform. This game will be used in the next workshop in Finland in its alpha stage.

References

1. Barba-Guaman L, Quezada-Sarmiento PA, Calderon-Cordova C (2017) Use of game jam model in the develop of a educational board game. In: 12th Iberian conference on information systems and technologies (CISTI), pp 1–5. IEEE
2. Blakely G, Skirton H, Cooper S, Allum P, Nelmes P (2009) Educational gaming in the health sciences: systematic review. J Adv Nurs, pp 259–269
3. Bochennek K, Wittekindt B, Zimmermann S-Y, Klingebiel T (2007) More than mere games: a review of card and board games for medical education. Med Teacher, pp 941–948
4. Bright GW, Harvey JG, Wheeler MM (1985) Learning and mathematics games. J Res Mathem Educ 1. Reston
5. Claypool K, Claypool M (2005) Teaching software engineering through game design. ACM SIGCSE Bull 37(3):123
6. Costa FC, Buratti G, Antonella S, Alessia B, Francesca T, Guven C, Barbaros B (2019) A CAD-based game for inclusive design
7. Drake P, Sung K (2011) Teaching introductory programming with popular board games. In: Proceedings of the 42nd ACM technical symposium on computer science education—SIGCSE '11
8. Fang Y-M, Chen K-M, Huang Y-J (2016) Emotional reactions of different interface formats: comparing digital and traditional board games. Adv Mech Eng
9. Fowler A (2016) Informal STEM learning in game jams, hackathons and game creation events. In: Proceedings of the international conference on Game Jams, Hackathons, and game creation events—GJH&GC
10. Fowler A, Khosmood F, Arya A, Lai G (2013) The global game jam for teaching and learning. In: Proceedings of the 4th annual conference on computing and information technology research and education New Zealand, pp 28–34
11. Gibson V, Douglas M (2013) Criticality: the experience of developing an interactive educational tool based on board games. Nurse Educ Today, pp 1612–1616
12. Hrehovcsik M, Warmelink H, Valente M (2016) The game jam as a format for formal applied game design and development education. Games Learn Allian, pp 257–267
13. Kultima A (2015) Defining game jam. FDG
14. Mikami K, Nakamura Y, Ito A, Kawashima M, Watanabe T, Kishimoto Y, Kondo K (2016) Effectiveness of game jam-based iterative program for game production in Japan. Comput Graph, pp 1–10
15. Nakao M (2019) Special series on "effects of board games on health education and promotion" board games as a promising tool for health promotion: a review of recent literature. BioPsycho Soc Med 13(1)
16. Sardone NB, Devlin-Scherer R (2016) Let the (board) games begin: creative ways to enhance teaching and learning. Clear House J Educ Strateg Issues Ideas, pp 215–222
17. Tuker C (2018) Redesigning Games For New Interfaces And Platforms. Encycl Comput Graph Games
18. Xu Y, Barba E, Radu I, Gandy M, MacIntyre B (2011) Chores are fun: understanding social play in board games for digital tabletop game design. DiGRA Conf

Raising Awareness Through Games: The Influence of a Trolling Game on Perception of Toxic Behavior

Gökçe Komaç and Kürşat Çağıltay

Abstract The use of video games for purposes other than entertainment has become an appealing area of research. In recent years, games have become actors that support social and political change by raising awareness, i.e., persuasive games. In this study, we focus on a persuasive game that portrays toxic online behaviors, often considered as trolling: spamming, flaming, trash-talking, misdirection and using offensive language. To observe the influence of a trolling game that we designed as a tool for raising awareness about toxic behavior, we applied a single-group pre-test and post-test design in a quantitative manner. We collected data via an online questionnaire (N = 111) to have a descriptive view at the results. Even though self-reports did not show a change in awareness and knowledge acquisition by playing the game, participants had a more negative perception of toxic trolling after the gameplay. All five of the types of trolling were successfully represented in an immersion-neutral but realistic setting. We aim to bring more insight into persuasive games literature by discussing the implications of this study.

Keywords Persuasive games · Trolling · Toxic behavior · Raising awareness

1 Introduction

Born with the sole purpose of entertainment, video games have evolved to provide surplus goals thanks to their ubiquitous nature and rapidly developing technologies. They have advanced in visual and audial elements, narrative capabilities, game mechanics and numerous other qualities, and can present authentic manifestations of our world. Players get immersed in these alluring *magic circles* to an extent of a completely immersive state during the play activity [1–3].

G. Komaç (✉) · K. Çağıltay
Middle East Technical University, Ankara, Turkey
e-mail: hello@gokcekomac.com

K. Çağıltay
e-mail: kursat@metu.edu.tr

A tool so powerful could not be dismissed: Scholars have discerned video games' potential to evoke emotions, influence audiences and transfer information. From this, novel ways to use games have emerged. The notion of combining education and games was born. The games that are designed to go beyond their entertainment quality to fulfill educational goals are called *serious games*. Despite the name sounding like an oxymoron, they do not lack the entertainment ingredient per se [4]. The 'serious' property of the game implies that its content is learning-oriented. Hence, the main aim of serious games is to be educational rather than entertaining, without necessarily sacrificing the 'fun' essence of the game.

Embedding 'fun' into learning processes is effective and motivating [4–6]. Consequently, serious games have been specifically utilized for myriad different objectives. They were used for instructional activities in education, business and healthcare [4, 7]. A little more than a decade ago, a specific subgenre of serious games arose for a new mission, *to persuade*. 'Persuasive games' is an umbrella term for games that have a *potential* [8] to raise awareness, increase knowledge and influence attitudinal and behavioral change [9] in topics surrounding health, marketing, society, politics and others [7].

In this paper, we scrutinize raising awareness through games and observe the influence of a persuasive game about some of the toxic online behaviors in gaming context, often called 'trolling'. Even though trolling can be harmful, as well as non-harmful to others [10, 11], we only have harmful trolling behaviors under the spotlight in this study. The close ties of these toxic behaviors with often overlapping or otherwise interrelated concepts such as cyber-bullying make trolling worthy of concern [12]. These toxic behaviors act as manifestations of sadism [13] and they are associated with depression and anxiety [14, 15]. Interestingly, toxic players are sometimes unaware of being toxic [14, 16] and these behaviors are self-perpetuating [10, 17]. Considering the reasons stated above, researching the potential of a trolling game for raising awareness becomes a substantial priority for ending toxicity in online spaces and having safe online communities. To our knowledge, there are persuasive games studies targeting other phenomena about interpersonal harm like dating violence [8] but none covering this context specifically.

To conduct the research, we designed a trolling persuasive game based on the guidance from the literature. Even though this study is derived from a larger study published as the first author's master's thesis, here we cover only the influence of the game on raising awareness to change the perception of toxic behavior. Before proceeding further to the research, we will continue with the theoretical background to get a better grasp of games for raising awareness and toxic behavior in online games.

2 Games That Raise Awareness

Persuasive games convey messages by presenting abstractions of problematic real-life narratives in the form of interactive media to allow players to explore these issues

[7]. To expand this definition, these games often promote critical thinking and tackle difficult and controversial questions together with ethical challenges [18–22]. Often acting as ambassadors of progression [23], persuasive games encourage people to be proactive about the world's problems, may they be social or political. These games have a multitude of applications like urging better habits [24], triggering empathy or sympathy towards a certain group [25–28] and fostering help for those in need [29–31].

Constructing persuasion in games is assisted by a game-specific rhetorical device called *procedural rhetoric* [7]. This term briefly translates to the game mechanics that demonstrate action-outcome relationships in a clear way with the purpose of persuasion [7]. Some scholars argue that procedurality alone is insufficient: persuasive processes in games require other measures [32] and a player-centric approach rather than the designer-centric approach that procedural rhetoric employs [33]. However, recent studies developed a more nuanced framework to read the multi-layered structures of in-game persuasion [8, 34]. Moreover, our understanding of persuasion in games can be expanded by also including persuasive processes taking place outside of the persuasive content in play, e.g., one's susceptibility to be persuaded by the game's message or games that are used as supplementary tools for persuasion [8, 35, 36].

3 Trolling and Toxic Behavior in the Gaming Context

Trolling is a phenomenon appearing in online spaces like social media platforms, forums, communities and online games [12]. Despite the lack of consensus on the definitions and taxonomy of trolling [10, 12, 37], it is often characterized by deceptive, disruptive and destructive actions [13] where enjoyment is experienced only by the perpetrator [11].

Even though the empirical research for trolling, especially in the gaming context, is scarce, recent attempts have revealed a sound comprehension of this behavior. Verbal trolling in games may appear as text or voice chat and includes actions like insulting (using offensive language/hate speech), spamming, faking/intentional fallacy, misdirection, flaming, trash-talking and inappropriate roleplaying [10, 14, 17]. The types of trolling are expanded by the addition of gameplay-specific behaviors. Behavioral trolling usually occurs as a result of intentionally abusing the game mechanics to perform actions that were not intended to be made available for the players in the game design. These can be exemplified by contrary play/griefing, inhibiting team, aiding the enemy/feeding [10, 14, 17].

Although literature succeeded in identifying many types of trolling, we took into account only a few of them in the game design of this current study due to several restrictions concerning convenience to simulate these behaviors [12]. Trolling types represented in our game are in Table 1.

Table 1 Definitions of trolling types in the game and reference studies

Trolling type	Explanation	Study
Trash-talking	"Putting down or making fun of others"	[10, p. 3329]
Flaming	"Presenting emotionally fuelled or contrary statements with an instrumental purpose"	[10, p. 3329]
Misdirection	"Spread false information among targeted or general players"	[10, p. 3329]
Spamming	"Repeating game-unrelated chat"	[10, p. 3329]
Offensive language/hate speech	Insulting using offensive language and hate speech	[14, 17]

4 Operationalizing Persuasive Games for Raising Awareness About Trolling

As prior work noted, raising awareness and improving knowledge about an issue is one of the primary goals of persuasive games [9, 26]. Another popular concept in game studies is immersion. In this context, immersion is having a strong focus on the gameplay activity and a sense of being in the game [2, 38]. Although complementary or affiliated concepts like *flow*, *engagement* and *involvement* also often appear in literature [12, 38, 39], in this study, we use the term immersion to simplify matters. Recent studies investigating the role of immersion in persuasion provide remarkable cues, however additional empirical methods are necessary [31, 38]. One of these cues that requires further research is perceived realism because immersion, together with perceived realism, acts as a critical component of persuasion [38]. In our approach, we assess the perceived realism of trolling and victim behaviors. Moreover, an investigation about the effects of the persuasive message in the game on perception of trolling would give us more insight. Another thing to consider is the accuracy of representations of trolling types in the game. As aforementioned, trolling is an ambiguous concept without a universally agreed-upon definition and taxonomy. For this reason, implementing a check about the accuracy of trolling representation in the game becomes essential. Lastly, game enjoyment and game difficulty need to be addressed in order to validate that they are not interfering with the persuasive process.

In the light of the mentioned considerations above, we operationalized persuasive games for raising awareness about trolling to explore (1) influence of the game on trolling knowledge, (2) influence of the game on trolling awareness, (3) influence of immersion and perceived realism on persuasion, (4) influence of the game on trolling perception, (5) accuracy of trolling representation in the game, and (6) game difficulty and game enjoyment. In pursuit of finding answers, we asked the following research question:

RQ: What is the influence of a persuasive game about trolling on the perception of toxic behavior?

5 Persuasive Game Design: Troll Simulator

We designed a game called *Troll Simulator* (TS) that simulates the pre-game lobby of a fictitious multiplayer online game, as trolling can be circumstantially initiated in these chat rooms [10]. The game follows an unorthodox approach in design; the player takes the role of the perpetrator and trolls others. There are four dialogue options that vary in intensity of toxicity, or sometimes a combination of different types of trolling behaviors. They also include at least one neutral option in most of the cases (Fig. 1). There are 14 dialogue blocks and the player proceeds by selecting a single choice from each block. The story is mostly linear and the game ends with the troll being kicked out. Although the scripts include offensive language, throughout the game, profanity and racist slurs are censored. TS intends to present a distressing experience that could possibly evoke an antipathy for the perpetrators by utilizing *rhetoric of failure* [7], e.g., a persuasive game that can never be won. Since perpetrators are sometimes unaware of their toxicity, this approach could potentially help raise awareness.

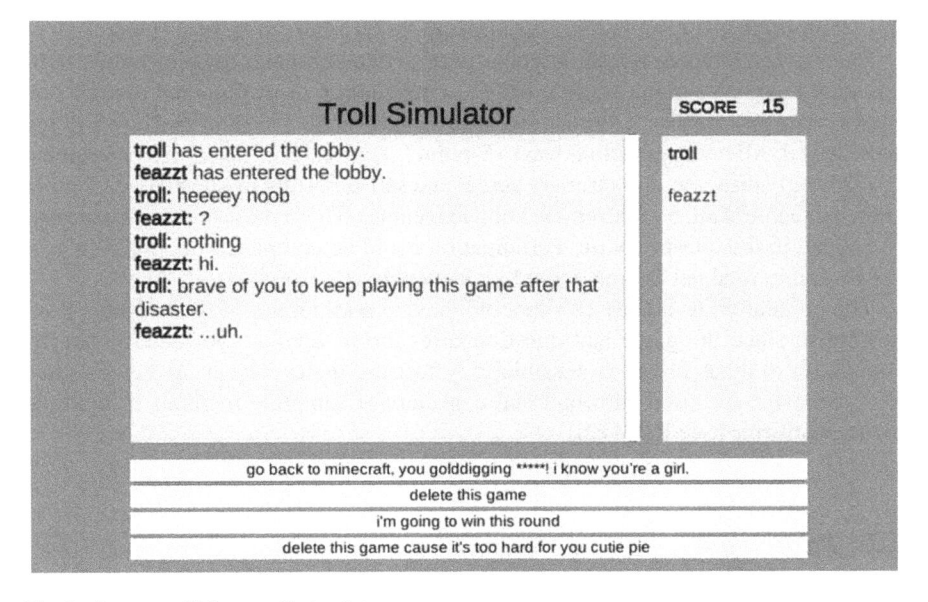

Fig. 1 A game still from troll simulator

6 Method

6.1 Design, Instrument Development and Procedure

We designed a descriptive study to find answers to our research question using a one-group pre-test and post-test approach [40]. Persuasive game effectiveness measuring studies often deployed also a follow-up questionnaire [9, 25] or had a different design strategy that involves control groups with conditions including informative or game-watching [9, 29]. However, previous approaches were not suitable for this study because of the lack of prior research to back up the toxic behavior context. Besides this, being a young research area, a comprehensive and appropriate instrument that fulfills our research goals did not exist to our knowledge. Therefore, we had developed the material inspired by relevant research in persuasive game and trolling studies [17, 24, 25]. Moreover, we developed Attitude Towards Toxic Trolling Scale (ATTTS) to compare the results from the pre-test to post-test. After two pilot tests were conducted to improve the measurement instruments, we decided to finalize them since we did not encounter any issues with the final version. Then, we collected quantitative data from the sample using an online questionnaire in October–November 2019.

The pre-test includes questions about general demographics, gaming habits, self-reported knowledge about trolling behavior, perception of trolling and thoughts on games raising awareness. The post-test has questions about the game and how trolling is perceived. All rating questions used a 5-point Likert scale for the level of agreement (1 = strongly disagree; 5 = strongly agree) and self-reporting of knowledge (1 = not knowledgeable at all; 5 = extremely knowledgeable). The game is browser-based and embedded in the questionnaire. Participation could be completed in approximately 10–15 min in total per person, including gameplay.

The population is at least 18 years old, having a minimum of intermediate level in English since the game and questionnaires are in English. We determined the population to be as broad as possible to reflect the multi-present nature of online toxic behavior and used snowball and convenience sampling methods in multiple online platforms (See Ref. [12]).

6.2 Participants

The sample (N = 111), having an age range from 19 to 39 (M = 28.62, SD = 4.54), consisted of 76 males (68.47%), 35 females (31.53%) and no participants of other genders. The sample predominantly lived in Turkey (94; 84.68%). Most participants completed at least a bachelor's degree (71; 63.96%) and had an advanced level in English (88; 79.28%). The majority of participants reported playing multiplayer online games; 70 of them reported currently playing and 31 of them having played in the past but not any longer. The current-players game on computers (64), mobile devices (35) and consoles (16). The most popular multiplayer genres are FPS (45),

MOBA (37), MMORPG/RPG (37) and board/card games (36). In an average week, most current-players (47) play multiplayer online games for at least 5 h. Nearly all (65) have been playing them for at least 4 years. A majority (63) play games with random players and of those, most (48) encounter trolls sometimes or more frequently. Among the sample, 99 reported finishing TS and 12 said they played the game up to a point before quitting.

7 Results

Influence of the game on trolling knowledge. Participants self-reported as moderately knowledgeable about online trolls and trolling behavior in online games. They weakly disagreed on having learned something new about trolling (Table 2).

Influence of the game on trolling awareness. Participants think games could be effective in raising awareness. They slightly agreed this game could be effective. They were neutral about being more aware after playing this game (Table 3).

Influence of immersion and perceived realism on persuasion. The gameplay experience was not found to be immersive or non-immersive. Troll and victim behaviors were found to be slightly realistic (Table 4).

Table 2 Influence of the game on trolling knowledge [12]

	M	SD	Var
Self-reported knowledge about online trolls (pre-test)	3.56	1.11	1.24
Self-reported knowledge about trolling in online games (pre-test)	3.48	1.21	1.46
I have learned something new about trolling by playing this game	2.8	1.42	2.01

Table 3 Influence of the game on trolling awareness [12]

	M	SD	Var
Video games could be effective in raising awareness about disruptive behaviors (pre-test)	3.75	0.94	0.89
This game is effective in raising awareness about disruptive behaviors that trolls perform	3.23	1.29	1.66
I am more aware about trolling after playing this game	2.93	1.43	2.05

Table 4 Influence of immersion and perceived realism [12]

	M	SD	Var
The gameplay experience was immersive	3.03	1.16	1.34
Trolling behavior was realistic	3.5	1.22	1.49
The behavior of other players who were trolled was realistic	3.46	1.18	1.4

Influence of the game on trolling perception. Participants agreed stronger about trolling being a serious problem after the gameplay. Trolling was already perceived as a harmful behavior before gameplay and it stayed the same. Participants were slightly disagreeing, and they tended to disagree a bit more about trolling being just for fun and trolls should not be taken seriously. Disagreement about trolls being free to play around unless the situation puts the victim in a life-threatening danger has slightly strengthened after playing the game. We observed an unexpected slight decrease in the level of disagreement for the victim-blaming statement (Table 5).

Representation of trolling/toxic behaviors in the game. The game was found to demonstrate all five of the behaviors by the majority of participants, with having trash-talking (95) and misdirection (92) as the most noticeable, followed by offensive language/hate speech (84), spamming (79) and flaming (74) (Fig. 2). However, 3 participants noted not observing any of them.

Table 5 Attitude Towards Toxic Trolling Scale (ATTTS) pre-test and post-test values [12]

	PRE-TEST			POST-TEST		
	M	SD	Var	M	SD	Var
Trolling is a serious problem	3.41	1.05	1.11	3.59	1.14	1.3
Trolling is a harmful behaviour	3.84	0.96	0.93	3.85	1.02	1.05
Trolling is just for fun and trolls should not be taken seriously	2.8	1.19	1.42	2.55	1.14	1.31
Trolls should be free to play around unless the situation puts the victim in a life-threatening danger	2.46	1.11	1.24	2.29	1.13	1.29
When a player is being trolled, it is their own fault	1.69	0.86	0.74	1.76	0.93	0.87

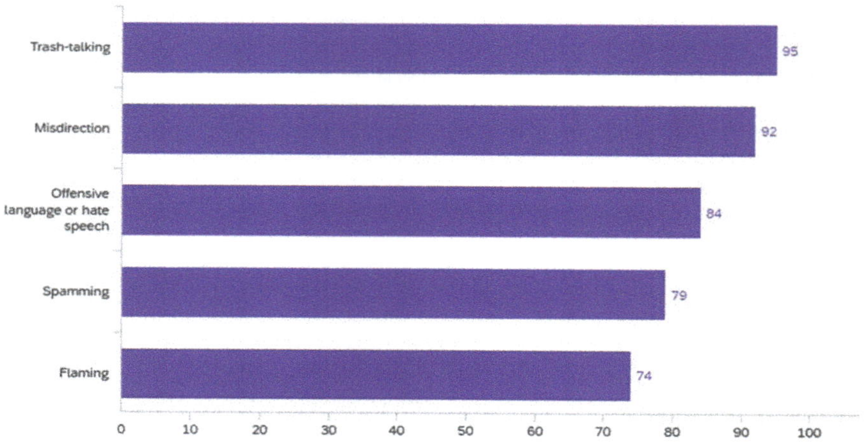

Fig. 2 Behaviors observed in troll simulator by the participants [12]

Table 6 Difficulty and enjoyment [12]

	M	SD	Var
The game was easy to play	4.18	0.85	0.72
The game was entertaining	2.98	1.27	1.60

Game difficulty and game enjoyment. Participants thought the game was easy to play and were indecisive about the game being entertaining (Table 6).

8 Discussion

The results indicate a few remarks to be considered. For instance, participants were indecisive about whether they have learned something new or whether they are more aware of trolling after playing the game. This might be due to participants considering themselves to be already knowledgeable about trolling. Literature acknowledges prior knowledge is a factor that can assist or hamper persuasive processes in games [8, 36]. Another case seems to be valid where participants correctly estimate their knowledge and therefore are not persuaded, while they think that TS could be effective for raising awareness for others, possibly with less knowledge. Interestingly, the investigation of the results of ATTTS indicates that the game had slight influence on participants and trolling is perceived to be more negative after playing the game. In this sense, the first explanation fits better: Participants might be overestimating their knowledge on trolling before the stimulus and the game did succeed in influencing their trolling perception.

As for the immersion, gameplay experience is neither immersive nor nonimmersive, however trolling and victim behaviors are perceived to be realistic. Previous studies note that together with perceived realism, immersion is also tied to narrative depth and identification [38]. However, this study only deals with the contribution of perceived realism to immersion. The complex nature of immersion and the different layers it has [1] might help explain why the game was found to be immersion-neutral. Even though measuring identification might also be interesting in this context [31, 38], the game in our case is irrelevant for this observation. TS aims to promote the opposite of this while forming an identification with the perpetrator means deviating from the goal of the persuasive content. A further measurement of *cognitive identification* [8] (i.e., experiencing a negative experience in a safe setting), rather than *character identification* [8] meshes with this study better. As utilizing negative experiences for learning outcomes is not uncommon [28], further empirical research is needed to understand its effectiveness in persuasion fully when dealing with toxic behavior.

Moreover, the game successfully demonstrated all five types of trolling for at least two thirds of the participants in spite of the lack of agreement on what constitutes trolling [12]. We also need to note that our sample consisted of English-speakers. However, how trolling is performed or perceived might differ depending on the language, culture, game or context [11, 14]. In order to achieve more realistic and accurate representations of trolling behavior in a simulated environment, these should be considered.

Finally, game difficulty does not seem to be interfering with the persuasion. Having a neutral score for game enjoyment reflects the commonly accepted meaning for enjoyment. However, the concept of enjoyment in this study aligns with *eudaimonic appreciation*, "how an experience makes someone reflect or become a better person" [8, p. 165], rather than *hedonistic enjoyment* paradigm.

As being a preliminary study in addressing toxic behaviors in a persuasive game, this study had a number of limitations. First and foremost, it has the common concerns of studies with newly designed instruments: Further methods need to be applied to ensure reliability and internal validity. Even though we had an adequate number of participants, heterogeneity of the sample was very limited, and therefore generalizability becomes an issue. On a different note, considering persuasive games' impact can reach to a certain extent [30], TS could potentially be insufficient in forming a full comprehension of toxic behavior in gaming context as it had limited content and only manifested five types of trolling. Besides this, duration of gameplay, hence the exposure to the toxic content was very short. Moreover, by following another research design strategy like including a control group and applying a follow-up test could be interesting to see the effects compared to other media and if the influence of the game persisted.

9 Conclusion

In this study, we observed the influence of a persuasive game about trolling on perception of toxic behavior. We found that participants had a more negative perception of toxic trolling after the gameplay. This study was a part of a larger study (first author's master's thesis) which presents the research in more detail. Although further empirical research is necessary for acquiring a complete comprehension of mechanisms behind raising awareness about toxic behaviors, this study was a small step towards understanding how games could teach us about these behaviors and how they can raise awareness. Hopefully, it will help develop more advanced methods in pursuit of eradicating toxicity.

References

1. Calleja G (2011) In game: from immersion to incorporation. MIT Press, Cambridge, MA
2. Csikszentmihalyi M (1990) Flow: the psychology of optimal experience. Harper & Row, New York
3. Huizinga J (1955) Homo Ludens: a study of the play-element in culture. Beacon Press, Boston
4. Michael D, Chen S (2006) Serious games: games that educate, train, and inform. Thomson Course Technology PTR, Boston, MA, USA

5. Abt CC (1970) Serious games. Viking Press, New York
6. Gee JP (2003) What video games have to teach us about learning and literacy. Palgrave Macmillan, New York, NY
7. Bogost I (2007) Persuasive games: the expressive power of videogames. The MIT Press, Cambridge, Massachusetts
8. Jacobs RS (2017) Playing to win over: validating persuasive games (PhD Thesis)
9. Soekarjo M, van Oostendorp H (2015) Measuring effectiveness of persuasive games using an informative control condition. Int J Serious Games 2:37–56. https://doi.org/10.17083/ijsg.v2i2.74
10. Cook C, Schaafsma J, Antheunis M (2018) Under the bridge: an in-depth examination of online trolling in the gaming context. New Media Soc 20:3323–3340. https://doi.org/10.1177/1461444817748578
11. Bishop J (2014) Representations of "trolls" in mass media communication: a review of media-texts and moral panics relating to "internet trolling". Int J Web Based Commun 10:7–24. https://doi.org/10.1504/IJWBC.2014.058384
12. Komaç G (2019) A study of using a persuasive game as a tool to raise awareness about trolling behavior (Master's Thesis). http://etd.lib.metu.edu.tr/upload/12625082/index.pdf
13. Buckels EE, Trapnell PD, Paulhus DL (2014) Trolls just want to have fun. Pers Individ Dif 67:97–102. https://doi.org/10.1016/j.paid.2014.01.016
14. Kwak H, Blackburn J, Han S (2015) Exploring cyberbullying and other toxic behavior in team competition online games. In: Proceedings of the 33rd annual ACM conference on human factors in computing systems—CHI'15, pp 3739–3748. ACM Press, New York, USA
15. Coyne I, Chesney T, Logan B, Madden N (2009) Griefing in a virtual community: an exploratory survey of second life residents. Zeitschrift für Psychol J Psychol 217:214–221
16. Lin H, Sun C-T (2005) The "white-eyed" player culture: grief play and construction of deviance in MMORPGs. In: DiGRA 2005 conference: changing views—worlds in play
17. Thacker S, Griffiths MD (2012) An exploratory study of trolling in online video gaming. Int J Cyber Behav Psychol Learn 2:17–33. https://doi.org/10.4018/ijcbpl.2012100102
18. Frasca G (2001) Videogames of the oppressed: videogames as a means for critical thinking and debate. http://www.ludology.org/articles/thesis/FrascaThesisVideogames.pdf
19. Flanagan M (2009) Critical play: radical game design. MIT Press, Boston, MA, USA
20. Brathwaite B, Sharp J (2010) The mechanic is the message: a post mortem in progress. In: Schrier K, Gibson D (eds) Ethics and game design: teaching values through play, pp 311–329. Information Science Reference. https://doi.org/10.4018/978-1-61520-845-6.ch019
21. Pedercini P (2019) Videogames and the spirit of capitalism https://molleindustria.org/blog/videogames-and-the-spirit-of-capitalism/. Last accessed 2019/11/02
22. Genvo S (2016) Defining and designing expressive games : the case of keys of a gamespace. Kinephanos J Media Stud Pop Cult Spec Issue Explor Front Digit Gaming Tradit Games, Expressive Games, Pervasive Games 90–106
23. McGonigal J (2011) Reality is broken: why games make us better and how they can change the world. THe Penguin Press, New York, New York, USA
24. Knol E (2011) Effects of serious game EnerCities on energy-related attitudes and behaviours
25. Lavender TJ (2008) Homelessness—it's no game: measuring the effectiveness of a persuasive videogame (Master's Thesis)
26. Antonacci F, Bertolo M, Mariani I (2017) In migrants' shoes. A game to raise awareness and support long-lasting learning. Ital J Educ Technol 25:55–68. https://doi.org/10.17471/2499-4324/858
27. Gerling KM, Mandryk RL, Birk MV, Miller M, Orji R (2014) The effects of embodied persuasive games on player attitudes toward people using wheelchairs. In: Proceedings of the 32nd annual ACM conference on human factors in computing systems—CHI'14, pp 3413–3422. ACM Press, New York, USA. https://doi.org/10.1145/2556288.2556962
28. Mariani I, Gandolfi E (2016) Negative experiences as learning trigger: a play experience empirical research on a game for social change case study. Int J Game-Based Learn 6:50–73. https://doi.org/10.4018/IJGBL.2016070104

29. Peng W, Lee M, Heeter C (2010) the effects of a serious game on role-taking and willingness to help. J Commun 60:723–742. https://doi.org/10.1111/j.1460-2466.2010.01511.x
30. Guardiola E (2019) Game and humanitarian: from awareness to field intervention. In: Game On 2019
31. van't Riet J, Meeuwes AC, van der Voorden L, Jansz J (2018) Investigating the effects of a persuasive digital game on immersion, identification, and willingness to help. Basic Appl Soc Psych 40:180–194. https://doi.org/10.1080/01973533.2018.1459301
32. Evans MA (2011) procedural ethos: confirming the persuasive in serious games. Int J Gam Comput Simul 3:70–80. https://doi.org/10.4018/jgcms.2011100105
33. Sicart M (2019) Against procedurality, http://gamestudies.org/1103/articles/sicart_ap. Last accessed 2019/10/18
34. De la Hera Conde-Pumpido T (2015) A theoretical model for the study of persuasive communication through digital games. In: Parreno IJM, Mafe CR, Scribner L (eds) Engaging consumers through branded entertainment and convergent media, pp 74–88. IGI Global, Hershey, PA. https://doi.org/10.4018/978-1-4666-8342-6.ch004
35. De la Hera Conde-Pumpido T (2017) Persuasive gaming: identifying the different types of persuasion through games. Int J Serious Games 4. https://doi.org/10.17083/ijsg.v4i1.140
36. Klimmt C (2009) Serious Games And Social Change: Why They (Should) Work. In: Ritterfeld U, Cody M, Vorderer P (eds) Serious games: mechanisms and effects, pp 248–270. https://doi.org/10.4324/9780203891650
37. Komaç G, Çağıltay K (2019) An overview of trolling behavior in online spaces and gaming context. In: 2019 1st international informatics and software engineering conference (UBMYK). IEEE. https://doi.org/10.1109/UBMYK48245.2019.8965625
38. Hafner M, Jansz J (2018) The players' experience of immersion in persuasive games: a study of my life as a refugee and peacemaker. Int J Ser Games 5:63–79. https://doi.org/10.17083/ijsg.v5i4.263
39. Ruggiero D (2015) The effect of a persuasive social impact game on affective learning and attitude. Comput Human Behav 45:213–221. https://doi.org/10.1016/j.chb.2014.11.062
40. Creswell JW, Creswell JD (2018) Research design: qualitative, quantitative, and mixed methods approaches. SAGE

Game Design Experiment

Using Mathematical Models in Game Design: A Survival Mechanics Case

Kutay Tinç and Reyhan Eren

Abstract Game Mechanics are the methods that players use to interact with and play the game; each stage's progress depends on their design. The type of mechanics employed at a game depends on the feelings that game designers want the players to feel. Most mechanics are straightforward and require little to no optimization whereas some mechanics can be complex enough to make players spend hours, if not days, to learn and master them. While every game revolves through a set of rules, the element of unpredictability should be integrated in the game so as to sustain the player's eagerness to keep playing. The design should be focused on setting scenarios that allow the players to show their skills and strategies. The game as an end product is obtained through a complex trial and error process, which can be better handled by the fundamentals of mathematics. Starting from the basic mechanisms to the most essential ones, a variety of factors influence their development throughout the game. Especially for survival games, stats such as thirst, stamina, hunger, sleep requirements, might be modeled as dependent on the effects of variations on these elements. Also, the correlation between each variation's effects to mechanic elements can only be explained by clear mathematical models. In this study, we will be creating a mathematical model framework for survival mechanics that will consist of various nonlinear functions that affect each other, and in exchange affected by different consumables or states that players will face in the game.

Keywords Video games · Survival games · Game design · Mathematical modeling

1 Introduction

People play games to win. This is not always the case but it is the most common case of playing a game and enjoying it. Whether it is a simple game like tic-tac-toe or a fully-fledged mmo-rpg like World of Warcraft, players always want to win,

K. Tinç (✉) · R. Eren
Istanbul Technical University, Maçka 34367, Turkey
e-mail: tinc@itu.edu.tr

© The Author(s), under exclusive license to Springer Nature Switzerland AG 2021
Ö. Cordan et al. (eds.), *Game + Design Education*, Springer Series in Design and Innovation 13, https://doi.org/10.1007/978-3-030-65060-5_13

but winning by itself is not always enough. Players also want immersion, depth, playability and many other aspects of a game to be able to enjoy it more.

This is true for survival games as well. We play survival games to stay alive, which is an important requisite of winning the game, but we also play them for immersion and sometimes for their story. As some aspects of a game add to our enjoyment, they can also take away from it as well. Game mechanics, when not optimized or built the right way, can take away from the player's expectation of reality, hence lower the immersion and enjoyment of the player.

In this study we are building a framework for survival mechanics using mathematical modeling to connect different attributes together to make it more realistic.

2 Survival Games

Survival games in general use bars to represent characters' life-related factors—mostly hunger, thirst, sleep, and health rates. Even though the most realistic approach is used in the background to model them, players are hard to satisfy. As a result of competitive market demands on the requirements of "How games should reflect the reality?", game designers struggle with satisfying the expectations of players. Previous generations of video games, both single and multi-player, on average maintained a focus on players becoming more than themselves within the virtual realm [1]. Game mechanics used in each level should be realistic enough for players to be live the experience of the virtual realm. Thanks to the analysis and studies made on the physical and mental limitations of humans, references can be taken for modeling the survival-based mechanics of a character on a game. Especially the horror segmented games are known by the goal of reflecting real anxiety of human being in the virtual world [1].

Such environments require the need for mathematical modeling of game bars representing the level of mental weight, for external effects. Virtual world and real-world transitions can be modeled concerning the reality of the story designed in the game. Needs, expectations, interactions, and their results can be carried to the game environment regarding real-world observations. Survival elements are the key to a game story to satisfy the game player.

In the game, first player survival game-themed horror game Outlast [2] power of story-telling is the mainly use technique. Missions given to players are simple and basic, yet interaction with the environment base factor for the effective changes in in-game mechanics. As investigative journalist Miles Upshur, explore Mount Massive Asylum and try to survive long enough to discover its terrible secret [2]. During the game players witness, many horror scene and intensity of the story followed gets higher in a way that pulls players into the story deeply. The health bar is not highlighted elements of the game. Players mostly depend on stealth elements, as such hiding in lockers, sneaking past enemies, staying in the shadows, and hiding behind or under things to survive [3]. This type of undirect survival mechanics is mainly preferred on the stealth category games and used for most of the horror games. This example shows the intangible usage of survival elements in the games.

> Perhaps the earliest, and certainly the earliest commercially successful game that includes survival elements, such as acquiring and managing scarce resources, permanent death and/or injury of player characters and companions, and confrontations with human, animal, and environmental threats. These elements remain central to the genre, and in summation can be viewed as a specific design orientation toward player agency, its recognition, confinement, and role in the player experience, but also as reflective of player demand for and acceptance of a fundamentally different orientation to power within games [4].

Additional to survival mechanics, game designers consider the external effects that characters interact within the games. Realistic, game experiences design comes with many interaction possibilities of a character with its environment and reactions to those interactions. Like real life, although it is so hard to model, in games surviving depends on many factors. Other than the physical needs of a character, also, modeling the cognitive reactions to an interaction, may help to catch more to players' attention. A psychological concept of Maslow's hierarchy of needs, the hypothesis that human lives are organized like a pyramid built from all our needs and we can only reach the pinnacle of the pyramid [5]. Similar to that in the games level designs are considered as a dynamic representation of life experiences. For each level design, the survival rate of a character can be modeled by the designer by using different approaches of mathematical modeling in which incorporate Dynamic Difficulty Adjustment (DDA) [6].

> According to Maslow, we can only reach the pinnacle of the pyramid, usually described as "happiness" or "self-actualization", if we meet the requirements of each of the layers that prop it up. You can't be spiritually fulfilled, for example, if you don't have a basic shelter or are starving and thirsty [7].

To own the players' eagerness to keep playing, the case of reflecting daily life items on mechanics within a harmony of the game concept and level should be actualized.

Competition is another methodology that can be used as leverage between players to create differentiable conditions and permutations of conditions created by players themselves. In a competition-based game, the clan approach is mainly used to reach new players by using the network of existing players. Space concept game Dark Orbit [8] nudge player to be a part of a clan to achieve missions. Players group up corresponding to their class of wealthy. They fight in the space to rule the planets in the orbit. Players share their experience abut different missions on the forum or they may look for a new clan to be a member.

Because it is an intergalactic struggle for a high level of survival, being a clan member reverberated. Additional to that, survival mechanics are designed as being affected by shields [9]. Moreover, safety elements offered to players that also have different effects on survival rates.

Players' interaction with the game and with each other can be limited in the worst-case scenario without achieving an emotional attachment to the story told by the game designer. In cases like these, thanks to the forums of players, the value of the game created loses its demand on the market. Avoiding that would be possible if the creators of the story well-defined, the conditions of the environment and interaction limit of a player on the play. Also, rank systems between player and provisions of level-based survival mechanics, makes the player feel more addicted to different concepts than their area of interest. In a rank system by matching the player with the opponent rivalry is creates more eagerness for players. To hook up the player to become a part of the game consistently, many tactics can be used, with supportive mechanics design. Correct usage of survival mechanics in a reaction between players increases the reliability of a player to the game. Players bond with the story of the game if they feel as they are in control as they think in real life. The best survival games are the ones that get under your skin, where dealing with the many sides of your character is so engaging that it leads to emergent gameplay and emotional attachment [7]. How realistic or utopian or dystopian a game story is, changes the segments of the players who are interested in the game. While some players looking for educational missions in a game, some players just go after challenge.

One of the top five best rated survival game [10], Forest [11] address to players of all counted categories. Chop down trees, build fires, and create your camp to protect yourself. Explore in the daytime and defend your belongings at night, and then when you think you're strong enough, fight off the cannibals [12]. It is the most common storytelling on survival games. These type of survival games requires more complex mechanics design than basic strategy or just a war game. Because the story is tangible to players action correlations between elements, players interact with, should be modeled in detail. The next move of the player can only be predicted in possible actions with—other words probabilities. With stochastic modeling, technique mechanics may reflect the real-life conditions at some level. Yet, without trial of the functions—written for the character's world—on a data collected or created for simulation, optimizing the boundaries of survival bar values would be unsubstantial. More to that question of "Is one life (permadeath) okay for the game character, or more is needed?" has seen key question for between game designers, likewise, the question of "If a character may reborn in the game, shall it start from scratch with a full life and zero resources, or shall they be able to save collected items for their second life?". Answers to those questions change players' moving patterns and responses to changes in survival rates, fundamentally. As an example, multiplayer battle royal games go for the strategy of starting naked each game with one life given. Because each player starts the game in fair conditions given to all of them, competition between them gets sharpened by the fight got furious. Survival becomes more important for such occasions. Animations, sound-effects, external effect change the decision-making of each player, by affecting them cognitively. Battle royal concept games, like PUBG [13], Fortnite [14], Apex Legends [15], are mostly focused on scorecards and surviving. Because most of the game's levels are identified as one area getting to shrink, to survive, players have to keep moving and be the last one alive. Animations can be added to survival mechanics for those concepts of battle royal to warn players about the current level of the game and the factors causing them to be injured, like staying outside of the shrunk map. Those effects guide the players, without the need of a player check the survival rates in the middle of the fight. In some survival games, additional to the basic genre, the designer adds extreme unexpected conditions to the story, for the game character, that pushes their survival limit.

> Don't Starve by Klei Entertainment does this through a mechanic of shifting seasons over the year. These force you to alter the character's diet introduces a freezing mechanic requiring the player to keep warm, and largely change the available resources and creature types [7].

Players in some cases, enjoy struggling with ultimate survival conditions. If complex health systems preferred by the designer, changing circumstances, turns the game experience into a surviving experience with adapting skills developed. An example of this system is the game Metal Gear Solid 3 Snake Eater [16]. In the mission, a player may lose an eye. For the rest of the mission, the first-person camera view even became limited around the edge, making it more difficult to shoot for players [7].

In addition to Horror games, survival games, war games, games in which the space life simulated are facing high demands by improved graphics and available game engine capabilities. Story of space life colonization games varies from a basic story of the game Space Colony [17], strategy game. With enhanced animations and game design Space Colony-Idle [18] exemplify the well-combined mechanic within the game. Even though it may look like a simplified version of the original strategic game from 2003, it dissociated by its well-defined game economics that drives player for continuous research [19], and the adventure presented to by the game endures players to be addicted to this extraordinary Sci-Fi journey. The game also differs from the first created genre of other space colony games by both the category it created and the goals directed to players—like relocating the humanity within the space rockets and discover 16 different planets by traveling from one to another- and the mechanics used [18].

3 Game Mechanics

Many aspects of a survival game hinges around the fact that the player needs to survive. Whether it's the enemies, the terrain, the weather, the hunger or thirst, the player has some sort of challenge presented to him that needs to be overcome. These challenges drain on the resources of the character that the player controls and require the player to be witty and plan ahead to stay alive.

The resources that a character has can be categorized into two segments: Internal and External. Internal resources are the character's abilities, stats and conditions, like stamina, health, strength or having sharper senses than normal people. External resources are mostly consumables that help Internal ones. Like water to keep the thirst at bay so that stamina drains slower or replenishes faster.

All these resources can be linked to each other through mathematical models, and formulating these models has always been a challenge for the game designer. Most games keep these formulas simple: consumables have constant values of effect, like drinking clean water always replenishes 50% of the bar out of 100, whether the water level (100—Thirst) is at 10 or 90. This is clearly not the case in real life as a very thirsty person gets more value out of the same glass of water then a person who is not felling thirsty at all. This is also true for hunger, someone who hasn't eaten breakfast would look at stale bread for lunch differently from someone who had a lavish breakfast and is still feeling full.

These connections between different aspects of a survival game is crucial for immersion and player satisfaction. Hence, establishing these connections should be a top priority for a game designer. In the next part of this study we will show what these connections can mathematically look like. All values used in these formulas will be time dependent which will be shown with the index i. Each increment of i can be taken as one second. Both crisp and fuzzy functions can be used in these formulas, according to the needs of the game.

4 Survival Bars

All survival bars and their related attributes and stats will be explained in this part of the study.

4.1 Health/Hit Points (H_i)

The life of the character. Decreases due to combat and injuries, can be regained through sleep or consumables.

4.2 Stamina (S_i)

Stamina is the amount of energy a character can use to take physical actions like running, climbing, swinging melee weapons. While any taxing physical action reduces the amount of stamina a character has, walking or resting in place refills this bar.

Fatigue (f_i)

Fatigue is directly related to stamina. It acts like an upper limit setter to stamina and diminishes the length of the stamina bar as it accumulates.

Maximum Stamina (S_{max})

$$S_{max} = 100 - f_i \tag{1}$$

4.3 Water Level (W_i)

Water Level shows how thirsty the character is. As water level drops the character gets thirstier. Water level slowly drops with time, but exertion might hasten the drop rate. Refilling this bar requires consumables. Different consumables can have different effects. Even negative ones at times.

4.4 Food Level (F_i)

Food Level shows how hungry the character is. Just like in water level, as food level drops the character gets hungrier. Food level also slowly drops with time, and exertion might hasten the drop rate. Again, like water level, refilling this bar requires consumables. Different consumables can have different effects. Even negative ones at times.

4.5 Other Mechanics

Activity (a_i) Activity shows the exertion amount of the character in a given time. Any taxing physical action will have a value between 0 and 1, depending on its severity, which will affect the survival bars mentioned above.

Weight Carried (w_i, w_{max}) This shows the amount of weight a character is carrying at the moment and the maximum amount he is allowed to carry.

Run Speed (R, R_{max}) This mechanic shows the speed a character can run as a function of the maximum speed it can run, the current fatigue he has and the weight he is carrying.

$$R = R_{max} s(f_i, w_i, w_{max}) takecare \qquad (2)$$

where s is the percentage calculating function of fatigue, weight carried and max weight allowed. It's usually a good idea to pick s as a fuzzy function instead of a crisp one to prevent over complicated statements.

Perception (P, P_i, P_{max}) Perception is the awareness of the character. This mechanic will be used in two different ways. One is the object highlight range (P_i), which will be shown as:

$$P_i = P_{max} P(f_i, a_i) \qquad (3)$$

where P is the percentage calculating function of current fatigue and current activity.

The second way perception will be used is as a blur effect (B_i), where the screen will get blurrier as certain conditions are met, like being poisoned, letting a disease advance to a critical level or a high level of fatigue.

Sleep
Sleeping is automatically done for a period of time the player chooses. Sleeping, with respect to the time spent doing it, might remove any fatigue a character has, worsen some conditions like poison or cure them if an antidote or medicine is taken before sleep. It will also decrease levels of Food and Water slightly.

Consumables Consumables have different effects on the bars. Some will work instantly while others work over time.

5 Mathematical Model

The differences for the bars are shown with Δ versions of each stat.

$$S_{i+1} = S_i + \Delta S_i \tag{4}$$

$$W_{i+1} = W_i + \Delta W_i \tag{5}$$

$$F_{i+1} = F_i + \Delta F_i \tag{6}$$

$$f_{i+1} = \Delta f_i + f_i \tag{7}$$

$$\Delta f_i = f(a_i, w_i, w_{\max}, S_i, W_i, F_i) \tag{8}$$

$$\Delta S_i = S(a_i, w_i, w_{\max}, W_i, F_i) \tag{9}$$

$$\Delta W_i = W(a_i, w_i, w_{\max}, F_i) \tag{10}$$

$$\Delta F = F(a_i, W_i) \tag{11}$$

As seen in the formulas, all increment functions S, W and F are dependent on the activity of the character, which makes this the most crucial variable in our formulas.

5.1 Stamina Function

The stamina function S is dependent on five other stats and each of them is either direct or inverse proportional to stamina. As activity level rises the stamina spent will increase as well so ΔS_i will be in the negative direction, it is the same for weight carried as well. On the other hand, maximum weight that can be carried, current water and food levels would affect positively on the stamina spent, decreasing the amount spent when they are at a higher level. If each action has a constant value of stamina expenditure, we can use the other parameters to decrease or increase this amount using them as a percentage value. An example of the stamina function can be modeled as:

$$\Delta S(a_i, w_i, w_{\max}, W_i, F_i) = c_s * a_i * \left(1 - \frac{1}{1 + c_{w_i} e^{-w_i}} + \frac{1}{1 + c_j e^{-w_{\max} - W_i - F_i}}\right) \tag{12}$$

5.2 Water Function

The water function can be modeled like the stamina function as well:

$$\Delta W(a_i, w_i, w_{\max}, F_i) = c_w * a_i * \left(1 - \frac{1}{1 + e^{-w_i}} + \frac{1}{1 + e^{-w_{\max} - F_i}}\right) \tag{13}$$

5.3 Food Function

Same type of mathematical modeling can be applied here as well:

$$\Delta F(a_i, W_i) = c_f * a_i * \left(1 + \frac{1}{1 + e^{-W_i}}\right) \tag{14}$$

It should be noted that even while resting food and water levels may drop due to the constant values.

6 Conclusion

The mathematical functions given in this study are just simple examples that can be improved and made more complex. One of the negative feedbacks that players give about food and water level bars are that after a full meal, the characters' water and food levels max out but they don't last maxed for long and start dropping immediately and this fact disrupts immersion as players start worrying about food and water almost immediately. To combat this phenomena, a lag can be implemented for food and water level change after a meal that takes into account the activity amount and sets the constant value to zero or very close to zero so that the bars do not diminish for some time after getting full.

References

1. Reid S, Downing S (2018) Survival themed video games and cultural constructs of power, 23 July 2018, Date accessed 24 Mar 2020. journals.sfu.ca/loading/index.php/loading/article/view/202
2. Outlast, Red Barrels, Steam (2013)
3. Ben S et al (2020) Episode 008. Level 403 Games Podcast OUTLAST 2 Part 2, Mar. 2020. Date accessed 24 Mar 2020. www.fsproductions.ca/level-403-podcast/tag/Level+403+Games
4. Lindley C (2005) The semiotics of time structure in ludic space as a foundation for analysis and design. Game Stud 5(1)
5. Improbable IO (2020) Design toolkit: 5 core elements from survival games. Improbable, 21 Nov 2017. Date accessed 24 Mar 2020. improbable.io/blog/design-toolkit-5-core-elements-from-survival-games
6. Hunicke R (2005) The case for dynamic difficulty adjustment in games. ACE'05
7. Improbable IO (2017) Design toolkit: 5 core elements from survival games. Improbable, 21 Nov 2017. Date accessed 24 Mar 2020. improbable.io/blog/design-toolkit-5-core-elements-from-survival-games
8. Dark Orbit, Bigpoint Games, Online (2006)
9. The Art of the Escape: Surviving in Dark Orbit. Edited by Wirwerdenniesosein, Dark Orbit, 5 Jan. 2020, Date accessed 24 Mar 2020. board-en.darkorbit.com/threads/the-art-of-the-escape-surviving-in-dark-orbit.122951/
10. 33 Best Survival Games on PC as of 2020. Slant, 19 July 2016, Date accessed 24 Mar 2020. www.slant.co/topics/6350/~survival-games-on-pc
11. Forest, Endnight Games, PS4 (2014) Date accessed 24 Mar 2020
12. Vincent B (2019) The 25 best survival games. Popular Mechanics, Popular Mechanics, 16 Dec 2019. Date accessed March 24, 2020. www.popularmechanics.com/culture/gaming/g30223018/best-survival-games/?slide=23
13. PUBG, PUBG Corporation, Krafton (2018)
14. Fortnite, Battle Royale Mode, PS4 Pro (2017)
15. Apex Legends, Respawn Entertainment, PS4 (2019)
16. Metal Gear Solid 3 Snake Eater, PS2, 2004, Date accessed 24 Mar 2020
17. Space Colony, Firefly Studios, Mac OC (2004)
18. Space Colony Idle, Veloxia, Appstore (2019) Date accessed 24 Mar 2020. https://apps.apple.com/tr/app/space-colony-idle/id1476713225
19. Space Colony Idle, Veloxia, Appstore, 2019, Date accessed 24 Mar 2020. https://apps.apple.com/tr/app/space-colony-idle/id1476713225

The Impact of Human-Centered Design of Game Mechanics on Feelings of Belonging

Gina Al Halabi, Kutay Tinç, and Ertuğrul Süngü

Abstract As the population increases, the amount of different people and different cultures also expands. With that comes major problems, one of which is our strong and inevitable need for a sense of belonging to a group of people. As social beings who depend on a sense of common values and beliefs, and seek commonality, the feeling that we belong is very important. The aim of this paper is to reflect on how games can increase our sense of belonging through the human-centered design of mechanics and games. The method used to do so will be a survey conducted with people from different backgrounds and nationalities, which explores the factors that make us feel that we belong. As a result of the survey, a list of things that increase our feeling of belonging was introduced, such as coming from different cultures, yet being supported and not judged, understanding each other's jokes, or having similar interests. The sense of belonging of the participants was also measured when they've lived in countries different from their own. The survey's results allow us to pick out things that revolve around that feeling and to design game mechanics that empower the feeling of belonging between groups of people. This paper's aim is to define such mechanics and to contribute to the impact of games on feelings of belonging. It also contributes to the debates on whether games should be recognized as a source of social support, especially since video games have grown out to be a popular medium, which connects people from all around the world and provides them the opportunity to foster connections and build skills.

Keywords Belonging · Video games · Game design · Human-Centered design · Serious games · Prosocial games

---

G. Al Halabi
Istanbul Bilgi University, Eyüp 34060, Turkey
e-mail: ghina7alabi@gmail.com

K. Tinç (✉)
Istanbul Technical University, Maçka 34367, Turkey
e-mail: tinc@itu.edu.tr

E. Süngü
Bahçeşehir University, Galata 34425, Turkey

1 Introduction

The game industry has evolved over time and games have transcended the media medium into other mediums and areas such as education, counseling, and the workforce. This evolution has sparked an interest in games as tools of education, which in turn created the research area of serious games.

People have the need to belong somewhere [1], this feeling stems from the fact that humans are social creatures at heart. Some people around the world are uprooted from their homes and are forced to relocate to unknown parts of the world, whereas others never feel they belong to where they were born. Both kinds, and many others, have the need belong to a group or society [2]. This also brings forth the question of acceptance, which is a change of behavior and can be imparted via a serious game.

This study set out to investigate the factors that increase our sense of belonging by surveying participants who have lived in countries different from their origin countries and whether those factors can be applied to games or not. The research question this study sought to answer was: Can these factors be implemented into well-defined game mechanics?

2 Serious, Impact and Prosocial Games

Serious games are named as such in 1970 by Clark C. Abt [3], where he describes them as games played for intent rather than fun. The term was popularized by Ben Sawyer in 2002 and has been a focus of interdisciplinary research since then. Although it is mostly used and known in that way, the definition of serious games does not only include games for learning new things, but also games that influence attitudes and change behavior.

Serious games are widely used in education and contrary to their name they are accepted as a social learning method that, supports the teaching process with fun, has instant feedback and is focused on problem solving [4–7]. These attributes are also true for when a serious game is used to change behavior or influence attitude instead of teaching.

Although Serious Games have been in literature for a long time and is still studied extensively, a lot of game researchers and designers dislike the name and find it oxymoronic. Researchers and designers that have issues with the name have banded together to (re)introduce a new name, Games for Impact or Impact Games. The main difference between a Serious Game and an Impact Game is that for a game to be considered an Impact Game it requires a goal that is for the good of the society. Hence an army training simulator can be considered a Serious Game, but it would be highly debatable whether it can be considered an Impact Game or not. Most experts would probably not consider an army training game as an Impact Game.

Table 1 Game types and their goals (Kutay Tinç)

Game type	Goals
Serious games	Education or behavior change
Impact games	Helping society through games
Prosocial games	Reducing aggression or ingraining a helpful attitude

Impact games have a clear goal in mind which help shape society in a positive way. One of the first, and probably the best, examples of impact games would be Re-mission. In 2019, Pappas introduces Re-mission with these lines:

> A white-helmeted nanobot swoops across the screen, hurling icy fire toward a stream of blank-eyed, gaping-mouthed villains. Blast! They've got their shields up. The nanobot calls in backup, and a white worm rises from beneath, destroying the enemy. More pour in. The bot reaches for another weapon, sending a river of radiation into the baddies below. They fall. Victory!

The enemy vividly pictured in this game is cancer. And the hero, the white-helmeted nanobot, is using chemotherapy, the white fire, while trying to awaken and get help from the immune system, the white worm. This game helps kids understand how chemotherapy works and why they need to keep taking it despite its horrible side effects. Re-mission clear has a goal of increasing public health through acceptance of medicine, which makes it an impact game.

Prosocial games, on the other hand, are either games that have mechanics based on helping others or games that do not contain any violence or much less violence than neutral games. The most known example of prosocial games is the Lemmings[1] series, where a group of Lemmings try to escape from certain death by taking on different jobs that complement and help each other.

Researchers have been examining the positive effects of prosocial video games, especially their effects on aggression reduction. According to behavioral research, playing prosocial video games has not only shown decrease in aggressive cognition [8], but may also diminish aggressive emotions and behaviors along with hostile attributes [9–13].

When all three types of games are compared to one another, it is clear that serious games are the greater set of educational and behavior or attitude manipulating games, while impact games and prosocial games have a more specialized field as seen in Table 1:

The mechanics of belonging we discuss in this study apply to prosocial games as they are designed to help members accept foreigners as part of their group and give them a sense of belonging.

---

[1]Lemmings is a series of video games in which the goal is to rescue the biggest number of lemmings possible through a set of levels. The player must give simple orders to the lemmings to attain the goal. Each level requires a minimum number of lemmings to be rescued.

3 Methodology and Results

To define well-designed mechanics that focus on increasing the belongingness of individuals playing a game, the methodology used was that of conducting a survey that measures these feelings and the factors that affect them. The survey conducted was designed based off the 27-item self-report instrument, Sense of Belonging Instrument scale (SOBI), which is a valid reliable measure of senses of belonging [14], as well as off the Generalized Belonging Scale (GBS) [15].

The survey was designed to ask the participants of their demographics; such as age, gender, nationality, countries they have lived in, and whether they are currently residing in a foreign country, and its two main important parts were as follows: The first part evaluated the factors that help us feel we belong, and the second part evaluated the degree of belonging of every participant in the survey based on the country they were currently living in.

The survey had a sample of 104 individuals, all of whom were from different countries. The mean age of the participants was 24 and consisted of 42.3% males and 57.7% females. 61.5% of these individuals were living in a place different from their origin countries. The survey results show that there is a significance between feelings of belonging and the participant living in their origin country ($p = 0.00 < a=0.05$). Individuals living in a place different from their origin country had a lower sense of belonging (3.14/5.00) than those living in their origin countries (3.38/5.00) (Table 2).

To measure their sense of belonging, the participants were asked to evaluate 24 sentences, based on the Likert scale (a scale that measures agreeability out of 5), that describe their experience of living in the country they are present in. The sentences include statements such as "I can be myself in this country", "I see myself as part of the society", "Locals here treat me with respect", and such.

We can understand from the mean averages of the results that the mostly agreed with statement was "I could ask another acquaintance for help if I had a question on how certain things work in the country," with an average of 3.82/5.00, and the mostly disagreed with statement was "I sense tension between me and other locals," with an average of 2.57/5.00.

Those results show us that at a social level, when individuals depend on each other for help and interact with each other, they contribute to their own sense of belonging and to others' as well. It proves a strong link between belongingness and games that focus on mechanics where helping others and interacting with the environment is emphasized.

Table 2 Belongingness in terms of being foreign (Gina Al Halabi)

	Are you living in a place different from your origin country?	N	Mean	Std. deviation	Std. error mean
Belonging	Yes	64	3.14	.614	.07
	No	40	3.38	.593	.09

To study the factors that may contribute to increasing belongingness, the participants were also required to imagine what would allow them to fulfill that need. Out of 21 scenarios, the factors the participants agreed they'd feel a sense of belonging the most were if they understood each other's jokes (4.33/5.00), shared similar interests (4.22/5.00), came from a different culture but weren't judged and were supported regardless (4.17/5.00), and shared similar manners among people (3.94/5.00) alongside other factors. The most disagreed to factor was if they had shared the same physical attributes (2.67/5.00).

Again, there is a link that can be established between belongingness and games. It starts with the highest scored factor out of the 21 others that the participants, understanding each other's jokes. The factor's position in the results of the survey is important. In this case, humor contributes to fulfilling a "fundamental social need… the need to belong" [16], yet "playfulness is considered the basis of humor (a play with ideas)" [17]. From that understanding, it is concluded that when a player reaches the state of finding "meaningfulness" [18] while playing a game, and they are interacting playfully and are inside the "magic circle" (a space created for playing) the game is offering [19, 20], they are contributing to their belongingness because of the humor and playfulness the game offers.

From the results, we can also understand that the participants feel they would belong when they have a strong support system and share similar manners. Manners here can be defined from the sociological aspect, where the concept of manners "refers to patterned interactions, prevailing norms and customs, and contextually dependent and socially anticipated behaviors," and also refers to "more formally codified standards of behavior" [21]. These behaviors are behaviors that the participants act upon regularly and are frowned upon when they break the code of honor or behave outside the norm.

It is also important that the most disagreed to factor was of sharing "physical attributes". The results show that when a group of people support, help each other, and share the same standards and normative patterns of thoughts, they contribute to each other's belongingness, in where physical appearance does not matter, "differences are a matter of culture, not race or appearance or taste or anything else," [22].

4 Games and Belongingness

Before defining mechanics based on these factors, it would like to be elaborated how existing games already provide a sense of belonging through mechanics that offer a forced interaction such as massively multiplayer online role-playing games (MMORPGs).

In an article on MMORPGs and intrinsic motivation, Michele D. Dickey explains that in such games, players are set in social environments in which they communicate, collaborate, strategize, and socialize with other players. She suggests that MMORPGs provide a model that fosters intrinsic motivation because they provide choice, control, collaboration, challenge, and achievement while players have to think, plan, and act critically and strategically due to the choices they are faced with in real-time [23].

Another study on the influence of belonging on MMORPGs has elaborated that MMORPGs are typical hedonic systems that "aim to provide self-fulfilling value to the user, … [which] is a function of the degree to which the user experiences fun when using the system" [24].

To explain how this directly relates to belongingness, the definition of the sense of belonging should be elaborated: It is a human need where one sees themselves as connected and accepted as a member or part [25]. This definition supports another that states that belongingness is an intrinsic motivation with self-fulfilling value, and fulfilling it offers internal rewards that naturally satisfy us [1].

Another factor that allows MMORPGs to contribute to our belongingness is the conflict and challenges of competing against others that the game offers, there we can present an argument which states that "violence and conflict can heighten need… to belong at both individual and group levels," [26].

5 Game Mechanics Designed Around Belongingness

The aim of this paper is to define abstract mechanics that revolve around the factors that help us increase our belongingness. Based on the results of the surveys, these factors are (a) receiving and giving help from and to the environment, (b) shared humor or playfulness, (c) support, and (d) a set of normative patterns. Other factors that can contribute to belongingness analyzed from MMORPG games are mechanics that provide choice, control, collaboration, challenge, and achievement in settings where we are playing with other players, as well as game environments that offer conflict.

These mechanics will be demonstrated using a Game Design Tool called "Machinations". Machinations is a framework that is designed to model the interaction between the parts of a game's internal economy [27]. To allow the reader to understand the schemes, first, some of the basic and essential elements of the Machinations diagram should be introduced (Fig. 1).

In Machinations, the most basic node type is the "pool", it is where the resources gather in the diagram. The opposite of the pool is a "gate", it does not collect resources, its main function is to immediately distribute them. Sources are nodes that create resources. The main difference between them and pools is that sources are unlimited, meanwhile the resources in the pool are limited. Drains have the opposite function of a source, we differentiate them by their upside-down shape, their function is to consume resources. Converters convert one resource into another, an example of that is mill machine that turns cotton into cloth. Traders allow players to exchange resources. The difference between them and converters is that converters affect the number of resources in the game, meanwhile traders do not. Resource connections allow resources to move from node to node. State connections work as triggers. They

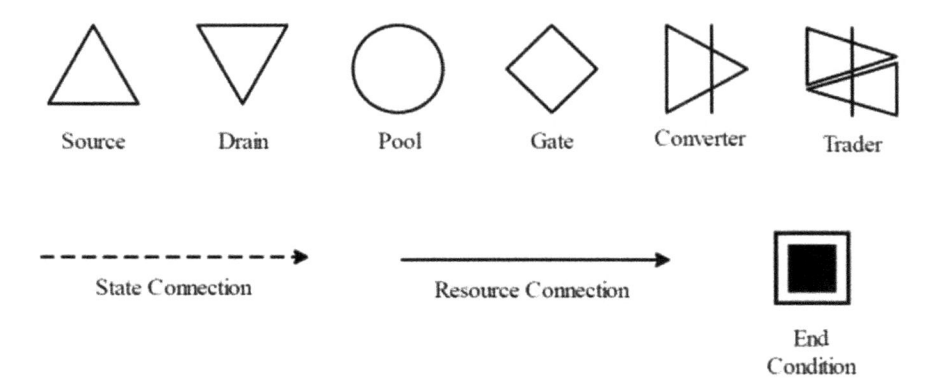

Fig. 1 Machinations essential elements (Ernest Adams and Joris Dormans)

update the nodes based on the state the game is at. Finally, end conditions specify end states, the tool checks the end conditions every time it runs [27].

Based of the factors; support, receiving help, choice, and conflict, this abstract mechanic was put together:

In Fig. 2, a simple mechanic is demonstrated. The player has 2 opportunities to cooperate with others. Every time he tries to, he has a 50% chance of achievement. If the player is unlucky and does not achieve, he will lose 5 safety points. If he was willing to try although he may lose 5 safety points, yet he achieves, his opportunity will be "converted" into 15 safety points. When the player achieves in cooperating with others 2 times, he will constantly gain safety points every interval until he reaches 100 points and wins the game. We can imagine the constant gain of safety points as

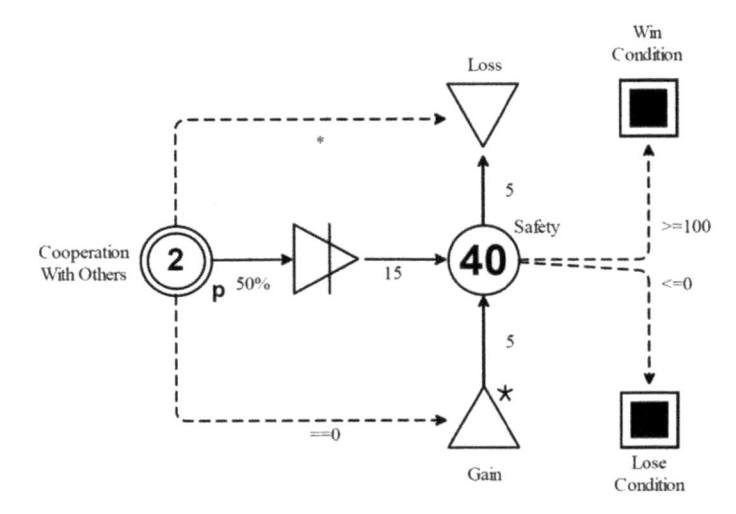

Fig. 2 Cooperating with the environment (Gina Al Halabi)

other people returning the favor for the first cooperation tries and as feedback for the loss of the points. The point of this mechanic is that there is conflict between risking safety and cooperating with others. Yet, trying to cooperate leads to reward. The same applies to belongingness in a foreign environment.

Based of the factors; receiving and giving help, support, and a set of normative patterns, alongside other factors like choice and challenge, another mechanic was put together:

In Fig. 3, a strategic trading mechanic was designed. The goal here is for Blue to produce as many reds as possible and vice versa. Although, the way to produce them requires the players to cooperate. Blue cannot produce without Red, and Red cannot produce without blue. In this design, Blue starts off with no reds at all and 2 blues, the opposite applies to Red, so they need to trade 1 token with each other to start the production. After doing so, Blue can produce reds. He now has 2 reds in his production pool and no blues. The only way to get a new blue for the next production is to trigger the blue source by giving Red one of his newly produced reds. Red does the same. Now both Red and Blue have returned to the initial state of the game and need to trade again to get the production going. In this design, receiving and giving help is the only way to reach the goal. The design falls into a normative pattern where it is not possible for any of the players to move forward without the other. They need to support and depend on each other.

Using the factors and the concept of the Prisoner's Dilemma from game theory, another mechanic which demonstrates all four factors can be demonstrated:

In Fig. 4, when both players cooperate, they both gain a total of 2 coins. Although, as demonstrated in Fig. 5, when a player cheats (the first player), he gains more (3 instead of 2), his total wealth increases, but at the expense of the other player (he loses 1). When both players cheat, the diagram looks very similar to Fig. 4, but instead, they both do not gain any coins. This dilemma and its mechanism support the factors

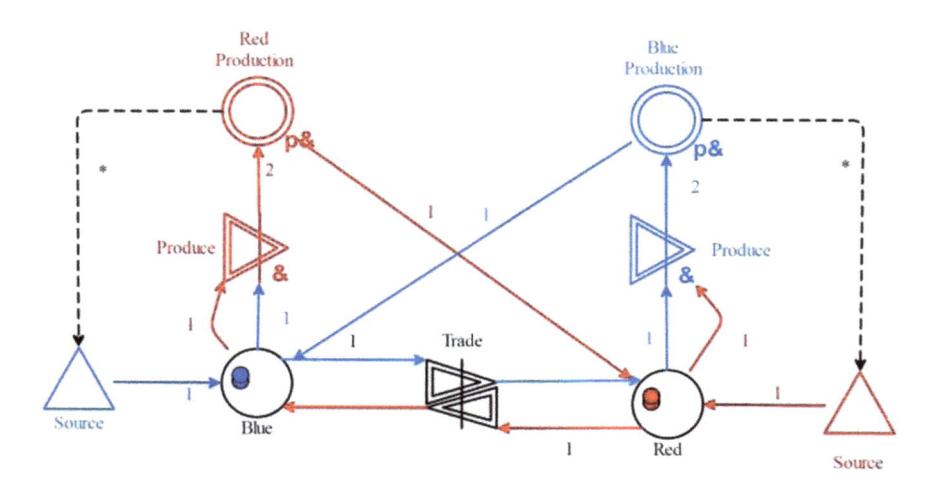

Fig. 3 Strategic trading (Gina Al Halabi)

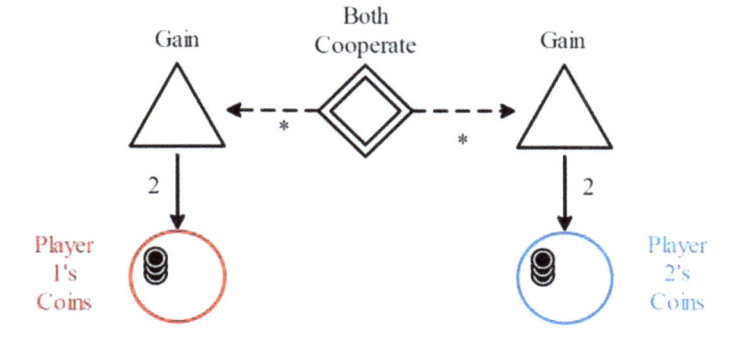

Fig. 4 Cooperation in the Prisoner's Dilemma (Gina Al Halabi)

Fig. 5 Cheating in the Prisoner's Dilemma (Gina Al Halabi)

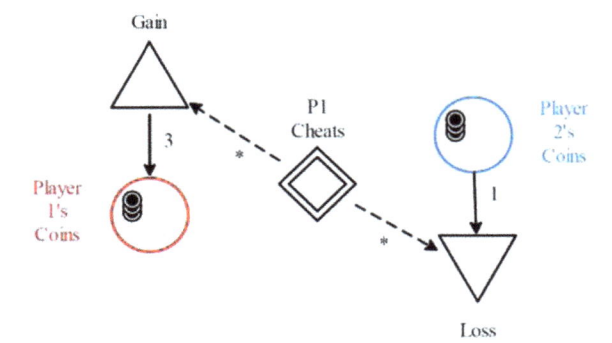

that increase our belongingness, especially after it becomes a norm to cooperate and help instead of focusing on personal gain. Humor is also supported if we imagine a scenario where two people always cooperate and then one of them decides to cheat to break the norm.

As demonstrated above, the set of factors analyzed in this study can help in designing mechanics that focus and contribute to our sense of belonging.

6 Conclusion

The goal of this study was to investigate the factors that contribute to belongingness and to study whether they could or could not be implemented into game mechanics. To achieve that goal, a survey was conducted and analyzed. The results of the survey presented that the contributing factors are (a) receiving and giving help from and to the environment, (b) shared humor or playfulness, (c) support, and (d) a set of normative patterns. Other factors that can contribute to belongingness were also analyzed from the mechanics of MMORPGs. Games with such implemented mechanics were defined as prosocial games because of their design and helpful attitude.

There has been earlier research on cooperative game mechanics and on how games can contribute to belongingness. Compared to earlier research, this study aimed to define mechanics that focus on increasing the sense of belonging of individuals. It also aimed to define the factors that can help in defining such mechanics.

The main limitation of the study is the size of the sample of participants and the variety of backgrounds. Further work should involve extensive testing of the mechanics in various types of games and testing their impact on the individuals.

References

1. Schneider ML, Kwan BM (2013) Psychological need satisfaction, intrinsic motivation and affective response to exercise in adolescents. Psychol Sport Exerc 14:776–785. https://doi.org/10.1016/j.psychsport.2013.04.005
2. Pillow DR, Malone GP, Hale WJ (2015) The need to belong and its association with fully satisfying relationships: a tale of two measures. Personal Individ Diff 74:259–264. https://doi.org/10.1016/j.paid.2014.10.031
3. Abt CC (1970) Serious games. Viking Press, USA
4. Garris R, Ahlers R, Driskell JE (2002) Games, motivation, and learning: a research and practice model. Simul Gam 33:441–467. https://doi.org/10.1177/1046878102238607
5. Kirriemuir J, McFarlane A (2004) Literature review in games and learning: a report for NESTA futurelab. NESTA Futurelab, Bristol
6. Petko D (2008) Unterrichten mit Computerspielen. Didaktische Potenziale und Ansätze für den gezielten Einsatz in Schule und Ausbildung. MedienPädagogik: Zeitschrift für Theorie und Praxis der Medienbildung Computerspiele und Videogames in formellen und informellen Bildungskontexten 15: 1–15. https://doi.org/10.21240/mpaed/15_16/2008.11.07.x
7. Tobias S, David YD, Wind AP (2011) Review of research on computer games. In: Fletcher JD (ed) Computer games and instruction, pp 127–221. IAP Information Age Publishing
8. Greitemeyer Tobias, Osswald Silvia (2009) Prosocial video games reduce aggressive cognitions. J Exp Soc Psychol 45:896–900. https://doi.org/10.1016/j.jesp.2009.04.005
9. Liu Y, Teng Z, Lan Z, Zhang X, Yao D (2015) Short-term effects of prosocial video games on aggression: an event-related potential study. Front Behav Neurosc 9. https://doi.org/10.3389/fnbeh.2015.00193
10. Gentile DA, Anderson Craig A, Yukawa S, Ihori N, Saleem M, Ming Lim Kam, Shibuya Akiko et al (2009) The effects of prosocial video games on prosocial behaviors: international evidence from correlational, longitudinal, and experimental studies. Personal Soc Psychol Bull 35:752–763. https://doi.org/10.1177/0146167209333045
11. Greitemeyer T (2011) Effects of prosocial media on social behavior. Curr Direct Psychol Sci 20:251–255. https://doi.org/10.1177/0963721411415229
12. Greitemeyer T, Osswald S (2011) Playing prosocial video games increases the accessibility of prosocial thoughts. J Soc Psychol 151:121–128. https://doi.org/10.1080/00224540903365588
13. Greitemeyer T, Agthe M, Turner R, Gschwendtner C (2011) Acting prosocially reduces retaliation: Effects of prosocial video games on aggressive behavior. European Journal of Social Psychology 42:235–242. https://doi.org/10.1002/ejsp.1837
14. Hagerty Bonnie MK, Patusky K (1995) Developing a measure of sense of belonging. Nurs Res 44. Doi https://doi.org/10.1097/00006199-199501000-00003
15. Malone GP, Pillow DR, Osman A (2012) The general belongingness scale (GBS): assessing achieved belongingness. Personal Indiv Diff 52:311–316. https://doi.org/10.1016/j.paid.2011.10.027

16. Baumeister Roy F, Leary MR (1995) The need to belong: desire for interpersonal attachments as a fundamental human motivation. Psychol Bull 117:497–529. https://doi.org/10.1037/0033-2909.117.3.497
17. Willibald R, Tracey P, René PT, Chen H-C (2019) Editorial: humor and laughter, playfulness and cheerfulness: upsides and downsides to a life of lightness. Front Psychol 10. https://doi.org/10.3389/fpsyg.2019.00730
18. Rodriguez H (2006) The playful and the serious: an approximation to Huizinga's homo Ludens. Game Stud. http://www.gamestudies.org/0601/articles/rodriges. Last accessed 2020/08/29
19. Huizinga J (1950) Homo Ludens: study of play element in culture. Beacon Press, Boston
20. Stenros J (2014) In defence of a magic circle: the social, mental and cultural boundaries of play. Trans Digit Games Res Assoc 1: https://doi.org/10.26503/todigra.v1i2.10
21. Voyer A (2018) Sociology of manners. Oxford Bibliographies Online Datasets. https://doi.org/10.1093/obo/9780199756384-0214
22. Levy MM, Mendlesohn F (2019) Aliens in popular culture. Greenwood, Santa Barbara, CA
23. Dickey MD (2006) Game design and learning: a conjectural analysis of how massively multiple online role-playing games (MMORPGs) foster intrinsic motivation. Educ Tech Res Dev 55:253–273. https://doi.org/10.1007/s11423-006-9004-7
24. Ernst C-PH (2017) The influence of perceived belonging on massively multiplayer online role-playing games. In: Proceedings of the 50th Hawaii International Conference on System Sciences (2017). https://doi.org/10.24251/hicss.2017.494
25. Hall K (2014) Create a sense of belonging. Psychology Today. Sussex Publishers. https://www.psychologytoday.com/us/blog/pieces-mind/201403/create-sense-belonging. Last accessed 2020/03/24
26. Nadler A, Malloy TE, Fisher JD (2008) The social psychology of intergroup reconciliation. Oxford University Press, New York
27. Adams E, Dormans J (2012) Game mechanics: advanced game design. New Riders, Berkeley, CA

Virtual Reality Experiment

Design Process of a VR Sports Games Trilogy for Paraplegic Players: VR4Inclusion Case Study

Semih Bertuğ Benim, Mehmet İlker Berkman, and Güven Çatak

Abstract Individuals with Spinal Cord Injury, has problems with their motor dysfunctions and Physical Therapy is an important process in order to prevent those problems dramatically. Motivation plays a key role in this part. People with the SCI, don't want to be separated from the others yet they require to be attended like the others. Aim of this project is about how to design an inclusive game and interaction and to empower young people with disabilities both socially and physically. In order to do that, Three Paralympic sport games—Boccia, Handcycling and Sledge Hockey—were produced. During the game production, focus group played the game. Playtesting sessions were conducted as a part of a social inclusion event in Istanbul with the support of Tyrtaois Sports Club and International Association of Spinal Cord Paralysis. During the playtesting, disabled people participated as well as non-disabled people, who got together in order to play the games and share their opinions. Game production continued with the feedbacks received from playtesting sessions. After the beta phase, there was another meeting in Ankara, with the hosting of the International Association of Spinal Cord Paralysis, and people who played the old version and the others play a newer version of the games. After each session, they expected to fill a questionnaire about their experience. The results evaluated in order to make it more inclusive and more user-friendly for all type of players.

Keywords Virtual reality · Interaction design · Paralympic games · Inclusion · Sports games

---

S. B. Benim (✉) · M. İ. Berkman · G. Çatak
Game Design Graduate Programme, Bahçeşehir University, İstanbul, Turkey
e-mail: bertugbenim@gmail.com

M. İ. Berkman
e-mail: ilker.berkman@comm.bau.edu.tr

G. Çatak
e-mail: guven.catak@comm.bau.edu.tr

© The Author(s), under exclusive license to Springer Nature Switzerland AG 2021
Ö. Cordan et al. (eds.), *Game + Design Education*, Springer Series in Design and Innovation 13, https://doi.org/10.1007/978-3-030-65060-5_15

1 Introduction

According to the World Health Organization (WHO), about 15% of the world's population is disabled individuals [1]. Every year, around the world, between 250,000 and 500,000 people suffer a Spinal Cord Injury (SCI). An estimated 20–30% of people with spinal cord injury show clinically significant signs of depression. They bear the feeling of dysfunction and exclusion.

SCI can be treated with the exercises to ease the pain and also make the motor functions work better. Making a couple of motions over and over without any short-term objective can be painful, exhausting and boring progress. Also, each individual has a specific amount of energy to spend daily to maintain essential body functions. Energy Expenditure (EE) is a definition which refers to that amount and is determined by resting, metabolism and nutrition [2]. Unused energy expenditure can cause obesity, resting issues [3]. To add an objective, Activity Promoting Video Games (APVG) can help. One hour of APVG can increase daily energy expenditure by about %6–15 [4].

Unlike the other gaming platforms, the HMD (head-mounted display) based VR allows the players to move independently, without any limitations due to the position of the screen. For this reason, it is a suitable platform for games that require physical activity [5]. Although it is relatively novel as a consumer product, Virtual Reality (VR) is a fast-growing technology area and is expected to reach 98.4 million sales by 2023. This means that the VR will be a comprehensive technology and easy to reach in a few years for nearly everybody yet also means that the development in this area will be dramatic.

VR4Inclusion is an Erasmus + project, realised with the partnership of Bahçeşehir University, International Spinal Cord Injury Association, Development and Innovation Office from Turkey, Trytaios Disabled Sports Club from Greece and Politechnica Slaska. The project includes the development of 3 Virtual Reality Games for both people with and without disabilities. It makes them compete against each other in the same competitive conditions while using the feedback from both sides and making them as reachable as possible. The project aims to create an opportunity for social interaction for physically disabled individuals through virtual reality technologies and gaming.

As an output of this project, boccia, hand-cycling (hand biking) and sledge hockey VR games were designed and implemented, which were evaluated by a group of disabled and non-disabled individuals.

This paper explains the design and development process of these VR sports games.

2 Design Decisions

2.1 Content Decisions: *Determining the Sports*

We followed a player-centred approach in order to decide the sports games that would be developed for the inclusion of disabled young individuals. We ran three focus groups with young disabled participants to determine the content of the games. The first group included 9 participants aged 14–23 and the second group included 8 participants aged 15–18. They were students of a special educational institution in Athens. The last group of 9 participants were para-athletes, aged 23–54. Their physical disabilities vary, as some had paraplegia, some had quadriplegia while some have disabilities of walking without aid or moving their arms. In the first part of the focus group sessions, participants were asked to explain about their disability, daily activities, use of a wheelchair if they do, their involvement into sports, digital media use and gaming, prior VR experiences and expectations of VR in terms of realism and physical activity. Later, they were exposed to sport-themed games, skiing, basketball, ping pong and archery game that they played on either Oculus Go or Gear VR.

On the second part of the session, they were asked to discuss their likelihood to own a VR system, and the match of between their prior expectations and what they experienced and the qualifications of their experience such as ease of use, challenge, interactivity and realism, as well as the experience of physical activity in terms of appropriateness of the level of exercise for disabled people, disabled athletes and non-disabled people. Finally, the participants were queried on their knowledge of adaptive sports for disabled people, followed by a discussion on the content of the games.

For the younger students, most of them have been born with a disability, but the majority of the elder athletes group were injured in an accident. The younger students are involved in sports because they are encouraged by the others, while most of the athletes were involved in sports before they got disabled.

Some of the wheelchair users use it at home most of the time, while they were dining. Some use it also while they rest, watching TV. Some use other aids at home, like canes. Caregivers usually help the younger kids to move around whşle they are at home, instead of using wheelchairs or other aids. They exercise at home, using dumbbells or a particular set-up of ropes. Youngsters also got visits from physiotherapists.

Boccia is a popular sport activity that is practised regularly by most of the young students and all of the athletes. Other sports activities mentioned as a regular occupation was swimming, ping pong, taekwondo, javelin throw and chess. One of the participants tried mono-ski, and many declared that they are anticipated in javelin throwing and swimming.

In-line with their experiences, they anticipated that they would like to see a boccia game on VR. Swimming and skiing were other popular answers as a VR experience, along with ping pong. Basketball and volleyball are mentioned frequently followed by water sports such as rowing, surfing, canoe and kayak; with a few mentions to cycling, curling and archery.

Their digital habits are similar to their non-disabled peers; as all own a mobile device. Young students play games on mobile, tablets, computer and engage with social media. A few participants have game consoles. Male participants are more likely to play on computer and consoles while female play mobile games. Being likely to own VR, its price is important. Elderly disabled athletes play less digital games compared to young students. They said that they have prior knowledge on VR, but not tried it before.

They describe VR as "Great"—a vague definition by younger students, "Like living it", "7.5 over ten realistic", "like a dream—than come back to reality", "like to live the experience by doing things I couldn't do in real life", "what you see will be something moving but not real".

After they experienced VR, they were asked again about their likelihood to own a mobile VR system. One of the participants in Group 1 already owns a Playstation VR. He said he would not own a mobile one. This affected others for their likelihood to own a mobile VR headset.

Group 2 and 3 participants were likely to own, but have concerns on cost.

Although they were satisfied with what they have experienced, some participants had mild cybersickness symptoms after they played the games. The controls, which especially require sharp head movements, were reported to be unsuitable. We also observed that some participants experienced difficulties in reaching the control buttons on the side of the Gear VR headset. They said the handheld-controller of Oculus Go is more suitable for them.

The last part of the discussion was about the content of the games. The younger participants claimed that VR could be an opportunity for them to try out the sports activities that they cannot do in real-world, due to physical limitations. When they were suggested to experience a paralympic sport on VR other than boccia, such as hand-cycling or curling, they were not attracted by the idea. When the moderator reminded them that they have recently tried some VR sports games for non-disabled people and there is not any adaptive sports VR game already available, they agreed with the idea of having an adaptive sports game for VR. However, they said that they still want to try sports for non-disabled people as a VR game.

On the contrary, the disabled athletes were highly supporting the idea of having adaptive sports as VR games, as it would increase the awareness of these sports among both disabled and non-disabled people.

Due to its popularity among the disabled people based on ease of access according to the simplicity of equipment, boccia was the highest-rated option as a VR game. It is followed by team sports such as wheelchair basketball, followed by curling and ice-hockey. Even the participants did not remark the hand-cycling, they did not refuse it when suggested.

Evaluating the focus group results and technical limitations, we decided to create a boccia game, a hand-cycling and a para ice hockey experience for VR. The main reason for choosing to make a boccia game was its popularity among the audience. Although it is a competitional team game, it is less complicated to make it a game that is played against the computer for its turn-based gameplay, compared to other competitional ball games such as basketball.

The ice-hockey is selected since it is suggested by participants but simplified as a "skating and shooting practice" due to hardware, budget and time limitations.

The hand-cycling is determined since it offers continuous physical activity through a handheld device.

2.2 Technical Decisions: Determining the Platform

Unity3D is a game development focused, 3D development environment which also supports Extended Reality solutions [6, 7]. Besides that, there is a vast repository of programming and visual components that can be used when developing applications using Unity, namely Unity Asset Store, along with rich documentation and great community support. Therefore it is decided to be the primary tool to develop the games explained in our study.

Making the game easily reachable by any user is one of the critical objectives. In order to achieve this, Mobile VR devices were considered. At the time of the development, three types of mobile VR solutions were available commercially. On the other hand, we also aimed to increase the physical activity of users, which requires using handheld controllers. At the time of the development, 3DoF controllers were available for mobile VR, which are depending on the accelerometer data inside the controller, rather than a combination of accelerometer and optical tracking used in 6DoF controllers used with HMDs attached to personal computers.

DoF(Degree of Freedom) is a term for motion about an axis or along an axis [8]. 3DoF Controllers are controllers where it detects the 3-axis rotation of the device. An upgraded version, 6DoF detects the 3-axis movement of the device too.

The state-of-the-art platforms available for our games were:

1. Cardboard: Google's easy to use, highly compatible semi-VR solution. It works with almost any smartphones, but the interaction is limited to the head movements, touchscreen, and the magnetometer on the mobile device.
2. Daydream: Google specific VR solution. It supports a pair of 3DoF Controllers that enables users to interact with their both hands, but compatible with a limited number of mobile phone models.
3. Gear VR: A mobile VR system that runs on several Samsung mobile phones. It supports 3DoF controllers and it is compatible with the applications developed for Oculus Go
4. Oculus Go: A standalone HMD display that includes an Android mini computer and a 3DoF controller. As a result, no cell phone is required and device compatibility issues are less problematic (Fig. 1).

Among these options, we decided to use Oculus Go as our primary targeted platform, since it also covers the Gear VR systems and Daydream supporting devices.

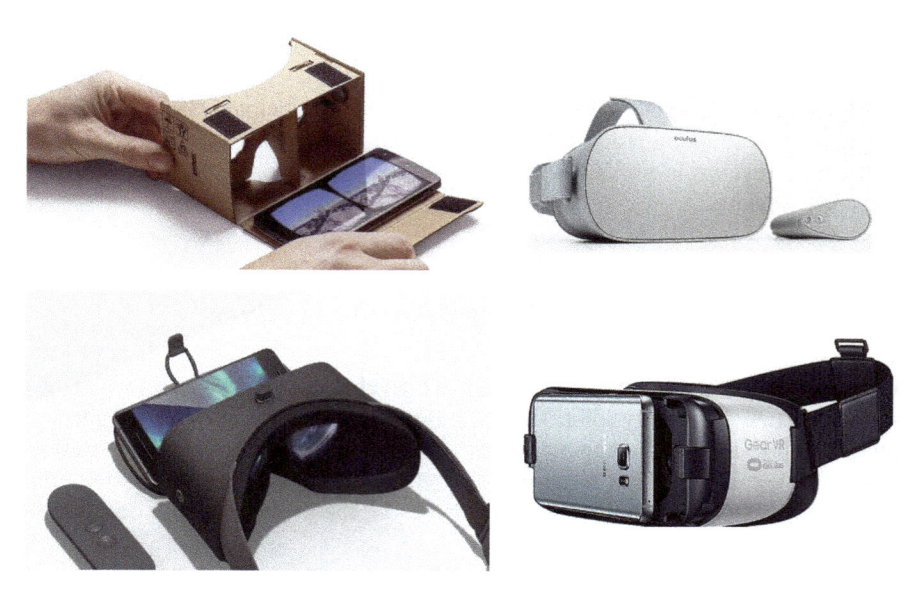

Fig. 1 HMD virtual reality devices, Google Cardboard (upper-left), Oculus Go (upper-right), Google Daydream (lower-left), GearVR (lower-right)

Compared to a mobile phone based system, it is relatively cheaper, if the user does not already own a VR-ready mobile phone.

On the other hand, we wanted to make our games available for the people who have any kind of mobile phone that can run VR applications. For this reason, we focused on using 3rd party 3DoF controllers with the Cardboards. After a couple of tryouts, the first pitfall encountered. Google Cardboard doesn't support the low budget 3DoF [5] that were available on the market at the time of the development. This situation forced us to narrow down the target audience to Daydream and Oculus Go users or make the games work with only clickers instead of motion controllers.

As we eliminated the cheap 3DoF controllers since they were not compatible with mobile phones, we still had to develop games that involve a high level of physical activity. But having a specific VR device is not a common thing amongst the target audience. In order to reach a larger audience, we decided to fork the project in order to support cardboard compatible mobile devices without any controllers and the Oculus Go/Gear VR devices with single 3DoF controller option.

The two forks were as follows:

1. Cardboard + any controller version: This game should be played only with one extensive button while any cardboard is compatible. Highly reachable but offers a limited experience.
2. Oculus Go and Daydream version: It has the full potential of the game itself by supporting 3DoF player motions.

3 Design, Development and Implementation

3.1 First Trials with Google Cardboard

Google Cardboard is a cardboard box with lenses which has a place for smartphones. Besides its low price, it supports most of the smartphones [9]. To use it, users place their compatible smartphones after they open the desired software.

During the project's early developments, it focused on the Boccia game in Cardboard environment. This game defines the theme, controllers and style of the game. But the main issue was developing a Boccia game that is playable by only one button. Paralympic games inspired the design of the game. In paralympic boccia where the players are profoundly disabled, that can't throw balls, plays the game with a ramp. Players have one helper that responsible with the ramp position and angle of it. Player instructs the helper by head gestures or voice as they try to move it into the desired angle and position as you depicted in Fig. 2. Helpers leave the box and player release the ball either by their hands or with the stick that is attached to their heads. In the original game is mimicked by putting a ramp which controlled by the head of the player.

In this case, the button can not be defined as a specific button to make it more compatible with any 3rd party controller since all may change the button layout on their devices by default. Unity solves this case by "Input.anykey" method [10]. It detects any key input from any connected controller device. In each button detection, game is progress according to Fig. 3.

Boccia game requires two teams to compete. In this project, making it real multiplayer is a hard task to achieve with VR support, and also it requires two players, two cardboards and two controllers which makes it less reachable. This issue solved by making the players compete against an AI player which has a robot appearance with

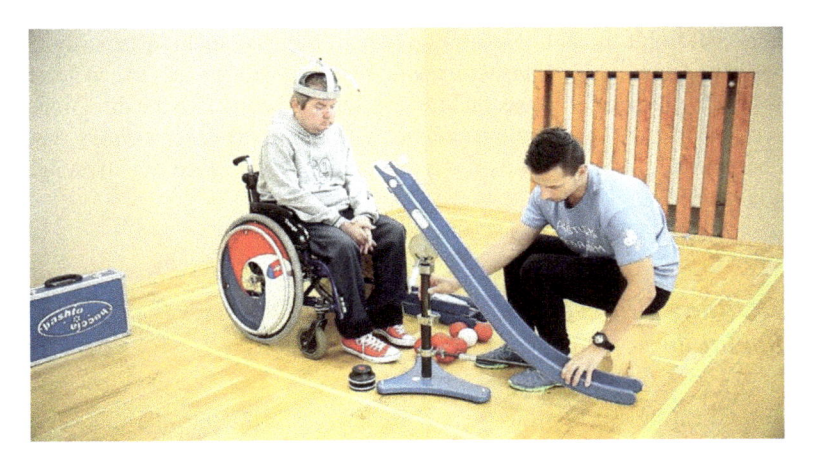

Fig. 2 Boccia ramp BASHTO athletic profi promo video [11]

Fig. 3 VR4Inclusion Boccia gameplay

a ball throwing hole on its chest. Afterwards, we use that robot to help the player in any matters such as guidance, menu controls and even as a scoreboard.

Hand-cycling is similar to regular bicycles, yet it functions with drivers hands. While there is no possible motion control for the cardboard version, acceleration is made by a button press, and after another button press, it starts decelerating. The bike makes the turns right as the player leans their head on the right side and vice versa.

Sledge-hockey is played while the players are on a sledge. They are supposed to play a classic hockey game where each player got a pair of special sticks. Those sticks got a hit side where it looks like a typical hockey stick while on the other side, they got a surface to make them push forward like a ski. Due to limitation of controls, Hand-cycle controls were also applied to the ski. Since it has to change the mode for movement and to hit the ball with only one button, phase method from the Boccia game has been taken. This means with the first button, sledge starts to accelerate, and as the button is pressed for the second time, it shoots the puck to the direction where the player is looking. Due to the problems with the multiplayer options described above the gameplay simplified as the player supposed to make ten shots against a robot goalkeeper.

3.2 Iterating Project into Daydream and Oculus VR Technologies

After limited cardboard versions were completed, 3DoF controller motion control features should be added. As mentioned before, Oculus Go and Daydream devices have a narrow audience, yet they have support for 3DoF motion amongst the mobile VR devices that means you can move your hand, and it detects your hand's rotation.

Since they use the same controller binaries, Oculus features a Unity APK for both Oculus Go and Daydream [12, 13]. First, ready-made assets that using this APK are inspected. As it turns out, they are not so customisable for the games already made, this feature is started to make from scratch.

When a human throws an object with hand, its movement happens as rotation and movement at the same time. This is equal to 6DoF movement. Due to our limitation to 3DoF, the movement supposed to be simulated. To calculate the throwing motion of players, as long as the player press the trigger button of the controller, rotation value is stored. As the trigger button released, the system detects the difference between the current rotation and the rotation value from the previous frame. The difference between the two values gives the data for projection and speed. After the calculation of the vector and speed, related force applied to the ball.

As for the hand-cycle game, the rotational movement was not possible to calculate accurately by only rotation values. Therefore, the game detects only the movement of the controller and the speed of that movement. As the player moves their hands faster, the bike goes faster while the trigger button function for braking. Head rotation system directly applied from the cardboard version.

Head rotation and speed-up systems from the hand-cycling game applied directly to Sledge Hockey movement system. Brake button transformed into a shooting mode. As the players press that button and move their hands, it calculates the speed of that movement and shoots the puck into the direction of players view.

Due to lack of detailed controls on cardboard games, there was no main menu. Instead, the game scene is loaded as it runs. But for the Oculus and Daydream version, the main menu is implemented (Fig. 4), which also contains settings and instructions. For the main menu controls, the same robot used to assist the player. Players select the options from the face of that robot, which is also a screen. After the end of each game, players return to the main menu scene, as a design decision based on the playtesting observations (Fig. 5).

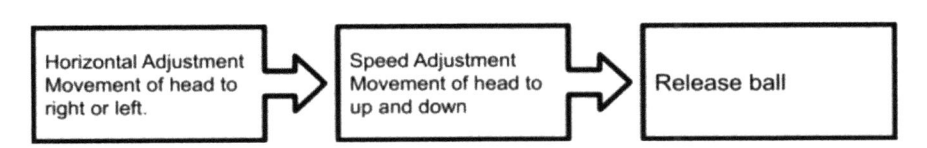

| Horizontal Adjustment Movement of head to right or left. | ⟹ | Speed Adjustment Movement of head to up and down | ⟹ | Release ball |

Fig. 4 Boccia gameplay sequence (created by authors)

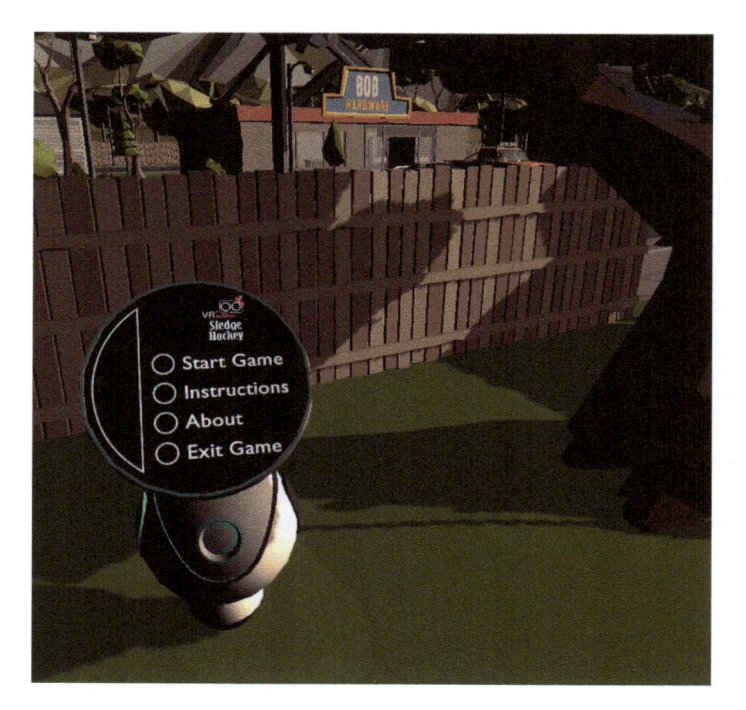

Fig. 5 Main menu scene

3.3 Playtest Sessions and Design Improvements

The game described above were evaluated by a group of 124 participants [14], which includes both disabled and non-disabled participants. Afterwards, they tend to experience games with Oculus Go. At the end of the session, a small tournament happened in order to encourage inclusion. The initial results of the competition show that the performance between people with and without disabilities are comparable. However, since the target audience is not capable of doing the same movements as the others do, some specific and unseen fixes must be made. Feedback sessions made with each individual, in the form of semi-structured interviews. Considering the feedback through these interviews, several improvements would be made on the game controls and the interface elements, as this initial playtesting activity is considered as formative evaluation.

During the first play sessions, we observed that many players throw the boccia ball with high speed. As a result, the ball disappears from the visual field of the player. This frustration is lowered by assisting the player by establishing a constraint on the throwing speed. Similarly, we also defined a speed limitation for the sledge hockey puck. Also for the readability problems, some UI improvements have been made such as additional indicator robots and font updates. After some quality improvements, second playtest session and closure event handled at the International Spinal Cord Paralysis Association (Uluslararası Omurilik Felçlileri Derneği) in Ankara.

4 Conclusion

In this paper, we explained the design, development and implementation of three VR adaptive sports games, developed for both disabled and non-disabled individuals. Due to the interaction limitations of the state-of-the-art mobile VR in the time of development, we had to split the project into two forks: one that is for mobile phone based VR, and the other is standalone headsets with 3DoF single-handed interaction. We adapted the gameplay according to the technological limitations of the targeted devices.

The playtests revealed several issues of in-game mechanics, which were later calibrated through limiting the game physics. As the disabled users had difficulties in controlling the games, we also simplified the game mechanics.

Through the initial formative evaluation sessions, we observed that both disabled and non-disabled players perform similarly while they engage with the games.

Another set of playtest sessions are planned to be executed in order to understand the requirements of disabled players in comparison to non-disabled individuals.

References

1. World Health Organization [and] The World Bank (2011) World report on disability. World Health Organization, Geneva, Switzerland
2. Heaney J (2013) Energy: expenditure, intake, lack of. In: Gellman MD, Turner JR (eds) Encyclopedia of behavioral medicine. Springer, New York, NY. https://doi.org/10.1007/978-1-4419-1005-9_454
3. Naish J, Court DS (2019) Medical sciences. Elsevier, Edinburgh
4. Gaffurini P, Bissolotti L, Calza S, Calabretto C, Orizio C, Gobbo M (2012) Energy metabolism during activity-promoting video games practice in subjects with spinal cord injury: evidences for health promotion. Eur J Phys Rehabil Med
5. Aksayım A, Berkman MI (2020) Effect of physical activity on VR experience: an experimental study. In: Richir S (ed) Proceedings of virtual reality international conference (VRIC), 22–24 April, Laval, France, Publisher: Laval Virtual. www.laval-virtual.com, ISBN 978-2-9566-2517-9
6. Dillet R (September 5, 2018) Unity CEO says half of all games are built on Unity. TechCrunch. Archived from the original on December 20, 2018. Retrieved 3 Dec 2018
7. Grubb J (February 10, 2016) Unity game-making tool gets native support for Google's 5 M cardboard virtual reality devices. VentureBeat. Archived from the original on March 22, 2019. Retrieved 3 Dec 2018
8. What is a 3 DoF versus 6 DoF in VR? (n.d.). Mechatech. https://www.mechatech.co.uk/journal/what-is-a-3dof-vs-6dof-in-vr
9. Google Cardboard. (n.d.). Google Cardboard. https://arvr.google.com/intl/en_gb/cardboard/
10. UT (2020) Input-anyKey. Unity Documentation. https://docs.unity3d.com/ScriptReference/Input-anyKey.html

11. Bashto Sports (2017) Boccia ramp BASHTO athletic profi promo video ENG (Video). Youtube. https://www.youtube.com/watch?v=O6ruUQC-LI8
12. Introducing Oculus Go|Oculus. (n.d.). Oculus. https://developer.oculus.com/blog/introducing-oculus-go/?locale=tr_TR
13. Downloads Oculus Go (n.d.). Oculus. https://developer.oculus.com/downloads/
14. İstanbul Dissemination Summit (2019) Retrieved from http://vr4inclusion.org/istanbul-dissemination-summit

Use of Virtual Reality in Participatory Urban Design

Zeynep Burcu Kaya Alpan and Güven Çatak

Abstract This paper focuses on providing a comprehensive look at the use of virtual reality in participatory urban design practices. Immersive virtual environments are used in many areas of design, one of them being participatory urban design. Interactive, multisensory three-dimensional environments prove to be engaging for the public and illuminating for the designer. Presence can be benefitted for several layers of participatory urban design process: understanding the proposed design, commenting on the proposed design, contributing to the design. To this end, a review of the literature on the area is conducted and human-centered design considerations are noted. A human-centered VR experience is not proposed as the only component of the participatory design process, but one of them. The process should be designed by experts such as urban planners and designers with the input of all the stakeholders. This model should be included in the process design and tested in such a process in further studies.

Keywords Virtual reality · Participatory urban design · Human-centered design · Experience design · Interaction design

1 Introduction

Design as a notion has similarities and differences in its many disciplines. For example, architecture and urban design can be considered as siblings. Software design and interaction design are intertwined. And even though they seem to be very different fields, urban design and interaction design may be more similar than they look like at the first glance, since they have a human-centered design approach in common.

Z. B. Kaya Alpan (✉) · G. Çatak
Bahçeşehir University, Kemeralti 24/A 34425, Turkey
e-mail: zeynepburcukaya@mekan.space

G. Çatak
e-mail: guven.catak@comm.bau.edu.tr

© The Author(s), under exclusive license to Springer Nature Switzerland AG 2021
Ö. Cordan et al. (eds.), *Game + Design Education*, Springer Series in Design and Innovation 13, https://doi.org/10.1007/978-3-030-65060-5_16

This commonality is more evident in participatory urban design practices than other urban design processes. Starting with the 60s, emphasis was made on the user's experience of the built environment. Urban design processes were designed to gather information and arguably give back some of the power over the decision-making process to citizens.

New technologies have often been implemented in participatory urban design studies. Democratization of the computer and the internet has affected participatory urban design significantly. As an extension, virtual reality has been a recurring topic in participatory urban design.

With this paper, we suggest that Immersive Virtual Reality designed with human-centered design and body-centered interaction design may enable laypeople understand the design proposals and help them develop a sense of belonging.

2 Evolution and Components of VR

Immersive virtual reality (IVR) or virtual reality (VR) for short is extremely compelling in the sense that it provides seemingly endless amount of possibilities to the designer. Nevertheless, designing and developing an impressive VR experience is a complex challenge. If the experience is designed well, the outcome may surpass anything that would be possible in the physical reality. But a poorly designed VR experience may result in more than discomfort, it may make the participant ill.

The reason of the difference between a well and poor design in VR is complex to decipher. Some failures are caused by the limitations of technology, but many come from a lack of understanding perception, interaction, design principles, and real users [1].

2.1 A Phenomenological Approach to Realities

The term virtual reality (VR) is an oxymoron. An adjective meaning "not physically existing" and a noun meaning "physical existence" are combined to represent a computer technology. A technology that provides sensory information and feedback to the user, in order to immerse them into an artificial world that only exists inside a computer [2].

However it is named, virtual reality has opened new philosophical discussions about reality, mind and body. Heidegger's phenomenological approach and rejection of Cartesian dualistic reality (clear distinction between the thinking subject and the world of objects) means that all reality is affected and altered by the interpreter. Heidegger's being in the World (Dasein) points to the basic experience of being in the process of making and doing, where the person who is engaged in the process doesn't perceive a divide between subject and object [2].

According to Coyne, Heidegger would view VR as a literal enactment of Cartesian ontology, as VR seems to isolate the subject within a field of sensations and claim that everything is there, presented to the person in a cocoon. Also, the idea of constructing a reality through data and algorithms would hypothetically be argued strongly. Things are not a collection of properties.

A designer with a phenomenological approach who is designing an immersive virtual environment would not see the virtual world they are building as the sum of the parts; as a collection of assets and scripts. An intrinsic design education would guide them into building obscure connections, a system, within a context. The context would guide the connections, as well as the parts. Such an approach is very similar to what is called human-centered design.

2.2 A Brief History of VR

If VR is the illusion of another reality, then it has been around since humans learned how to tell stories through words and images such as cave paintings. The medium and the technology may change, but the main goal is the same.

Perhaps the most significant feature of VR, the stereoscopic imagery, has been around since before the invention of photography. According to sales records, the first hand-held stereoscopic devices were quite popular as they sold over half a million products by 1856 [3]. Self-assembled cardboard stereoscopes from 1860 with analogously moving images are basically the same concept as Google Cardboard VR [1].

In addition to this, records also state an immersive room screening experience from 1895 called "The Haunted Swing". The horror theme may bring to mind the first wave of countless VR experiences made for phone-based VR in 2016.

In 1928, the first known flight simulator was developed by Edward Link. This device was first sold to amusement parks instead of the military.

As technology evolved, science fiction writers started to write about what we call VR today. Science fiction is still an inspiration for VR developers and an interest for popular culture, from 1935s Pygmalion Spectacles to 2011s Ready Player One.

In 1960, Morton Heilig patented the Stereoscopic Television Apparatus. This would become the Sensorama with stereoscopic color and a wide field of view, stereo sounds, seat tilting, vibrations, smell, and wind [4]. This device had a fixed world view. the first actual head tracking HMD would be built in 1961.

Advanced flight simulators for the Air Force were developed with very specific purposes. These simulators would only work for specific scenarios.

In 1965, Ivan Sutherland wrote an article exampling some of the newest technologies of the day and some novel ideas of non-existing technologies such as various input and output devices [16]. The idea is to connect the body and its many senses to the computer. With today's language, he proposes gaze tracking, full body tracking, controllers with 6 degrees of freedom, mixed reality with occlusion, all part of a system he calls "The Ultimate Display" [16]. Along with his prototype "Sword of

Damocles" built 3 years later, this 3-page long essay affected the world to give birth to what we call virtual reality [17].

In 1985, Scott Fisher and other NASA researchers developed the first commercially viable, stereoscopic head-tracked HMD with a wide field of view, called the Virtual Visual Environment Display [1]. 1990s saw an explosion in commercial interest for VR, as well as a booming interest in popular culture. However, this interest eventually died out in the commercial market, while research continued. This changed with the launch of the Kickstarter campaign of Oculus VR, when a new era for VR started.

The leading hardware and software that qualifies as VR has changed significantly throughout the centuries. However stereoscopic headgear or glasses that track the head movement, the ability to change perspective in three-dimensional space and computer-generated imagery are key features of VR.

2.3 Being "There"

Humans perceive realities, physical or virtual, through their bodies. Our sense of being in the world is primal and fundamental. It is difficult to analyze its components. However, developing and using hardware and software to accommodate our body into the built (virtual) reality can be analyzed with two main components; immersion and interaction.

Mel Slater defines immersion as an objective description of the technology, which can be compared with degrees [5]. The degree of immersion is increased with by adding sensory modalities (visual, tactile, auditory, kinesthetic). A non-immersive or less-immersive system can be fully simulated with an immersive or more-immersive system [6]. Immersive technology may lead to, and is necessary for presence; a psychological property of immersive systems and a state of consciousness known as the sense of being there [7].

The subjective experience of immersion is known as presence. Presence is limited by immersion that the experience is offering. In this psychological and physiological state, the participant's attention is not directed at the technology, but it is directed at the content, the objects, the events, the characters [1]. Presence can be examined in three core concepts: place illusion, plausibility illusion and body ownership illusion.

Place illusion is the strong illusion of being in a place, while knowing for a fact that the person is not there. Place illusion can occur with non-immersive virtual reality (for example computer games) to an extent as well. But this happens through the player's or user's engagement in "additional mental recreation" [6].

Plausibility illusion is the illusion of believing in the things that are happening, even though the person knows that it is not happening. Actions and interactions in the virtual environment help make or break this illusion. Actions and interactions outside of the virtual environment may also break the illusion. For example, talking to a person outside the virtual world would break the illusion, while place illusion may still be intact [6].

Body ownership illusion occurs by looking at yourself in VR and seeing a virtual body. If the body is tracked fully or partially, movements of the person and the movement of the virtual body align. Proprioceptive signals that provide information about the position and movement of the body or body parts become overlaid with consistent sensory data coming from the virtual body. Interaction techniques that are unnatural or artificial may reduce presence, while natural and intuitive interaction may increase the sense of being there. This paradigm is called Body Centered Interaction [7].

VR may be the ultimate "empathy machine", a term first used by film critic Robert Ebert about cinema, and later by Chris Milk about VR. But empathy isn't a fixed quality. And results of studies on empathy and VR often show interesting results, such as an increase in racial stereotypes in one study and a decrease in another [8].

3 Participation in Urban Design

There was a simpler time, when the division and specification of professions were not so clear, when people simply lived and built. However, the development of complex systems such as cities has always demanded a division of roles. Therefore, in traditional practice, the architect worked for an individual or a small group such as the government, the Church or a company [9]. This was a time with shared values between the architect and the client.

This division of roles evolved into highly specialized and classified professions after embracing the Cartesian theory. The architectural profession became exclusive and separate from the society, similar to many other professions. With this ideology, roles became more defined with explicit protocol creating a division between specifically educated professional and uneducated layperson [10]. Ideals of the architect as a professional were reflected onto the city's form. Thus, the architect and the city builder lost touch with their client.

In the 60s, community participation and citizen involvement were widely discussed issues. Though, many participatory urban design cases were criticized as pseudo participation as there was no real redistribution of power.

At any level of participation, pseudo or genuine, designers must take the current division of specifically educated professional and uneducated layperson into account. In common participation practices, laypeople are presented with plans, sections and perspectives. However, they cannot be expected to understand and visualize 3D space from 2D plans and sections. Even with perspective renders, human scale and human experience is hard to mentally construct without moving around in 3D space at human scale.

Today, Immersive Virtual Environment is speculated to facilitate an instrument that enables laypeople to actively take part as designers in the early stage of urban design process [11].

3.1 Participatory Urban Design Process

An architect draws with pen, paper or digitally through a computer. Need, purpose and aesthetics structure the concept. Then, the design is realized using material and construction techniques. The architect is supposed to think about the material and the construction method while designing on paper. If they do not, the design is more similar to sculpture than architecture. Perhaps more importantly and practice-deficiently, the architect should intrinsically imagine bodies moving through the would-be-built environment. Today, this last part is necessary for a human-centered design process.

Urban designers and planners may be more familiar with the human-centered design approach than architects. Surveys, charettes, focus group interviews are often used to gather information about the human need in the environment. Moughtin states that man is central to the study of urban design, his values, aspirations and power or ability to achieve them [9]. This statement may feel similar to Don Norman's ideals of human-centered design.

The participatory urban design process should be well planned. This is a design in itself. An existing framework, such as the Social Impact Design Toolkit from Kentsel Strateji [12] may be used to design the process. If VR is going to be used in the process, it should comply within such a framework.

4 Using VR to Build Better Cities

So, can we use VR to build better cities? VR allows policy makers and local communities, as well as urban planners, designers and further stakeholder groups, to experience and better understand the changes in the environment under planning before the development takes place, thus enables information sharing and consensus building throughout the planning process [13]. By using VR in urban design, participation in the early phases of project development is possible, which may result in a high level of participation that may result in the redistribution of power.

4.1 Design Considerations for VR in Urban Participation

There are many design considerations for the use of VR in participatory urban design. The architect draws on paper while imagining the realization, with a clear division from the building stage. However, a software or interactive experience designer's actions are directly guided by the medium (the platform, the technology). The line between design and realization is blurred in interaction design. Even a primary prototype is formed through the medium.

VR experiences differ greatly with different hardware and software. There are tethered and untethered devices; mobile and PC-based devices. Content wise, there are interactive and static content, realistic and stylized art styles, photogrammetry or modelling techniques. Even modelling techniques differ greatly, organic assets are keener to be digitally sculpted while hard surfaces can be polygon based. When modelling a city, the designer should perhaps consider parametric or generative design techniques.

Place illusion is strongly linked to environment design. And today it is relatively easy to achieve place illusion by transferring 3D data onto game engines using templates or virtual reality frameworks.

Allowing interaction such as a conversation between the person in IVR and the person in VR (flat screen) may be beneficial for the design process but it interrupts some modalities of the place illusion, such as auditory place illusion.

When using technology-based design instruments, the technological skills required to operate the instrument should not prohibit the participant from participating. Required skill should be easy to learn on the spot. A human centered design approach with natural and intuitive body-based interactions would be useful.

The level of agency, interactivity should be limited in this regard. Some interactions may be optional. More agency may result in less accessibility. Citizens who wish to have a high level of participation and skills to use the instrument should be able to co-design while other participants should be allowed to have a low level of participation, perhaps with no agency except free movement in the virtual environment.

Accessibility mods are useful to develop. Highly realistic environments may be difficult for color blind citizens. In locomotion (movement in VR) design, interaction designer must consider that standing might not be an option for every citizen.

Some special cases such as an urban space that is free to navigate in physical reality with no current construction going on could be more fit for AR than VR.

Basic game design principles such as level design, lighting design, sound design may be useful to analyze.

Embodiment in VR may be a very useful feature in participatory urban design projects, as it allows the participant to experience the space with another body/bodies. Using full or partial body tracking, the participant possesses a body that may be the opposite gender, another skin color or altered scale to mimic a child. Disabilities may be mimicked for example with a chair or cane. Moving through the urban design with "another body" would be very impactful and would raise concerns that may otherwise be unnoticed. The impact of embodiment to empathy should be explored in order to build better cities.

4.2 Examples of VR in Participatory Urban Design

Augmented Urbans is a cross-border collaboration platform for Central Baltic cities that co-develops integrated urban planning practices through Extended Reality

Fig. 1 Helsinki, Bruno Granholm Square [14]

(VR, AR, MR) Technologies [14]. In 2019, Augmented Urbans presented stakeholders a VR experience to show them 3 versions of Bruno Granholm Square in Helsinki (Fig. 1). The software allowed some interactivity. Users were guided by a real guide on one-on-one. Traditional plans and sections were present, however they were not used very actively.

The second example is from a case study in a public park in the Hague. Here paper, computer, mobile VR and immersive VR were compared (Fig. 2). Results show that immersive VR results in more vivid memory of the viewed content than computer monitors, which may be important in terms of making informed decisions. Also it is stated that the effect of human interaction should not be neglected in decision-making processes when harnessing engaging technologies [15].

The last example is different in its technology as it is from 2007 (Fig. 3). Because of a new tramvay rail, several designs of a public square in Nice were presented to the public. A 3D display with spatialized 3D sound, photographic capture of existing buildings, high-detail vegetation, and perspective shadow maps, as well rendered crowd simulation were used.

The results of the study point to similar conclusions. Even though the technology has changed, and will change, the use of natural interaction and different viewpoints at human scale are very important.

Fig. 2 The Hague, Public Park [15]

Fig. 3 Nice, place Garibaldi [18]

5 Conclusion

To conclude, further studies involving a case study with a preferably real participatory urban design process to be implemented on urban space. An experiment on the success of the study should be conducted with real citizens. A collaboration between local administration, project developers, NGOs, CBOs (community-based organizations), experts such as urban designers, planners and architects and the research team is necessary. It would require funding to develop this concept into an implementable case study. Virtual reality laboratories are necessary conduct such a research process.

Using a well-designed VR experience with multi-sensory modalities and human centered interaction design approach in a participatory urban design project would increase interest in the proposed design and encourage the participant to think about and comment on the proposed design. If the participation process has a high participation level that allows the design to be changed by the participant; intuitive, natural body centered interaction is necessary. Full or partial virtual body not only increases the level of presence but also might provide interesting design opportunities for empathy in the community and shape the design in a way that practices universal design principles.

References

1. Jerald J (2015) The VR book: human-centered design for virtual reality. Association for Computing Machinery and Morgan and Claypool
2. Coyne R (1994) Heidegger and virtual reality: the implications of Heidegger's thinking for computer representations. Leonardo, pp 65–73
3. Brewster SD (1856) The stereoscope: its history, theory, and construction, with its application to the fine and useful arts and to education. John Murray, London
4. Heilig ML (1992) El cine del futuro: the cinema of the future. Presence Teleoper Virtual Environ 279–294
5. Slater M, Wilbur S (1997) A framework for immersive virtual environments (FIVE): speculations on the role of presence in virtual environments. Presence-Teleoper Virtual Environ 603–616
6. Slater M (2009) Place illusion and plausibility can lead to realistic behaviour in immersive virtual environments. Philos Trans Royal Soc B Biol Sci
7. Slater M, Usoh M (1994) Body centred interaction in immersive virtual environments. Artificial life and virtual reality. Wiley, pp 125–148
8. Bailenson J (2018) What virtual reality is, how it works, and what it can do. W. W. Norton & Company
9. Moughtin C (2003) Urban design: street and square. Architectural Press
10. Davis H (2006) The culture of building. Oxford University Press, New York
11. Chowdhury S, Schnabel MA (2019) Laypeople's collaborative immersive virtual reality design discourse in neighborhood design. Front Robot AI
12. Kentsel Strateji (2015) Social impact design toolkit. Kentsel Strateji
13. Wolf M, Söbke H, Wehking F (2020) Mixed reality media-enabled public participation in urban planning. In: Jung T, Tom Dieck MC, Rauschnabel PA Augmented reality and virtual reality: changing realities in a dynamic world. Springer, pp 125–138
14. Augmented Urbans About (2020) www.augmentedurbans.eu/about/. Last accessed 2020/03/05

15. Leeuwen JP, Hermans K, Jylhä A, Quanjer AJ, Nijman H (2018) Effectiveness of virtual reality in participatory urban planning: a case study. In: MAB18: proceedings of the 4th media architecture biennale conference. New York, Association for Computing Machinery, pp 128–136
16. Sutherland IE (1965) The ultimate display. In: Proceedings of the IFIP congress. New York, pp 506–508
17. Sutherland IE (1968) Head-mounted three-dimensional display. Association for Computing Machinery. New York, pp 757–764
18. Drettakis G, Roussou M, Martinez AR, Tsingos N (2007) Design and evaluation of a real-world virtual environment for architecture and urban planning. Presence Teleoper Virtual Environ 318–332

Virtual Reality Application for Relieving the Pain of Child Dental Patients

Fatma Betül Güreş and Gökhan İnce

Abstract In this paper we develop an application that eases the anxiety of the child dentistry patients by taking them into a virtual environment. This virtual environment is a friendly and calming place, thus making it possible to minimize the pain and hard-ship caused by the dental procedures. The main aim of this study is to improve the user experience and usability elements of previous research with the use of a new technology (virtual reality). The main restriction of the application is the fact that the user has to stay still in the dental unit, since the child patient is not allowed to give a verbal input or use a controller during a treatment procedure. It can be dangerous for the child to move his/her head during treatment, therefore novel techniques are adapted to overcome these issues and create a user-friendly application. The movement restriction makes it possible to work with a three degrees of freedom VR headset, which is the most affordable type and can be easily purchased by dentists. One crucial part of this study is the animation in the beginning of the application intended to calm down the children as much as possible. Friendly characters with realistic and appropriate movements will be created and 3D modeled. A fun and playful scenario with an educational dialog is designed. Finally, the effectiveness of the proposed approach is shown so that in future practical virtual experience applications will be adopted by many dentists to make their jobs easier with the patients.

Keywords Virtual reality · Child patients · Dentistry · Serious games

---

F. B. Güreş
Game and Interaction Technologies, Istanbul Technical University, Istanbul, Turkey
e-mail: gures19@itu.edu.tr

G. İnce (✉)
Computer Engineering, Istanbul Technical University, Istanbul, Turkey
e-mail: gokhan.ince@itu.edu.tr

© The Author(s), under exclusive license to Springer Nature Switzerland AG 2021
Ö. Cordan et al. (eds.), *Game + Design Education*, Springer Series in Design and Innovation 13, https://doi.org/10.1007/978-3-030-65060-5_17

1 Introduction

Dentophobia (odontophobia), or fear of dental treatment, is a common phobia among people of all ages, especially children One of the primary demands of dentists is to provide high quality dental treatment services to their patients in a stress free environment. It has been shown that dental anxiety before or during treatment is not only related to behavioral problems, but also increases the perception of pain, and as a result, nervous, anxious children feel reluctant to go to future treatment appointments in the literature.

The aim of this study is to reduce dental anxiety in children by using virtual reality glasses (VRG) with a special content and innovative interaction methods, to determine the level of stress experienced by patients during dental treatment and to prevent the workload of dentists.

Virtual reality (VR) technology is a simulated experience which tries to mimic real world beyond the flat monitor to give an immersive 3D (Three Dimension) visual experiences. Although they are regarded as expensive devices, a simple smart phone and a cardboard headset is enough for experiencing this technology. The aim of this project is creating an accessible application that all dentists could easily download, therefore the app is built on a smartphone and tested with the cardboard headset, also referred as mobile VR Headset.

Within the scope of the project, the patients who will be examined by the dentist will be in a controlled manner from the practice environment by attaching a VRG and headphones throughout the treatment. With the help of VRG, it will be ensured that the patient is prepared for treatment and the devices and equipment to be used will be explained visually. During the treatment, the patient's focus will be on various contents within the spectacle. These contents will include visual (video surveillance) and auditory (music listening) stimuli, and will provide information about treatment to the patient with the help of avatars (characters) and environmental elements to be placed within the VRG application. In addition, dental anxiety will be reduced by the fun content within the VRG and the goal is to increase the rate of dental treatment success in the child patient.

The effectiveness of these systems will be compared by testing three different groups of children, in the first group in which the dentist carries out the treatment alone, in the second group the cartoons are mounted on a screen mounted dental unit and the third group is VRG. In the course of these experiments, the effects of VRG on dental treatment (vital pulpotomy and dental filling) that requires local anesthesia will be examined in order to measure the effects of VRG on the level of stress on dental treatment. As a result of the study, it is thought that the distraction method applied by VRG will be beneficial for the children, especially during local anesthesia, by reducing their stress levels and the child will tolerate treatment more easily than other conditions. With the VRG content to be programmed, positive behaviors will be developed in children by creating a comfortable environment, as well as the use of dentists as a first tool in the field to enable them to perform their treatments in a more successful and comfortable way.

2 Literature Research

In recent years, researchers have been searching for new ways for overcoming this condition with the help of technology. Significant progress has been made in the management of pain and anxiety associated with dental treatment. Various pharmacological (eg general anesthesia) and non-pharmacological (distraction) strategies have been proposed to help pediatric patients adapt to dental stress factors [1].

Distraction is the psychological method of manipulating the child's attention towards something else, making him/her forget about the situation which is considered a threat. Visual or auditory stimulations can be used to alter behaviors in children with low and moderate anxiety during dental treatment [2]. In the children's departments of the hospitals, in the clinics specialized for children, iPad technology and MP3 players connected to the headset have tried to draw the child's attention away from painful stimuli [3].

In some studies, in the field of medicine, there are data indicating that watching cartoons reduces pain and anxiety [4]. Watching movies on television screens in dental clinics is basically a distraction method, but the use of audiovisual glasses in dental treatments proved to be more effective especially in children [5]. For this purpose, a study was conducted to test the effects of audiovisual distraction on children's behavior during dental treatment. Fifty-six child patents were divided into two groups: a control group without distraction and a distraction group who had access to audiovisual content during the procedures. The conclusion of this study was that AV distraction proved itself an effective method in reducing fear and anxiety.

In studies conducted in the medical field, it has been reported that pain sensation can be reduced with virtual reality in interventions such as chemotherapy, physical therapy, care of burn wounds and surgery [6]. In dentistry, it has been reported that adult patients treated under virtual reality in the removal of the dental plaque have less pain compared to patients who watch movies or do not apply any distraction method [7].

In a similar study, researchers have compared different methods of pain management instead of the mainstream method done with anesthesia. Thirty-eight patients were divided into three groups who had different distraction conditions: virtual reality, watching a movie and the third group had no distraction at all. Virtual reality has proven itself to be the best way for distracting the patients, followed by watching a movie. The no distraction method was the least preferred one. The result has shown that immersive VR distraction may be an effective method of pain control [8].

Therefore, the studies have shown that distraction methods are a good mean to reduce both the fear of dental treatment and the pain of the procedures. From these researches came the idea of creating a VR application, designed specifically for children which would minimize the pain and hard-ship caused by the dental procedures.

3 Design and Implementation

3.1 Analysis

After a solid research process on the relationship between anxiety and dental procedures, some main anxiety reducing techniques have emerged. During the development process of this application, the main purpose was the implementation of these techniques in the best possible manner. The following main questions have guided the design process.

Q1: Which type of VR headset is targeted?
Q2: What kind of an environment is displayed in the application?
Q3: How can user interaction be achieved in the restricted conditions?
Q4: How can the animations be improved?

3.2 Modeling

In this section, the answers to the questions listed above were explained thoroughly.

A1: Mobile Headsets, which combine a smartphone with a mount are the most accessible and affordable type of VR device, that allows the standalone phone to also serve as a tethered headset. Therefore, the application was designed and built on an android device so that it could reach as many users as possible. The hardware that the dentists have to invest in can be any android smart phone (at least Android 5.0) and a compatible mount display.

A2: As the child is in a dentist environment, the first approach is to explain the procedures to be performed. After the educational introduction part, the child is allowed to choose a movie and watch it. For making the user feel in a different environment, the app opens another scene where the movies are projected in a movie theatre environment. The movies that are displayed on the application were suggested by the dentists from Istanbul University Pediatric Dentistry Department.

A3: As explained in A1, this project is targeting mobile headsets to achieve the virtual reality technology. In this case there is no controller device. Additionally, due to the posture restrictions of the dental patient, only subtle gestures can be done. These two restrictions have determined the interactivity of the project. Gaze selection is an input method that makes use of the user's gaze direction. The application was designed so that when the user was expected to make a selection, he/she used his head orientation to look at the option he wanted to choose and keep the camera positioned at that point to verify to selection.

A4: The introductory part of the application is where the designed and rigged character is communicating with the patients in the hopes of calming them. A child model was chosen for the users to feel connected. This child-dentist character is wearing adequate clothes and has a friendly smile. Before the explanatory speech, the character is performing a small dace to a song about brushing teeth, for being appealing to the children. While the dance is a generic movement taken from an online source (Mixamo), the gestures in the introductory speech are captured with Perception Neuron. At the moment, all the basic animations are accomplished. For further polishing, the future studies aim implementing the 12 principles of animation designed by Disney.

3.3 Hardware and Software

Unity. Unity is the world's most popular development platform (game engine) for creating 2D and 3D multiplatform games and interactive experiences. Unity is highly compatible with most of the platforms (PCs, gaming consoles, web browsers, mobile devices, VR headsets) therefore, developers frequently prefer this game engine [9].

In the case of this application, Unity is an adequate choice, as the in-built features allow virtual reality integration for Android application, without any other extra coding. Any application that is developed in Unity can be turned into a virtual reality application by changing the built environment and player settings.

Perception Neuron. During the alpha release development process, Perception Neuron motion capture device was used for recording the initial animations. As the name suggests, it captures the movements of the user and turns them into rigged humanoid animations. This technology is common in the film and game industries and is the fastest way to create digital characters from actual actors. There are two types of motion capture devices: optical and non-optical.

Although optical motion capture technology is more professional and is offering smoother results, they require a setting and extra equipment for optical monitoring (cameras, special clothing etc.).

For this project non-optical motion capture was used. This technology is more practical and does not require extra devices. The disadvantage is that it is more prone to creating errors, which require to be corrected in other software programs.

Autodesk Maya. Autodesk Maya is a 3D design software that is mainly used for creating animations. In this project, only its animation tools were utilized (mainly its graph editor) for correcting the errors that arouse from Perception Neuron, as explained above.

Autodesk 3ds Max. Autodesk 3ds Max, formerly 3D Studio and 3D Studio Max, is a professional 3D computer graphics program for making 3D animations, models, games and images. It is developed and produced by Autodesk Media and Entertainment.

This program was used for the 3D modelling of the dentist environment. Additionally, it was also used for the character rigging. Afterwards, both models are exported in fbx format and imported in Unity.

Accelerometer. Accelerometers are devices that can measure acceleration (the rate of change in velocity), but in smartphones, they're able to detect changes in orientation and tell the screen to rotate. Basically, it helps the phone differentiate up from down.

For the use of Virtual Reality obtained from smart phone and cardboard VR headset combination, this in built hardware device is one of the most important features buried in the everyday smartphone experience This is how the app tracks the head movement of the user.

3.4 Visual Design

Scene Design. While developing the beta release, the design process began with an architectural research on creating child-oriented interior design. A mood board is a type of visual presentation or a collage consisting of images, text, and samples of objects in a composition After analyzing real world case studies, an arrangement of images—known as mood board—that displayed the pediatric dental clinic was created. Figure 1 was realized in Adobe Photoshop, which is a software used worldwide for design, photography, video editing and more.

After the concept was decided, the 3D modeling process began. The interior design of the dentist was modeled from scratch, with the only imported model being the dentist chair (imported from Sketch-up 3D Warehouse). For this part of the project 3ds Max was used. Among other uses, this program serves not only modeling but also rendering. By using the V-ray plugin for 3ds Max, assigning materials, lighting and camera, the scene was rendered. Figure 2 shows the rendered image, with a slight touch of the previously mentioned image editing software Photoshop.

Character Design. The last step before importing all assets into Unity was the character design and rigging process in 3ds Max. Skeletal animation or rigging is a technique in computer animation in which a character (or other articulated object) is represented in two parts: a surface representation used to draw the character (called the mesh or skin) and a hierarchical set of interconnected parts (called bones, and collectively forming the skeleton or rig), a virtual armature used to animate (pose and keyframe) the mesh. The process can be divided into three steps: creating the skeleton, skinning the character and building animation controls. Animation controls are external geometries that change the posture of the character when moved or rotated as shown in Fig. 3.

After importing the previously described models as fbx files into Unity (Fig. 4), the building process of the application began. This game engine was used because Unity provides an easy application development process and it provides a native support for Android and virtual reality applications. Unity prevents unnecessary setup time for initial development stages, so the application development started with a project and build up from there step by step until the release.

Gaze Selection. Gaze Selection technology in a head-mounted display has undergone rapid advancement in recent years but frequently, virtual reality systems involve controllers that provide the necessary user input for the applications. Such input from a controller is not practical to the purpose of this project because of three main reasons:

Virtual Reality Application for Relieving the Pain ... 211

Fig. 1 Mood board for concept design of the scene

Fig. 2 Rendering of the 3D model of the scene

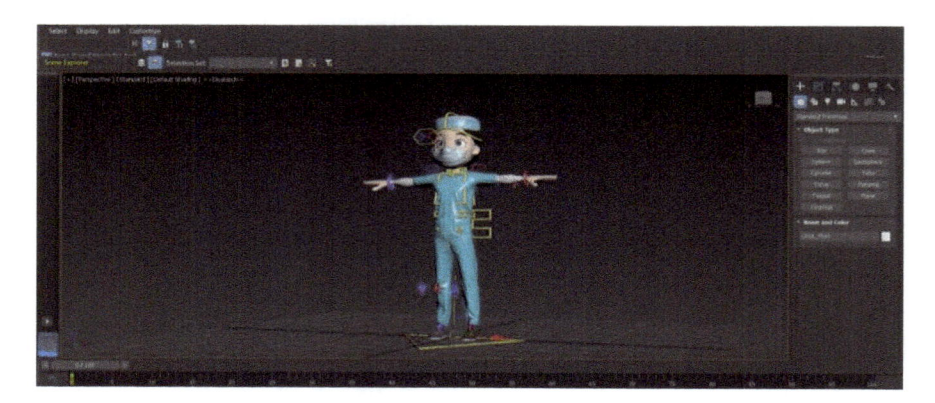

Fig. 3 Character creation and rigging

- in a dental procedure, the patient can not be expected to handle a controller
- as the target audience involves child patients, the interactions must be as simple and intuitive as possible
- an additional controller brings unnecessary cost of hardware to the project

The only way to achieve interactivity without a controller, is to use Gaze Selection.

In Unity, the user view is defined as a camera that the user sees the virtual world from. Locating the exact position at which the user's view is centered, this point can be used as an input. This kind of control can be achieved with Unity's raycasting and collider systems. Raycasting can be imagined as a point with a specific direction that is shooting an invisible ray. Colliding this ray with an object for a certain period

Virtual Reality Application for Relieving the Pain ... 213

Fig. 4 Game scene

of time determines the user input. Unity measures the direction of the ray in each frame and in case of collision with the desired object for a certain period the object becomes red. The origin of the ray is the location of the camera, and the direction of the ray is the camera's orientation, which is bound to the head orientation of the user. Thus a ray is cast in the direction the user looks at the time. When the user is required to make a selection, the appropriate choices are displayed as 3D models in the virtual environment to make them accessible for gaze selection interaction. Adding rigidbody and collider components to the selectable objects makes gaze selection method possible.

Movie Selection. For this application, the gaze selection was implemented mainly because the user was to select a film of his/her choice. After the gaze selection code had been implemented, adapting it to the selection of films was an easy task. The movie tiles displaying the posters of the available films are put close to each other, in the user's center of view, to minimize the required head movement. Once the user looks consistently at one of the film tiles, the film is picked with gaze selection (Fig. 5). The application opens another scene a movie theatre- and on the white screen, the selected video is shown. The change in the environment is hoping to make the child patient forget about the real place and treatment by creating an illusion of a cinema.

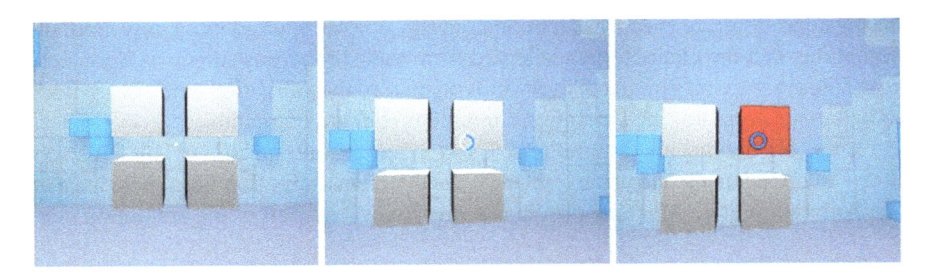

Fig. 5 Gaze selection

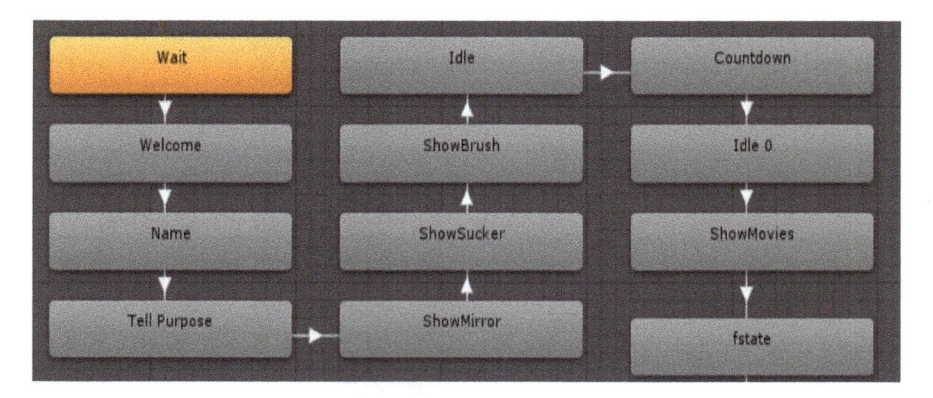

Fig. 6 Animation state machine in unity

Head Tracking. Vr technology requires head tracking, in order to process the simulated space. The user's view must be changed in tune with the head rotation; therefore, head orientation measurement is required. This is done by an internal sensor in virtual reality headsets, which in the case of this project refers to the mobile phone. Smartphones and other mobile technology identify their orientation through the use of an accelerator, a small device made up of axis-based motion sensing. It is the accelerator that enables the head tracking.

Animations. After the creation and rigging process of the character explained in Sect. 3.4, the humanoid model is ready for being animated. For this process, mainly two steps are necessary:

First, creating and finding humanoid animations that move a rigged character and second, assigning the animation to the desired character by suing Unity's in-built Animator. For the first step, animations were captured via motion capture as the default animations found on external sources did not cover the scope of this project. So new animations have been created with Perception Neuron motion capture device. The device itself consists of numerous sensors fixed to a wearable suit. The suit makes it possible for the sensors to record the movements of the body parts.

For the second part, in order to make the assigning procedure possible, the animation file and targeted character must be of the same type. The animations recorded are not for a particular character but for a generic human rig. The character model has the bone structure specific of a humanoid rig. When imported into Unity, both the animations and the character are selected from their properties screen as humanoid rigs. This allows Unity to match every moving part of the animation to the character's body parts. Therefore, the animations and the model are compatible.

Lastly, for playing the animations, Unity offers a state machine [10]. This tool allows the structuring and arrangement of the different animation files, called states. The Animation State Machine provides a way to overview all of the animation clips related to a particular character and allows various events to trigger different animations and switching the animation files between them. Figure 6 demonstrates the linearly evolving state machine that was designed for this project.

4 Conclusion

In conclusion, this project's main goal is to create a virtual reality application that will soothe the pain experienced by child patients during dental procedures by offering a virtual environment. The realizations so far can be summed up as follows. The ambiance of the child is turned to a place of happiness, designed carefully for this purpose. The explanatory introduction part takes place in a vivid dentist room while the movies are watched in a movie theatre for detaching the user from the actual place and context. The virtual environment has been enhanced by specially created animations. The application was designed to function in such a way that outside intervention is not required. The application will interact with the user from start to finish via gaze selection and head tracking mechanism.

For further development, the animations can be polished according to Disney's twelve principles of animation. In addition, the scope of the study can be enlarged such that the use of this program will not be restricted to dentists. New usage areas can be explored starting from other medical fields. For example, a child who is scared of vaccines may use another extended version of the application to overcome the fear and get easily vaccinated. This form of usage areas can be expanded after consultation with doctors from various medical fields. The use of the virtual reality in fields like dentistry is still experimental but with the help of the researchers, experts, scientists and industry leaders compelling advancements can be seen in this field.

Acknowledgements The research reported in this paper was supported by The Scientific and Technological Research Council of Turkey (TUBITAK) under the grant 119S618. We are thankful to İlkan Engin, Elif Benli, Ahmet Karagöz, Yelda Kasımoğlu and Elif Bahar Tuna İnce for their guidance and helpful comments.

References

1. Schienle A, Kochel A, Leutgeb V (2011) Frontal late positivity in dental phobia: a study on gender differences. Biol Psychol 88(2):263–269
2. Armeld J, Heaton L (2013) Management of fear and anxiety in the dental clinic: a review. Aust Dent J 58(4):390–407
3. Scharmuller W, Ubel S, Leutgeb V, Schoengassner F, Wabnegger A, Schienle A (2014) Do not think about pain: neural correlates of attention guiding during visual symptom provocation in dental phobia, a forestudy. Brain Res 1566:69–76
4. Yasemin M, Kasimoglu Y, Kocaaydin S, Karsli E, Ince EBT, Ince G (2016) Management of dental anxiety in children using robots. In: 24th Signal Processing and Communication Application Conference (SIU). IEEE

5. Ram D, Shapira J, Holan G, Magora F, Cohen S, Davidovich E (2010) Audiovisual video eyeglass distraction during dental treatment in children. Quintess Int 41(8):673–679
6. Mazuryk T, Gervautz M (1996) Virtual reality-history, applications, technology and future
7. Upload VR Homepage. https://uploadvr.com/wp-content/uploads/2015/02/intro1.png. Last accessed 2020/08/27
8. Google VR Homepage. https://developers.google.com/vr/develop/unity/get-started-android. Last accessed 2020/08/27
9. Unity Homepage. https://unity3d.com/unity. Last accessed 2020/08/27
10. Unity manual: state machine transitions. https://docs.unity3d.com/Manual/StateMachineTransitions.html. Last accessed 2020/08/27

Audio Centered Game Development in Mobile VR

Ece Naz Sefercioğlu and Hatice Köse

Abstract Audio is one of the essential elements of game design. Even in virtual reality applications, visuals have been thought to have more importance to create impressiveness. However, using its stereo or surround capabilities, it is possible to improve the effectiveness of the game, on the players. Also, creating an audio rich game increases its accessibility to a variety of people. This study involves a game setup with 3D audio used in virtual reality (VR), design of audio games, and Google Cardboard development. Using this game setup, a highly audio dependent mobile virtual reality game is developed and tested by 10 users. The performance of the users and feedback from the qualitative and quantitative comments were analyzed and reported. The main aim of this work is to show that audio can be a powerful game element, based on an explemantary work involving a game developed with audio experience on its focus.

Keywords Audio game · 3D audio · Mobile virtual reality

1 Introduction

Audio is an undervalued medium compared to the other elements of game development. While there could be severe criticism towards the visuals of a game, criticism on audio components may be negligible to the game's success. What's more, muting a game and continuing to play is a general practice when the player does not have a way to personalize audio output or would listen to other sources while playing but muting the visuals of a game is not a common tendency. Lastly, an audio element in interactive experiences could help the navigation training of blind people as well as sound source training of semi-deaf people. Using this feature enables accessibility

E. N. Sefercioğlu (✉) · H. Köse
Istanbul Technical University, Istanbul 34469, Turkey
e-mail: sefercioglu@itu.edu.tr

H. Köse
e-mail: hatice.kose@itu.edu.tr

for a wide variety of people including people with disabilities, to enjoy the gaming experience.

The main aim of this paper is to present an audio-based mobile virtual reality game to show the effect of audio in virtual reality experiences. The background research contains many layers to present knowledge on the aspects of developing a virtual reality game based on sound. The game platform is virtual reality so the sound source carries 3d sound aspects, which leads to the research of 3d sound and its usage in virtual reality. Moreover, to bring a better experience for the players in this niche genre of audio-based games, previous works are inspected and summarized. Lastly, the development medium should be distinguished among others. The objective of this research is to create an example project that utilizes the findings by combining previous topics and providing an intuitive game design that supports the importance of audio in the experience.

2 Literature Review

2.1 3D Audio

Virtual reality cannot exist with only immersive visuals. To provide a more immersive experience one should appeal to more than one sense of experience. One of the unattained senses is hearing. To start to create an immersive sound experience the basic start point is stereo sound. The stereo sound consists of two channels for left and right for each ear. To increase immersiveness surround systems could also be considered. These systems try to provide more directions variations of the sound sources, such as front-left, rear-left. Surround and stereo sound called channel-based sound formats. These are simulated outputs of speaker replacements. For stereo, it is accepted that there is one speaker on the left and one speaker on the right of the listener. Surround accepts that there are speakers on the front in the left, center, and right positions and on the rear in the left and right positions.

It is accepted that these output formats do not always produce the best results as they do not consider the effects of the shape of the head, ears, and torso of the listener. The systems that take these into accounts called Head-related transfer functions (HRTF). These also carry some problems. One of the problems is deciding the position of the source if it is in the vertical center to both ears such as back or above directions. The human brain could decide the source by looking into the smallest details perceived by ears. To achieve this HRTFs should be individualized for each person. Another problem is sound generated from HRTFs perceived artificial. Even though this is not a huge problem with careful listening the quality could be spotted. The assumption of a static body and torso state is another thing that damages the experience. Lastly, there is the time and material cost of creating HRTFs. With dynamic HRTFs that use dynamic head orientation to determine sound output, these disfavors are aimed to be reduced. To create a dynamic system, sensors to record head orientation is needed. VR headsets play an important role to meet this need [1].

Geronazza et al. propose personalized HRTFs. A tool that maps anthropometric features of an ear from its image to HRTF functions is created. After the system decides which HRTF to use an experiment is carried with testers. In this experiment, testers are provided with 25 different directions randomly for each subject. It is carried out in a virtual environment where head motion is tracked with a VR headset. The core approach of the test was asking testers to point to the direction where they assume the sound comes from with a pointer [2].

In their work, Faria et al. target proposing a solution for audio immersion into CAVE(Cave Automatic Virtual Environment) systems. Based on the perceived attributes of sound a 6 level perception scale is proposed. Level 0 represents a simple sound signal resulting in no immersion. Level 1 provides effects such as echo to be felt there is an ambiance, space. Channeled sounds included in level 2 of the scale and provide a direction and a primitive movement. Using amplitude panning techniques a higher level of immersiveness could be reached positioning can be determined in limited areas. Level 4 and 5 are composed of using HRTFs or high-level approaches such as Ambisonics to simulate what would ear hear, 2d sound field, and 3d sound field respectively. In the paper, Ambisonics is used to simulate surround sound in a CAVE system. The challenges of installing the system can be summarized in speaker positioning, acoustic of environment, and system adaptation to the environment [3].

Wu et al. remarked on the importance of latency and head movement for sound detection in VR environments. Two experiments were carried out concerning using headphones and head tracking magnetic sensors. In the experiment on latency, subjects asked to turn to the sound source that is given randomly and click on the mouse button if they are sure of their success. If the azimuth of the head is under the threshold the sound stops otherwise it continues. This procedure is carried with latency and latency compensated sounds. One of the outcomes of this experiment was that the accuracy of pinpointing the place of sound increases if both ears have balanced signals. The final outputs show that subjects had a %50 faster sound localization results with latency compensation applied sounds. The second experiment focused on the impact of head movement in sound localization. Similar to the latency experiment, subjects were listened to sounds in space and asked to locate the sound direction by rotating and clicking a mouse while their head is free to move and not allowed to be moved. The outputs show that dynamic head movement had a mean of 9° error while the fixed head had a mean of 18°. One of the hardships of the fixed head movement was to locate the sound source that is above or rear of the object. Results show that head movement increases the ability of users to locate a sound source in the 3D environment. In light of this finding, the importance to prompt the user to move their heads in the experience and investing in a sound latency compensation strategy should be very clear to consider [4].

Doornbusch presents the importance of sound immersion in VR experience in other areas than the games. Such as surgeon simulations, in the operation, the direction of sound coming from the body could lead to different diagnoses. Moreover, in real-life scenery operators have the aid of many devices to carry out an operation with many people. To reach a better simulating training design sound should express all these factors. In a more generalized manner sound is as important for on the job training. For example, in an emergency scenario, a miner trainee should understand the direction of an explosion and estimate how destructive it was [5].

Santini exhibits a way to visualize spatialization of sound as well as create spatial sound in AR and VR environments. The difference in realities not exactly changes the experience but only changes the perceived reality. In AR, users see the real world and in VR, they interact with the sound in virtual worlds. Moreover, the AR platform provides a collaboration space for multiple users to create and sense the sounds. In the application, users can choose among provided sounds, and with the toolset put these sound around them. The sounds also could be placed to run on trajectories drawn with the controllers. The running of sound then decided with the speed of the gesture that drew the trajectory. In the visualization, the place of the sound and its trajectory is shown. When the scene played a place of sound source simulated as differently colored spheres [6].

2.2 Virtual Reality Audio Based Experiences

Lumbreras and Sanchez created a hyper story for blind children to train and test their navigation skills using 3D spatial sound. Players can navigate in the world and interact with creatures using a keyboard or a joystick. In the story, children go through a path consisting of standing and moving objects and doors that divides the path. Each object has its unique sound and sound behavior. They would emit sound in different proximities to the player and with different patterns. For example, there are monsters on the road and the children are expected to shoot at them using a keyboard. The output method was left for children's choice of speakers or headphones. The frequent choice was speakers which concluded as they want to not to be isolated by the researchers and real environment. At the end of the experiment subjects required to recreate the environment with Lego pieces. After several plays children could achieve this. After the experiment, the children stated that they felt competent and accountable in their navigation skills [7].

A similar study to improve navigational skills of blind children was carried out by Allain et al. A game that is played with a keyboard but head tracking done with Oculus headset was developed. The game provides the headset scene to be inspected through monitors and the ability to play the game with disableable visuals. Auditory skills of sound position detection, detecting a sound in the presence of many sounds, using sound detecting objects and interacting with them, adjusting orientation regarding environmental sound, and training spatial memory to remember places of sound sources are aimed to be improved. The test was run with a group of blind teenagers and visually healthy people. Teenagers stated that the game element provided a more engaging training experience and they would have liked to experience this game when they were younger as well [8].

Balan et al. proposed a different experience for training and testing navigational skills of visually impaired people not limiting subject age to children. To eliminate the rear-front confusion of determining sound direction, two noise is used. One is only applied to the noises in front of the player and the other is applied to the ones in the rear. With this pattern infusing, sound perception is aimed to be improved. Auditory icons meaning instinctively matching sounds such as footsteps and earcons which are sound that is special to application and need time to get accustomed are implemented to improve the game experience. In the game, there is a target source emitting sound constantly an obstacle emitting sound if the player is in their peripheral. When the player reaches the source a new source is created on the map. Navigation is done by mouse, with no head tracking. 3D sound is provided with the movement of the game avatar [9].

Sanchez and Saenz modeled small representation of 3 Chile cities and created hyper stories about them for training auditory skills of children. This way children are expected to have confidence in navigating outside environments while having an experience based in Chile. Interactions included moving objects, storing, sharing them moving inside the map. The application went through many iterations by having feedback from users. At the results, it was shown that children with residual vision were satisfied with the experience more than the blind children [10].

2.3 Audio Games

Friberg and Gardenfors present a guide on how to develop audio games while inspecting existing games and developing examples. The aims are creating audio games as compelling as normal games and emphasize the audio-based experience in games. 3 games were developed having an audio output in center and visuals in complementary levels. The first game consists of 5 worlds, that is fought with monsters in them. The game is aimed to be self-explanatory by having different background music for each world and giving an estimation of the state of the monsters that sounds come from them. The second game is more like a mixer, having its interfaces as spoken audio. Using a predefined sound set player can create his/her composition and save it afterward. The last game is the most complex one, which is a 3D world exploration game. It contains different themes such as desert or forest and each theme has its unique sound set. Moreover, auditory navigational aids are another important part of this game. These aids are explained in 4 ways. Enabling users for a limited time to only hear interactable objects, providing the material of the ground with footstep sounds, placing NPCs to help players, and sounds that signals where the player is in the special parts of the map. The type of sound used in games is also classified under avatar sounds, object sounds, character sounds, ornamental sounds, and instructional sounds. Letting player know that sounds other than ornamental sounds are played by the actions of the players were a big goal in the design process. Likewise, auditory icons and earcons are used in game development to increase similarity with the game environment. To give the constant information of surrounding emitting sounds from objects in brief durations in a looping manner was chosen instead of emitting sound constantly. Lastly, for the interface design, the lack of common convention was stated. The implemented approach was to have an auditory menu scene and each element is read when focused. Focus moved by gestures of the player [11].

Targett and Fernstörm transformed two classically known games to non-speech audio games using auditory icons and earcons. The aim was to determine if non-speech audio games provide a normal game feel and see if audio games could be used for talent acquisition. The first game developed is XOX with a 3×3 game mat setup. The grids are represented with earcons. Rows of the grid presented with different pitches and columns have different volume behavior(increasing, decreasing, constant). The player always put X so the computer puts O. These symbols have its earcons. The player moves around the game mat using a keyboard and listening earcon feedback. The second game is a copy of Mastermind, with three colors instead of numbers. The player places colors in order. Feedback sounds given after the player finalizes their answer. In these games, giving auditory feedback to let the player know they made a choice and start of their turn was put on big importance. In the results, it was found that keeping earcons short would provide a better experience. Moreover, designing earcons for the end of the tour, win, lose states was stated as a good fit for future research topics. Lastly, it was seen that non-speech audio games could be a benefit to areas of memory training and sound interpretation for different outputs [12].

Fizek et al. examine audio game examples from Audio Game Hub. Audio Game Hub contains audio experiences of casual games that similar for common cultural games like Tetris and activities aimed to improve skills such as navigation and memory. Hub is a research project with a framework to unite audio games under common design practices. The game menu is placed in the corners of the game scene. To activate an element double-tap gesture is required. Another way to browse the menu is to use a swipe gesture. In-game, experience includes giving different audio feedback for each user action [13].

Liljedahl et al. proposed that a rich soundscape could compensate for the fewer details on graphics and still provide a satisfactory game experience. The game is an adaptation of a part of the Scandinavian hero Beowulf defeating a monster. The design is aimed to be a mostly audio-based game with the least detailed graphics possible for sighted players. There is a wide range of audio output for different cues. Changing footsteps sound helps the player to distinguish the type of environment he/she is in with environmental sounds. A whole environment also consists of dynamic elements such as waterfalls and lava flow sound. Moreover, alive animals, bug sounds also add detail to the environment. Lastly, there are sound effects for movement and combat. Such as sword-swinging and bumping into a wall. After questionnaires, interpretations of the game environment and objects that were highly dependent on sound were very divided and sometimes different than their design purpose. This showed how the sound-based game experiences are open to interpretation with the imagination of the player [14].

Miller et al. have taken another approach to develop an audio game. Instead of changing sensory input through mediums, the sound is used directly to play the game. Finger Dance is a rhythm game that performance of the player is determined by their precise touch with the current keystroke of the note playing. Success and failure feedback given by audio plays. The goal is to catch the perfect rhythms with the notes. Performance is calculated by the players' response duration to listened sounds. Lastly, the instructions are provided to the player at the start of the game as an audio explanation. The explanation was a synthetic sound with the feed-backs pointing out it was hard to understand the sound source was improved [15].

2.4 Mobile Virtual Reality as a Development Platform

Perla and Hebbalaguppe point out the lack of academic resources on google cardboard and proposes a comprehensive review of the device. Launch date in 2014, Google Cardboard interactions went underway changes in each version. The first one uses the built-in compass of smartphones as an extra medium but the next one has a touch button that touches the screen. The more technologies evolve now even speech can be used as an input medium. On some applications, hand gestures are used through vision processing. With an example questionnaire application designed some limitations of Google Cardboard pointed out. The field of view is around 90° leaving designers a small area to work with and users to interact with. For interaction head rotation and speech recognition are used. The performance of speech recognition highly reduces in noisy environments. Moreover, Cardboard applications need high power usages leading to fast battery discharges and inconveniences. If the user device has low camera quality, vision processing would not improve the experience. Lastly, Cardboard being a new technology has a small community and support for developers. Some user based subjective limitations includes motion sickness, rendering text in 3D, and brightness of the scene content. These would harm the experience and adaptation of technology. The application was tested in an outdoor and indoor environment. After the questionnaire results inspected, not using speech input in outdoor applications is advised [16].

Moural and Oritsland conducted a review of user experience in mobile virtual reality. The areas are divided into four to determine the quality of UX. Comfort put to the main importance. It is the physical relationship between the application and the user. Which include the comfort of the headset and the safety of the surroundings while the user is in the virtual world. Moreover, to improve in-game comfort, the perimeter and the places objects put carry importance for users' visual perception. Another aspect impact UX is interpretability. The visual world cuts most of the ties of the user from the real world and with limited guidance, they are expected to interact with the virtual world. The created worlds should appeal to the instincts of the user. The important objects should emit feedback that they are important for the experience. Users should grasp how to navigate in the virtual world easily to adapt quicker. The last significant question to create a good UX for mobile VR is whether the experience is useful or satisfying to be experienced in mobile VR. There could be cases using a different medium would be more suitable for the experience. Mobile VR should not be chosen for the sake of the medium in any experience. All in all, to achieve an optimum UX these factors should be taken into consideration [17].

In their work Yoo and Parker lists the controller-less interaction methods for Google Cardboard. As of 2015, 32 applications from the Google Play Store were inspected and 5 interaction methods were listed. The magnetic sliding switch being the most popular, focused gaze, dynamic gaze, head tilt, and external controllers are used [18].

3 Methodology

In the lights of previous research, a mobile virtual reality game experience based on audio was developed. Then it was tested by a group of people. Finally, the results are interpreted for further insight into the performance of the game on conveying sound as a core game design element.

3.1 Development Tools

Unity: Unity is a multi-platform game engine enabling game developers to create 2D/3D games and port them to different platforms with ease. It is chosen as this project's core development software due to its capabilities on audio management, compatibility with mobile virtual reality software development kit (SDK), and proficiency of the developer.

Google Cardboard SDK: Google Cardboard SDK enables developers to create mobile virtual reality applications. The application runs in smartphones with Android operating system. No controllers needed to interact with the game, the phone's gyroscope is sufficient. This project utilizes its compatibility with Unity and practicality of converting a 3D game into a virtual reality game.

3ds Max: 3ds Max is a 3d modeling software. In this project, it is used to create the sphere with the inversed face which is the main game environment.

3.2 Game Setting

Player tries to tell apart and detect the places of same-looking good and bad objects solely from the sound they emit. Objects are 3d audio sources, therefore if the player not directly looking at them they could pinpoint the objects' places with stereo sound. The objects start from the bounds of a sphere towards the player. Their lifetime, if not

Audio Centered Game Development in Mobile VR   225

before destroyed by the player, ends when they collide with the player. Bad objects harm the player if it contacts with him/her. That's why they should be destroyed before the collision. On the contrary good objects beneficial to the player so destroying them before the collision is not a wise decision. In the game loop, the player should detect the bad objects and destroy them while leaving good objects to continue their life until the collision with the player.

3.3 Game Environment

The game is played in a sphere-shaped world. Where the player is at the center and objects are spawned from the borders of it. To give the player the cue of he/she turns his/her head the inside face of the sphere has a sparse noise texture. The top and the bottom of the sphere excluded from being a spawn area as having players bend his/her neck over 40° down and 60° up causes discomfort for the player [19]. The degree to limit the spherical segment is decided to include areas of 40° up and 40° of down. The half radius of the sphere is 20 units of Unity meaning the player is away from the bounds by 20 units.

3.4 Game Mechanics

Gaze Power: When the user locks his/her gaze for 3 s on a game object, he/she destroys the object he/she is looking towards. In Fig. 1 player locked her/his gaze

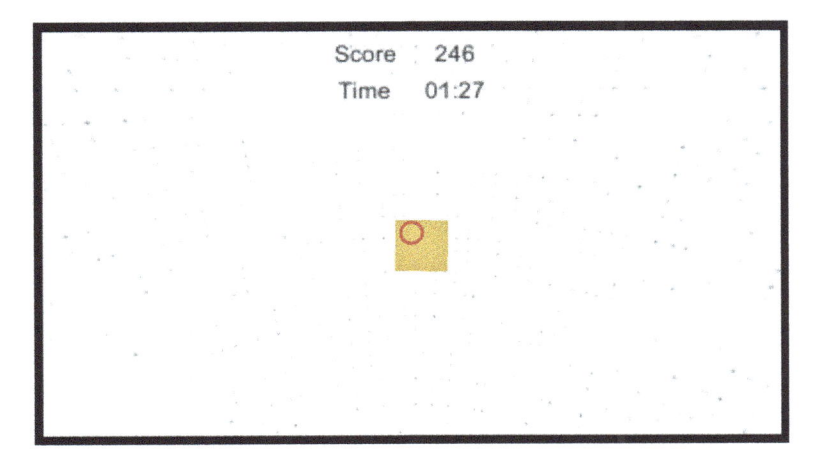

Fig. 1 Player can destroy objects by looking at them for 3 s. [Created by writers]

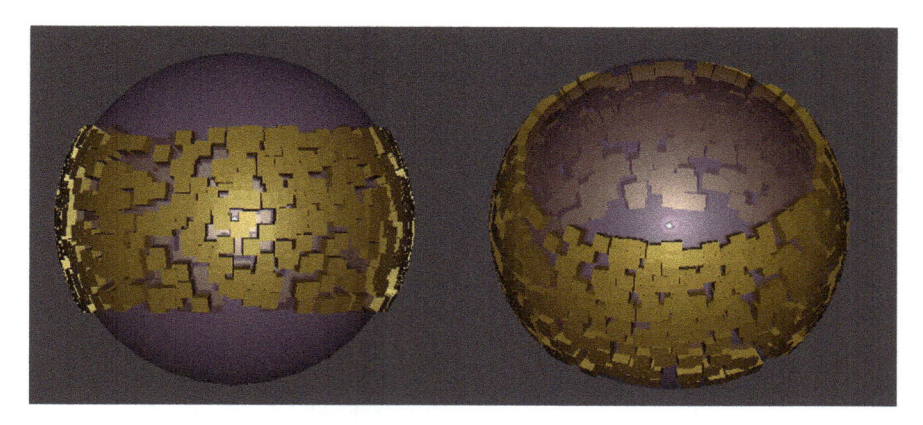

Fig. 2 3D representation of spawn area. [Created by writers]

to moving object. If another object interprets, the gaze time is reset. When the user moves his/her gaze from the object the timer resets.

Spawn Logic: The places, the duration between, and the types of the objects to be spawned are decided to be random in certain bounds. The spawn could appear from anywhere between the 40° up and 40° down of the middle section of the sphere that can be inspected in Fig. 2. The duration of the spawn interval decided to be between 1 and 6 seconds after a spawn. The weights of the randomness of object types are given equal.

3.5 Training

The game contains several sounds with different meanings. To accustom the player to the sounds an audio player training scene is created. Figure 3 shows the training panel when players enter this scene. In this panel when the player looks at a state of an object, the sound of that state plays in the loop. There is also a list of main instructions of the game listed on the right side of the panel to give a brief introduction about the game.

3.6 Audio

The game aims to provide to give audio feedback to players every-way possible as to how visuals would give feedback. That's why it includes two sound sets special to each type of the game object, the signaling audio that there is an object in gaze and audio cues for game state.

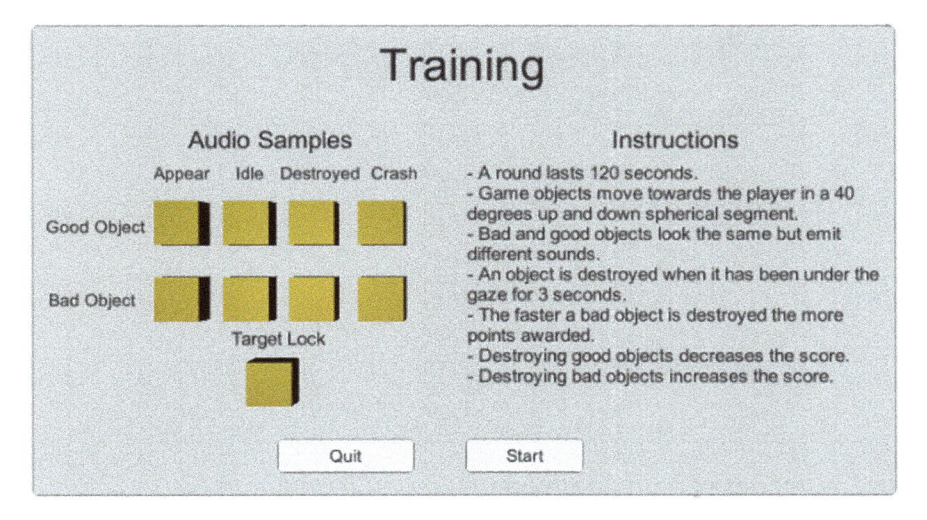

Audio Centered Game Development in Mobile VR   227

Fig. 3 Training UI consists of audio sample players and instruction text. [Created by writers]

Object Specific Audio: An object has audio clips to play when created, destroyed, crashed to the player, and moving towards to player. Each audio clip except moving clip plays once, moving clip plays in loop. When a good object is created the audio clip aims to be a soothing sound. On the contrary, the bad object's audio is decided to be a more disturbing sound. The looping movement sound of a good object has a similarity of bells while bad object's sound brings a tension creating rhythm. For both objects, the more they are close to the player the higher the audio is perceived from them. Destroying a bad object plays a victory sound whose counterpart is a sad sound for good objects. Lastly, when objects crash to player, bad object emits a harsher sound than the good object.

Target Lock Audio: When the gaze locked to an object, the lock signal is given by playing a thumping sound on the loop in the background. When the gaze is free, the sound stops.

3.7 Performance Evaluation

The game expects the player to destroy the bad objects with his/her gaze and do not engage with good objects. When a bad object is destroyed, the player gains points. On the contrary, when a good object is destroyed the player loses points. The crashing of bad objects makes the player lose points. Player gains point linear to his/her speed to destroy a bad object. The farther the object is destroyed, the more points the player gains. The player gains a constant amount of points in the crash with a game object. To keep the game-play short and simple, the game duration is limited to 120 s.

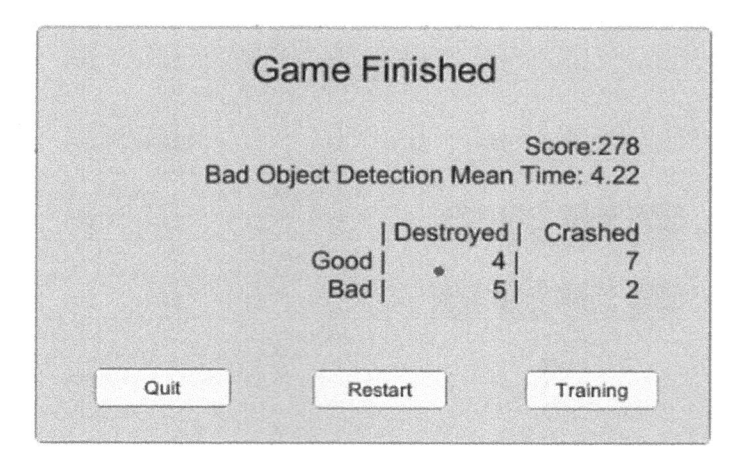

Fig. 4 A game performance report was shown to the player. [Created by writers]

Table 1 Contingency table of game actions [Created by writers]

	Bad object	Good object
Destroyed	True positive	True negative
Crashed	False positive	False negative

At the end of the game, the player is shown a performance report of a contingency table of destroys and crashes of objects. An example report output is provided in Fig. 4. In the contingency table presented in Table 1, destroying an object labeled as a positive action, as it is the main interaction of the game. If the destroyed object is bad, it is truly positive. This was an expected action to be taken. If the destroyed object is a good object, it is a false positive action. There is not a big negative effect but it reduces life sources. Since crashing is a secondary happening of the game, it is labeled as a negative action. The crash of a good object is expected and no actions needed to achieve. Therefore, crashing with a good object is true negative, and crashing with a bad object is a false positive. The report includes a mean time of detecting bad objects and scores as well.

3.8 Player Testing

The game was tested with 10 people between ages 19 and 26 using stereo headphones and an Android phone in a mobile VR headset case. It was all the testers' first time playing the game. After a brief explanation of the game and the aims of the project, players requested to listen to the training sounds and read the instructions. When players felt ready they started playtesting of a 120 s game session. Then the game reports of each play saved for future inspection and their comments on the experience were recorded.

4 Results

The MVR game was implemented in Unity game engine using Google Cardboard SDK. An iterative software development approach was taken during development. At the start, the game objects had different colors but that lead players choosing their target mostly by their color, not the audio they emit. After this observation colors were set the same to force players to distinguish game objects only by their sound. The destruction of game objects had no visual feedback, they abruptly disappeared. Visual feedback of destruction improved by adding a particle effect of an explosion. The addition of a striped game environment has arisen from the problem when the player turned his/her head they could not get any feedback of it if there were no game objects in his/her sight. After these modifications, the development of the game concluded with a playable version.

The audio in the game was chosen to satisfy the feeling/situation they are aimed to convey. Creation, approach, and collision of a good object emitted sounds that evoke nice feelings. whereas destruction of it evoked a saddening sound. On the contrary for bad objects, the sounds played on creation and approach had threatening tunes while on collision had an effect resembling a high impact crash. As destroying bad objects is the main practice to keep alive, at the destruction a victory sound plays. Lastly, the visual of the gaze has a target that was given, an audio feedback counterpart plays along when this event occurs.

The game was tested by 10 people. The testers' age was between 19 and 26 with 23.6 average all university students from different degrees of education level. The game allowed negative scores, the average absolute score was 144.1, the maximum score was 300 and the minimum score was − 331. The following Table 2 gives the summary for average durations as follows, the average bad object detection duration was 6.7 s, the maximum duration was 13.98 s and the minimum duration was 2.32 s.

More than half of the players said the sound emitted from the good and bad objects were hard to distinguish. Most of the players stated that they liked the gameplay, and would be more satisfied if the sounds were more distinguishable. Target lock sound was also a feature that reduced game enjoyment by getting confused with bad object idle sound. During the testing, second plays were requested. Even the audio received to be hard to distinguish in the second play of a tester, his score increased more than double.

Table 2 Contingency table of the test results [Created by writers]

	Bad object	Good object
Destroyed	2.5	5.3
Crashed	3.4	4.1

5 Discussion

The game requires the user to turn to an audio source if they want to destroy the game object otherwise they should avoid it by not directly looking at it. When there are multiple objects of the same type, it confuses the player. This could be prevented by at any time allowing only one game object from each type. On the downside, this reduces the excitement and hardship of decision-making elements of game design. To have a better game experience using stereo headphones are a requirement. The audio sources move closer in their lifetime but the player can turn and the direction of the sound changes. Conveying this action depends on different volumes of sound in different ears.

Comments coming from the testers on sound source confusion shows itself a significant problem for the aim of audio-based game design. Even though some testers could share common ways to interpret the difference between the object sounds, most of the testers had problems distinguishing objects. Another reason caused this confusion was the similarities between target lock sound and bad object idle sound. Aim of using target lock sound was to give audio feedback as well as visual feedback of gaze on an object. The use of a target lock sound may be left for the player's choice or different audio can be chosen. To give objects more distinguishable audio, future research on audio and interpretation may be needed.

In the game, players expected to destroy the bad objects and avoid destroying the good objects. Therefore, for a good player performance destruction of bad objects should be higher than the crash of bad objects. This holds reversely for good objects. When the means for 10 tests inspected from Table 2, the results show undesirable behavior. The game performances differ from player to player severely, which also explains the standard derivation of absolute values of scores is 108.9. With that high of a standard derivation, it is hard to comment on statistical data. The causes may include many factors of the player such as experience with mobile VR, attention to instructions, audio selectivity skills, and emotions at the test moment. Even, the standard derivation should have been lower to remark the success of the game.

6 Conclusion

In this project, an audio-based mobile virtual reality game is implemented as the aim was to show that it is possible to create virtual reality games highly dependent on audio output. The game is developed in Unity game engine using Google Cardboard SDK. The game experience was iterated by the feedbacks from playtesting. With the final version, testing was performed with 10 higher education students who played the game for the first time. Even though the sounds used in the game were chosen to complement the effects of the results of the actions, their distinguishability quality underperformed. To increase the interpretability and distinguishability of the sounds used in the game future study on audio is needed. While this research shows that it is possible to create playable audio-based mobile virtual reality game but it also raises the challenge of creating a solely audio dependent mobile virtual reality experience.

7 Future Work

Moving the game platform to a head mouth display VR system with controllers is planned. This way game-play would be faster as there would be no wait time for gaze events. Moreover, having the haptic feed-backs from controllers should provide another dimension of dialogue between the experience and the player filling the lack of detailed visual feedback. Lastly, in the lights of the feedback from the player testing, the issues that hurt the game satisfaction will be worked on. Scoring and spawn strategies will be iterated to bring the player a more balanced experience. To reduce the naivety of the player to the game faster current plans include reduction of sound set variety and providing a demo trial before the recorded test. To increase the interpretability of the sounds, the final decision could be made with the aid of surveys on audio samples.

References

1. Johansson M (2019) VR for your ears: Dynamic 3d audio is key to the immersive experience by illustration by Eddie guy. IEEE Spectr 56(2):24–29. https://doi.org/10.1109/MSPEC.2019.8635813
2. Geronazzo M, Kleimola J, Sikström E, de Götzen A, Serafin S, Avanzini F (2018) Hoba-VR: Hrtf on demand for binaural audio in immersive virtual reality environments. In: Audio engineering society convention 144. https://www.aes.org/e-lib/browse.cfm?elib=19546
3. Faria RRA, Zuffo MK, Zuffo JA (2005) Improving spatial perception through sound field simulation in VR. In: IEEE Symposium on virtual environments, human-computer interfaces and measurement systems, p. 6. https://doi.org/10.1109/VECIMS.2005.1567573
4. Wu JR, Duh CD, Ouhyoung M, Wu JT (1997) Head motion and latency compensation on localization of 3d sound in virtual reality. In: Proceedings of the ACM symposium on virtual reality software and technology. VRST '97, Association for computing machinery. New York, NY, USA, pp 15–20 (1997) https://doi.org/10.1145/261135.261140
5. Doornbusch P (2003) Sound and reality
6. Santini G (2019) Composing space in the space: an augmented and virtual reality sound spatialization system. Zenodo. https://doi.org/10.5281/zenodo.3249329
7. Lumbreras M, Sánchez J (1999) Interactive 3D sound hyperstories for blind children. In: Proceedings of the sigchi conference on human factors in computing systems. CHI '99, Association for computing machinery. New York, NY, USA, pp. 318–325. https://doi.org/10.1145/302979.303101
8. Allain K, Dado B, Gelderen MV, Hokke O, Oliveira M, Bidarra R, Gaubitch ND, Hendriks RC, Kybartas B (2015) An audio game for training navigation skills of blind children. In: 2015 IEEE 2nd VR workshop on sonic interactions for virtual environments (SIVE), pp 1–4. https://doi.org/10.1109/SIVE.2015.7361292
9. Balan O, Moldoveanu A, Moldoveanu F, Butean A (2015) Developing a navigational 3d audio game with hierarchical levels of difficulty for the visually impaired players. In: RoCHI

10. Sánchez J, Sáenz M (2005) 3D sound interactive environments for problem solving. In: Proceedings of the 7th international ACM SIGACCESS conference on computers and accessibility. Assets '05, Association for computing machinery. New York, NY, USA, pp. 173–179. https://doi.org/10.1145/1090785.1090817
11. Friberg J, Gärdenfors D (2004) Audio games: New perspectives on game audio. In: Proceedings of the 2004 ACM SIGCHI international conference on advances in computer entertainment technology. ACE '04, Association for computing machinery. New York, NY, USA, pp 148–154. https://doi.org/10.1145/1067343.1067361
12. Targett S, Fernström M (2003) Audio games: fun for all? All for fun, pp. 6–9
13. Fizek S, Woletz JD, Beksa J (2015) Playing with sound and gesture in digital audio games. In: Mensch Computer Workshopband
14. Liljedahl M, Papworth N, Lindberg S (2007) Beowulf: A game experience built on sound effects. In: Proceedings of the 13th international conference on auditory display. pp. 102–106
15. Miller D, Parecki A, Douglas S (2007) Finger dance: a sound game for blind people, pp. 253–254 https://doi.org/10.1145/1296843.1296898
16. Perla R, Hebbalaguppe R (2017) Google cardboard dates augmented reality: issues, challenges and future opportunities. ArXiv abs/1706.03851
17. Moural A, Øritsland T (2019) User experience in mobile virtual reality: an on-site experience, pp. 152–159. https://doi.org/10.14627/537663016
18. Yoo S, Parker C (2015) Controller-less interaction methods for google cardboard. In: Proceedings of the 3rd ACM symposium on spatial user interaction. SUI '15, Association for Computing Machinery. New York, NY, USA p. 127. https://doi.org/10.1145/2788940.2794359
19. Alger M (2018) Visual design methods for virtual reality. https://aperturesciencellc.com/vr/VisualDesignMethodsforVR_MikeAlger.pdf, https://aperturesciencellc.com/vr/VisualDesignMethodsforVR_MikeAlger.pdf. Accessed 02 Jan 2020

VR and AR in Teaching 3D Environment Design for Video Games

Çağlayan Karagözler and Didem Dönmez Karagözler

Abstract VR (Virtual Reality) and AR (Augmented Reality) are two different technologies that bring alternative or projected realities to our life [1]. They allow us to imagine and simulate any non-real sense of space as if it were real [2]. When teaching 3D design, a common problem would be being forced to look at the design through a 2D screen trying to navigate around it. Especially to a person who is not a professional on the field [3]. In this research we aim to provide details on how VR and AR technologies can be useful to fill this gap and provide better cognition by simulating the feeling of the real space and thus, better and faster learning curve for 3D design students. The method of this research is both experimentation and observation. We started to use these technologies in numerous classes and, important results started to emerge as we observe the improvement on the student's understanding of 3D space and geometry. The students' impressions along with their ability to create 3D geometry are observed. There is a clear and a considerable gain in favor of students when it comes to understanding and visualizing 3D spaces for environmental design when experienced through a VR or AR device. This way, students gain a big benefit on understanding the basics of 3D space and they visualize their own ideas and creations better as they also gain better reference points to establish a basis for their design.

Keywords Virtual reality · Augmented reality · Lecture · Environment design · Video game

1 Introduction and Literature Review

One purpose of the innovation of virtual reality (VR) and augmented reality (AR) is to indulge the user in a digital world that is distinguished from physical reality. While for virtual reality, displaying a digital environment from a head mounted display (HMD) can make a participant feel like they are in a different place physically, the

Ç. Karagözler (✉) · D. D. Karagözler
Faculty of Engineering and Architecture, Department of Interior Design, İstanbul Arel University, Türkoba Mahallesi, Erguvan Sokak No: 26/K 34537 Tepekent—Büyükçekmece, İstanbul, Türkiye
e-mail: caglayankaragozler@arel.edu.tr

augmented reality "mixes" physical and simulated objects together; in turn, interactive components are arranged and balanced to behave as part of the physical world respective to the user view[4, 5]. For both technologies, in this digital environment, feeling spatially positioned or rather as more known as spatially present either for the user's body or the objects placed in the scene is central to the experience[5, 6]. This practically applies to any application of these technologies, which includes video games and game design.

When it comes to video games, Dondlinger indicates that there are 4 different and important aspects for an exceptional game design. Motivation, Narrative Context, Goals & Rules and Interactivity & Multisensory Cues. While these are not the only requirements or aspects that make a video game design efficient, they certainly play an important role. For our paper, especially when it comes to environment design, the notes on Interactivity & Multisensory Cues can be considered as a starting point which states; One aspect inherent in the story background and goals of the game is the relationship between the player (or players) and the game world. Effective games weave objects and characters into a game world which provides feedback and clue structures for successful playing. The level of interactivity is further constituted by the degree of user control over the game environment. The best games are "highly interactive, deliberately generating tension between the degree of control that the story imposes and the freedom of interaction of the player," reasoning that play experience can be boring and unchallenging in games with complete freedom of interaction [7].

Combining these two phenomena of a multisensory video game environment and VR/AR development perks, one may be able to achieve total spatial visualization dominance. So, what really is Spatial Visualization? It is defined as "the ability to mentally rotate, manipulate, and twist two and three-dimensional stimulus objects"[6]. Most of the time, terms of visual imagery, 3D skills, visualization, spatial recognition, spatial reasoning, and much more were interchangeably used to define whole or at least certain parts of the field. The words skill and ability have also been widely and interchangeably used, although the former stresses that these properties are linked to genetic inheritance, but the latter highlights the positive effects of training on the improvement of the particular property. This skill, can be considered as the main requirement for creating or designing an environment in 3D space, in a digital work station [6, 8].

On the subject of improving the aforementioned skill, it is observed that despite increased VR/AR adoption, relatively little research has been done to expand VR/AR usage outside of visualization applications. However, the studies have been done has indeed been encouraging to use VR/AR to enhance design creation. The combination of video game engines and VR has shown that it can be used to teach the principles of design [9]. With certain shortcomings, VR is being increasingly implemented in the design fields and a recent ASLA survey showed that 82% of organizations in the U.S. now include VR in their workflow or intend to implement it [10]. In Hill's research, there is a clear consensus that using VR in design process, helps with 3D understanding and spatial visualization, along with actual designing. Figure 1, taken from the research is shown below.

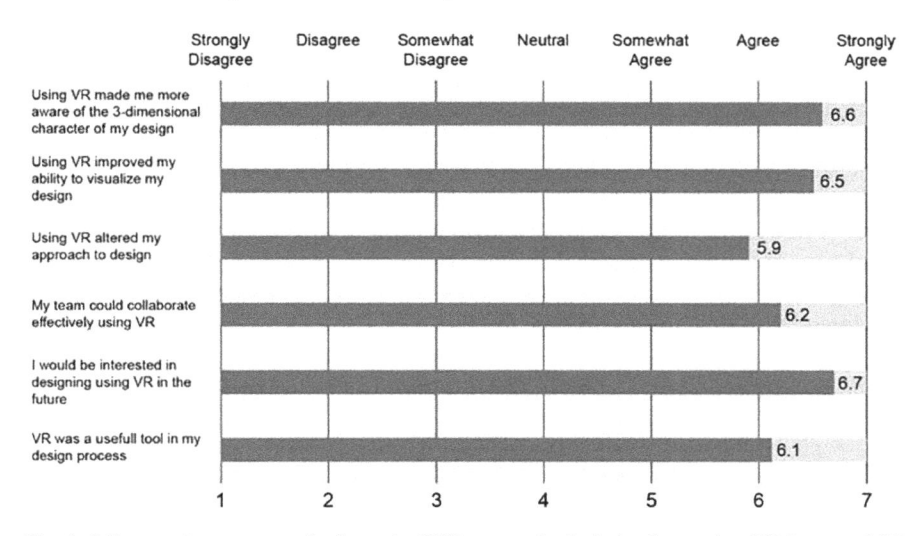

VR and AR in Teaching 3D Environment Design for Video Games 235

Fig. 1 Likert-scale survey results from the Hill's research, depicting how using VR improved 3D design in a landscape village design project [9]

Initially, for AR, the key applications that showed the promise of the technology were architectural designs, videoconferencing, mall visits, apps, etc. [11]. AR models were often used to grasp whole-scale building designs development sites too which leads us to also ability to visualize buildings used in video game environments as well [12].

Brit et.al. used these words to describe how the two technologies can be utilized to allow better visualization of a digital environment and design education:

> Results showed that the experts valued the ability to switch between different modes, and gave a positive rating to the memorability, manipulability, navigability, real world aspects, communication, creativity and engagement of the multiple simulations. A simplified workflow will facilitate increased uptake in both educational and professional setting, further adding to the value of these mixed reality visualization methods.

The aim of this research is to understand if we can indicate that using VR/AR technology in design process, helps designing better received and perceived game environments, see whether there is a difference in designing an environment for a video game using the technologies and also to see if they render the entire process easier and more entertaining.

2 Methodology

The method of this research is both experimentation and observation. Our main intent was to utilize VR/AR technology found in Virtual Experience Design Lab (SANLAB) at Istanbul Arel University to see if we can use it to improve the design skills of the students which we also lecture in the very same institution. The courses and classes cover many fields and disciplines of design but for this research, we focused on one important discipline of digital design: Improving the process of environment creation and spatial visualization for video games. We used a structured interview tailored to understand how VR/AR helps specifically for artificial, not-necessarily but generally unreal, fictional environment (including props) design aimed to be used in a video game. Two main sessions were conducted among all peers in select classes that incorporate the lab. The classes include Interior Architecture Project III-IV-V, Design Criteria for Fictional Spaces, Architecture in New Media and Interactive Media and Furniture Design.

The first session included the popularly acclaimed video game named *The Elder Scrolls V: Skyrim (Skyrim in short)*. The mentioned game has both a version which is experienced through a traditional screen, with a keyboard and a mouse and a version that adopts virtual reality and is experienced through an HMD with hand controllers [13, 14]. This enabled the participants to clearly compare and differentiate between the two methods of visualizing the environment and perceiving details inside.

The participants played a saved game for approximately 10 min where the player is located in a castle named Whiterun which contains a good amount of detailed buildings, props and environment ranging in scale from tiny nails to big dragon cage towers. After experiencing the game environment, the students were asked only two open-ended questions:

1. Did experiencing the environment in VR affect your perception of it? If yes, describe how.
2. How would you describe the differences between the two experiences in terms of noticing details and spatially understanding the size and coordinates of a digital environment?

In the second session, the participants were asked to create and/or place environmental props or pieces, or even entire basic shaped spaces using a VR application and also were presented with a pre-compiled app running in a tablet to alter furniture and props in terms of design to make realistic, collaborative choices in an AR environment. The pre-compiled app was designed and deployed by the researchers using Unity 2019.3.1f1 software and AR Foundation as one of the packages that company incorporates within the software. After the experience, they were asked two open-ended questions:

1. How does making design choices and implementing your ideas in VR/AR feel compared to designing in front of a traditional screen?
2. Considering ease of use and designing speed, which experience would you think to be the best and why?

Both sessions were conducted in the lab and during the class and all students participated as a part of their learning process.

3 Findings

As shown in Figs. 2 and 3, participants used an HMD named Vive from HTC for the VR experiences and an Apple iPad for the AR experiences. After the two experiments, our interviews with the students revealed very clear and distinctive findings.

For the first session with Skyrim, the answer to the two questions were almost conclusive. Our deductions from the open-ended answers came down to a few key points. Questions were 'Did experiencing the environment in VR affect your perception of it? If yes, describe how' and 'How would you describe the differences between the two experiences in terms of noticing details and spatially understanding the size and coordinates of a digital environment?' From a total of 45 students and 5 lecturers, none answered no. All participants seem to agree on at least some level, the VR experience affected their perception of the environment.

Over 95% of the participants stated that they feel more like inside the environment. Especially, being not limited by a computer screen, they felt all the space including the environment behind them and thus, immersed themselves with the environment. One participant described it as 'feeling physically in Whiterun' which is more formally known as being spatially present.

Another common response found was that the participants could notice the details found in the environment that they would normally miss far easier compared to looking at them from a computer screen. Also, being able to get as close as desired, made them feel more in control and more immersed even if the environment could not be physically real as opposed to the computer screen.

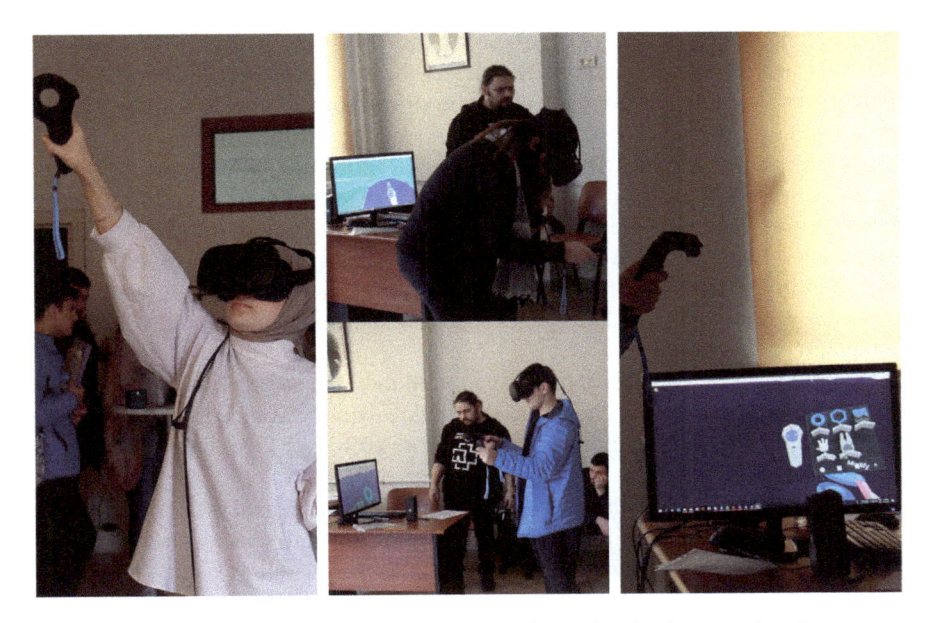

Fig. 2 Participants taking part in the VR experiment (Photo taken by the researchers.)

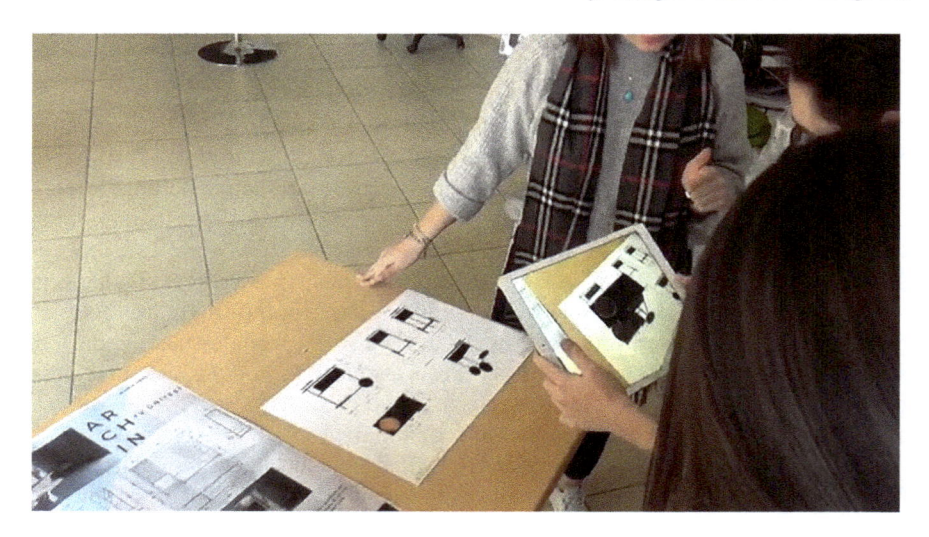

Fig. 3 Participants taking part in the AR experiment (Photo taken by the researchers.)

Again, over 95% of the participants agreed that experiencing a game environment in VR makes it much more believable and livable inside. More importantly, once the game environment satisfies the need for multisensory stimuli and makes itself also believable and real enough, it highly improves spatial visualization of the participants, as also they state the same.

When it comes to understanding the size and coordinates of a given object or a bunch of objects, even the entire environment, most of the participants used words like positively much more different, better, clearer than computer screen due to actually being able to reach in and compare the environment to their own body parts or their entire bodies.

For the second session with implementing design ideas, the answer to the two questions were yet again, almost conclusive. The interpretations from the open-ended answers and the interviews pointed out several common findings from all participants. The questions were 'How does making design choices and implementing your ideas in VR/AR feel compared to designing in front of a traditional screen?' and 'Considering ease of use and designing speed, which experience would you think to be the best and why?'

Over 90% of the participants answered with the very same sentence with a few alternative word and syntax choices to the first question; It is much better and much more sensible than the traditional way. The other 10% stated that they would prefer a traditional way.

One consensus was that the VR/AR design experience, helped them to understand and better visualize what is in their mind. It helped them to express their ideas in a unique and eventually easier way.

Also, one more key point was that the digital environment also made a way for different tools to provide inspiration to the participants as well. Using the tools they have as an extensions of their bodies, not a mouse with a pointer on the screen, made them feel in much more control and they could create whatever is on their mind without relying on heavy one handed cursor work.

All participants agreed on that using VR or AR in design process, would make it immensely faster compared to the traditional way. Being able to almost touch the design piece physically, made them to iterate their ideas more efficiently and speedily.

As a final deduction, almost all participants stated that using VR and AR in their design processes, would make it easier, faster and overall better when designing environments.

4 Conclusion

Based on the findings we deducted from the open-ended questions and interviews with the participants, an obvious outcome particularly emerged. Using VR and AR when designing environments for video games, actually has a very good chance to basically render the design process faster, generally easier and overall better for the designer and the viewer/reviewer, according to popular belief among participants.

Any designer can benefit from the usage of these technologies in many different levels. But especially, when it comes to environment design, it has an actual clear impact on producing better environments in general. Being able to spatially, almost literally feel in the environment being designed for all intents and purposes helps with understanding and visualization of the main design, which specifically is fairly significant.

More importantly, since a game environment can be non-realistic and physically impossible to exist, having the chance to definitely explore the environment like if it was real, basically makes one of the biggest differences on the design process, or so they particularly thought. Understanding different objects in comparison to the human body enhances the ability to create fairly more realistic and generally more spatially believable environment.

Also, trying to visualize the design and transferring it to the digital environment through a screen, a keyboard and a mouse proves to mostly be a very slow process for the designer, after experiencing the VR/AR version of editing and designing, or so they mostly thought.

An almost physical touch to the virtual environment, changes how a designer thinks and creates objects compared to the untouchable 2D flat-screen. Seeing the possibility, spatial presence, detailed close-up look of the virtual object, sometimes also mixing it with actual reality, specifically makes the designer think more detailed and envision a pretty much more believable design in a robust way.

In conclusion, while including VR/AR helps in any design discipline and field, it is especially useful when creating video game environments due to the environment's nature of fictionality and the need of believability, where the technology helps to perceive the fiction almost as if it was real.

5 Future Research

For more data collection and analyzing the differences in the equipment to achieve these technological phenomenon, and for including more fields from video game design like prop and character design, motion capture with VR support, more interviews and tests can be done using different mediums of VR and AR.

Mixed reality devices like HoloLens, Magic Leap, advanced virtual reality body suits, whole environment tracking systems with multiple participant support, different realization and visualization mediums like Leap Motion, Kinect or other different peripherals can be included to better analyze and deduct a more detailed research on how these immersion technologies help video game design processes and fields.

References

1. Bastug E, Bennis M, Medard M, Debbah M (2017) Toward interconnected virtual reality: opportunities, challenges, and enablers. IEEE Commun Mag 55(6):110–117. https://doi.org/10.1109/MCOM.2017.1601089
2. Burdea GC, Philippe C (2003) Virtual reality technology. 2nd edn
3. Weng T-S (2016) Use of social networks to affect the teaching and learning effectiveness of 3D design. Comput Technol Appl 7:1–10. https://doi.org/10.17265/1934-7332/2016.01.001
4. Sanna A, Manuri F (2016) A survey on applications of augmented reality. Adv Comput Sci Int J 5(1):18–27, [Online]. Available: https://www.acsij.org/acsij/article/view/400/350
5. Coxon M, Kelly N, Page S (2016) Individual differences in virtual reality: Are spatial presence and spatial ability linked? Virtual Real 20(4):203–212. https://doi.org/10.1007/s10055-016-0292-x
6. Tuker C (2018) Training spatial skills with virtual reality and augmented reality. In: Encyclopedia of computer graphics and games, pp 1–9.
7. Dondlinger MJ (2020) Educational video game design: a review of the literature. J Appl Educ Technol 4(1):21–31. Accessed: Jun 16 2020 [Online]. Available: https://www.researchgate.net/publication/238444705.
8. Duwain Brazley M (2018) Architecture, virtual reality, spatial visualization, learning styles, and distance education. Int J Archit Arts Appl 4(2):10. https://doi.org/10.11648/j.ijaaa.20180402.11
9. Hill DM (2019) How virtual reality impacts the landscape architecture
10. George BH, Summerlin P, Fulford T Teaching and learning software in landscape architecture: a survey of software use amongst faculty and students. Full Paper J Digit Lands Arch 354–362. https://doi.org/10.14627/537663038
11. Fernandez M (2017) Augmented-virtual reality: how to improve education systems. High Learn Res Commun 7(1):1. https://doi.org/10.18870/hlrc.v7i1.373
12. Birt J, Manyuru P, Nelson J (2019) Using virtual and augmented reality to study architectural lighting. In: ASCILITE 2017—conference proceedings—34th international conference of Innovation. Practice and research in the use of educational technologies in tertiary education, pp 17–21
13. Simkins D, Dikkers S, Owen E (2012) Unbroken immersion: the skyrim experience. Well Play 2(1):13–25
14. Studios B (2015) The elder scrolls v: Skyrim

A New Environment: Augmented Reality

Hakan Anay, Ülkü Özten, and Merve Ünal

Abstract In brief, augmented reality can be defined as a new "environment", which is created by simultaneously transferring virtual data such as sound, image, graphic produced in virtual environment to real environment.It is seen that the augmented reality has great potential in idea generation, development, presentation to users and information transfer as a representation (presentation) tool with its current applications. Accordingly, the purpose of this study is to evaluate the use of AR technology in cultural heritage areas, to study application examples in archaeological sites and to examine the potential contributions that different uses can provide. Within the framework of this research, AR application is planned to be developed for the ancient city of Alexandria Troas, one of the important cities of the Troas region, located in Çanakkale. With the application created, it is aimed to understand the value of the historical artifacts and structures unearthed during the excavation, to transfer them to the people who will experience the area, and to keep the city alive within the framework of virtual heritage values.

Keywords Augmented reality (AR) · Environment · Archeology · Cultural heritage

1 Introduction

In the field of information technology, the rapidly developing augmented reality technology has the opportunity to apply itself in many fields such as medicine,

---

The work described here is a part of an ongoing master thesis project at Eskisehir Osmangazi University (ESOGU).

H. Anay · Ü. Özten · M. Ünal (✉)
Eskişehir Osmangazi University, Eskişehir, Turkey
e-mail: mrve.unal97@gmail.com

H. Anay
e-mail: info@hakananay.com

Ü. Özten
e-mail: info@ulkuozten.com

entertainment, engineering, architecture, education, art. It can also be said that it has become accessible to the ordinary user and has started to become a part of everyday life in this direction.

In summary, AR is a technology that enables users to experience augmented media by simultaneously transferring virtual data such as audio, images, graphics generated in their virtual environment to the real environment. AR systems are also used in cultural heritage areas. The historical significance of a ruin, the culture it reflects, the processes it goes through are very difficult to understand by only looking at the ruin. Augmented reality seems to be a very convincing tool in cultural heritage sites with its powerful presentation technique and interactive experience that it combines various layers of data. AR is a valuable technology in terms of increasing the awareness of the masses in the areas of cultural heritage, experiencing the real place of the historical environment, as well as the survival and sustainability of historical environments that are threatened with extinction by environmental factors.

In this research, the use of AR technology in archaeological areas, will be examined through different examples. This information will be used to understand another ancient site: Alexandria Troas. This study aims to develop a location based AR application in order to understand and explain the cultural value of Alexandria Troas, one of the important ancient cities of Anatolia, where excavations have been carried out since the nineteenth century. The main purpose of the application is to understand the historical value of many ruins in the ancient city of Alexandria Troas in the Dalyan district of Çanakkale, to ensure the sustainability of the ancient city and to pass it on to users.

2 What is Augmented Reality?

Viewed from a certain perspective augmented reality is accepted as a special branch of virtual reality. And for another perspective augmented reality has a more general scope than virtual reality. Virtual reality puts the person in a fully synthetic world with the generated virtual data, but augmented reality overlaps the real world with virtual data produced in digital media such as sound, picture and video. Instead of creating a fully synthetic world or displaying the real world as it is, it creates a new environment by mixing these two environments. Therefore, it is certain that augmented reality does not detach the person from the real world like virtual reality [1, 2]. Milgram and Kishino described the relationship between augmented reality to virtual reality with concept of virtuality continuum. As shown in Fig. 1, they described an axis with virtuality at one end and reality at the other. At the left side the environment consists of entirely real objects while at the right side the environment consists of entirely virtual objects. The virtual world with added real world views is called augmented virtuality, and AR is between the real world and augmented virtuality [3].

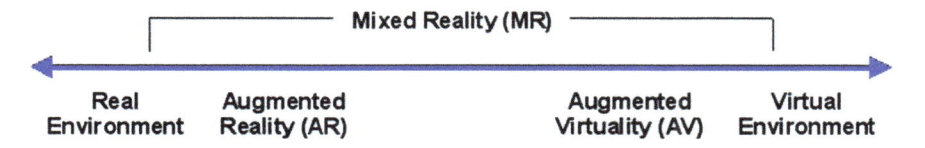

Fig. 1 Milgram and Kischino's virtuality continuum [3]

3 Why New?

Briefly, AR consists of adding virtual data produced in computer environment, 3D visuals and animations, and video to the physical environment simultaneously [4]. With AR, the user does not step into a fully synthetic, real-world independent environment, where the real world is not perceived as pure and complete, but also filled with virtual objects. Instead of all this, it is a new and increased level of perception where virtual and real environment overlap each other, where virtual data is fed from real environment components and the real environment can be experienced with objects that cannot be physically located.

With AR, users who are able to experience the virtual data added to the environment as well as the physical environment are faced with a new level of perception. Through this environment, where the level of perception is increased visually and audibly, the obstacles become unobstructed for the users, and the invisible becomes visible. At the same time, the user moves out of the passive audience position with the interactive aspect of AR technology, making it an active part of the experience. It is thus a new environment in which the user becomes an active part, both mentally and physically, between all the embodiment of real life and the infinity of the virtual world.

4 Potential Uses

AR technologies, which can be defined as the simultaneous transfer of visual and audio virtual data produced in digital environment to the real environment, come up with different applications in every area of our lives. AR applications have become more accessible with the development of technology [5]. Today, there are examples of application in many fields such as entertainment, health and architecture.

Many games for entertainment purposes have been produced with AR technologies that enable users to enjoy pleasant moments by adding virtual data to the real world view. The most known application of such games is Pokemon GO application. With this application, the user tries to find the location of the virtual characters and collect them. When the user reaches the location where the character is located, the virtual character appears on the screen, as shown in Fig. 2, and the user taps the screen to collect the character [6]. Such games are used for educational purposes today, besides providing users with pleasant moments.

Fig. 2 Pokemon GO application [20]

Due to its structure that enriches the real world with virtual data, AR technologies are also used as a presentation tool with the possibility of effective visualization. Audio, video and 3D visual support help architects to visualize their projects more effectively, while providing an impressive display of historical buildings and artifacts in museums and historical sites. Figure 3 shows as an example of use for presentation purposes.

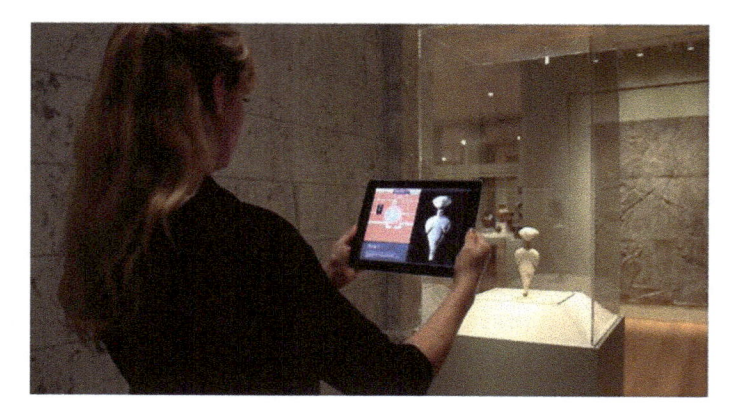

Fig. 3 AR application for presentation [21]

A New Environment: Augmented Reality   245

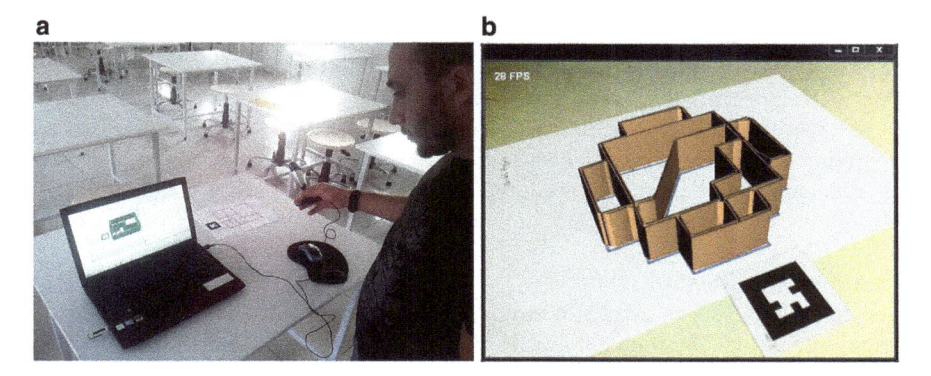

Fig. 4 a and **b** Various examples from SketchAR program [7]

AR, which provides the opportunity to translate information into practice with its interactive structure, is also used for educational purposes. SketchAR developed by Köymen can be given as an example for AR applications produced for use in architectural education. 2D sketches drawn in the early stages of architectural design are made digitally with SketchAR. It is an educational application that aims to improve students' 3D perception and at the same time enrich the architectural design stage [7]. Figure 4a and b shows a student experiencing the program.

5 Possible Uses of AR in Archeology

Augmented reality with its advantages is also used for many different purposes in archaeological areas, which are important representation sites of cultural heritage. With the virtual heritage it creates, AR offers the opportunity to combine past culture with today's user [8]. El-Hakim and others explain the motivations of creating virtual heritage as follows; [9]

Documentation for Restoration and Reconstruction of Historic Buildings
Historical buildings that are in danger of extinction as a result of natural disasters such as earthquakes, floods or various human activities need to be documented in order to ensure restoration or reconstruction in the ongoing process. At this point, AR technologies are an aid to architects, archaeologists and art historians. With the help of the data transferred from the paper plane to the virtual database, documentation of the historical structures can be provided and it can make it easier for the experts to continue their work.

Virtual Reconstruction for Historical Buildings that no Longer Exist
For historical structures that cannot be physically sustained or partially sustained for various reasons, even if AR cannot eliminate these factors, AR can ensure that it is kept alive with virtual reconstructions and passed on to future generations.

Interacting With Structures and Objects Without the Risk of Damage
In places that are cultural heritage sites, users cannot physically connect because there is a danger of damaging historical buildings and objects. However, due to the interactive environment that AR systems offer to the user by combining real environment and virtual data, it can connect with the historical environment without any risk factor and the user who is dominating the field has a sense of belonging. As a result, the user gets more information about the field.

Creating Educational Resources
AR technology, which creates a strengthened perception level with the overlapping of the virtual environment and the real world, makes the learning activity easy and permanent. AR applications, which transform information into practice with its interactive structure, are also educational resources.

Visualizing Scenes
AR technologies are an important tool for archaeological sites, in terms of inaccessible locations or the reconstruction of virtual assets of historical environments for users with physical disabilities.

6 Why AR for Archeology?

Various methods are used to understand the importance of archaeological sites and develop cultural heritage awareness. Augmented reality allows virtual objects to be exhibited in real environments, while interacting with the user, enabling them to be used for reasons such as exhibiting, documenting, training [10]. With different uses augmented reality is a powerful presentation technique as it transfers information interactively with the simultaneous expression technique enhanced with video, sound, 3D visuals and presents the past-today comparison in a comparable way to the user. In this way, the navigation becomes enjoyable for the users who experience the area and the information is provided to be more descriptive and permanent [11]. With AR technology, the ruins that contain a certain historical process are exhibited not only in the present state but also in the three-dimensional virtual representation of the past, and enables it to navigate around like a real object. A complete view of the ruins provided with AR sheds light on the past and allows the user to learn more about the ruins It is useful not only for tourists, but also for architects, archaeologists and art historians [12]. They can better conduct their work with augmented data. Also in areas of cultural heritage that are threatened with extinction due to environmental factors, data can be reproduced in virtual ways to ensure that historical remains can live in their own place as long as desired. With such contributions, AR provides many potential uses in cultural heritage areas.

7 Research Focus: AR and Archeology

Archaeological sites are of great importance because they have witnessed history and have a certain cultural heritage. The fact that physical intervention is not possible in such cultural heritage areas causes different solutions for keeping history alive and transferring it to the masses. At this point, AR enables the redefinition of these environments with virtual data without any intervention. It makes it easier for users to access more information about the historical environment by not only seeing the ruins but also experiencing the original state of the structures. In addition to the physical environment, virtual data that are experienced interactively by the user during the navigation, increase the interest in the field, and gain the awareness of the historical heritage, thus transferring that culture to other generations.

In the light of the advantages it provides, AR technologies are used in many different ways such as presentation technique, documentation method, and educational purposes in archaeological areas that have important cultural heritage. AR expands its usage area with the development of technology day by day.

8 Various Cases

8.1 The Ancient Pompeii Project

Many archaeological and research studies have been done to show the history of Pompeii and the effects of the disaster it experienced, and much work is still being done today. Technology is also used to protect the cultural heritage and display it to the masses. One of these is the LIFEPLUS project, which adds virtual data to real scenes in the cultural heritage site, completed in the year 2000. It is an electronic tour guide for tourists coming to the site. Based on the fresco paintings in the area, plant and animal models were made and an artificial life was designed with human simulations reflecting the lifestyle of the period. Face and speech simulations, voice data, and clothing simulations were made to the characters according to the stories [13]. Figure 5 exemplifies the production of virtual clothing.

In the Pompeii project, users get the chance to experience an interactive environment with animations acting according to fictional stories, enriched with virtual data during their visits. As Pappagiannakis and others explain, the opportunity to experience with storytelling broadens the visitor's perspective. With AR technology and virtual storytelling technique, which is the main purpose of the study, as shown in Fig. 6, visitors have stepped into the past and went on an interactive and immersive trip [13].

Fig. 5 Virtual garment based on a real ancient dress [13]

Fig. 6 The user who experiences the created story [22]

8.2 Archeoguide Project

Archeoguide is an application that offers guidance to the user using augmented reality technology. By using the user's location, it enables the historical buildings to be displayed without any intervention by providing augmented reality reconstructions. It presents the reconstruction of the historical buildings in the area with AR technology, on-site and full-time to the user. This project, which has been tried in the ancient city of Olympia in Greece, also offers access to virtual tours and database with internet access [14].

Three different mobile units were implemented in Archeoguide Project; laptop, pen-tablet and palmtop. With this hardware, many 2D pictures, 3D models, audio, video and information content articles were provided to the users. With its GPS support, the system can overlap the actual data and virtual ones provide the user with increased views [14]. In Figs. 7a and b, the comparison of the real environment and the augmented environment is presented.

In addition to tangible heritage objects, abstract cultural actions are also included. As an example as shown in Fig. 8, the Ancient Olympic Games reconstruction was exhibited to the user with athletes competing in the stadium. In order to do this, Olympic athletes and virtual human models were created. It is animated by adding the necessary movements related to the sports on the created models [14].

Fig. 7 **a** Real environment, **b** augmented environment [14]

Fig. 8 Ancient olympic games virtual reconstruction [14]

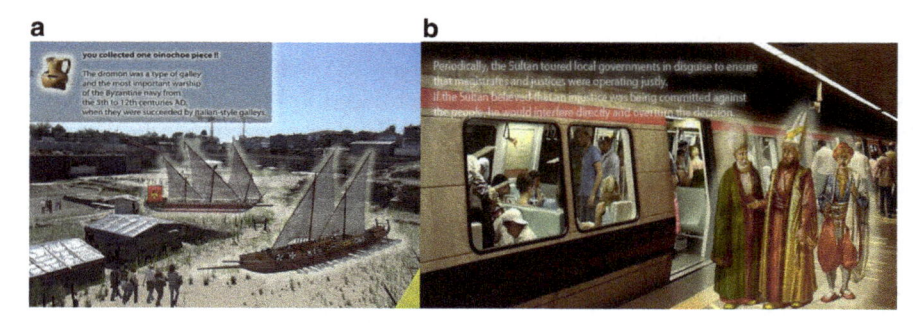

Fig. 9 a and **b** images from the game [16]

8.3 Yenikapı Explorer Project

Recent studies have shown that mobile games made with AR applications are also educational. With these games, it has been observed that the users interact more strongly with the space they are in. Yenikapı Explorer is also an AR supported mobile gaming platform created in 2012. The purpose of the study is to show the historical richness of Yenikapı to the users with the game designed. In order to solve the transportation problem of Istanbul, a transportation network project was wanted in Yenikapı, but archaeological excavations were carried out due to the historical importance of the area [15]. In these excavations, a lot of historical elements emerged. Necessary symposiums and competitions were organized in order to find a solution because it is impossible for the works to remain in place.

Özgan, who emphasizes the potentials of augmented reality in cultural heritage areas, proposed an AR game to display the history of Yenikapı. In order to achieve this, 3D reconstruction of historical objects in the area has been carried out and characters belonging to different time periods have been created. Users participating in the application have experienced these historical objects virtually in their original places [16].

Yenikapı Explorer is a location-based AR game where the user has the chance to watch virtual scenes by collecting all virtual objects. The user must answer the questions asked about the object correctly in order to collect the objects. All objects belong to a certain collection. When all the pieces are collected and the collection is completed, the user gets the chance to observe scenes, exemplified in Fig. 9a and b with more detailed information and data about the area [16].

8.4 Research on Alexandria Troas Ancient City

The region located in the northwest of Çanakkale in 1000 BC was called Troas. It was the most important region of Anatolia due to its connection point between Anatolia and Thrace and its location on trade routes in ancient times. There were 18 cities in the region. One of these cities was the city of Alexandria Troas, famous for its trade and maritime activities.

The ancient city of Alexandria Troas is located within the borders of the village of Dalyan in the Ezine district of Çanakkale. The city BC Antigonos, the commander of Alexander the Great (Alexandros) in 310, is a port city founded by Monophtalmos under the name of Antigoia. The city took its present name as Alexandria Troas, which means the city of Alexander (Alexandros) by Lysmimakhos after the death of Alexander the Great [17].

The city has become one of the most important cities with its theater, stadium, baths, temples, fountains, waterways and the walls surrounding the city. It has attracted the attention of many researchers and archaeologists because it is home to many civilizations. The city, which has attracted the attention of travelers since the sixteenth century, has hosted research and excavation works since the nineteenth century [18]. Excavations were carried out in the city for a short time in 1997 by a German team. Since 2011, archaeological studies are ongoing by Prof. Dr. Erhan Öztepe [19].

Within the framework of above-mentioned approaches, this research plan to carry out a BAP project in ESOGU. The project aims to set out the interconnection of scientific fields (such as architecture, computation, archaeology, history, psychology), trying to emphasize issue of user experience in a multi-layered historical/archeological field. It plans to develop and test a location-based mobile application supported by AR system, which is a powerful tool in terms of identifying and documenting the remains in the Alexandria Troas ancient city and reflecting the historical significance by transferring the discovered remains to the users who experience the area. In line with the data acquired from the field, it is aimed to bring users to the past while experiencing the physical environment by making 3D models together with various audio and visual data, and to demonstrate the historical importance of the field in an educational and enjoyable way.

9 Conclusion

AR technology has found many uses for itself with the new environment created by the combination of virtual and real world. It has been determined that with the contributions of AR technology, different applications have been developed with various motivations. Different examples of AR applications in the archaeological areas, which are the main subject of the research, have been examined and their advantages have been revealed at points such as protecting the historical structures and cultural values of the environments by understanding them and transferring them to future generations.

It is seen that historical artifacts and structures presented using AR in archaeological areas make the experience enjoyable as well as the ease of learning with the interactive structure provided by AR technology. Learning action, which has become enjoyable for users, is very important in terms of reaching different audiences and triggering cultural heritage awareness. AR applications, which are documented not only for tourists who experience the area but also for architect archaeologists and art historians, facilitate the interpretation of historical works. Many historical monuments can be transferred to future generations by ensuring that historical environments, which cannot be destroyed due to various human activities and environmental factors, are kept alive with virtual reconstructions. Due to such reasons, AR technologies are seen as a powerful tool in archaeological areas day by day.

Based on these motivations, the application, which will be developed for the Alexandria Troas region in the continuation of the study, aims to reveal the cultural value of the area and to present it to the users and to provide the historical accumulation that has come up to centuries ago.

References

1. Azuma RT (1997) A survey of augmented reality. Presence Teleoper Virt Environ 6(4):355–385
2. Bimber O, Raskar R (2005) Spatial augmented reality: merging real and virtual worlds. CRC Press, FL
3. Milgram P, Kishino F (1994) A taxonomy of mixed reality visual displays. IEICE Trans Inf Syst 77(12):1321–1329
4. Raskar R, Welch G, Fuchs H (1999) Spatially augmented reality. In: Proceedings of the international workshop on augmented reality: placing artificial objects in real scenes: placing artificial objects in real scenes. CRC Press, FL, pp. 63–72
5. Coşkun C (2017) Bir Sergileme Yöntemi Olarak Artırılmış Gerçeklik. Sanat Ve Tasarım Dergisi 20:61–75
6. Bingöl B (2018) Yeni Bir Yaşam Biçimi: Artırılmış Gerçeklik (AG). Üsküdar Üniversitesi İletişim Fakültesi Akademik Dergisi Etkileşim 1:44–55
7. Köymen E (2014) Mimari Ön Tasarım Sürecinde Eskizleri Gerçek Zamanlı 3B Modelleyen, Arttırılmış Gerçeklik Destekli Bir Yazılım Denemesi: "Sketchar." Yıldız Teknik Üniversitesi, Fen Bilimleri Enstitüsü, Doktora Tezi, İstanbul
8. Noh Z, Sunar MS, Pan Z (2009) A review on augmented reality for virtual heritage system. In International conference on technologies for E-learning and digital entertainment. Springer, Berlin, Heidelberg. pp 50–61
9. El-Hakim SF, Beraldin JA, Picard M, Godin G (2004) Detailed 3D reconstruction of large-scale heritage sites with integrated techniques. IEEE Comput Graphics Appl 24(3):21–29
10. Höllerer T, Feiner S (2004) Mobile augmented reality. Telegeoinformatics: Location-based computing and services
11. Bernardini A, Delogu C, Pallotti E, Costantini L (2012) Living the past: augmented reality and archeology. In: 2012 IEEE international conference on multimedia and expo workshops pp 354–357
12. Akkuş G, Akkuş Ç (2018) Tarihi turistik alanlarda kullanılan mobil artırılmış gerçeklik uygulamalarının değerlendirilmesi. J Tour Gastron Stud 6(1):83–104
13. Papagiannakis G, Schertenleib S, O'Kennedy B, Arevalo-Poizat M, Magnenat-Thalmann N, Stoddart A, Thalmann D (2005) Mixing virtual and real scenes in the site of ancient Pompeii. Comput Animat Virtual Worlds 16(1):11–24
14. Vlahakis V, Ioannidis M, Karigiannis J, Tsotros M, Gounaris M, Stricker D, Almeida L (2002) Archeoguide: an augmented reality guide for archaeological sites. IEEE Comput Graphics Appl 22(5):52–60
15. Kocabaş U (2012) Yenikapı Batıkları Kazısı ve Araştırmaları. Tina Denizcilik Arkeolojisi Dergisi, 26–42

16. Özgan SY (2012) Use of augmented reality technologies in cultural heritage Sites; Virtu (re) al Yenikapı, Doctoral dissertation, Master Thesis (M. Sc.), Department of Informatics Architectural Design Computing Programme, Istanbul Technical University Graduate School of Science Engineering and Technology, İstanbul
17. Kaşka M, Fırat M (2012) Aleksandrıa Troas Kazısı 2013 Yılı Hellenistik Dönem Seramiği Bulguları. Hacı Ali Ekinci Armağanı/Pisidian Essays in Honour of Hacı Ali Ekinci, 47–56
18. Şimşek A (2010) Alman bilim adamlarının Troas Bölgesi'ndeki arkeoloji çalışmaları. Doktora Tezi, Selçuk Üniversitesi Sosyal Bilimleri Enstitüsü, Konya
19. Çavga Ö (2005) Herodes Attikus Hamamı Gün Yüzüne Çıkmayı Bekliyor. Arkeologlar Derneği Dergisi 7(26):43
20. https://www.mobil13.com/pokemon-go-benzeri-en-iyi-ar-oyunlari-21922.html. Last Accessed 20 June 2020
21. https://www.augmentedrealitytrends.com/augmented-reality/new-museum.html/. Last Accessed 20 June 2020.
22. https://www.vi-mm.eu/2016/12/20/862/. Last Accessed 20 June 2020

A Novel Approach in High School Design Education Using Virtual Reality

Tuğba Çelikten and Gökhan İnce

Abstract Design education aims to develop creativity ability, gain production knowledge and technical knowledge. Design education is given at many different levels from high school to doctorate level. Project This project focus on high school level of design education. Virtual reality technology enables users to enter a virtual scene by isolating them from the environment with the help of glasses. This experience, which generally appeals to the sense of vision, can also be supported by the senses of touch and hearing, and is largely disconnected from reality and creates a virtual environment. We have collaborated with Kartal Yakacık Vocational Technical Anatolian High School furniture and interior design department students. This study was carried out in order to solve the needs of the students as a result of the researches conducted using observation, interview and survey methods. The existing curriculum was examined and the target group as well as the course content subject to change were determined. In order to measure the influence and effects of education in the virtual reality environment, tests were applied before and after the students received training with virtual reality glasses. Within the scope of the study, 13 students at three levels of high school and 22 students at two levels of high school were studied. Finally, the outcomes and results of the experiments involving teaching basic practical production and material usage information that is supposed to be learned in furniture design education at high school level were explained.

Keywords Virtual reality · Design education · Practical education · Usability · Furniture design

T. Çelikten
Game and Interaction Technologies, Istanbul Technical University, Istanbul, Turkey
e-mail: celiktent19@itu.edu.tr

G. İnce (✉)
Computer Engineering, Istanbul Technical University, Istanbul, Turkey
e-mail: gokhan.ince@itu.edu.tr

© The Author(s), under exclusive license to Springer Nature Switzerland AG 2021
Ö. Cordan et al. (eds.), *Game + Design Education*, Springer Series in Design and Innovation 13, https://doi.org/10.1007/978-3-030-65060-5_21

1 Introduction

Technological developments change needs and methods in last years. It has an impact on people's perspectives and educational methods. One of the latest technological developments affecting our lives is virtual reality technology that entered our lives with VR glasses. It is an undeniable fact that this technology, which has been applied and studied in many different fields, has greatly contributed to making education interactive. Virtual reality; The simplest level is to appeal to the sense of vision with the help of glasses, to greatly break the relationship with the real world and experience a virtual world. More advanced products of technology also appeal to the sense of sound and touch to enhance the experience. Virtual experiences that can be developed with computer-aided or mobile-supported software can be used with different types of virtual reality glasses. This technology, which enables the development of different methods in every field, also enables the development of more efficient methods in design education.

Design education is one of the disciplines that can effectively use virtual reality technology. Design discipline is divided into different branches and levels. Industrial design is one of the design areas that are trained from high school to doctorate level. At the earliest stage, vocational education is provided at high school level. Industrial design vocational education has different skills. Technical drawing training, which is one of them, is important for students to visualize products suitable for production and to contribute to the production of products by reading technical drawings of the products. Technical drawing plays a key role in determining the ultimate quality of a product, good technical drawing is one that properly and conveniently communicates all of the information needed to transform a design into a product that meets or exceeds all customer expectations. There are different technical drawing technics but 2 of them are commonly used. These are first angle projection and third angle projection. The main difference of the two systems is the position of the projection plane. While technical drawing, the regions are divided into four quadrants and the part is placed in the first partition in the first angle projection method, but in the third angle projection method it is placed in the third region. After this process, reflection of the product on each surface gives orthographic drawings.

In this study, we have worked with 10th grade and 11th grade students in order to make the technical drawing education, which we mentioned in this project, more effective. We aim to create solutions with VR technology so that students can keep up with current technological developments in the industry and receive more interactive education.

2 Literature Review

Developing technology is used to make technical drawing education, which is one of the cornerstones of design education, more interactive. In addition to the commonly used technical drawing teaching methods, virtual and augmented reality technologies are designed to be integrated into the education curriculum. When traditional teaching methods are used alongside AR and VR, students have a much higher engagement rate and perform significantly better on tests [1]. Technical drawing training basically brings two important acquisitions. One of them is to take out the appearance of the product or piece, and the other is to explain the production technique and materials of the product with a sectional drawing. The orthographic views of all surfaces required in technical drawing surface views are drawn according to certain grammar and drawing rules. The necessary angles and dimensions for the production are obtained by looking at the different views of the product. The section drawing is cut like a knife perpendicular to the specified surface and the places touching the blade are scanned. Thus, the details inside the product and its wall in production are determined.

Many different projects are running with AR and VR technologies [2]. They developed a study that they can see in augmented real environment. They concluded that the project developed for ease of use and effective training of students should be a user-friendly product.

Usability principles aim to make the product to be user-friendly and sustainable by adding disciplines that aim to make the interaction between human and industrial products more efficient and healthier. Process materials will be developed based on the principles of usability in the planning, design, development and testing processes of the project. The aim of our project is to achieve the most efficient way of projecting the targeted group, and to determine the needs and responsibilities of the project manager, end product user and institutions or individuals that provide the product by using the user journey map, and control of each stage and stakeholder of the research process [3]. Concludes that it can be used in a functional and interactive way in industrial design education as a result of its studies and reports that flexible and easy tools can be introduced. There are many different methods and development techniques. Although VR technology has been developing for many years, applications in the field of education are still developing and recognizing new areas. Applications that have developed the applicability of the technology should be accessible as well as providing ease of use. The fact that the glasses with the developed software are expensive also slows down the use of this technology, especially in the field of education. This project has been developed with all this in mind.

3 Field Study and Observation

In the current curriculum at the school where the project was passed educate through the first angle projection technical drawing regulations this project is developed according to the first angle projection method on application [4]. The training of the pilot school Kartal Yakacık Vocational Technical Anatolian High School furniture and interior design students which we conduct the project, proceeds in two different branches. Furniture design and interior vocational education of students who have been trained in two different ways, namely theoretical and vocational starts in the 10th grade. Lessons are divided into modules according to their subjects. They receive theoretical and practical training in the atelier. In their theoretical training, they acquire the information they may need at every stage of design and production such as manual technical drawing, material, production, CAD drawing. In addition, they acquire practical knowledge such as machine usage, production processes and prototyping.

They start their technical drawing training in the 10th grade by hand with a curriculum consisting of 3 modules. These three modules are sequentially divided into drawing geometric shapes, removing part appearances and scaling furniture pieces. As the second module is the module where the technical drawing views are taught, thus we aim to support the project in this part of the curriculum (Table 1). In the 11th grade, they learn to make technical drawing on a computer. Students coming to grade 12 see a one-year internship to improve their professional knowledge, and at the end of the year they are graded by both the school and the company where they are trained. After understanding the educational process of the department, after conducting interviews and observation studies to understand where students have difficulties in their lessons to identify problems, the education methods and methods of teachers were also examined. Teachers support the course with animation videos in addition to textbooks and technical drawing tools during the education process [5]. Technical drawing education, which is the subject that students and teachers have difficulties in common, is one of the most important acquisitions of vocational education. After determining the points that students and teachers had difficulties in their vocational education processes, we would be positioned in one of the manual technical drawing modules, which is the first stage of technical drawing education.

4 Proposed VR System for Technical Drawing Using Camera

In this project, we have developed a process and product that enables students who are trained in high school level furniture and interior design to integrate them into the curriculum in technical drawing lessons, so that they can obtain technical drawing and reading information more easily and interactively. Since the technical drawing education starts with hand drawing, we aimed to improve the teaching process by adding a more interactive and controllable method to the technical drawing processes in order to eliminate the pain points of the students. The project is experienced with mobile based VR glasses and is developed using UNITY 3D.

The way of using VR glasses are basically divided into three. Computer aided glasses can be used with computers with good processors and are supported with arms. Thus, they also allow control by hand-arm movements. Some products offer a stronger experience by sensing pressure as well as motion according to the level of development, but computer aided glasses are difficult to price and need a powerful computer. Mobile-based glasses are the most economically applicable glasses that

Table 1 10th grade technical drawing lesson's curriculum

1. MODULE: Geometric polygons	2. MODULE: Appearance removal	3. MODULE: Furniture combinations and measurement
A-Text and number 1-The place, importance and definition of technical drawing in the industry 2-Drawing tools and materials *Papers, rulers, squares	A-Appearance removal 1-Definition and classification of the concept of projection 2-Definition and types of projection planes	A-Perspective 1-Definition and importance of perspective 2-Perspective types
3-Text and numbers 4-Line and its types 5-Geometric drawings about Lines	*Conical (Central) projection *Parallel projection *Point projection *Projection of the lines	*Isometric perspective *Dimetric perspective *Trimetric perspective
*Dividing the line segment into two equal parts *Compass help from the point on the line to erect with *Straight up the end of the line	B-Rules of appearance 1-Definition of faces and types 2-Parts expressed in one view	3-Perspective drawing rules 4-Dimensioning perspective drawings *Isometric perspective applications
B- Lines, circles and planes 1-Geometric drawings about Angles *Drawing angles *Moving angles *Dividing an Angle into two equal parts	3-Parts expressed in two and three views 4-Common looking parts Evaluation Exam	*Dimetric perspective applications *Trimetric perspective applications
C-Polygons drawing 1-Triangle drawing 2-Quadrant drawing 3-Hexagon drawing	C-Perspective pictures and model parts 1-Missing views 2-Parts that need auxiliary views	B-Furniture combinations 1-Types, features and drawings *Top joints *High joint drawing with lamp Evaluation exam
4-Hexagon drawing 5-Heptagon drawing 6-Octagonal drawing	D-Sectional view 1-Definition of sectioning concept 2-Section view types *Full section	C-Dowel coupling drawing 1-Drawing and dimensioning of 1/10 scale clear picture 2–1/10 scale perspective drawing and dimensioning
7-Drawing of a regular or an octagonal with general method application	*Half section *Partial section *Stage section *Profile section	3-Frame corner joints *45° frame corner joint drawing with dowel
D-Circle, tangent and line drawings 1-Tangent drawing from a point on the circle, 2-Tangent drawing from a point outside the circle	*Rotated section 3-Sectioning rules	4-Foot record joints *Open mortise foot registration assembly drawing *Dimensioning

(continued)

Table 1 (continued)

1. MODULE: Geometric polygons	2. MODULE: Appearance removal	3. MODULE: Furniture combinations and measurement
4-Oval drawings 5-Ellipse drawings 6-Helix drawings Module evaluation exam	4-Section drawing applications Module evaluation exam	5-Drawing of mortice foot Module evaluation exam

do not have control arms that can only interact with head movement and focus. Since the most suitable VR is mobile based for the feasibility and accessibility of our study, we carried out our studies with android supported mobile based VR glasses.

With the application we have developed, the student takes the technical drawing views he/she draws in accordance with the third angle projection method by using the camera from within the application. When he looks at the errors he noticed for a long time, he can see and compare the appearance of the 3D product on the wall compared to the wall he is looking at, and a red dot is formed in that area so that when he takes off the glasses, he has the chance to check and correct his mistakes. Since the student is dependent on the teacher in order to notice and correct the errors in the current education, he has to wait for the whole class to be able to improve himself and continue his studies. In addition, in two-dimensional papers and videos, the students reported that they had difficulty reducing a three-dimensional product to two dimensions because they could not think of the pieces and the drawings they had together.

With our application developed, the student was included in his technical drawing system and had the opportunity to compare what he drew in the virtual reality environment and see the product together (Fig. 1). In addition to the appearance drawings in the technical drawing training, the section drawing is also of great importance.

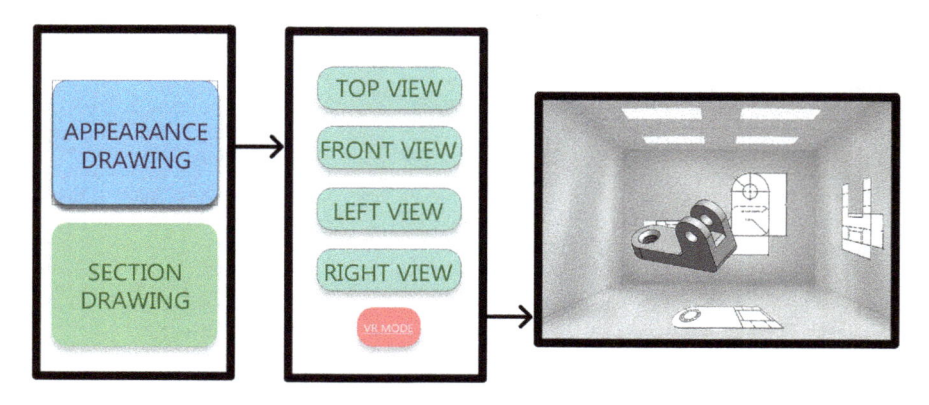

Fig. 1 Orthographic appearances of technical drawing in VR environment

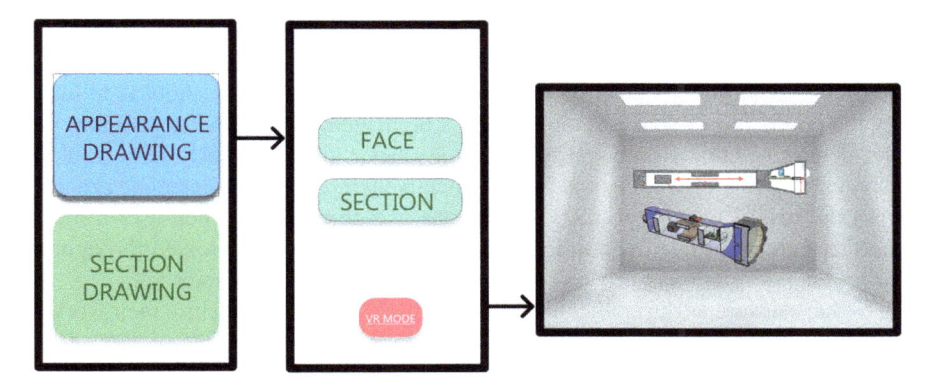

Fig. 2 Section appearance of technical drawing in VR environment

Therefore, when the student starts the section drawing education process, he/she will be able to have this experience by entering the section drawing section of the application.

Students who have difficulty in section drawing as well as appearance drawing education will use the application by taking a photo of their sections by choosing which surface they are cut from. When they wear the glasses and enter the virtual environment, they will be able to compare the cut version of the product cut from the specified surface with their own works (Fig. 2). While developing the project, we aimed to develop the application so that teachers and students can easily use the application, as well as we aimed to create a common language as each of the students had different perspectives and habits. Considering the usability principles to develop easy-to-use interfaces for everyone [6], we proceeded in our work by listening to users' troubles and relying on observations. We selected the pieces used in the application from the furniture pieces educated in the curriculum and used in the atelier. In this study, which we conducted in cooperation with teachers, we selected the parts by determining at which points the students had difficulties thanks to their experience in the education processes up to now. The application allows new items for technical drawing homework to be added in line with the wishes and results of teachers and students.

5 Conclusion

In summary, VR glasses have begun to enter different areas of education and help students get more interactive education. It will be a refreshing development for students and teachers to integrate this technology by identifying the area where design education students have problems most. For this purpose, we interviewed students and teachers and observed the course processing processes. In addition, we examined their curricula and learned the lessons they experienced with course materials. After examining the existing solutions targeted in this project and identifying the problems faced by them, the research process with the pilot school is to identify the points of problem and to establish a permanent virtual reality solution. We have determined that virtual reality technology can achieve the most useful result in technical drawing education, and we can effectively integrate an interactive process. From the results of current AR/VR solutions, we observed that non-user-friendly interfaces create problems in use. For this reason, we have progressed throughout our product development process, considering the usability principles [7].

We have developed an application that will enable students to control their work in two dimensions by transferring them to three-dimensional virtual environment. They have the opportunity to compare the technical drawings of the smart phones with their cameras by looking at them from different sides with the three-dimensional version of the product they draw in 3D virtual environment. This application, which they can use on their own, can also support homework given by teachers. Three dimensional models added to the application are selected from the furniture pieces covered in the course. In addition, it enables the addition of new models in the process. There will be testing process after Covid-19 pandemic situation.

This study conducted at vocational high school level can be adapted for many departments that receive technical drawing training. Technical drawing trainings in all areas of industrial design and engineering education may differ. After examining each curriculum, new versions can be created by updating as needed. CAD modeling education, which is the next stage of technical drawing education, is also included in the 11th grade curriculum of furniture and interior design vocational high school students. In this process, students learn to draw in technical environment. In this process they learn, Autodesk-AutoCAD program can help them advance in technical drawing education in a study where they can transfer their drawings to the computer environment and compare them with their 3D views in virtual reality and take their orthographic views.

References

1. Bodekaer M (n.d.) Bu sanal laboratuvar bilim derslerinde devrim yapacak, https://www.ted.com/talks/michael_bodekaer_this_virtual_lab_will_revolutionize_science_class?language=tr https://www.ted.com/talks/michael_bodekaer_this_virtual_lab_will_revolutionize_science_class?language=tr. Last Accessed 01 July 2020
2. Ivan H, Abdil K, Ertuğrul U, Rıdvan A, Muhammed D, Muhammed K, Vlademir I (2019) A design-based approach to enhancing technical drawing skills in design and engineering education using VR and AR tools
3. Jonna H, Ashley C, Jani V, Antti-Jussi Y (2018) Introducing virtual reality technologies to design education
4. David G, William C, John N, Raynmond R (2005) Technical drawing, 5nd edn. Cengage Learning
5. Esparza M (2017) Intermediate drawing: technical drawing course

6. Bettina L, Martin S, Theo H (2008) T.Construction and evaluation of a user experience questionnaire. In: Holzinger, A. (Ed.): USAB 2008, LNCS 5298, pp 63–76
7. Denizhan D, Çağla Ş (2018) A Turkish translation of the system usability scale: the Sus-Tr. Uşak Üniversitesi Sosyal Bilimler Dergisi 11(3):237–253
8. Lise öğrencilerinin çalışma alışkanlıkları anketi. National Institution for Youth Education (2017)
9. Pierre G, Paul R, Yann P, Sébastien G, Emmanuelle R (2019) Simulation tools for the design of virtual training environments. In: International conference for multi-area simulation (ICMASim). Angers, France, pp 293–298
10. Murat Y, Birsen K (2015) Developing innovative applications of technical drawing course at the maritime education. Procedia Soc Behav Sci 195:2813–2821. https://doi.org/10.1016/j.sbspro.2015.06.399
11. Noureddine E (2019) Augmented reality and virtual reality in education. Myth or reality. Int J Emerg Technol Learning
12. Murad S, Passero I, Francese R, Tortora G (2011) An empirical evaluation of technical drawing didactic in virtual worlds. Int J Online Eng (iJOE) 7(S1). https://doi.org/10.3991/ijoe.v7is1.1733

Smartphone as a Paired Game Input Device: An Application on HoloLens Head Mounted Augmented Reality System

Mehmet Sonat Karan, Mehmet İlker Berkman, and Güven Çatak

Abstract From social media filters to medical applications, AR (augmented reality) is a rapidly growing technology. On the other hand, AR gaming is a popular application of this field of study. Microsoft's see-through augmented reality headset HoloLens is one of the first and powerful headsets in the market today but it has limited interaction methods especially for gaming. This study deals with enhancing gaming experience in augmented reality devices by creating new interaction methods through a smartphone used as a game-controller an input device. We developed the Remote Input SDK (software development kit) to allow users to share input data between Unity applications to use a smartphone as remote controller while playing a game through HoloLens. This study explains the design and implementation of our SDK, which is available as an open-source component for Unity game development platform.

Keywords Augmented reality · Game development · HoloLens · Game controller

1 Introduction

Smartphones are the most common technical gadget and a large amount of the population own a smartphone in advanced and developing countries [1]. Today, sensors like accelerometers, magnetometers, light sensors and gyroscopes are standard components of smartphones along with the touchscreens. These sensors have become a rich data source [2]. By using these sensors, it is possible to create a virtual 6-DoF (6 degree of freedom) controller to interact with virtual world, using the data that collected from sensors to manipulate virtual elements. The sensor data

M. S. Karan
Bahcesehir University Game Design Graduate Programme, Istanbul, Turkey

M. İ. Berkman (✉)
Department of Communication and Design, Bahcesehir University, Istanbul, Turkey
e-mail: ilker.berkman@comm.bau.edu.tr

G. Çatak
Department of Digital Game Design, Bahcesehir University, Istanbul, Turkey

of mobile phones has been used by game designers to develop interesting interaction schemes for mobile games, but rarely investigated for their potential as a peripheral controller device that is to be connected to a gaming platform. Although there are many studies on possible interactions schemes for multi-display systems using several mobile phone sensor capabilities, e.g. [3–5], only a few studies have employed the cross-device approach in game design.

In this study, we explored the possibilities of enhancing gaming experience in HoloLens augmented reality device by creating new interaction methods through a smartphone. We developed a SDK (software development kit), which we call Remote Input SDK, to allow developers share sensor input data between applications to use a smartphone as remote controller in order to engage with a game-like interactive environment through HoloLens.

Current input methods do not closely map to the interactions required for an enhanced gaming experience and there is a conflict with realism of the augmented world and limitations of the available interaction methods supported by current AR HMD sets.

2 Related Studies

2.1 Previous Attempts to Employ Mobile Devices as a Game Input Device

The idea of employing a mobile phone as an input device attracted designers and developers for various types of interactions. Ballagas et al. [6] reviewed several applications that employ mobile devices connected to other systems as input devices and categorize the inputs directed through by mobile devices as position, orient, select, path, quantify and text inputs. Some of the mobile phones employed in the applications they investigated were not smartphones and users were interacting through numeric keys, trackpads or velocity controlled keys on these devices. On the other hand, some of the applications employ smartphones to use their, accelerometers, cameras, RFID readers and microphones with voice recognition capabilities. These applications were mainly designed for ubiquitous computing purposes, such as allowing interactions on public displays.

Vajk et al. [7] had an early attempt to use mobile phone as game controller. They used a Nokia 5500 as a gaming interface for a multiplayer car racing game by developing an application to run Nokia's Symbian operating system that transfers data to computer through Bluetooth connection. Their system, namely Poppet Framework, was an extension of their previous study [8]. Their gameplay allowed multi-user interactions. Malfatti et al. [9] demonstrated a similar system that they had named as Bluewawe, based on Bluetooh signal transmission for a multiplayer game. Joselli et al. [10] also developed a system to control a 2D space shooter single player game running on an Apple tablet computer running IOS via an Apple I-Phone device.

The data connection between devices was using TCP-IP protocol through wireless network.

Finger Walking In Place (FWIP) is proposed as a navigational solution for CAVE virtual environments [11]. Originally it was implemented for the Lemur touchscreen midi controller and then exported to run on Apple IOS devices [12]. In a recent study, Liang et al. [13] employed a tablet computer as a controller for a virtual reality game. Using their system, players experienced a more efficient gameplay compared to their performance with a gamepad device.

Touchscreen handheld devices and their accelerometers had also been implemented in along with AR HMDs. Ha and Woo [14] developed a mobile application to control the positions of augment 3D objects viewed through a HMD, exploiting the phone's internal sensor information.

Several interaction and object manipulation methods were evaluated using a handheld device for input on an AR HMD system [15], revealing that interactions using devices with motion sensors and touch screen capabilities are applicable to AR.

2.2 Defining Augmented Reality

The journey of augmented reality started with the Sutherland's research on head mounted displays in the early days of computer graphics [16]. His prototype still inspires the researchers and developers who are working on virtual reality and augmented reality even though it is only capable of drawing simple vectors and detecting walls of a room.

Milgram and Kishino [17] placed augmented reality between virtual environment and real environment in their mixed reality continuum where real environments are located at the left end of continuum. Azuma [18] suggested that augmented reality is a technology that has three key requirements: (1) It combines real and virtual content. (2) It is interactive in real time (3) It is registered in 3D.

These requirements also define the technical requirements of augmented reality systems. First, it has to have a visualization mechanism that can combine virtual and real content. Secondly, there must be a software which is enabling a user to interact with the virtual environment. Finally, a tracking system is a must. An AR system has to find the position of the user's viewpoint in three-dimension environment and overlap virtual image successfully [19]. Augmented reality is aiming to make user interfaces invisible and improve user interaction with the real world environments at the opposite extremum.

Wearable technology means an electronics or a computer that embedded into clothing or designed as an accessory that can be worn on the body [20]. Wearable computers enhanced the connection between user and application by providing the data that is collected from directly user's body. For this reason, Starner et al. [21] had defined wearable systems are a natural platform for augmented reality.

2.3 Design Methods for Augmented Reality

There are too many interaction methods exist in the AR applications. These are mostly forming of existing interaction methods in desktop, mobile or VR applications. According to Billinghurst et al. [22], there is a need to develop interaction metaphors specialized for AR The author also found that when a new interface environment, such as AR is developed, it typically follows these steps: (1) Prototype demonstration (2) Adoption of interaction techniques from other interface metaphors (3) Development of new interface metaphors appropriate to the medium (4) Development of formal theoretical models for modelling user interactions. In addition, they suggest that for design of the physical and virtual objects of the application, the interaction metaphor needs to be developed. In this case, there are three elements that must be designed in the AR application; physical object, virtual element to be displayed, and the interaction metaphor.

Using design patterns is another approach in designing interaction of augmented reality applications. In order to improve game design of AR games and make them more enjoyable and intuitive [23]. Xu et al. [23] present nine design patterns for Handheld AR Games: Device metaphors, control mapping, seamful design, world consistency, landmarks, personal presence, living creatures, body constraints and hidden information.

2.4 Complexities in AR Software Development

Augmented Reality technology now available at outside of the laboratories. Nevertheless, AR technology have to solve some problems like mobility, tracking, cost, power usage and ergonomics, to be accepted as everyday technology such as smartphones or smart watches [24].

Mobility and outdoor usage are one of the main problems of AR. Most of the complex AR system requires powerful hardware and this means heavy machine with cables. Large devices with limited battery and cables create bulky experience for user [25].

Billinghurst et al. [19] point out that tracking and calibration are the major problem for AR systems especially for optical see-through AR displays. Because of the calibration parameters are spatial dependent it is hard to calibrate wearable device where the device position keeps changing with user's movement. Calibration failures causes misalignment between real and virtual view images. On the other hand, tracking and calibration problems bring the non-immersive experience together. In recent years, the tracking and calibration problems are not an issue any more, as AR development frameworks offer these functions as a standardized software feature.

Since the AR overlaps to user's view, some design guidelines must be followed to preventing user to overly rely on the AR application and missing important cues from the environment [24]. Bengler and Passaro [26] suggested guidelines to design

AR for cars. They focus on driving task, no moving or obstructing imagery. They provide information that improves driving performance.

Social acceptance has also been declared as important issue for wearable technologies like augmented reality by number of researchers. According to Billinghurst et al. [19], the reasons behind this reluctance are privacy concerns, or fear of looking silly, or being a target for thieves.

In addition to technical aspects of designing augmented reality experience, there is also commercial and ethical aspects. For example, if the application can only be runnable on specific devices, users have to buy them. This concept has been exploited by gaming console manufacturers. Thus, designing game for this concept is attractive under commercial perspective [27]. However, it is disadvantage under ethical perspective due to economical differences of players.

3 Development Environment

One of the first head mounted augmented reality headsets available on the market today is Microsoft's HoloLens. It comes with Universal Windows Platform (UWP) which offers powerful development environment. So, it is easy to develop games for HoloLens since developers can export their game via Unity3D to UWP.

HoloLens comes with 32-bit Intel processors, custom-built Microsoft Holographic Processing Unit (HPU 1.0) a coprocessor manufactured exclusively for HoloLens by Microsoft, 64 GB Flash, 2 GB RAM and built-in rechargeable battery. All of these processing units provide 2–3 h of active standalone usage (headset fully functional while using with power cable plugged in). It also has Inertial Measurement Unit (IMU) (including accelerometer, gyroscope and magnetometer), four environment-processing cameras (two on each side), a depth camera to map its surroundings and allow interaction between the real and virtual world while tracking the device's position, a 2.4-megapixel camera, microphone, and an ambient light sensor. HoloLens features Wi-Fi and Bluetooth for wireless connectivity. The headset uses Bluetooth to pair with the Clicker, a thumb-sized finger-operated input device that can be used for interface scrolling and selecting.

While using HoloLens, users need to be at least 1.25 m away from holograms. If users get closer the holograms for more than one meter, virtual objects rendered by the HoloLens will begin to fade out, and they will actually disappear as they close to 0.85 m away. The device has a very narrow field of view of just 35°. Although augmented reality and mixed reality has to fill user's view to provide truly immersive experience, in HoloLens users can only see holograms at the center of their vision in a small letterbox.

There is certain memory limitation for HoloLens app. If an application exceeds the memory limit, resource manager of HoloLens will terminate the application. Also, device has passive cooling. That means if its internal temperature spikes too high, the system will shut down the offending applications.

Developing application for HoloLens requires high-end system configuration. Although it is not necessary to own a HoloLens headset in order to develop applications for it, a special system configuration with a specific operating system version is required to run an emulator [28].

Unity is one of the most powerful game engines available in the market and it is possible to develop games with free plan of Unity. During the Build 2015 keynote, it was revealed that Unity is partnering with HoloLens. After that partnership they worked together to strengthen the integration between Unity and Visual Studio which results more efficient development environment for creating non-gaming 3D experiences and that's make the Unity is the best choice for developing applications on HoloLens. In addition, that partnership, Unity has large community, hundreds of tutorials online and Microsoft has released tutorials so it is easy to learn how to develop an application in Unity for HoloLens.

For the reasons mentioned above, we decided to use Unity versions released after version 2018.2 running on a computer with the Windows 64-bit Pro operating system with an eight-core AMD Ryzen 7 1700 3.0Ghz CPU, NVIDIA GTX 1060 6 GB GPU, 16 GB of RAM. We used both the HoloLens emulator and the headset itself during the development process.

4 Design and Development

Our Remote Input SDK allows users to share predefined input data such as sensor data and virtual gamepad button states over Wi-Fi between applications which were built in Unity3D game engine. SDK was written in C# and it uses Transmission Control Protocol (TCP) for wireless communication. It can be added to any Unity Project by just extracting the unity package file which is available to download at GitHub page of SDK or it can be also downloadable from GitHub as Unity Project, via the URLs given in supplementary data.

4.1 The Structure and Flow in Remote Input SDK

Developing a Universal Windows Platform game with Unity using.NET may require extra coding because some of the.NET libraries are not available. When building a game with Unity for multiple platform including UWP, Microsoft suggest that using platform-dependent compilation to make sure that UWP is only run when the game build for UWP.

Remote Input SDK is requiring Networking namespaces such as System.Net, System.Net.Sockets and these namespaces are not available when building a Unity game for UWP with.Net scripting backend. While developing network part of the Remote Input SDK, the strategy software design pattern has been used to overcome this problem. The strategy software design pattern is a behavioral pattern that allows

Fig. 1 Usage of strategy software design pattern in remote input SDK. *Source* Mehmet Sonat Karan

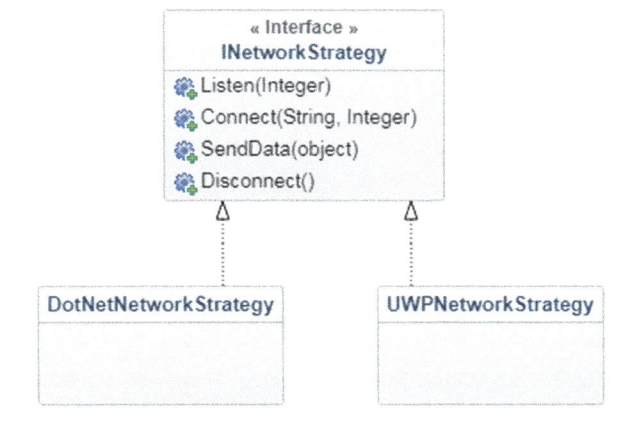

selecting algorithm at runtime. Remote Input SDK has two different network strategy one for specially UWP, UWPNetworkStrategy class and the other one for all other platforms DotNetNetworkStrategy class, which can be inspected on Fig. 1.

At the application startup, NetworkStrategyFactory class decide which network strategy class should be instantiated with help of platform-dependent compiling. See the following code on Fig. 2.

Once the network strategy instance is created, all methods of the INetworkStrategy interface will be implemented with the correct algorithm based on the runtime platform. Since the Unity support IL2CPP scripting backend for UWP, DotNetNetworkStrategy implementation works for all platforms when building applications with IL2CPP. So this approach became unnecessary.

SDK can be used as Host or Controller. A state machine is used to handle this states and transitions between states.

There are two different state in Remote Input SDK; MainMenu and GamePad states. MainMenu states can act differently according to SDK's working mode which

Fig. 2 Sample for strategy software design pattern. *Source* Mehmet Sonat Karan

```
#if NETFX_CORE

    _networkStrategy =
NetworkStrategyFactory.Instance.CreateUWPworkStrategy();

#else

    _networkStrategy =
NetworkStrategyFactory.Instance.CreateDotNetworkStrategy();

#endif
```

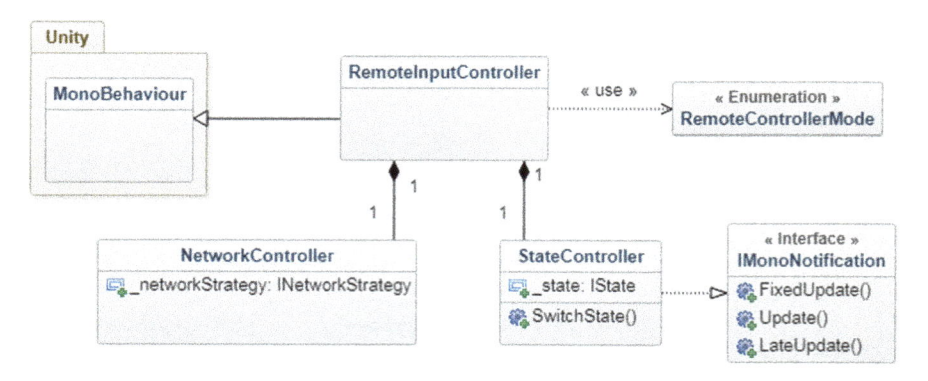

Fig. 3 Remote Input SDK class diagram. *Source* Mehmet Sonat Karan

can be change between two modes; Host or Controller. If Host mode selected, Main-Menu state create a view for host application which allows users to Listen specific port to any possible controller connection. If controller mode is selected state will create a view that allows users to enter host's IP address and let them connect to host. GamePad state is only available if application is running on controller mode. When SDK is connected to host application, state controller will automatically switch state to GamePad state and a gamepad view will be created.

As on overview of Remote Input SDK, there is one MonoBehaviour which is main controller of the system (See Fig. 3). It is a component added to a GameObject in initial scene and it does not affect from scene loads. Lifetime of this controller starts when the application start, and end when user terminate the app. RemoteInputController has two sub-controllers; NetworkController and State Controller. NetworkController is responsible for wireless communication and StateController is controlling the SDK's states. StateController uses IMonoNotification interface to get update calls from MonoBehaviour.

While developing Remote Input SDK, UnityMainThreadDispatcher, VirtualJoystick, FollowCamera and Unka the Dragon asset [29] external components are used. While working with Unity, if an operation modifies engine's properties it has to be done in main thread of Unity. To do this we use UnityMainThreadDispatcher. It is a thread-safe way of dispatching coroutines to the main thread in Unity [30]. VirtualJoystick is small component which is developed by researcher that allows user to interact with unity application by using virtual joystick. Finally, Unka The Dragon is an asset which is available in the Unity Asset Store [29]. The asset contains high quality 3D model and predefined animation sets.

The interface for our Remote Input SDK is prototyped as depicted in Fig. 4. Prototype was tested on Android and iOS devices as Controller and a PC used as host. Prototype can act as both Host or Controller. If user pressed Listen button application simply listen to predefined port and when a controller enters the host's IP to address bar and simply pressed to Connect button data transfer will start from Controller to Host.

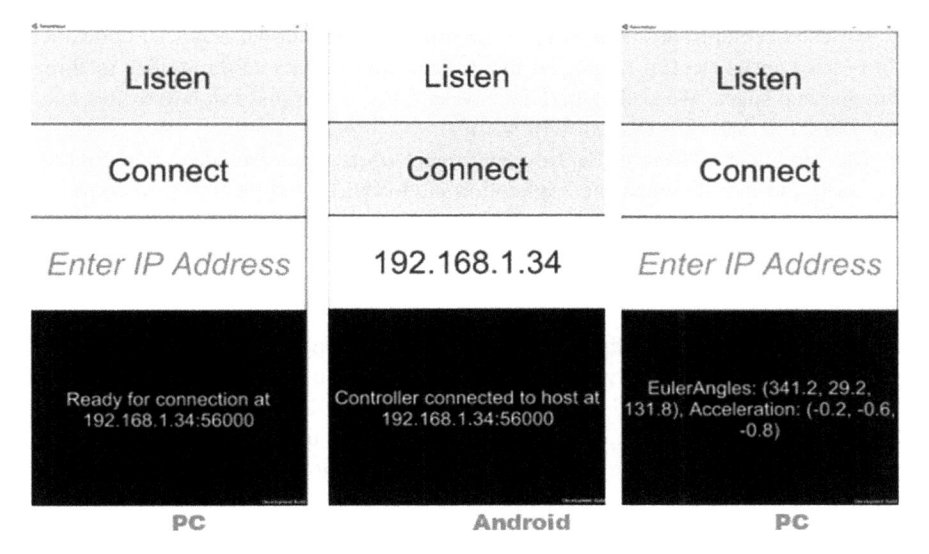

Smartphone as a Paired Game Input Device: An Application ... 273

Fig. 4 Remote Input SDK running on Windows PC (Host) and Android device (Controller). *Source* Mehmet Sonat Karan

4.2 Game Development and Use of Remote Input SDK in the Environment

Developing a Holographic User Interface was the first challenge we had to overcome while developing an application for HoloLens with Unity. It should be work on both Unity Editor and the HoloLens itself. So we follow the guideline that is described in Unity Forums [31]. First of all, we add HoloLens Input Module component to EventSystem object and leave Standalone Input Module attached so our UI still work with editor. After that, we changed canvas render mode to World Space so it can be registered in 3D space. Finally, we create virtual cursor to more easily tell to user where their gaze is pointed.

Microsoft developed a toolkit which is aiming rapid prototyping, accelerating content production and removing complexities in multi-platform XR solutions [32]. It is available at GitHub and also downloadable as a Unity package file. We use this toolkit while prototyping our HoloLens app. Toolkit contains examples that showing the best practices for mixed reality development specially with Unity. It also has ready to use prefabs which is really helpful while creating simple holographic user interfaces.

Unka the Dragon [29] asset provides high quality 3D animal models with fully functional animation setup. We have chosen to use this asset because their highly detailed and animated dragons can fly in the air and walk in the ground so it perfectly matches with our control-mapping method where the user's actions are registered in 3D space and mapped with avatar's actions.

We use accelerometer sensor to detect tilting up and down states of controller. Unity give access to last measured linear acceleration data of the device in three-dimensional space. We collect that data every frame and transform it to tilting states according the data change in last 10 frames.

The life cycle of Remote Input game object starts when the scene that contains it is load and it ends when the application is closed. So before trying to connect a controller, a scene with the Remote Input game object must be loaded.

Listen method of RemoteInputController class has to be called before trying to connect with controller application. After calling Listen method host will be ready for connection and ReadyForConnection event will be fired. Now controller application can connect to host. When the controller connected, ControllerConnected event will be fired and the controller will begin to start sending input data over WiFi. Every time an input data received an event called InputDataReceived will be fired. This event contains input data in it, and it can apply directly to the environment.

When a scene with Controller mode and RemoteInput game object is selected, the controller UI is shown. The user must type the IP address of the host in the address field and press the connect button to connect a host. The GamePad view is automatically displayed when the controller is connected to the host computer. GamePad view can be customized in consonance with the game requirements. The GamePad class that contains the input data must be modified according to the GamePad view.

As it can be seen in videos at supplementary material, when the users run the game that contains Host application on their HoloLens devices, HoloLens device prompts the IP address of itself and tells them to run the Controller application on their mobile device. After doing this, users can control the Unka the Dragon [29] around the room they are in, by tilting up the mobile phone upwards to start its flight, which is an accelerometer based input to the gameplay. They can land the dragon by tilting their phone downwards. A joystick-like interface on the touchscreen of the mobile phone lets the users to control the dragon's direction in 3D space and a button on the phone touchscreen triggers flame throws, as depicted on Fig. 5.

Fig. 5 Screenshots from the user's HMD view. *Source* Mehmet Sonat Karan

5 Conclusion

In this study, we used smartphone as an input device and use the sensor data as an input data to enhance gaming experience on Microsoft's augmented reality headset, HoloLens. Although the idea of employing a mobile device as a game controller had been implemented for computer games and virtual reality applications previously, The SDK we developed is not only for connecting a smartphone to Microsoft's HoloLens AR device, but also it can be used to connect a mobile phone to any gaming platform such as desktop PC's and secondary mobile devices, which support applications created with Unity development platform.

The Remote Input SDK can create connection between Unity applications so an application developed with Unity for XR devices can be controlled by a smartphone. Users can add input methods to their application like gyroscope or accelerometer by using smartphone or they can use smartphone as an information browser. Since our SDK uses wireless network technology to connect other applications, users can also interact with their application out of the headset camera's boundaries.

The SDK has a restriction on connectivity. SDK can lose connection or transfer data with delay when network signal is weak. To overcome this problem other connection methods like Bluetooth can be added to system in the future. Second limitation is about HoloLens' development environment. HoloLens is an expensive device, if developer's budget is not enough to use a HoloLens, he/she needs to work with emulator. HoloLens emulator required more powerful hardware and experiences in the virtual environment may not coincide with the actual environment for some cases.

Considering the popularity of smartphones and their rich interaction capabilities based on their sensors and cameras, we believe that Our SDK could be an inspiration and a starting point for game development platform vendors such as Unity should include built-in functions to let game developers employ a mobile phone as controller in their games, either their game is developed to primarily run on a platform other than a mobile device, and even to control a game running on another mobile device such as a tablet computer. However, further research is required via involving the players, to explore the user performance and game user experience in order to develop rich and powerful interactions with smartphone based paired input devices.

Supplementary Material

User video captures of the application in action

https://www.youtube.com/watch?v=EIX19dNL65U

https://www.youtube.com/watch?v=_xVtDZa8d68

Source code of Remote Input SDK

https://github.com/karansonat/RemoteInput

References

1. Silver L (2019) Smartphone ownership is growing rapidly around the world, but Not always equally. Pew Research Center, [Online]. Available: https://www.pewresearch.org/global/2019/02/05/smartphone-ownership-is-growing-rapidly-around-the-world-but-not-always-equally/
2. Shoaib M, Bosch S, Incel OD, Scholten H, Havinga PJM (2015) A survey of online activity recognition using mobile phones. Sensors (Switzerland)
3. Paay J et al (2017) A comparison of techniques for cross-device interaction from mobile devices to large displays. J Mob Multimed
4. Ramos G, Hinckley K, Wilson A, Sarin R (2009) Synchronous gestures in multi-display environments. Hum-Comput Interact
5. Chong MK, Mayrhofer R, Gellersen H (2014) A survey of user interaction for spontaneous device association. ACM Comput Surv
6. Ballagas R, Borchers J, Rohs M, Sheridan JG (2006) The smart phone: a ubiquitous input device. IEEE Pervasive Comput
7. Vajk T, Coulton P, Bamford W, Edwards R (2008) Using a mobile phone as a 'wii-like' controller for playing games on a large public display. Int J Comput Games Technol
8. Vajk T, Bamford W, Coulton P, Edwards R (2007) Using a mobile phone as a 'Wii like' controller. In: Proceedings of the 3rd international conference on games research and development
9. Malfatti SM, Santos Dos FF, Santos Dos FF (2011) Using mobile phones to control desktop multiplayer games. In: Proceedings 2010 Brazilian symposium on games and digital entertainment SBGames
10. Joselli M et al (2012) An architecture for game interaction using mobile. In: 4th international IEEE consumer electronic society—games innovation conference, IGiC 2012
11. Kim JS, Gračanin D, Matković K, Quek F (2008) Finger walking in place (FWIP): a traveling technique in virtual environments. In: Lecture notes in computer science (including subseries lecture notes in artificial intelligence and lecture notes in bioinformatics)
12. Kim JS, Gračanin D, Matković K, Quek F (2009) iPhone/iPod touch as input devices for navigation in immersive virtual environments. In: Proceedings—IEEE virtual reality
13. Liang HN, Shi Y, Lu F, Yang J, Papangelis K (2016) VRM controller: an input device for navigation activities in virtual reality environments. In: Proceedings—VRCAI 2016: 15th ACM SIGGRAPH conference on virtual-reality continuum and its applications in industry
14. Ha T, Woo W (2011) ARWand: phone-based 3D object manipulation in augmented reality environment. In: Proceedings 2011 international symposium on ubiquitous virtual reality, ISUVR 2011
15. Budhiraja R, Lee GA, Billinghurst M (2013) Using a HHD with a HMD for mobile AR interaction. In: 2013 IEEE international symposium on mixed and augmented reality ISMAR, 2013
16. Sutherland IE (1968) A head-mounted three dimensional display. In: Proceedings of the December 9–11, 1968, fall joint computer conference, part I on—AFIPS '68 (Fall, part I), p 757
17. Milgram P., Kishino F (1994) Taxonomy of mixed reality visual displays. IEICE Trans Inf Syst
18. Azuma RT (1997) A survey of augmented reality. Presence Teleoperators Virtual Environ 6(4):355–385
19. Billinghurst M, Clark A, Lee G (2014) A survey of augmented reality. In: Foundations and trends in human-computer interaction
20. Wright R, Keith L (2014) Wearable technology: if the tech fits, wear it. J Electron Resour Med Libr
21. Starner T et al (1997) Augmented reality through wearable computing. Presence Teleoperators Virtual Environ
22. Billinghurst M, Grasset R, Looser J (2005) Designing augmented reality interfaces. Comput Graphics (ACM)

23. Xu Y (2011) "Pre-patterns for designing embodied interactions in handheld augmented reality games. In: 2011 IEEE international symposium on mixed and augmented reality—arts media, and humanities, 19–28
24. van Krevelen DEF, Poelman R (2010) A survey of augmented reality technologies, applications and limittions. Int J Virtual Real
25. Khor WS, Baker B, Amin K, Chan A, Patel K, Wong J (2016) Augmented and virtual reality in surgery-the digital surgical environment: applications, limitations and legal pitfalls. Ann Trans Med
26. Bengler K, Passaro R (2004) Augmented reality in cars requirements and constraints. BMW Gr. Forsch. und Tech
27. Lindt I, Ohlenburg J, Pankoke-Babatz U, Ghellal S, Oppermann L, Adams M (2005) Designing cross media games. In: Proceedings PerGames 2005—3rd International Conference on Pervasive Computing—PERVASIVE 2005. Munich, Germany
28. Community MD (2018) Using the HoloLens emulator. Windows Dev Center, [Online]. Available: https://docs.microsoft.com/en-us/windows/mixed-reality/using-the-hololens-emulator Accessed 18 Oct 2018
29. Malbers Animations, Unka the Dragon. Unity Asset Store [Online]. Available: https://assetstore.unity.com/packages/3d/characters/creatures/unka-the-dragon-84283
30. De Witte P UnityMainThreadDispatcher [Online]. Available: https://github.com/PimDeWitte/UnityMainThreadDispatcher.
31. Unity UI on the HoloLens Unity Forums, [Online]. Available: https://forum.unity.com/threads/unity-ui-on-the-hololens.394629/. Accessed 16 Nov 2018
32. D. (Microsoft) Kline Mixedrealitytoolkit-unity, GitHub, [Online]. Available: https://github.com/microsoft/MixedRealityToolkit-Unity. Accessed 10 Oct 2018

Playful Experience Design

Mapping Current Trends on Gamification of Cultural Heritage

Sevde Karahan and Leman Figen Gül

Abstract Gamification, employed to document, present, represent and disseminate the cultural heritage, is related with these practices as instruments, methods and mediums. The main purpose of the systematic approach of gamification in the area of cultural heritage interpretation is to achieve the positive results by effecting an individual/user on provoking/triggering/changing the attitudes/behaviors/thoughts on cultural heritage. In this context, it is important to adopt an interpretation and presentation approach that offers its users an enhancing experience. As a result of the features stated, gamification provides potentials on the interpretation and presentation of cultural heritage. With this paper, it is aimed to present a bibliometric analysis of the studies linking the terms of game/gamification and interpretation of cultural heritage, and to reveal developments and trends on this field. Within the scope of the study, the publications reached from the Elsevier Scopus© online database under the search term defined as "game/gamification and cultural heritage" were examined. The current status and correlation of the studies on gamification and cultural heritage is defined and tried to be revealed. The findings of the study are directed to the interrelation and key approaches on the use of game/gamification in cultural heritage studies. In the context of the findings obtained, this study deals with the current trends of the literature produced in the relevant field.

Keywords Cultural heritage · Gamification · Bibliometric analysis · Literature review

---

S. Karahan (✉)
Erciyes University, Kayseri 38280, Turkey
e-mail: svdgnr@gmail.com

L. F. Gül
Istanbul Technical University, İstanbul 34743, Turkey
e-mail: fgul@itu.edu.tr

© The Author(s), under exclusive license to Springer Nature Switzerland AG 2021
Ö. Cordan et al. (eds.), *Game + Design Education*, Springer Series in Design and Innovation 13, https://doi.org/10.1007/978-3-030-65060-5_23

1 Introduction

The game is a fictional, structured, meaningful entertainment medium and provides learning and social interaction opportunities [1, 2]. The proliferation and accessibility of the game environment, and the potential of using game elements to promote user motivation for non-game concepts highlight the trend of using the game and gamification as a method in studies on various of fields [3]. With these features, game environment and gamification provide a platform for the documentation, presentation and representation of cultural heritage and the possibility of creating a medium that enables the dissemination of cultural heritage. The literature shows that the studies in which the game is related to the cultural heritage increase with acceleration. This situation raises the necessity of revealing the current situation of instrumentalization of the game for the stated purposes and gamification of the cultural heritage object/knowledge. This study aims to reveal the literature in which these possibilities are discussed/presented/experienced by focusing on instrumenting game and highlight the gamification on cultural heritage field.

Cultural heritage is correlated with digital technology under the main objectives of documentation, representation and dissemination [4]. Interpretation of cultural heritage is considered as communication design that includes the integrity of these objectives, aims to fill the gap between cultural heritage and individuals. It is an effort to transform cultural heritage into a comprehension that everyone can understand without the need for the expertise. In the interpretation of cultural heritage, due to the nature of communication, it is necessary to define a provoking, triggering transmission strategy, and takes an approach that premises the individual experience in which the individual actively participates during the communication [5, 6]. Considering these features, the game-based approach allows for a wide spectrum of cultural heritage-related studies that include sorts of concepts such as digitization of cultural heritage, creating virtual and/or learning experience, addressing different age groups, defining a method for storytelling... etc.

With this study, a literature mapping is made within the framework of the aforementioned possibilities by examining the literature related to game-gamification and cultural heritage, and a bibliometric analysis is made to reveal the current trend.

2 Material and Methods

2.1 Data Collection

The bibliometric indicators developed within the scope of this study were built upon the data obtained from scientific publications through the use of the Elsevier's Scopus© Database [7]. Considering the relevant literature, Scopus database provides a comprehensive and accessible structure [8, 9] and this features are effective in selecting this database as the main source within the scope of this study.

The search expression consists applying the words "game", "gamification" and "cultural heritage" to the advanced search tool by using Boolean operators as follows; KEY(game OR gamification) AND KEY("cultural heritage"). Aiming to keep the data set wide, in the search results obtained no restriction has been made on the date, subject area, work type (article, book chapter, conference paper,…)… etc. fields (due to the consideration of the date this study was conducted, an exception has been made on this statement and the data provided from the year 2020 is not included). The final dataset consists of bibliographic data of 257 records including the information of citation, abstract text, author and indexing (determined by the database) keywords and has last achieved on June 2, 2020.

Science mapping is a representative bibliometric data visualization method to reveal scientific productivity contextually and socially [10]. The methodology of this study is built on the potentials provided by science mapping and Fig. 1 shows the brief methodology.

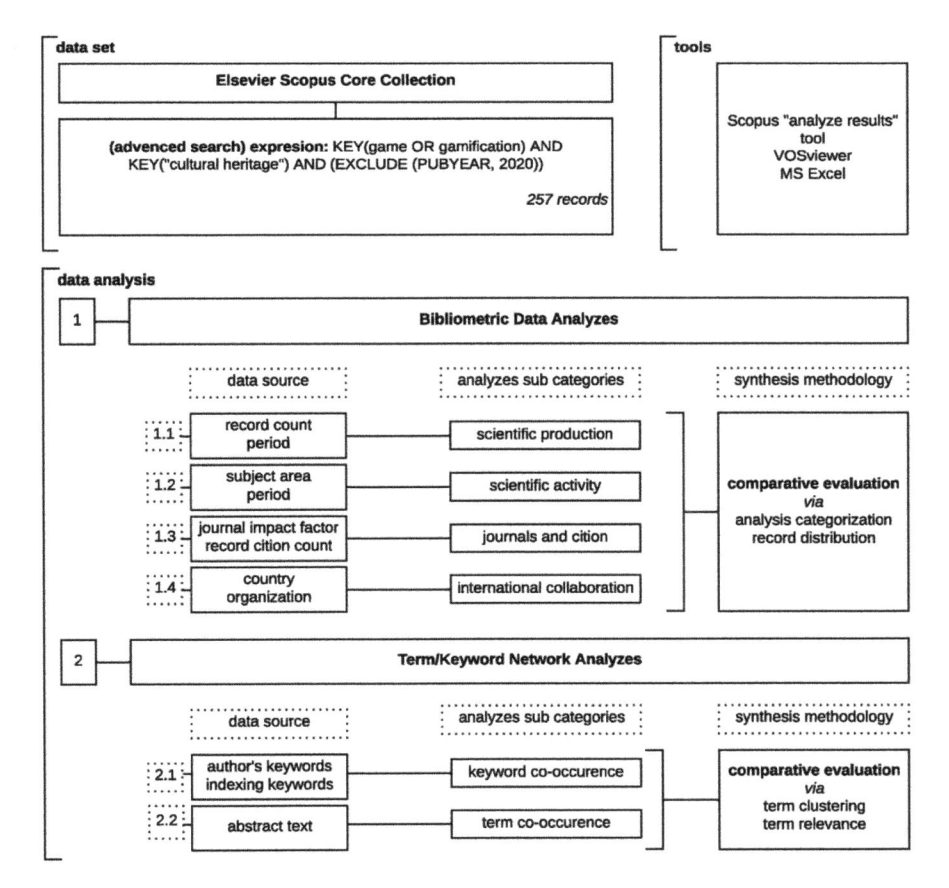

Fig. 1 The employed methodology

2.2 Data Analyzes

The analyzes were performed in two main stages: bibliometric data analysis using the "analysis search results" tool provided by the database with the support of Microsoft© Excel 2020, and the second, the term/keyword network including the analysis developed under the term co-occurrence and correlation consideration obtained using the bibliographic data mapping tool VOSviewer© software [11]. With the "Analysis search results" tool accessed from the database, the documents included in the data set were examined under the titles of publication year, subject area, document type, publishers and impact factors, and international collaborations. The examinations obtained under these headings were evaluated comparatively and presented through tables and graphics. VOSviewer©, selected for the analyzing the dataset in this study, is a the bibliographic data visualization-mapping software tool and has the functionalities of creating, visualizing and exploring maps based on network data [12, 13].

3 Results and Discussion

3.1 Bibliometric Data Analyzes

The literature, which associates game-based approaches with the cultural heritage, has been tried to be analyzed under the terms as follows; spread of production to the time period, the subject area to which it is associated, documents' citation counts and the journal the impact factors, international collaboration of the countries.

Scientific Production and Activity. Literature reveals the trend of applying the game-based approaches on cultural heritage area. Comparative analysis based on the years (2003–2020 time period) and numbers of the studies (257 records) on the literature in question reveals that scientific productivity in this field shows an increasing trend (Fig. 2). These studies are related to various scientific areas and the production in the field of computer science displays graphic in parallel with the total count. However, considering the number and distribution of records related to the arts and humanities area covering the cultural heritage studies, it is possible to conclude that the discussions about cultural heritage are relatively low referred.

Main Journals and Impacting Documents. Considering the document type of the records in the dataset, it is seen that the vast majority is conference papers (188 records) followed by articles (65 records), book chapters (2 records) and review articles (2 records). In order to evaluate the academic prevalence of the literature, the records in the dataset are sorted according to the citation counts of publications and journals, and the top 10 document and top 5 journals are presented in Tables 1 and 2. This analysis revealed that there is a close relationship between the number of citations from a specific publication and the most active journals in the area.

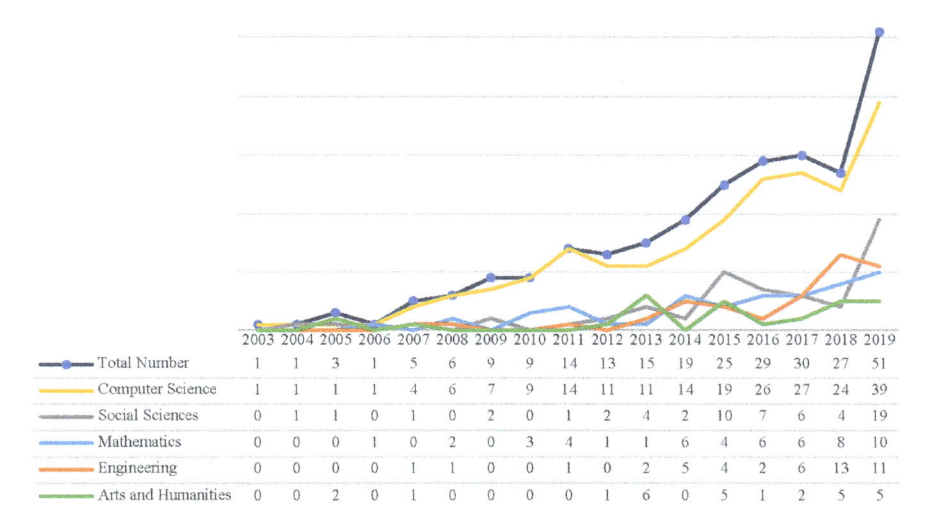

	2003	2004	2005	2006	2007	2008	2009	2010	2011	2012	2013	2014	2015	2016	2017	2018	2019
Total Number	1	1	3	1	5	6	9	9	14	13	15	19	25	29	30	27	51
Computer Science	1	1	1	1	4	6	7	9	14	11	11	14	19	26	27	24	39
Social Sciences	0	1	1	0	1	0	2	0	1	2	4	2	10	7	6	4	19
Mathematics	0	0	0	1	0	2	0	3	4	1	1	6	4	6	6	8	10
Engineering	0	0	0	0	1	1	0	0	1	0	2	5	4	2	6	13	11
Arts and Humanities	0	0	2	0	1	0	0	0	0	1	6	0	5	1	2	5	5

Fig. 2 Scientific activity and top 5 subject area distribution graphic

International Collaboration. In order to understand how countries and authors are organized and distributed in the literature, an evaluation of international cooperation has been made taking into account the total number of publications. The analysis showed that scientific production took place in 58 different countries all over the world, consisting of Italy (49 records), Greece (44 records), United Kingdom (26 records), China (20 records) and Germany (18 records) in order of total record count. The general distribution among countries shows that production is dense in European countries. The result of the evaluation, made on accordance of the total number of records and the linking strength of each other, revealed that the 5 countries with the strongest international relations among the publications are listed as; Greece, Italy, England, France and Turkey. When the results are compared, it has been concluded that Italy and Greece, which published a significant number of collaborative scientific studies and have a share of 19.06 and 17.12% in the overall number of publications, have contributed significantly to the production of the researches blending the game-based approaches on cultural heritage field.

3.2 Term/Keyword Network Analysis

Integrating the game-based approaches with learning is an increasing tendency [14]. It is seen that these trend approaches, utilizing the educational theories such as experimental-active-position learning [15] are mediated with technology, referring the blending the term edutainment [16], playful-learning [17], serious games [18], gamification [19]. Cultural heritage attracts the attention of researchers as one of potential areas of these blended approaches. The implementation of game-based

Table 1 Top 10 cited publications

R	Authors	Title	Source	PY	NC
1	Anderson et al.	Developing serious games for cultural heritage: a state-of-the-art review	Virtual reality	2010	147
2	Bellotti et al.	A serious game model for cultural heritage	Journal on computing and cultural heritage	2012	86
3	Coenen et al.	Museus: case study of a pervasive cultural heritage serious game	Journal on computing and cultural heritage	2013	52
4	Rubino et al.	Integrating a location-based mobile game in the museum visit: evaluating visitors' behaviour and learning	Journal on computing and cultural heritage	2015	39
5	Bujari et al.	Using gamification to discover cultural heritage locations from geo-tagged photos	Personal and ubiquitous computing	2017	35
6	Raptis et al.	Effects of mixed-reality on players' behaviour and immersion in a cultural tourism game: a cognitive processing perspective	International journal of human computer studies	2018	29
7	Antoniou et al.	An approach for serious game development for cultural heritage: case study for an archaeological site and museum	Journal on computing and cultural heritage	2013	22
8	Froschauer et al.	Art history concepts at play with ThIATRO	Journal on computing and cultural heritage	2013	22
9	Vourvopoulos et al.	Brain-controlled serious games for cultural heritage	Proceedings of the 2012 18th international conference on virtual systems and multimedia	2012	22
10	Raptis et al.	Do field dependence–independence differences of game players affect performance and behaviour in cultural heritage games?	Proceedings of the 2016 annual symposium on computer–human interaction in play	2016	18

Abbreviations R rank, PY publication year, NC number of citations

Table 2 Top 5 journals ranked by total citation count

R	Journal	DC	CC	CiteScore	SJR	SA	SC
1	Journal on computing and cultural heritage	8	242	1.83	0.429	Computer science arts and humanities	From 2008 to present
2	Virtual reality	3	162	3.87	0.480	Computer science	1995, from 1998 to 2000, 2002, from 2004 to present
3	Lecture notes in computer science	38	152	106	0.283	Computer science mathematics	1937,1955, from 1973 to present
4	ISPRS journal of photogrammetry and remote sensing	9	68	8.64	2.979	Computer science engineering physics and astronomy earth and planetary sciences	From 1989 to present
5	International journal of human computer studies	2	55	4.36	0.688	Computer science social science engineering	From 1994 to present

Abbreviations R rank, *DC* document count, *CiteScore* average citations received per document published in the serial (retrieved from Scopus), *SJR* scientific journal rankings score, *SA* subject area, *SC* scopus coverage

approaches requires the interpretations of cultural heritage on multiple stages such as the digitalization, (re)presentation and dissemination.

The pioneering charter of ICOMOS for the interpretation and presentation of cultural heritage declares that such approaches should be considered and based on seven principles including the terms as follows; *"facilitate understanding and appreciation, communicate the meaning, safeguard the values, respect the authenticity, contribute to the sustainable conservation, encourage inclusiveness, develop technical and professional guidelines"* [20]. These objectives emphasize the importance of conceptualization of sub-terms such as digitalization-representation-reproduction of cultural heritage, selection of interpretation tool-medium-environment-methods, and the terms of experience-perception-learning-interaction related to the user/individual. In addition to the potentiality of implementing the above-mentioned game-based blended-approaches, the insufficient consideration of these objectives raises the dilemma of commodifying cultural heritage and failing to achieve the ultimate goal of preservation/protection/maintenance.

In this section, which constitutes the second stage of the data analysis of the study, the author defined keywords and the indexing keywords of the records in the data set and the terms in the abstract text are examined according to their co-occurrences and association. It is aimed to question and interpret the literature in which the game-based approaches are related to the cultural heritage under the above-mentioned terms and the sub-terms.

Keyword Co-occurrence. The "indexing keyword analysis" was performed by using the VOSviewer© tool and obtained by fractalization of the co-occurrences and linking counts of the pre-defined index keywords of the dataset. Among the 1358 indexing keyword in total, the parameter of minimum number of co-occurrences of a keyword was setted as 5, and the dataset was cleared by using the thesaurus file created by the authors in order to merge the different variants of terms (such as game-games, three diamentional-3D, ...etc.). The result consists of 86 keyword and 1165 link among them and presented under 8 cluster by considering their co-occurrences (see Fig. 3). The "author keyword analysis", performed by using the same tool and parameters on in total 705 keywords, gives the result of 21 keyword and 92 links in 7 clusters (see Fig. 4).

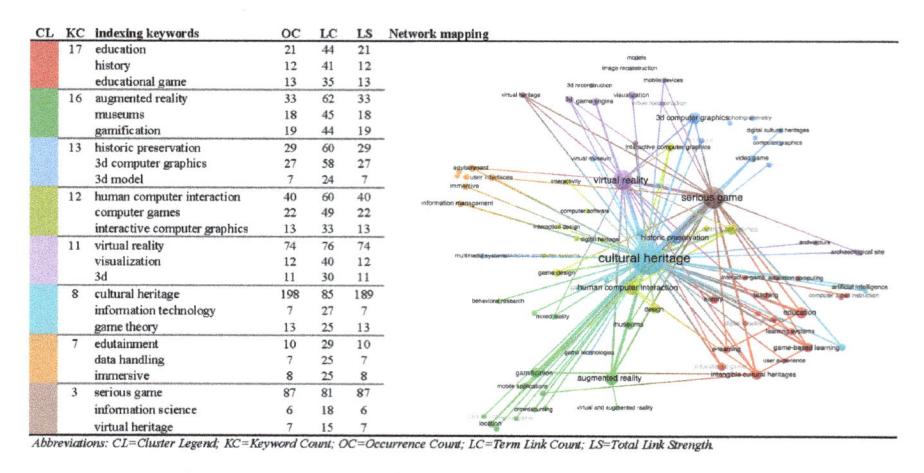

CL	KC	indexing keywords	OC	LC	LS
	17	education	21	44	21
		history	12	41	12
		educational game	13	35	13
	16	augmented reality	33	62	33
		museums	18	45	18
		gamification	19	44	19
	13	historic preservation	29	60	29
		3d computer graphics	27	58	27
		3d model	7	24	7
	12	human computer interaction	40	60	40
		computer games	22	49	22
		interactive computer graphics	13	33	13
	11	virtual reality	74	76	74
		visualization	12	40	12
		3d	11	30	11
	8	cultural heritage	198	85	189
		information technology	7	27	7
		game theory	13	25	13
	7	edutainment	10	29	10
		data handling	7	25	7
		immersive	8	25	8
	3	serious game	87	81	87
		information science	6	18	6
		virtual heritage	7	15	7

Abbreviations: CL=Cluster Legend; KC=Keyword Count; OC=Occurrence Count; LC=Term Link Count; LS=Total Link Strength.

Fig. 3 Indexing keyword analysis (top 3 keywords for each cluster according to the occurrence)

CL	KC	indexing keywords	OC	LC	LS
	5	gamification	26	12	22
		intangible cultural heritage	15	7	7
		tourism	9	8	9
		educational games	8	6	5
		crowdsourcing	7	7	6
	5	cultural heritage	114	19	85
		virtual reality	34	15	28
		game	12	9	9
		virtual heritage	5	5	5
		education	7	4	5
	3	augmented reality	15	12	14
		mixed reality	6	10	6
		storytelling	6	7	6
		user experience	5	7	5
	3	serious game	67	20	53
		game design	13	5	11
		heritage	6	3	3
	2	game-based learning	9	5	8
		museums	6	8	6
	1	3D model	6	4	5
	1	edutainment	8	7	6

Abbreviations: C=Cluster Legend; OC=Occurrence Count; LC=Term Link Count; LS=Total Link Strength.

Fig. 4 Author keywords analysis

The results of both analyzes have shown that the top 10 keywords directly related to "cultural heritage" keyword are "serious game, virtual reality, human computer interaction, augmented reality, education, 3D computer graphics, gamification, game design, game engine, computer games", respectively. Considering the conceptual relationships between keywords, the results of both analyzes overlap. As can be seen in the network map of the analyzes, there are keywords that are specific to the relatively specific area located away from these top 10 basic concepts. The concepts, interpreted through the keywords, do not include the concepts associated with the protection and dissemination of cultural heritage directly, and majority of the concepts is related to game-based approaches. In this context, literature, consisting the game-based approaches on cultural heritage subject area, is interpreted that they do not constitute a sufficient discussion medium on the cultural heritage area. The second observation of this analyzes is that "indexing keywords" contain relatively more specific definitions and the authors have a generalizing approach on the determination of the keywords. The descriptively and specificity of the indexing keywords assigned by publishers and databases facilitates access to the publications from the related literature.

Term Co-occurrence. The analyzes in this part of the study were obtained by using the term co-occurrence of text data function on the VOSviewer© tool. The abstract texts of the records in the dataset were examined. All occurrence numbers of the terms were taken into consideration, among the 5269 term in total, the 90 term meet the threshold of repeating minimum 10 times, were visualized according to the co-occurrence and linking strength (see Fig. 5). The terms/words (challenge, aim, methodology… etc.) that structure the abstract texts are not included in the visualization, the errors encountered in the previous analyzes that arising from different variations of the terms have debugged.

Visualization reveals that the concept sets do not diverge from each other. In the studies, the content of the clusters, which were formed on the basis of relativity, it was observed that blended approaches were made within the framework of game-based approaches, cultural heritage by concerning the terms user-player and technology-tool. The analysis result show that "game" and "cultural heritage" are the most occurred and linked term as it was foreseen with-in the scope of this study. These terms are followed by "user application, technology, experience, serious game, information, museum" terms respectively. Sub-terms, stated in the previous sections, related to the protection of cultural heritage and learning are at the lower parts of the ranking (for example; learning 25th, education 30th, understanding 47th, storytelling 53rd, dissemination 68th) (Table 3). Findings of this study pointed out the game-based approaches are dealt with cultural heritage within the context of the instrumentalization (VR, AR and MR…etc.), methodization (the serious game, gamification…etc.) and providing a medium (for education, learning…etc.). Discussing the potentials offered by the game-based approaches to the field of cultural heritage through by focusing on instrumentalization, methodization and providing a medium

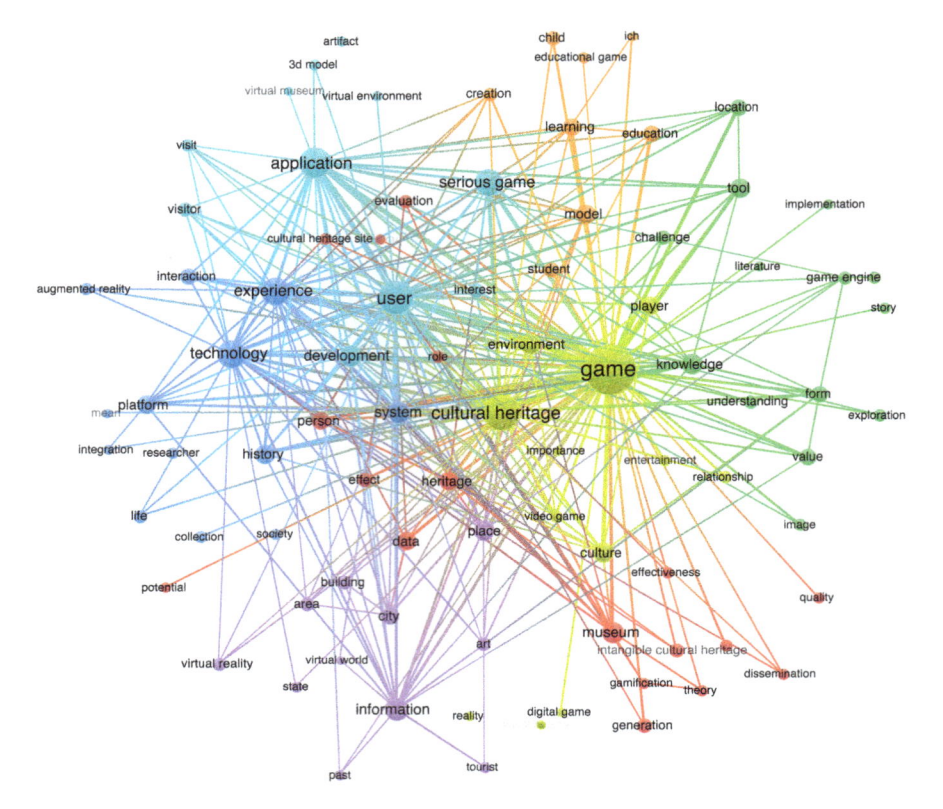

Fig. 5 Term co-occurrence analysis network visualization

but not addressing conservation-transfer-dissemination problems, causes the necessity of questioning scientific production to unveil the role of cultural heritage in game-based approaches. The condensation of the studies in above mentioned frameworks leads to the consequence that the potentials provided by game-based approaches in the field of cultural heritage have not yet been sufficiently discussed in the literature.

4 Conclusion

This paper presents a bibliometric analysis of literature about game-based approaches in cultural heritage field. It should be noted that the scientific production in this subject manner is its early steps and requires cooperation of the related disciplines. Bibliometric and visualization tools have been used to perform the analyzes on dataset records and it has been drawn the following conclusions of; first, the publication trend in this area has been in an increased tendency. Given the studies associated with learning theories, the learning habits of the current generation, targeted in game-based

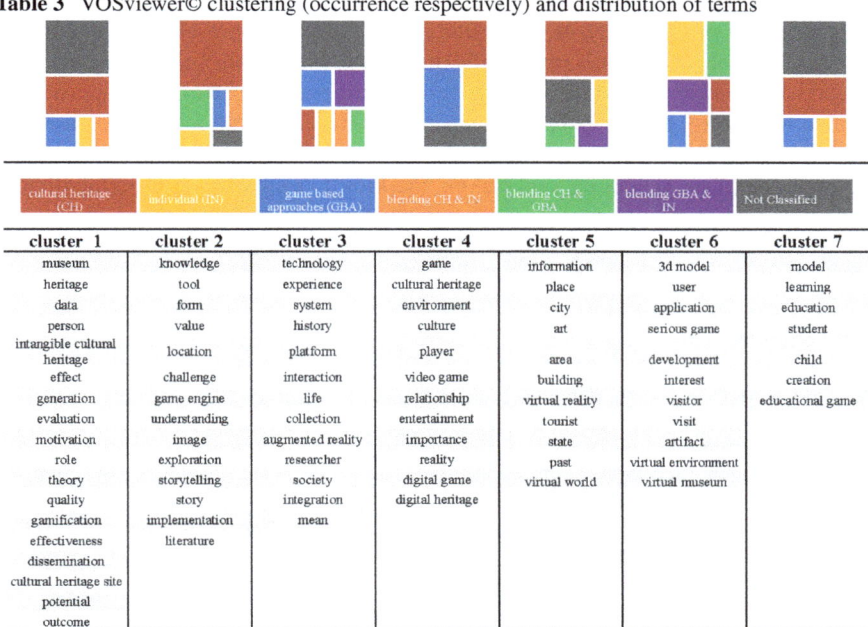

Table 3 VOSviewer© clustering (occurrence respectively) and distribution of terms

cluster 1	cluster 2	cluster 3	cluster 4	cluster 5	cluster 6	cluster 7
museum	knowledge	technology	game	information	3d model	model
heritage	tool	experience	cultural heritage	place	user	learning
data	form	system	environment	city	application	education
person	value	history	culture	art	serious game	student
intangible cultural heritage	location	platform	player	area	development	child
effect	challenge	interaction	video game	building	interest	creation
generation	game engine	life	relationship	virtual reality	visitor	educational game
evaluation	understanding	collection	entertainment	tourist	visit	
motivation	image	augmented reality	importance	state	artifact	
role	exploration	researcher	reality	past	virtual environment	
theory	storytelling	society	digital game	virtual world	virtual museum	
quality	story	integration	digital heritage			
gamification	implementation	mean				
effectiveness	literature					
dissemination						
cultural heritage site						
potential						
outcome						

approaches, are the main factor in the bias to use this method. Increasing support of UNESCO, European Commission and similar institutions/organizations to the studies produced within this framework, is evaluated as another parameter causing this trend. Second, the contributions on this area is accumulated in European countries. Supporting funds for the researches related to the cultural heritage provided by the European Commission can be considered among the factors that affect this situation. However, due to the universal nature of cultural heritage it requires to be more worldwide. Third, most of contribution to this field is related to the scientific subject area is "computer science", and the results of term network analysis confirm that the major concerns of publications are on the game-design approaches. Studies involving game-based approaches are associated with this field due to the requirements of the tools and method used. However, considering that these studies are related to the cultural heritage area and the possibilities it provides to this area, establishing the primarily relevance with the cultural heritage scientific area is important in terms of discussing its scientific contribution on literature.

This exploratory work has helped us make important statements about blending game/gamification approaches in cultural heritage. On the use of game-based approaches in the field of cultural heritage, basic strategies and relationships are mentioned. Scientific production on the possibility of these blended approaches to provide its user with a learning experience in the non-game area, and the relevance of conservation and dissemination of cultural heritage are revealed. Within the body of evidence identified in this study, there is a distinct lack of contribution on assessment of actual potentialities of games for interpretation and presentation of cultural heritage. The novelty of this research is that, to the best of our knowledge, the first research providing a systematic mapping covering research into game approaches applied to cultural heritage. The conclusions produced by the inferences from the current studies are expected to contribute to the future production of the literature on the terms of the mediating and linking theories/concepts in the implementation, evaluation and development of game-based approaches.

References

1. Mortara M, Catalano CE, Bellotti F, Fiucci G, Houry-Panchetti M, Petridis P (2014) Learning cultural heritage by serious games. J Cult Heritage. 15:318–325. https://doi.org/10.1016/j.culher.2013.04.004
2. Papathanasiou-Zuhrt D, Weiss-Ibanez D-F, Di Russo A (2017) The gamification of heritage in the unesco enlisted medieval town of Rhodes. GamiFIN conference. Pori, Finland, pp 60–70
3. Deterding, S., Dixon, D., Khaled, R., Nacke, L (2011) From game design elements to gamefulness: defining "gamification. In: Proceedings of the 15th international academic Mindtrek conference: envisioning future media environments. Association for Computing Machinery, New York, NY, USA, pp 9–15. https://doi.org/https://doi.org/10.1145/2181037.2181040
4. Rahaman H, Tan B-K (2011) Interpreting digital heritage : considering end-user's perspective. Int J Archit Comput 09:99–113. https://doi.org/10.1260/1478-0771.9.1.99
5. Tilden F (1957) Interpreting our heritage. The University Of North Carolina Press, United States of America
6. Ham S (2013) Interpretation: making difference on purpose. Fulcrum Publishing
7. Scopus—Document search. https://www.scopus.com/search/form.uri?display=basic&zone=header&origin=resultslist. Last Accessed 2 June 2020
8. Falagas ME, Pitsouni EI, Malietzis GA, Pappas G (2008) Comparison of PubMed, Scopus, web of science, and Google scholar: strengths and weaknesses. FASEB J 22:338–342
9. Salisbury L (2009) Web of science and Scopus: a comparative review of content and searching capabilities. Charleston Advisor 11:5–18
10. Cobo MJ, López-Herrera AG, Herrera-Viedma E, Herrera F (2011) Science mapping software tools: review, analysis, and cooperative study among tools. J Am Soc Inf Sci Technol 62:1382–1402. https://doi.org/10.1002/asi.21525
11. VOSviewer—Visualizing scientific landscapes. https://www.vosviewer.com/. Last Accessed 2 June 2020
12. Van Eck NJ, Waltman L (2013) VOSviewer manual, vol 1. Univeristeit Leiden, Leiden, pp 1–53
13. Van Eck N, Waltman L (2010) Software survey: VOSviewer, a computer program for bibliometric mapping. Scientometrics 84:523–538
14. Malegiannaki I, Daradoumis T (2017) Analyzing the educational design, use and effect of spatial games for cultural heritage: a literature review. Comput Edu 108:1–10. https://doi.org/10.1016/j.compedu.2017.01.007
15. Ortiz SA, Bowers CA, Cannon-Bowers JA (2015) Video game self-efficacy and its effect on training performance. IJSG 2. https://doi.org/https://doi.org/10.17083/ijsg.v2i3.89
16. Okan Z (2003) Edutainment: is learning at risk? Br J Edu Technol 34:255–264
17. Resnick M (2004) Edutainment? no thanks. I prefer playful learning. Associazione Civita Rep Edutainment 14:1–4

18. Backlund P, Hendrix M (2013) Educational games—are they worth the effort? A literature survey of the effectiveness of serious games. In: 2013 5th international conference on games and virtual worlds for serious applications (VS-GAMES), pp 1–8. https://doi.org/https://doi.org/10.1109/VS-GAMES.2013.6624226
19. de Sousa Borges S, Durelli VH, Reis HM, Isotani S (2014) A systematic mapping on gamification applied to education. In: Proceedings of the 29th annual ACM symposium on applied computing, pp 216–222
20. ICOMOS (2008) The ICOMOS charter for the interpretation and presentation of cultural heritage sites

Exploring the Future of Spatial Typography in Immersive Design Applications

Barış Atiker

Abstract Spatial typography is a concept where the text is in direct and instant relationship with the real or virtual space. The connections of spatial typography between space, time, and meaning interact with the movements of the reader. Reading the text from different angles, in particular, may change the message given with the perspective view. Spatial typography is the most obvious way to move beyond the physical boundaries of the screen for motion typography. Immersive Design practices such as augmented (AR), virtual (VR), and extended reality (XR) offer an excellent environment for the 'fluent' nature of spatial typography, although this issue has not been given enough weight. Spatial typography embodies challenges such as legibility, orientation, figure-background relation, and font selection, just like motion typography. Also, instantaneous change of the text according to dynamic content, motion tracking, the flexibility of transitions between different platforms, multi-user experiences, and even its interaction with artificial intelligence are among the current topics. Therefore, new approaches and techniques are emerging for spatial typography in both artistic and commercial products of immersive design applications. Designers accustomed to dealing with the flat, pictorial paradigms of print are now dealing with the architectural, ergonomic, and cinematic paradigms of environmental and immersive media. This paper explores future approaches in spatial typography by examining contemporary immersive design examples operating in different disciplines such as art, engineering, and medicine in comparison with the content analysis method.

Keywords Spatial typography · XR applications · Design principles

1 Introduction

Typography is getting rid of its meaning by the day and it is becoming more and more dynamic than just printed text. The reflection of the industrial revolutions of

---

B. Atiker (✉)
Visual Communication Department, Bahcesehir University, Istanbul 34725, Turkey
e-mail: baris.atiker@comm.bau.edu.tr

the twentieth century repeats itself as an approach in the twenty-first century and especially pushes the limits of typography at every opportunity.

Typography, which was saved from being the prisoner of the nails, brushes, or pen by movable wooden blocks, has turned away from three-dimensional production techniques with the invention of photography, has gained motion with the invention of cinema and has become an abstract commodity with the discovery of digital design.

Chartier [1] draws attention that typography has evolved from an environment that is mechanical, static and communication focused to one that is digital, dynamic, and experienced focused. Yet we still use print-derived terminology (such as x-height, counter, baseline, descender, ascender, kerning, leading, tracking, em, en, pica, and points) to continually describe screen-based typography. This is unsurprising, considering that we continue to think, write, and read using a print model.

The evolution of typography has accelerated in the last century, especially after digitalization, with motion typography gaining new functions on the axis of time and motion, and has turned into an image that is no longer read but watched.

From the Crystal Goblet approach in typography to the often playful interactions with type in new media, a 'new reader' emerges, who is at the same time reader in a classic sense but also viewer of a typographic performance, and finally user or even creator of technological mediated typography [2]

The biggest challenge typography faces today is; its relationship with immersive design applications such as AR and VR, which have been hugely popular recently. Because the relationship of typography to the reader was always restricted to a 2-dimensional frame (page, signage, screen, etc.) The concept of spatial typography has broken this frame, revealing the problem of the 'distance' between the text and the reader, and has allowed us to rethink typography principles in the immersive world.

Here immersion is a perception of being physically present in a non-physical world and the perception is created by surrounding the user of the system in texts, images, sound, or other stimuli that provide an engrossing total environment.

2 Spatial Typography and Immersive Design

The relationship between typography and space is as old as the relationship between architecture and design. The reason for this lies in the attempt to pass on one's own story to future generations. These stories, previously seen as murals in the caves, have turned into simpler symbols, letters, and scripts over time. The engraving of the first known inscriptions on huge rocks was not only an admirable effort according to the technology of that period, but also a result of the desire for eternity and immortality. This result bears great similarities to our re-look at typography in immersive designs.

2.1 Typography in Space

The relationship of typography with space has changed size and shape after it is 'portable'. Especially, the text was formulated on the two-dimensional plane of the paper, as it showed the effects of the search for an architectural order, the grid systems were taken under control with concepts such as different fonts, color, texture, weight.

Dadaism and futurism, the greatest anti-order movements of the twentieth century, broke all known rules by opposing the disappearance of text on the two-dimensional axis as an expressive indicator of meaninglessness and defiance. According to Blackwell [3], Dadaists and Futurists in the 1920s and 1930s—later Concrete Poetry during the 1950s and 1960s—freed type from the mechanical grid of reproduction.

This approach was not only limited to paper, but it also turned into a design philosophy and reconstructed the relationship of text with the 3-dimensional space. Bachfischer and Robertson [2] describe that this typographic space is neither a book space, where typography acts as the invisible servant nor film space where one attends an expressive typographic performance; it is something different, a truly enhanced typographic space, enriched by the possibility of user interaction.

Of course, what is mentioned here is that the relationship between typography and space is not only formal but also conceptual from the very beginning. Even though the mission of the text is to convey the message, how and why it has always been a question to be answered.

Our vision is the main reason why we perceive the text in two or three dimensions. When viewed from the right angle on a flat wall, the text may create the illusion of three-dimension which can be transformed into a meaningless block of shapes when viewed from different angles (see Fig. 1). What is needed here is for the reader to discover that 'true' point of view (POV) within the space so that the text can reach its meaning.

Fig. 1 Sebastian Lemm website, https://www.sebastianlemm.work/3d-type-installation [4]

This point of view is a coordinate. In a place where nothing moves, coordinates are also fixed. The movement of the text initiates a 'tracking' process with varying coordinates. The changing positions, dimensions, colors, and transparency of the text that moves in space directly affect this tracking process both formally and conceptually. According to Ayiter [5], a graphic designer can use size differences to visually distinguish certain elements in a text. In a (virtual) 3D space however, you cannot always resolve the relative size of two objects.

Muriel Cooper is one of the first artists to question the relationship between digital typography and space. Cooper saw typography as a prime element for visual experimentation. Students and staff at the workshop developed a whole range of tools to create a type that responds to its content and its environment.

Hillner [6] states that as long as text elements' relative positions remain consistent, they will be perceived as static environments. Only when their correlative positions change, will text elements be perceived as in motion. Similarly, virtual space appears three dimensionally only, as long as some or all of the elements vary in size, overlap, grow or shrink because the perception of movement within space relies on visual references.

2.2 Typography in Motion

Krasner [7] comments on the relation of the text with the moving image that has been abstracted unusual in artists' works, especially in avant-garde, has met new limits in terms of form and meaning. With the acceptance of time and movement as design elements, moving text has become a fluid and temporal phenomenon.

Since moving type was increasingly produced and viewed on computational devices, it seemed a clear progression to shift attention to the additional expressive possibilities of type in a digital computerized environment [2].

In his work called Virtual Shakespeare (see Fig. 2), Small [8] answers the question by saying 'Why should text move or change over time at all? At least five reasons were considered in the paper: "to convey information that itself is changing, to pace the observer, to save [screen or display] real estate, to amplify and to get attention." According to the Small 'by escaping the confines of the flat sheet of paper, we can arrange information into meaningful landscapes that exhibit qualities of mystery, continuity, and visual delight' [9],

The movement of the text also causes the transience and flow of the message in the axis of time and motion. In particular, screen-based motion text is constantly changing concerning itself and other graphic elements within the limits of resolution. This relationship is not only limited to the visibility and readability of the text but also affects the way the message is expressed and keeps the reader's mind busy.

The definition of transience is a trace of change, especially over time. This change can influence one or more of the basic design elements of the text at the same time. In the motion picture, which is time-based media, this change was always under the control of the designer.

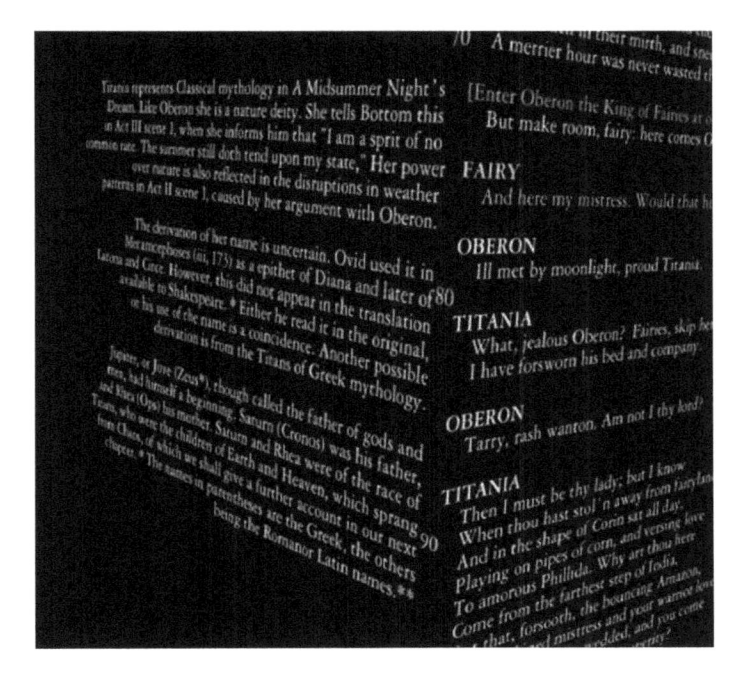

Exploring the Future of Spatial Typography in Immersive ... 299

Fig. 2 Virtual Shakespeare by David Small [10]

2.3 Typography in Interaction

Interaction has been the biggest acquisition that internet technologies have brought to text and typography. Hypertext, which was created by Vannevar Bush [11], with the idea of Memex, means linking the text to other texts, thus establishing bridges between themselves.

Hypertext provides a structure for non-linearity in texts, where in-text links connect a consecutive, linear piece of text with a conceptually connected text or image structure somewhere else in the information space of the internet [2].

The transformation of independent blocks of text into a meaningful road map through websites has revealed not only the formal but also the orientation features of the text. Of course, the fact that digital text is 'clickable' has given it new functions and changed its appearance. This change started at the very beginning with the fact that the type showed itself as hypertext (see Fig. 3).

Similarly, hypertext, which acquired flow and impermanence properties in the moving images, maintained these properties in interactive environments and turned into an image that 'response' to the user's movements.

The fact of text and typography are responsive means that it rearranges itself according to different frame sizes, i.e. adapts to the environment. This harmony applies not only to the composition but also to the ground-shape relationship. It is

Fig. 3 Dynamic typography in IKEA Place AR application [12]

now an act of awareness that the text color turns to light or changes its dimensions to maintain contrast on a dark background.

According to Yee [13], interactivity refers to the ability of users to select, change, or customize media elements that they access. Temporality refers to the passage of time through virtual environments. This concept can be discussed under two main themes: animation and dynamic content. Animated or kinetic typography is the most progressive area of screen-based typography and owes its development to the film medium.

3 Immersive Typography

The latest transformation of the typography takes place through immersive media. The digital text is now interacting with the new virtual and augmented reality which is copied from the real world.

The most important criterion for the interaction of typography with the virtual world is its perfect adaptation to the immersion. In other words, it is impossible to separate the text from the image. This brings 3 major challenges to virtual typography. The first is the distance between the text and the reader in the virtual world. The second is the movement of text in the virtual world. The third and last one is the dynamic source of the text.

The distance of text to the reader in the virtual world makes it both possible and necessary to be in constant change. In other words, as the reader relocates to the virtual world, the text must change according to the reader's changing position to

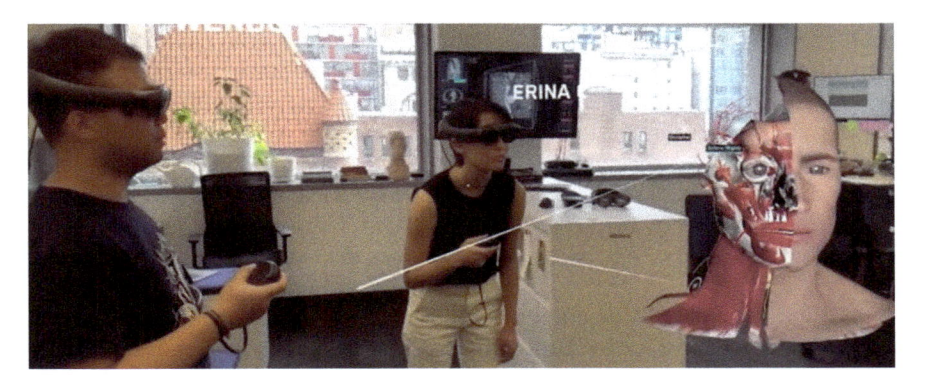

Exploring the Future of Spatial Typography in Immersive ...

Fig. 4 Medivis—AR health application interface [14]

maintain its position. Although this rule does not apply to the text in the device interface, it is of great importance in terms of the 'seamless' reading experience. So actually, even though the text is moving, it has to look like it is stable.

It is one of the most obvious tools that this text uses, especially in the virtual world, where it is not constrained by at least a two-dimensional frame, both to orient its position relative to the reader's position, and to highlight the message it wants to convey (see Fig. 4).

Again, the gestural interface and the interaction with type overpowers the content of the text but shows the possibility of engagements and enhancements in the experience people will gain from typographic interaction with textual entities [2].

The orientation of the text according to the reader is the result of motion tracking and real-time rendering technologies. Already immersive media is made possible by the development of these two technologies.

In the virtual world, the text is naturally related to the facts of time and motion. This relationship emphasizes the responsibility of carrying the identities of kinetic typography, such as transience and flow, to the virtual world. First of all, immersive media isolate or change the reader from his real world. In this case, the frame—in which the text is located—is no longer a two-dimensional plane, but a 'spherical' frame.

This spherical frame must necessarily make a hierarchical structure feel to the reader. This hierarchical structure requires proper use of movement and temporality as well as basic typography rules.

The third challenge that typography faces in immersive media is the source of the text. Typography, which has predominantly informative content, has been stripped of its features over time and has begun to be evaluated in a conceptual structure.

The content and meaning of the text relate not only to its form but also to its relationship with its environment. Immersive typography means the integration of the text with the story in terms of meaning and content, which must already be in harmony with its environment.

Of course, at this point, it should be taken into consideration that the text is fed from different sources. It is the diversity of these resources that have already changed the text. For example, in an application that is compatible with different languages and alphabets, the same design has to look different to users. Similarly, in cases where the typography generates itself, these sources gain great importance.

Ayiter [5] accepts that it might be wise to look for textual sources that would address a need for play, for personal readings and interpretations; in other words, text that is meant to be 'felt' as an artwork, rather than to be 'read' as information content.

It is also necessary to mention the other design elements that the typography competes in immersive media. Especially the 'faster' communication habit brought by social media has come to the agenda with the preference of symbols rather than writing. Especially, the limitations of the text in the expression of emotion caused the use of more pictorial signs (emoticons) with or instead of the text, and even more importantly, it gained a universal quality in terms of comprehensibility.

4 Spatial Typography with Immersive Design Principles

The basic design principles for the evaluation of text as spatial typography are effective but often inadequate. This is because the design principles are mainly determined by considering the static property of the text.

With the conversion of the text into a moving image, a problem of visibility, as well as legibility, arose, and with the acquisition of interactivity, the text has become a tool. In spatial typography, looking at the relationship of text with the 3-dimensional real and virtual world from this perspective is the first step in understanding the dynamics of interaction between designer-reader-text.

Typography, especially in immersive media, has its self-own characteristics. Of course, at this time when immersive media technologies are gaining momentum, these features are also developing and becoming the building blocks of a better experience.

4.1 Intelligibility

As with all typographic elements, legibility is a priority concept. Although the concept of legibility with moving typography has been replaced by the concept of 'intelligibility', it is still valid due to the informative nature of the text, especially in the immersive media.

It is possible to make any text legible by separating its characters from each other and also other design elements. In other words, the more difficult it is to transform the letters or word groups that are intertwined or far apart from each other into meaningful text, it is also difficult to achieve this in a 3-dimensional space where the

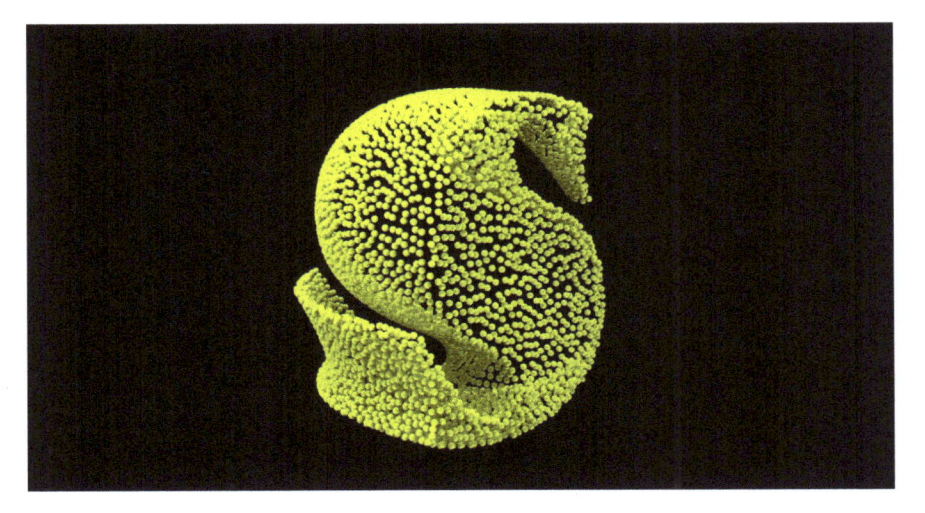

Fig. 5 Experimental VR typography by Juneza Niyazi [15]

reader is constantly in motion, the ground-figure relationship is constantly changing, and there is a perception of depth between the typographic elements (see Fig. 5).

For this reason, to give the text a hierarchical structure, it is necessary to consider the distance phenomenon as well as features such as size, style, color, texture, and weight. In this case, the text will be shaped according to the reader and other graphic elements and will try to fulfill its function.

4.2 Contrast

The color and tone of the text require high contrast use due to the shape-ground relationship. This contrast is sometimes provided to the text with a shadow effect, or through a virtual floor frame. While light text colors are preferred on dark grounds, especially white and tones may show excessive glare effect in immersive media. Besides, the image quality resulting from the screen resolution may cause aesthetic problems in cases of high contrast usage.

4.3 Display

According to Yee [13], differences in screen display (for example quality, surface, size, ratio, refresh rate, orientation), rendering technology and default system fonts have made type functionality a key consideration of digital design. The issue of usability has become more pertinent with the introduction of different rendering and imaging technology.

4.4 Style

Especially with the development of digital typography, the fact that the font styles that have diversified do not have the same effect on the screen and paper is a very important problem. The serif structure, which facilitates the readability of text on paper, can confuse due to the screen resolution. Similarly, the presence of different text styles in the same composition can disrupt the hierarchical structure.

4.5 Weight

Although thin typefaces are perceived more aesthetically on paper, they remain weak on the screen. Fonts of different weights in particular need to be optimized for the display. This optimization requires that many typographic principles, such as x-height and spacing, be taken together from the folds of the letter edges. Hardware developers, therefore, design and use their fonts.

4.6 Height and Width

When editing the page, the height and width of the text block is a factor that directly affects the legibility, since it makes a jump movement instead of a linear movement during eye reading. This movement is called saccades. This happens because the eye is focusing on a certain part of the text for a while. In immersive designs, this area is much narrower than a normal page layout.

4.7 Alignment

Aligning the text with different objects brings the problem of priority. In particular, motion design elements affect both the visibility and legibility of the text. This alignment can also change according to the perspective of the spherical frame and the reader's perspective (see Fig. 6).

Exploring the Future of Spatial Typography in Immersive ... 305

Fig. 6 WayRay's AR driving interface concept [16]

4.8 Perspective

Another important issue in spatial typography is how the text looks from different perspectives on 3-dimensional space. Most typefaces are designed according to 2-dimensional planes, and most characters become unreadable after certain angles. Similarly, there are types of fonts designed according to 3-D projection, the use of these fonts in immersive media is unlikely due to perspective overlap (see Fig. 7).

Fig. 7 AR 3D typographic poster for printworks by OMSE [18]

Miller [17], explains that as 'dimensional typography' and he refers to sculptural and three-dimensional forms of individual letters as an alternative to the spatial disposition of 'flat' letterforms as they occur in information landscapes.

The appearance of spatial typography as 3-dimensional instead of 2-dimensional planes is also a factor that increases realism. Of course, the text should not only look 3-dimensional but also be compatible with the lights and shadows of the environment.

4.9 Navigation

The use of text as an interface element is an important factor affecting the user, especially in complex immersive applications where multiple functions coexist.

The smooth transition between different texts according to the reader's preferences is one of the main reasons for its use in immersive media. In addition to the buttons on handheld devices, the 'click' action, which we are familiar with from web applications, can sometimes be performed with just one hand or head gesture.

Spatial typography, which constantly regulates itself according to the movement of the user, should respond to many actions of the reader such as touch, scroll, hold, release, break, expand. If this answer has a parallel approach to the general flow of the story, the user experience progresses positively.

Exploring VR UI beyond hand gestures opens up even more possibilities. We use a wide array of sensory cues to connect to the physical world, all fodder for virtual UI. Gaze-based interaction, audio, light-based and olfactory navigation—we've been considering many of these ideas in simulated spaces since the 1960s, but we just now can access the processing power to easily try them out [19] (see Fig. 8).

4.10 Haptics

It is theoretically possible for the text to acquire touch characteristics in addition to its visual and audio effects in immersive designs. Currently, haptic technologies can create different tissue sensations at your fingertips through sound waves and this can provide a new reality effect between the reader and the text.

The quality of the immersive experience depends on the effective use of open and hidden menus which contain not only visible but also auditory and tactile responses. A realistic immersive experience is possible with the reader requiring minimal physical and mental effort to interact with the text.

4.11 Occlusion

The fact that virtual objects appear in augmented reality as a transparent layer over physical objects is an important problem experienced by realism. Virtual layers can

Exploring the Future of Spatial Typography in Immersive ... 307

Fig. 8 Typographic interface design iterations' by Yoon Park [20]

appear as if they are behind real objects thanks to 3D object tracking and volume scanning technologies. This is especially important for typography in augmented reality compositions. Because texts can express not only objects but also the distances in between.

4.12 Focus and Depth of Field

Although immersive media aligns graphics to the world that the user sees, it does this through a screen between real objects and the eye. The focus of the eye only on the relevant area and the blurring of everything left behind is not yet fully achieved in the immersive applications. But it is possible to find exactly where the user's eyes are focused through specific sensors. In this case, texts that are out of focus of the user may become blurred just like in depth of field (see Fig. 9).

Fig. 9 When I am 64 by Tu Uthaisri. https://tuday.co/experimental [21]

4.13 Generative Text

As mentioned before, typography that feeds from different sources can acquire features such as position, size, color, texture, weight by itself, especially through technologies such as artificial intelligence and machine learning. It can even create the most appropriate composition for the reader by associating with different text groups through hypertext logic.

Ishizaki [22] explains that dynamic information systems "continuously adapt to the dynamic changes in information content and the information recipient's intention" However, authorial power in a hyper-textual environment has become less defined and has altered the relationship between author, designer, reader and text [13].

5 Conclusion

Immersive design technology is trying to respond to new emerging needs with a rapidly increasing popularity. Behind this effort lies the search for solutions to UX problems, especially in hardware.

First of all, this equipment is not yet as cheap as anyone can access. Immersive applications, in particular, are prepared in a helmet logic such as Oculus, Vive, and often operate dependent on computers because they require high processing power. Stand alone is still seen as a low-access tool despite its cheaper prices on hardware such as Quest, which does not require a physical connection to the computer.

Besides, more accessible and affordable smartphones, or equipment that offers an immersive experience with simple lens kits, have begun to take more place in everyday life. Especially guide and game applications are a factor that accelerates this development.

Although mobile (portable) technologies seem to be the pioneer of this progress, in fact, more predominantly industrial applications lead the real development of these technologies. The increasing number and quality of applications, especially in the military, medical, transportation, heavy industry, and education, bring the need for more and more effective use of spatial typography to the agenda and cause it to reach a competitive structure.

Communication is undoubtedly the most important actor in immersive applications. Spatial typography will be the only guide to both interpersonal communication and computer-to-human communication. Hillner states that the temporal disposition of contents which contrasts with Real-Time communication, but not with 'real world' communication constitutes the main value of virtual typography.

As Ayiter [5] ideates virtual dimensions can be instrumental in eliciting exciting alternative usages of text and typography which bring to the fore the allographic properties of text as an artistic/creative expressive media that may well bear further scrutiny and exploration.

In this case, typographers will have to understand the new opportunities and challenges offered by immersive designs, and they will design the fonts suitable for the best immersive experience in a more dynamic structure and context. According to Yee [13] in these environments, designers must consider the level of control and feedback given to users to deliver a coherent design experience. At the same time, designers must also accept that absolute control over typographic form is no longer possible, and they should design for multiple rather than single-user experiences.

References

1. Chartier R (1995). Forms and meanings: texts, performances, and audiences from codex to computer (New Cultural Studies) University of Pennsylvania Press, Pennsylvania
2. Bachfischer G, Robertson T (2005) From movable type to moving type—evolution in technological mediated typography. Paper presented at the Apple University Consortium Conference
3. Blackwell L (2004) 20th-century type, London/UK, Laurence King Publishing. (rev. edn)
4. Sebastian Lemm website. https://www.sebastianlemm.work/3d-type-installation. Last Accessed 18 Apr 2020
5. Ayiter E (2012) Further dimensions: text, typography and play in the metaverse. In: 2012 international conference on cyberworlds, Darmstadt, 2012, pp 296–303
6. Hillner M (2006) Virtual typography: time perception in relation to digital communication. Leonardo Electron Almanac 14(5/6)
7. Krasner J (2008) Motion graphic design, applied history and aesthetics. Focal Press/Elsevier, Amsterdam
8. Small DL (1999) Rethinking the book, Ph.D. thesis program in media arts and sciences. Massachusetts Institute of Technology, Cambridge
9. Ayiter E (2018) Playing with text in space. In: Khosrow-Pour M (ed) Enhancing art, culture, and design with technological integration. IGI Global, Pennsylvania, pp 114–130

10. David Small's "Virtual Shakespeare" artwork. https://www.research.ibm.com/journal/sj/mit/sectiond/small.html. Last Accessed 12 Feb 2019
11. Bush V (1945) As we may think, atlantic monthly, July 1945, pp 101–108
12. IKEA Place AR application. https://newsroom.inter.ikea.com/gallery/video/ikea-place-demo-ar-app/a/c7e1289a-ca7e-4cba-8f65-f84b57e4fb8d. Last Accessed 23 May 2020
13. Yee JSR (2008) A cross-media typographic framework: teaching typographic skills in a convergent media. HYΦEN 2008:91–110
14. Medivis—AR Application. https://www.medivis.com. Last Accessed 24 Jan 2020
15. Juneza Niyazi artwork. https://miro.medium.com/max/1400/1*lvCgBgv4D5fDmIO-27chgQ.jpeg. Last Accessed 20 Apr 2020
16. WayRay AR concept. https://www.wayray.com. Last Accessed 6 May 2020
17. Miller A (1996) Dimensional typography. Princeton Architectural Press, New York
18. Printworks AR billboard. https://www.dezeen.com/2019/07/29/omse-augmented-reality-printworks-campaign-technology. Last Accessed 7 Apr 2020
19. Armstrong H, Bone M (2017) Virtual reality. No one can tell you, you are doing it wrong yet
20. Yoon Park's "Typographic interface design iterations" artwork. https://medium.com/dongyoonpark/designing-typography-insight-for-hololens-a55fc5fe025. Last Accessed 8 Apr 2020
21. Tu Uthaisri's "When I am 64" artwork. https://tuday.co/experimental. Last Accessed 7 Apr 2020
22. Ishizaki S (2003) Improvisational design: continuous responsive communication. The MIT Press, Cambridge

A Critical Review of Video Game Controller Designs

Serefraz Akyaman and Ekrem Cem Alppay

Abstract The game understanding has changed shape according to the possibilities and needs of the digital age and gained a digital structure and penetrated to our homes and even our pockets. Increasing the rate of involvement of games in our daily lives has also provided diversification of the ways people play games. There are many computer-based platforms and game types that meet different game needs. Each platform brings with it various peripheral devices. Considering that the main purpose of the game is to enjoy, it is also important to discuss the designs of the products in question for the experience to be gained. Among the physical peripherals, controllers stand out as a remarkable area in terms of product design due to their visual and tactile (sometimes auditory) features and diversity. In this research, video game controllers discussed in terms of user needs, expectations, and academic researchers' dimensions such as natural interaction style or dimensionality. In addition to the mouse and keyboard, the current game consoles, VR game platforms, and some wearable controllers examined in the study. Also, the concepts used by users and researchers in evaluating control devices compiled and points that overlap with each other interpreted. The evaluation dimensions, which were deemed incomplete in both views, are expressed. The study, as a result, revealed the multidimensionality of the game controllers and the difficulty of making a complete comparison of the features of all the controllers.

Keywords Video games · Game controllers · Player experience

S. Akyaman (✉)
Art, Design and Architecture Faculty, Department of Architecture, Sakarya University, Sakarya 54050, Turkey
e-mail: serefraz@sakarya.edu.tr

E. C. Alppay
Architecture Faculty, Department of Industrial Product Design, Istanbul Technical University, Istanbul 34367, Turkey
e-mail: calppay@itu.edu.tr

1 Introduction

In the last few decades, digital games have become a common part of the entertainment, consumer culture, and people's daily lives. Computers, which are the critical elements of digital games and which further enrich the ability to play and entertain for both gaming and business-oriented devices due to their ability to perceive, interpret, and communicate with the environment, have managed to revolutionize the gaming area as well as in all other areas in the society [1].

Increasing the rate of involvement of games in our daily lives has also enabled the diversification of the ways people play games [2]. There are many different computer-based platforms and game types that meet different game needs—the growth and diversification in the game market progress in parallel with technological developments [3]. In particular, the development of graphics and processor technologies has an impact on the gaming industry. In addition to this, the act of playing the game is constantly changing by looking at the variation in the way of controlling the game through the control devices' designs. This study aims to make a general evaluation of video game controllers.

There are two research questions explored in this study: (1) What are the relevant dimensions of video game controllers as seen by players; and (2) What dimensions do researchers use to evaluate control devices? In this context, the main focus is to evaluate game control devices to discuss product features. As a result of this analysis, it is aimed to present a set of evaluation criteria in order to evaluate a game control interface.

2 Video Games and Human–Computer Interaction

Besides the social, cultural, economic, political, and technological factors, Newman [4, 5] states that video games are worth studying for only three features: the size of the video game industry, the popularity of video games, and the human–computer interaction in video games.

The environment where (video) gaming interaction typically occurs is called the user interface. The user interface acts as a translator between application and user semantics [6]. In the context of the game, user interfaces are called the way players interact with the game and get feedback on their interactions [4] through input (controller) and output (display) devices.

The realization of the game in the modern game layout (video games), is now dependent on the inter-layer relationship, which includes the world of the game and the way it designed, our perception of this world as a player (user) and the processes of controlling the game world. Video games reach large masses, and especially when it comes to popular games, the same games are played on very similar screens. If we consider the game interface that turns into shape, aside from the fiction or design of the game, playability has become more and more critical. In such a situation, to establish the relationship between the game layers, the interfaces become more important. Moreover, the relationship of the control or user input devices (which is related to our ability to play) to the human being begins to turn into a point that needs to emphasize.

Video games have been delivered to users through many different platforms since their emergence. Each platform has its technology, physical peripherals (such as display, controller), and features. These different platforms are listed by Wolf [7] as mainframe computer games, coin or token operated arcade video games, home video game systems, portable handheld games, and home computer games. Although basically, every platform uses computer infrastructure, computers differ from other platforms because their purpose is not just gaming. In addition to these platforms, the development of internet technology enables the emergence of new cloud game systems such as Google Stadia. Additionally, depending on the video game classifications, it is possible to see specialized controllers or accessory designs. For example, there are steering wheel controllers for only racing games, or there are tennis rackets, bow, and baseball bat-shaped accessories for sports games.

Over time, companies have diversified their controllers on dimensions such as control type (such as directional, gestural), the way of holding (such as one hand, two hands, the need to position the unit on the floor), the way of wearing (such as on the head, arm or foot), ability to move (3DoF, 6DoF, 9DoF). Variables such as gameplay time, user characteristics, comfortable and easy use have led the control units to develop continuously. While simple mechanisms used in the designs of the first control units, today's devices have state-of-the-art motion-sensing sensors [8]. With the inclusion of wearable technologies in the sector, the control unit, and the way it controls are irreversibly changed.

3 Game Controllers

The games vary in areas such as the graphic features they use, the design of the game, and the control dimensions required. To play the game, the player must take some action. Control interfaces that mediate this playing action constitute a common point of the games. Almost every game platform produces controllers with different shapes and features, which can be customized mechanically or physically. Also, the manufacturers' design process of control devices is an issue to compete with each other.

Game controllers are input devices that aim to transfer user commands appropriately mapped to the game mechanics for manipulating the game environment. According to Crick's [9] definition controller is "the fundamental aspect that allows a video game player agency in a virtual world is, of course, the control device—allowing the player to act directly on and in that world as an extension of the player's body". These gaming peripherals have seen as an essential element that has an impact on the gaming experience. Game controllers create a layer in the virtual game world and make sense within the framework of game mechanics. Also, the controllers create a layer in the real world for the user in terms of their physical properties and also create an interface for interaction with the game.

Many studies show that the game controllers' hardware and software components affect the way the game plays, the pleasure obtained from the game, the performance of the game, and engagement to the game [8, 10–16]. These studies are in the context of the user experience, which defined as "focusing on the experience resulting from the interaction with products" [17], which included in the field of human–machine interaction. However, in-game research, the term "player experience" (a.k.a gamer experience/gameplay experience) is used in a more specialized subform. While academic researchers use certain features in their studies, players make comparisons according to their own needs and expectations. This study aims to reveal the dimensions in which game controllers are evaluated from both perspectives and contribute to creating the most comprehensive game controller evaluation set possible.

4 Method and Scope

In the frame of research questions of this work, we decided to conduct descriptive research. A content analysis approach was considered appropriate within the design perspective to explore research questions.

In addition to the standard controllers and computer keyboard and mouse of consoles in today's market, the controllers of VR platforms also included in the study. Additionally, some wearable devices that allow playing in more than one type of game also examined.

For the first research question, user reviews and customer questions and answers section text on Amazon.com analyzed, and words of frequently pronounced characteristics identified. Controllers are classified according to these characteristics and evaluated accordingly. This question aims to discuss dimensions as the expectations of users from the product, the features they are satisfied with and dissatisfied, or the dimensions affecting the purchase decisions. Also, these dimensions can be useful when designing a new controller.

A literature review was conducted to answer the second research question. We included studies that compare multiple controllers into this research. This question aims to reveal the approaches in the evaluation of existing products by researchers.

For conducting this research content analysis method has selected. Content analysis, a tool for performing descriptive research is "a technique for examining information, or content, in written or symbolic material (e.g., pictures, movies, song lyrics)" [17].

The determined body of material to analyze is a user review and question and answers text of the game controllers on Amazon.com. Frequency analysis carried out to reveal how often the descriptive words or themes used in the texts examined.

5 Analysis

5.1 Controller Review Dimensions from Content Analysis

In the content analysis section that constitutes the first part of the study, game controllers sold on the Amazon.com website were examined. Among these devices, the products with the highest evaluation rate were chosen by the users because of the large number of mice and keyboards used in PC games. In the game consoles and VR game platforms, while controllers evaluated, the original products of the platform manufacturer companies selected, third-party manufacturers not included in the evaluation. Wearable devices also selected on Amazon.com based on the amount of sale and user evaluation. Control devices belonging to the latest platform were selected (see Table 1).

The contents of the texts in the question and answer and user reviews sections for the selected game controllers are analyzed, and frequently used specs were listed (see Fig. 1). According to the Fig. 1, compatibility is the most critical issue among gaming platforms, games, and accessories. "Compatibility" includes game, platform, and additional gaming related equipment such as headphones. "Compatibility with accessories" include additional physical parts shapes as wheels, tennis rackets or guns. Secondly, the battery life of controllers is one of the most concerning conditions for wireless controllers. Thirdly precision is significant issues for users. We grouped

Table 1 Game controllers selected to analyze

Keyboard and mouse	Gamepads	Motion controllers	VR controllers	Adapatale controllers	Wearable controllers
	• PS dualshock 4	• PS move	• PS move	• 3DRudder	
	• Microsoft Xbox one			• MXbox adapatable	
	• Nintendo switch Joy-Con & Pro	• Nintendo Joy-Con			
	• Steam		• Steam value index		• CaptoGlove
			• HTC VIVE and Cosmos and focus		• Hi5 glove
			• Oculus touch and Go Stadia		• Bcon
			• Samsung gear VR		• Tilted

Source Authors

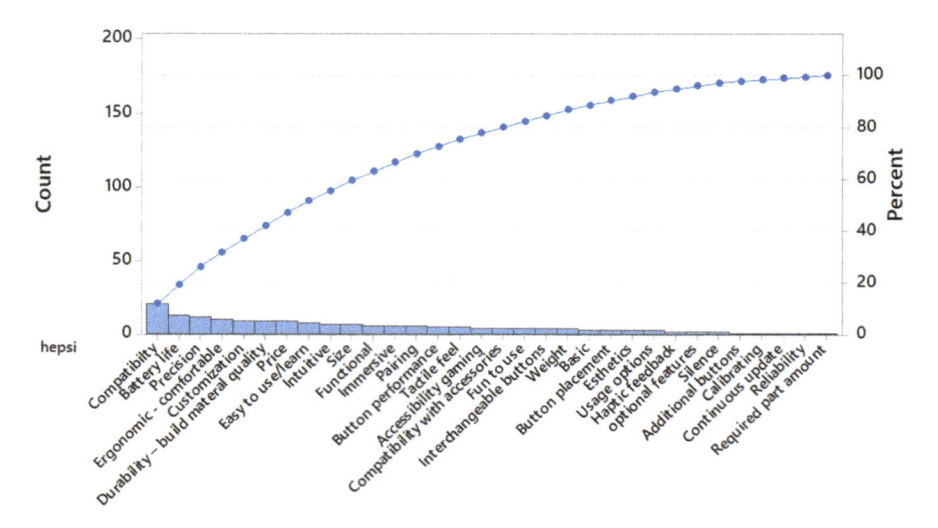

Fig. 1 Frequently used specs in the texts of questions and answers and reviews of selected controllers. *Source* Authors

all 32 keywords into four: Usability, physical specifications, other specifications, and experience related issues (See. Table 2).

According to Table 2, physical specification related comments are the most common in user reviews. In this group, compatibility, battery life, comfort and durability related specifications of controllers are the most interpreted dimensions. Secondly, in usability related review group, the most commented issues are ergonomics, precision, ease of use and learn, and intuitiveness. Thirdly, users comment about gaming experience related features such as comfort, intuitiveness, immersion and compatibility with accessories. As an economic dimension, price is another essential aspect for controller selection especially if the controller widely compatible with other platforms.

Mostly some adaptor hardware (game controller converter products) or software needed to make controllers compatible with other gaming platforms. Compatibility may be limited to some game types or games. For example, Tilted wearable controller can be used with consoles but work only games that support mouse and keyboard. Game controllers have listed in Fig. 2 according to their compatibility with other game platforms. The circle plot was generated with Circos [18]. As a reminder, for full compatibility, both platform's control requirements (such as gyroscope, accelerometer), and capabilities should fit.

Besides the compatibility with other gaming platforms, controllers can be compatible with certain game types. For example, racing wheels are suitable for racing games, or tennis racket shape controllers or accessories are meaningful for playing tennis, table tennis, or badminton games. Gun accessories to original controllers or new products like PS VR Aim Gun are usable in First Person Shooter (FPS) games, or guitar shape controllers can be used only in rhythm games like Guitar Hero (2005).

A Critical Review of Video Game Controller Designs

Table 2 Descriptive words grouped according to the terms with which they relate

Usability	Physical specifications	Other specifications	Experience related issues
• Accessibility gaming	• Additional buttons	• Basic	• Compatibility with accessorizes
	• Battery life	• Calibrating	
• Additional buttons	• Button placement	• Compatibility	• Ergonomic-comfortable
	• Compatibility	• Customization	
• Basic	• Compatibility with accessorizes	• Optional features	• Haptic feedback
• Button placement		• Pairing	• Immersion
• Compatibility with accessorizes	• Customization	• Update	• Intuitiveness
	• Durability-build material quality	• Price	• Silence
• Easy to use/learn			• Tactile feel
• Ergonomic -comfortable	• Ergonomic-comfortable		
	• Esthetics		
• Fun to use	• Haptic feedback		
• Functional	• Interchangeable buttons		
• Intuitiveness	• Silence		
• Precision	• Size		
• Reliability	• Tactile feel		
• Usage options	• Weight		
	• Required part amount		

Source Authors

They are specifically designed to be formally similar to non-game elements on which the game is based on [19].

There are limited amounts of controllers designed for only one type of game, but they have the advantage of feedback options from the point of immersive experience. Such controllers defined as realistic tangible natural mapped devices in the classification made according to the mapping style [11].

On the other hand, non-electronic accessories can simulate real experience on a limited degree, especially for motion supported games. For example, for the PS Dualshock4 controller, there are additional steering wheel-shaped attachments. For Nintendo switch joy-con and PS Move controllers, there are accessories such as tennis racket, steering wheel, bow, gun-shaped in the market.

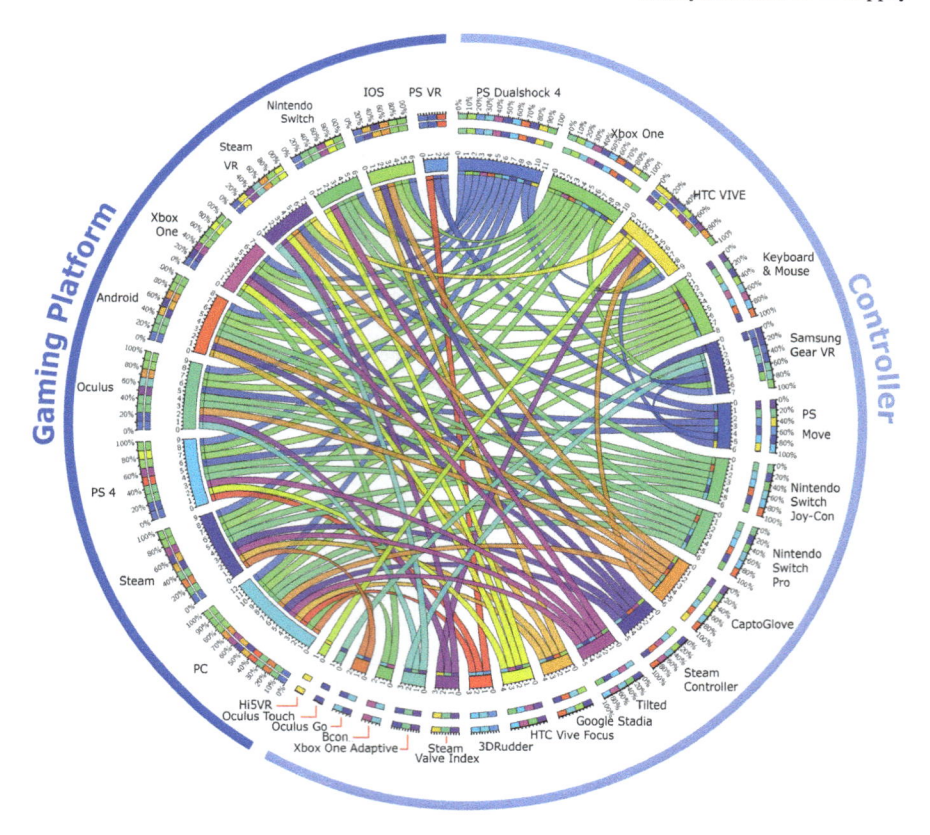

Fig. 2 Cross compatibility of video game controllers between gaming platforms. *Source* Authors

5.2 Controller Review Dimensions from Literature

Current research compare game controllers by naturalness [10, 13, 20–23], usability [24], control schemes [25], control techniques [26], realism level of the controller [27], in terms of semiotics [19], user performance [28–30], and compare existing controllers with prototypes designed [31, 32].

On the other hand, a large number of researches also focuses on the impact of controllers on player experience related terms as immersion, presence, engagement, enjoyment, flow, positive and negative affect [13, 19, 21, 25, 32–34].

The primary dimension for classification of the game controller made from *an intuitive interaction perspective* in related researches. Intuition is a situation involving the information processing processes applied in that product/interface rather than being a feature of a product or interface [35]. Therefore, intuition is an essential element of communication and interface design when controlling and using technological devices [36]. In the case of game controllers, "*natural mapping*" term appears. The most basic way of manipulating the controllers more naturally is to make a match between the directions used to interact with a controller and the results in the world or on the screen [11]. Steuer [37] defines the term mapping as "the ability of a system to map its controls to changes in the mediated environment naturally and predictably." Natural mapping uses physical analogies and cultural information to help users understand how to control devices [38]. The naturally mapped user interfaces offer the possibility to control the game mechanics more naturally instead of mastering the controller. For example, it is easier to remember to pull the trigger of the gun-shaped controller instead of remembering which key to press to shoot. Alternatively, instead of the key combination required to make a shot in a tennis game, it is enough to shake the motion controller like hitting the ball coming in that direction.

There are four different types of game controllers according to their mapping style: (1) directional natural mapping, (2) kinesic natural mapping (3) incomplete tangible natural mapping, and (4) realistic tangible natural mapping [16, 17, 27]. Birk and Mandryk [14], similarly classified controllers as traditional (e.g., Xbox GamePad), positional (e.g., PlayStation Move), and gestural (e.g., Microsoft Kinect) in their research.

The most basic way for controllers to be mapped more naturally is to establish a relationship between the directions used to interact with a controller and the results on the world or the screen [11]. This direction based control-interface mapping is called directional natural mapping. This relationship helps to achieve a real-world response through physical control, such as moving a bucket of an excavator machine and getting a virtual result from a virtual control interface, such as switching pictures on a smartphone.

Kinesic naturally mapped devices correspond to real-life actions and the movement of all or limbs of the human body with the game world, unlike controlling using handheld keys or analog sticks [11].

The main feature of the third group, which is called incomplete tangible natural mapping, is that they partially simulate the feeling that the real situation will give [11]. For example, using the Nintendo Joy-Con controller as a tennis racket in a tennis game is to associate the virtual object with a physical object as an imitation. They are called incomplete because the objects they substitute do not have precise features such as shape, weight, texture, haptic feedback [11].

The realistic tangible natural mapping defined as the state of simulating real-life feelings and feedback in a very similar way at visual, formal, and functional levels [11]. An example of the products included in this group today is the steering wheel sets used in racing games.

According to this classifications, gamepads, keyboard, and mouse listed under directional mapping. In this group, the Nintendo Joy-Con and Ps Move controller classified as incomplete tangible natural mapped devices because of the motion control abilities. VR platforms controllers other than gamepads also classified as incomplete tangible natural mapped devices.

From the other perspective, Natapov [39] categorizes game controllers as detached, immersive, and hybrid. Detached controllers defined as traditional and work as input message creators. Immersive controllers help gamers to engage in the game by enhancing the enjoyment. Hybrids, on the other hand, can be defined as controllers with immersive and detached features.

The control complexity of game controllers is also a practical dimension in classification. Control Dimensionality (CD) is used to grade a control mechanism by complexity [40]. CD is used for numeric comparison of video games, but it can also be used to see the maximum controller dimensionality of a controller (See. 42). Controllers have control abilities through parts like buttons, sticks, pedals, triggers, thumbs, or sensors. It is expected that the CD of a controller should coincide with the game mechanics. It is also possible to use the CD evaluation to classify player tolerances (See. 41).

According to Bateman and Boon [40], to calculate the CD, the "freedom of move" level should be defined first. If the game or controller can do only left and right moves (one-dimension), then $CD = 1$. If mechanics allow moving left–right, up–down (two dimensions), then $CD = 2$. If one can move left–right, up-down, in–out (three dimensions) in a game, then $CD = 3$. After that, as a secondary dimension, should add points according to:

- As an additional movement dimension (such as accelerate-brake, controlling the speed of time), add 1 point.
- As an embedded or hidden action (such as crouch, attack, jump), add 0.5 points.

However, this calculation method may include some subjectivity [41].

6 Discussion and Conclusion

Users evaluate existing game controllers based on the problems they face during their experience and their expectations from them. As revealed in the analysis, user requests appear to be directly related to compatibility, price, performance, battery life, and comfort. Additionally, as the natural mapping degrees of the game controllers increase, the frequency of expressions such as "intuitive," "fun to use," "easy to use, and easy to learn" increases in the review texts. This point corresponds to the focus of the studies in the literature. We observed that users tend to compare the same types of controllers when expressing their opinions in similar games, especially the directional mapped controllers in the form of gamepads compared with each other. There are many comments, especially on price and compatibility issues, especially in games that show both directional and incomplete tangible natural mapping features such as Nintendo Joy-con. There is no comparison of these two types of usage observed between different game types. However, there are some comparisons of the directional mapped version with other gamepads in the comments.

The vast majority of video game-related studies are on the design and usability of the video game itself. There is relatively little work on the peripheral elements of the game, such as game controllers. In the reviewed studies, the game controllers have studied in two main focus: usability and experience. In the studies based on usability and performance, game controllers compared to various game types or various tasks such as pointing. While making the evaluation, objective evaluations such as task completion time, amount of error, and subjective evaluations were made based on the comments of the players.

Similarly, at least two different types of controller comparisons made within the scope of one or more game types in studies focused on player experience. In these studies, the focus is on both game performance and enjoyment intersection. Studies also have many different evaluation tools (e.g., PENS, GExpQ, GEngQ, IEQ) created mostly based on motivation theories; the focus of evaluation differs from each other. These scales, which contain parts for evaluating the game controller, are formed in the focus of one or more terms such as immersion, presence, flow, enjoyment, competence, engagement, cognitive and emotional involvement. Moreover, they are limited in evaluating the control action independent of the game's design.

A comprehensive comparison is only possible by specifying and grouping the characteristics of the controller variants. However, this grouping may also fail to cover and evaluate all of the control devices. For example, we observed that wearable devices used in-game control were not included in the classifications. There is no criticism study from the design perspective in terms of the relationship with the body and product.

This research revealed that the multidimensionality of the game controllers and the difficulty of making a complete comparison of the features of all the controllers. Besides, looking at neither the size and availability of control devices nor the perspective of control schemes or natural match levels allows for a general assessment of the controller. On the other hand, comparisons made in a single game type also give results based on the game type. Evaluating the controllers in games that require different dimensionality will give us a more holistic understanding. It will be beneficial to make a more general evaluation to include design dimensions related to formal features and ergonomics in research.

References

1. Sicart M (2014) Play matters. MIT Press, New York
2. Hamari J, Tuunanen J (2014) Player types: a meta-synthesis. Trans Dig Games Res 1(2). https://todigra.org/index.php/todigra/article/view/13
3. Williams D (2002) A structural analysis of market competition in the U.S. home video game industry. Int J Media Manage 4(1):41–54
4. Poh M (2019) Evolution of video games user interface (UI). https://www.hongkiat.com/blog/video-games-ui-evolution/. Access date 8 May 2019
5. Newman J (2004) Videogames. Routledge
6. Turk M (2001) Perceptual user interfaces. Frontiers of human-centered computing, online communities and virtual environments. Springer, London, pp 39–51
7. Wolf MJP (2008) Chapter 3 Modes of exhibition. In: The video game explosion: a history from PONG to Playstation and beyond. ABC-CLIO. pp 13–16
8. Cummings AH (2007) The evolution of game controllers and control schemes and their effect on their games. In: The 17th annual university of Southampton multimedia systems conference, vol 21

9. Crick T (2011) The game body: toward a phenomenology of contemporary video gaming. Games Cult 6(3):259–269
10. Gerling KM, Klauser M, Niesenhaus J (2011) Measuring the impact of game controllers on player experience in FPS games. In: Proceedings of the 15th international academic MindTrek conference: envisioning future media environments. ACM, pp 83–86
11. Skalski P, Tamborini R, Shelton A et al (2011) Mapping the road to fun: natural video game controllers, presence, and game enjoyment. New Med Soc 13:224–242. https://doi.org/10.1177/1461444810370949
12. McEwan M, Johnson D, Wyeth P, Blackler A (2012) Videogame control device impact on the play experience. In: Proceedings of the 8th Australasian conference on interactive entertainment: playing the system. ACM, p 18
13. McGloin R, Farrar K, Krcmar M (2013) Video games, immersion, and cognitive aggression: does the controller matter? Media Psychol 16(1):65–87
14. Birk M, Mandryk RL (2013) Control your game-self: effects of controller type on enjoyment, motivation, and personality in game. In: Proceedings of the SIGCHI conference on human factors in computing systems. ACM, pp 685–694
15. Mueller F, Bianchi-Berthouze N (2015) Evaluating exertion games. In: Bernhaupt R (ed) Game user experience evaluation. Human–computer interaction series. Springer, Cham
16. Hassenzahl M (2010) Experience design: technology for all the right reasons. Synth Lect Hum-Centered Inf 3(1):1–95
17. Neuman WL (2014) Basics of social research. Pearson/Allyn and Bacon
18. Krzywinski M, Schein J, Birol I, Connors J, Gascoyne R, Horsman D, Jones SJ, Marra MA (2009) Circos: an information aesthetic for comparative genomics. Genome Res 19(9):1639–1645
19. Blomberg J (2018) The semiotics of the game controller. Game Stud 18(2)
20. McEwan MW (2017) The influence of naturally mapped control interfaces for video games on the player experience and intuitive interaction (Doctoral dissertation, Queensland University of Technology)
21. Cairns P, Li J, Wang W, Nordin AI (2014) The influence of controllers on immersion in mobile games. In: Proceedings of the SIGCHI conference on human factors in computing systems. ACM, pp 371–380
22. Hufnal D, Osborne E, Johnson T, Yildirim C (2019) The impact of controller type on video game user experience in virtual reality. In: 2019 IEEE games, entertainment, media conference (GEM). IEEE, pp 1–9
23. Seibert J, Shafer DM (2018) Control mapping in virtual reality: effects on spatial presence and controller naturalness. Virtual Reality 22(1):79–88
24. Brown MA, MacKenzie IS (2013) Evaluating video game controller usability as related to user hand size. In: Proceedings of the international conference on multimedia and human computer interaction–MHCI 2013, pp 114–1
25. Martel E, Muldner K (2017) Controlling VR games: control schemes and the player experience. Entertain Comput 21:19–31
26. Brown M, Kehoe A, Kirakowski J, Pitt I (2010) Beyond the gamepad: HCI and game controller design and evaluation. Evaluating user experience in games. Springer, London, pp 209–219
27. Kim KJ, Biocca F, Jeong EJ (2011) The effects of realistic controller and real-life exposure to gun on psychology of violent video game players. In: Proceedings of the 5th international conference on ubiquitous information management and communication. ACM, p 49
28. Napatov D, Castellucci SJ, MacKenzie IS (2009) ISO 9241–9 evaluation of video game controllers. In: Proceedings of graphics interfaces 2009, Toronto, Canada
29. Klochek C, MacKenzie IS (2006) Performance measures of game controllers in an three-dimensional environment. In: Proceedings of graphics interface 2006, Toronto, Canada
30. Isokoski P, Martin B (2007) Performance of input devices in FPS target acquisition. In: Proceedings of ACE 2007, ACM, New York, NY, USA, pp 240–241
31. Kwak M, Salem B (2009) Designing a game controller for novice HALO3 players. In: Proceedings of ICEC'09. Springer Verlag, Berlin, pp 325–326

32. Krekhov A, Emmerich K, Bergmann P, Cmentowski S, Krüger J (2017) Self-transforming controllers for virtual reality first person shooters. In: Proceedings of the annual symposium on computer-human interaction in play, pp 517–529
33. Wyeth P (2008) Understanding engagement with tangible user interfaces. In: Proceedings of the 20th Australasian conference on computer-human interaction: designing for habitus and habitat. ACM, pp 331–334
34. Nijhar J, Bianchi-Berthouze N, Boguslawski G (2011) Does movement recognition precision affect the player experience in exertion games? In: International conference on intelligent technologies for interactive entertainment. Springer, Berlin, pp 73–82
35. Blackler AL (2008) Intuitive interaction with complex artefacts: empirically-based research. VDM Verlag
36. Becker S (2008) Intuition. In: Erlhoff M, Marshall T (eds) Design dictionary. board of international research in design. Birkhäuser Basel
37. Steuer J (1992) Defining virtual reality: dimensions determining telepresence. J Commun 42(4):73–93. https://doi.org/10.1111/j.1460-2466.1992.tb00812.x
38. Kohn LT, Corrigan J, Donaldson MS (2000) To err is human: building a safer health system, vol 6. National Academy Press, Washington
39. Natapov D (2010) The empirical evaluation and improvement of video game controllers (Order no. MR68294). Available from ProQuest Dissertations and Theses Global (816700801). Retrieved from https://search.proquest.com/docview/816700801?accountid=13654
40. Bateman C, Boon R (2006) 21st century game design. Charles River Media Inc., Hingham, Massachusetts
41. Swain C (2008) Master metrics: the science behind the art of game design. In: Game usability: advice from the experts. Morgan Kaufmann, San Francisco

Proposal and Requirements for a Platform that Assists Teaching–Learning in the Problematization of Design Projects

Luiza Grazziotin Selau, Julio Carlos de Souza van der Linden, Carlos Alberto Miranda Duarte, and Teemu Leinonen

Abstract Design methods are a way to guide the project development process in the area. During the years of graduation students show more interest in the creative phase of the process, and less involvement with the research phase and understanding of the opportunity of the project, as well as the phase of finalizing and adapting the solution for delivery. Since the problematization phase is more theoretical and reflective, it is easy to understand this academic preference for the creative phase of the projects before the others, but mainly in relation to the understanding of the opportunity. Knowing the importance of research and analysis in the design process, the article shows the structured logic to define the development of a platform that aims to assist the realization of this important part in the project process. The approach of the article highlights the observation of classroom contexts in disciplines of graduation projects in Design in Brazil and Portugal. As a proposal, it presents the definition and requirements of an interactive digital platform as a way to assist undergraduate students in problematizing design projects.

Keywords Design · Method · Problematization · Teaching and learning · Digital platform

---

L. G. Selau (✉) · J. C. de S. van der Linden
Universidade Federal Do Rio Grande Do Sul, Porto Alegre, Brazil
e-mail: luizagselau@gmail.com

J. C. de S. van der Linden
e-mail: julio.linden@ufrgs.br

L. G. Selau · C. A. M. Duarte
IADE Universidade Europeia, Lisbon, Portugal
e-mail: carlos.duarte@universidadeeuropeia.pt

L. G. Selau · T. Leinonen
Aalto University, Espoo, Finland
e-mail: teemu.leinonen@aalto.fi

© The Author(s), under exclusive license to Springer Nature Switzerland AG 2021
Ö. Cordan et al. (eds.), *Game + Design Education*, Springer Series in Design and Innovation 13, https://doi.org/10.1007/978-3-030-65060-5_26

1 Introduction

The design process is based on the development of projects, which have in their process a path based on project methods. The design methods help the understanding and lead the designer and his team from the assimilation of the project opportunity to the solution to be delivered to the applicant.

It is noticeable that during the moment of learning design methods at graduation, students tend to have a greater interest in the creative phase of the process, paying less attention to the research phase and understanding of the project opportunity and also to the phase of finalizing and adapting the solution for delivery.

It is considered that if the design process was divided into three major phases: the initial phase, of understanding the project opportunity, is the one that demands a lot of research, reading, data interpretation and analysis of several factors, thus being the most theoretical of a design project; while the creative phase is known as one of the freest in the design process and allows the imagination to create countless possibilities of outcomes for the context worked; and finally, that the last phase is the one that requires greater technical skills and attention to technological and aesthetic details, in addition to necessary specifications and prototyping with tests. Thus it is not difficult to understand the reasons why there is this academic preference for the stage of creativity.

Thus, the first phase, better known as problematization, impacts directly on the form of development of the others, after all, if academics learn to define correctly the opportunity of the project and the need to research and collect the relevant data at the beginning of its development, they are likely to achieve better final results due to a consistent basis.

The project orientation that aims to assist teaching–learning in the design problematization proposed as a result in this article was developed after descriptive research, which presents the theoretical basis of the theme; and exploratory, which is based on data collection through observation (participant and non-participant) in Higher Education Institutions in Brazil and Portugal. Therefore, the present article intends to present the path taken to define the development of an aid to the realization of this important part in the design process.

The indicated option is one of four opportunities identified as possible responses to the observed demand and will also be tested in the same institutions where the data were collected, in order to allow comparisons of the development of the project by academics with the use of the platform as a support tool for the design project.

The study is a cutout of a doctoral thesis that shows the relevance of understanding all phases of a project by academics and also the importance of working efficiently with the problematization phase of design projects during graduation, since the project results are directly linked to the data collected and the requirements found in this early phase of the project. The result is the requirements and definition of the proposal so far identified as an option that can be the path to assist undergraduate students in problematizing design projects through an interactive digital platform.

2 Methodological Procedures

The research was of descriptive approach aiming to present characteristics, recognize variables and find associations between them [1]. It is also possible to frame the expected outcome of this research as exploratory and applied, as it seeks to produce knowledge for application of the results in contributions with practical purposes.

The realization began with classroom findings, in view of the form of carrying out activities in design projects of undergraduate academics, especially in southern Brazil. This triggered searches in the literature of the area, i.e., bibliographic survey, which are based on material already published to provide the necessary grounding, through data collection from different bibliographic sources in order to ensure the theoretical basis [1]. The initial objective of the bibliographic survey was to analyze the existence of records of other teachers' perceptions of the same situation: the lack of motivation of the design student in research, and the recognition of relevance and understanding about the initial stage of projects in the area. Finding publications that described the same finding, it was considered that the theme could be worked on in the search for strategies that aim to assist the undergraduate academic in the initial conception of their projects. Thus, this stage of bibliographical research had the purpose of verifying the relevance of the theme of the project method in design, analyze the importance given to the stage of problematization and the need to use strategies that raise awareness of the relevance and impact of this stage in the projects.

From this, we have the second stage of exploratory research that tends to provide greater familiarity with the problem and help identify the relevant facts that should be investigated [1]. The approach used qualitative research, which is used to obtain more data, based on people's behavior in relation to an experiment.

Qualitative research aims to describe the complexity of a given problem, make an analysis with variables, understand and classify the dynamic processes involved in the experience of social groups. Qualitative methods bring as a contribution to the research work a mixture of rational and inductive procedures capable of contributing to a better understanding [2]. Thus, in this case, it served to analyze the behavior of undergraduate academics while working and researching the area in relation to design problematization.

In this sense, in this project the data collection was carried out both in Brazil and Portugal, collecting the HEI data from both countries. The qualitative stage was carried out through observation (participant and non-participant), in which the observer and the observed are side by side and the objective is not omitted, seeking a relationship of trust for the understanding of the data [3]. With this it was possible to observe the behavior and the way of working of the students in relation to the project method in their work, this happened in three moments of graduation focusing on the stage in question. The definition of the use of the observation technique aimed to perceive the decision making of the students in a free way in their work process.

After this investigation, it was possible to construct a panorama regarding the use of methods and the problematization stage and not only based on the Brazilian context, but also in a context of the same language (which allows a more assertive understanding in relation to the teaching–learning context, without linguistic interference or terminologies that can be used). The objective of the data collection is, together with all bibliographic material analyzed and compiled, to organize an overview of how scholars deal with the problematization stage in the design project process. Everything that was applied by the professors of HEI of Portugal in 2019.1 was replicated with the students of the Brazilian HEI in 2019.2, and these results were analyzed and compared, which is not necessary to deepen in an article, but to consider the result of this analysis. With this information it is possible to define the inclusion and exclusion criteria, in order to prepare proposals for solutions that may help academics at the stage of problematization of projects. All of this seeks to collaborate with the understanding of some pedagogical issues of project teaching that according to [4] are still poorly assimilated, both on the part of academics, and also by teachers, who in some cases do not dispense with due importance to the subject.

The comparison occurs between two private institutions of higher education, both with degree courses in design in generalist format, with six semesters of duration, which within its scope define moments for product development projects (among other types of branches of design, but there are disciplines at compatible moments of the curriculum matrix that request product development). The institutions have a similar number of academics in design courses (about 500 students involved in the courses offered in the area), both are part of large groups of the education branch in their national scenarios. They already have a consolidated history in their contexts and a recognized brand in each location.

Three undergraduate moments were defined for the stage of observation because they are very different moments, the first in the disciplines LP (Brazil) and MD (Portugal) because they are the initial disciplines of project in graduation, are previous disciplines of project activity where the academic learns what is project and its stages. After that, the analysis becomes in the disciplines PDS (Brazil), and DP (Portugal) which are subjects in the middle of the courses and the first to require the development of a product during graduation. And finally, the PDI (Brazil) and DI (Portugal) disciplines which are equivalent to the last product development disciplines in the courses. This targeted comparison is possible due to the variables already mentioned that are compatible between the courses and because they are the subjects that can be considered equivalent between the courses of the participating HEIs.

The objective of the data collection is, together with all the bibliographic material analyzed and compiled, to verify the similarities and divergences between them. This analysis serves to enable the crossover of methods and tools verified, making the understanding of steps and their objectives defined and serve as a basis for a platform—of a format not yet defined—which aims to assist in understanding and initial use of methods in design. The platform aims to provide a structure for organizing the problematization and possible tools for this step. This makes each definition made to be thought in search of the solution of the project in question and tends to collaborate with a scope of project process always coherent and well established, allowing the designer to organize each project according to their real needs.

Not always well developed steps guarantee a satisfactory project result in design. And an unstructured design process also does not condemn the result of the project. It happens because the evaluation of what is delivered as a solution is done in a qualitative way, that is, it is perceived by the user or the large group of stakeholders. This justifies the need for understanding the client's wishes in an absolute way, and for consistent research that can provide the designer with a concrete basis when defending his design choices, thus reinforcing his role in the design processes, with the necessary knowledge for decision making. These practices and knowledge intrinsic to the designer find support in the National Curricular Guidelines for Undergraduate Design Courses [5] in which attitudes, skills, competencies and knowledge are specified. Also, the project is highlighted in the form of two specific items in the current legislation, reinforcing its primary role in the area of design:

> The first is the systemic view on the project, manifested through material and immaterial components (manufacturing, economic, psychological and sociological aspects of the product), and the second, mastery of the stages of development of a product (definition of objectives, techniques of data collection and treatment, generation and evaluation of alternatives, configuration of solution and communication of results), demonstrated through the study of the Project methodology [4] (our translation).

The objective of comparing realities and contexts between two institutions that present several similarities—one in Europe (Portugal) and another in South America (Brazil) was to not allow the researcher to be in a situation of authority in view of the context observed throughout the analysis period. In this way, performing observations in the classroom where the researcher is the teacher makes it possible to compare the context carried out in Portugal, where the researcher was a listener participant in the discipline. Putting the researcher in two different positions, but with the same conditions and research resources available, enables greater validation of the data collected, without threatening the "status-quo of educational research" [6]. The realities are similar in terms of the teaching format in design, language used in class, undergraduate design course offerings, course structure, IES infrastructure, IES format (private), academic profile. The analyses take into consideration several relevant issues for comparison, such as: curricular matrix, workload and credits of the subjects, menus, bibliographies, schedule of the subjects, activities, evaluations and project development of the semester.

The focus of analysis is how the academic works the problematization stage in a design project. Since all the background demonstrate the relevance of the stage and the perception experienced in the classroom together with the research carried out demonstrate that academics tend not to carry out this stage with due diligence, making this stage shallow and insufficient for the development of the project, thus often reflecting on the final result. The research done in Brazil about the use of project methods is usually worked through reports of classroom experiences, therefore, it is known that the minority of project cases passed to scholars are based on real experiences or simulations of market situations in partnership with external entities [4]. The purpose of the research period abroad also makes it possible to analyse—even if specific—the approach format used in Portugal.

With all the analyses carried out, it is possible to cross-check the data of the teaching methods and strategies verified, specifically analyzing the stage of problematization and making these data and contexts serve as a basis for the platform proposal. In relation to the research format, in face of the data collection and analysis stage, this presents itself as a case study in the investigation, a comprehensive empirical strategy of investigation of a contemporary phenomenon within its real life context, especially when the boundaries between the phenomenon and the context are not visibly defined. It is a methodological approach employed to understand, explore or describe events and contexts in which several factors are simultaneously involved [7].

The study in question, in addition to contributing its results aimed at undergraduate students in design, also intends to cooperate with teachers in order to provide reflections on their activities, since it is a case study of teaching, in which the teacher is also a researcher and a central figure in his own understanding while describing and analyzing the case, serves "as lenses to think about his own work in the future" [8]. The data collection of the present research is composed of a format combined with a triple focus on data collection and interpretation, so it is called the Triangulation Technique [3].

The triangulation took place through the combination of the two stages already mentioned, the bibliographic and documentary survey; with the participant observation performed; and also with the analysis, which was of a comparative nature, of the documents developed by the academics of the HEI during the period of observation of academic realities. Resulting in the definition of requirements and presentation of the platform proposal.

3 Analysis and Discussion of Results

Analyses and reflections were made on the subject studied in order to propose a contribution to the area of design in relation to the project methods for the problematization stage, that is, understanding the project opportunity. For this, the exploratory stage of the research was initiated, where the qualitative approach is used, it intends to understand the context and the important aspects of the question observed through the analysis of people's attitudes towards what is being studied. In this way, it is a question of understanding the way undergraduate design scholars work understanding the problems identified as design project opportunities. This means the way they approach the issue, how much they investigate what is presented as an opportunity, the questions they ask themselves in the face of the above, how much they use the information collected in the later stages of the project, when they evaluate that they already have enough information to follow up on the project, how the data work, what links are made regarding this information in order to seek innovation, differential and quality in the solution they will propose, how they analyze the solution of this data when they conclude that they have found an assertive solution and finally they verify the solution in front of the initial project opportunity and its requirements.

Thus, what was possible to observe in the two contexts of higher education in design where the immersion occurred was that the academics:

- do not feel safe at the beginning of any design project about using the method,
- are not sure about the flexibility that exists in using the method in their projects,
- don't know what to do with the information they collect in project surveys;
- are eager to start designing the solution even if they don't know the context of the project;
- lacks organization and planning at the beginning of the project (structuring of schedule for the development of the project);
- the information researched has no relation with the rest of the project; it is no longer used after the data collection stage;
- the objective of many is only to meet the discipline's requirement, there is no commitment, they only meet requested steps;
- do not understand what it is to do when receiving the project demand;
- their own repertoire, knowledge, skills, experiences and personal experiences have a great influence on the development of the project;
- even those who know that the phases of the project are flexible develop the project in a linear way;
- feel supported (in case of possible mistakes) by following an entire method to the letter;
- do not relate the phases of the project using information from one another for decision making;
- repeat what has already worked once in another discipline to avoid the error;
- need constant approval of their choices or stagnate in a tool-step;
- follow the whole project with the first idea of a fixed solution, even if there are indications that something should be changed;
- they're not at risk;
- hardly return to earlier phases to review, redo, or when they realize they need to complement something in the project that depends on this "backward step";
- the experience of the labor market of some impacts directly on the way of acting before the project—for those who already act in the area, especially observed in Brazilian academics;
- for not using an organization with a schedule, they accumulate work for dates close to the deliveries and evaluations, not being able to develop the project in a satisfactory way.

These observations were noticed in the activities developed throughout the immersion period, but also in the dialogues and reports from academics. In view of this, the reasoning that serves as a guide for the analysis is based on a triad (see Fig. 1), which involves the process of the designer as an academic: a) Lack of personal repertoire; b) Fear when making decisions; c) Low knowledge and project practice with methods.

Thus, the problem of the future designer, while he is still an academic, is related to the flexibility of methods, decision power and personal repertoire to be converted into project insights. All this has a great impact in the initial phase of projects, because is when they need to work on the project opportunity. When the academic

Fig. 1 Triad of an academic designer [9]

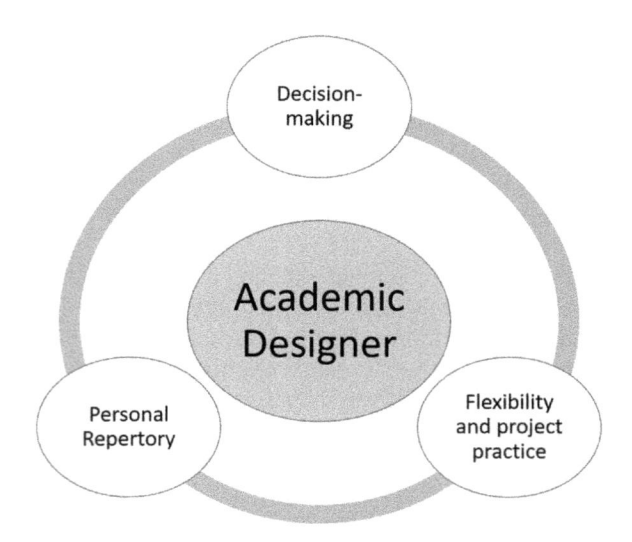

receives the project demand the problem needs to be restructured to be understood, the information needs to be worked in a way that supports the project and all this needs to be converted into project requirements so that the result is related to what was actually requested, improving the assertiveness of the proposal.

The problematization stage involves the understanding of the project opportunity, numerous questions must be analyzed to understand the specificities and needs that a project has, for this it is necessary to make studies, research and analysis of different areas. The methods propose some analyses that help this phase of the project, the study of the opportunity of the project is considered in different ways in the models of project scope published internationally, but in the search to group the largest number of observed analyses in proposals of studied methods is presented in Fig. 2.

In this way, it is realized that these analyses can (in the same way as the names of the phases and project phases) have more than one nomenclature depending on the author who proposes it. Some of them can even be indicated for other moments of the project beyond the initial stage, serving to support the creative process, supporting the final choice of project, sustaining the choices throughout the process. The truth is that the problematization occurs throughout the project, the discoveries are not only in the initial phase, sometimes a question is already considered with the project in the final phase, which may trigger the need to redo some choices or even return with the project some steps. The method, and the problematization stage mainly, serve for the academic to understand that: method is different from a cake recipe; as the author of the project itself he has the power of decision and needs to make choices in front of his project. Even if taking risks, the academy is the place where the future designer need to ask the following questions: 'how to do the project, what do I understand? what background do I already have in the subject? what knowledge do I have? how far do I go? when the result is satisfactory? who decides this?', without fear, because it is the only time when the project results will be evaluated with the

Proposal and Requirements for a Platform that Assists ... 333

Fig. 2 Analysis in design process [9]

objective of improvements, constructive criticism that will enable growth and better future productions in projects.

The objective of carrying out analysis in the search for understanding the project context is to provide the designer with a specific view of reality that surrounds the issue to be developed in the project so that his project choices are guided by relevant data and can direct the project to solutions more consistent with the existing request in the briefing. For this, it is concluded, after analysis of several methods proposed by the authors in the area, project development and monitoring of graduation projects as a guide that, if performed in the initial stage of the project, familiarizing the designer to the project context, tend to help and clarify the situation that involves the project opportunity, in addition generates security for the designer in their choices and decisions throughout the project process.

Basically, it can be said that the logic and the need for problematization in design are illustrated in Fig. 3:

The fact that it allows solutions means that the problem is the result of the designer's reading of the data and information that are already available, but that were collected to be worked on in front of the project in question. Problematizing is precisely to take this information into consideration throughout the project process and from it generate the requirements to be considered in the other stages of the project, especially in the creation and selection of alternatives as the final result. As much as it involves research, analysis, information and data, problematization

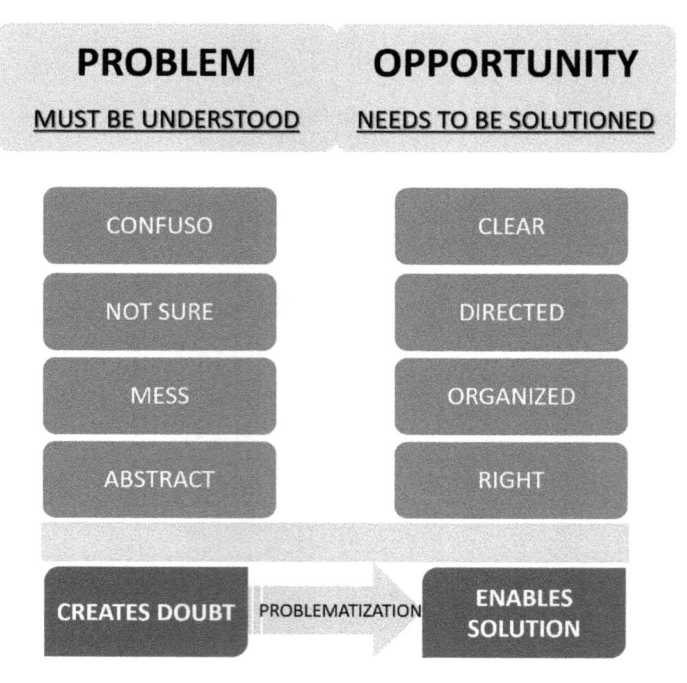

Fig. 3 Problematization in design [9]

actually aims to guide the process, define what will be the requirements, directions, limits and guidelines that need to be taken into consideration in every project act, in addition to guiding creativity within plausible possibilities with the existing need.

In this sense, the research stage is summarized in the realization of analyses of available information, but which need to be worked on within the perspective of the project in question. In order to answer some possible questions, such as: 'how to know which research to do? how to know how many analyses to do? how to know if I already have enough information? how to use this collected data?', it is intended to present a way to help the academic to know how to answer these very questions at the beginning of the project. Thus, the analyses and research proposed in most of the studied methods and also analyses observed in classroom practice for more than five years were listed and grouped by similarities in their objectives, resulting in about ninety possible analyses or researches that can help in the problematization stage of the projects. Here, all research directed to a particular purpose in projects is considered analysis. For better organization they were divided into eight dimensions by areas, which: contextual, conceptual, ergonomic, technological, environmental, economic, forecasting and public.

Before generating possible solutions to assist academics in this context, requirements were defined for this platform that is intended to be delivered as a result:

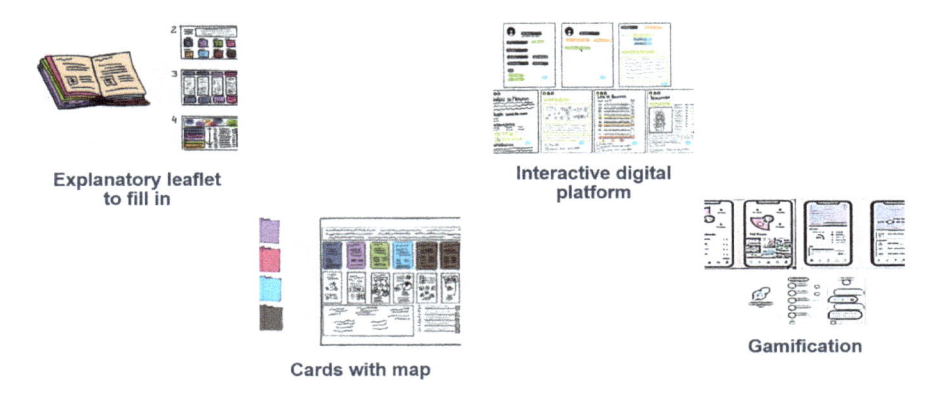

Fig. 4 Four possible solutions [9]

A. serve as a way to raise academic awareness of the importance of problematization;
B. be of intuitive use;
C. fit into the context of study, but can also cover other realities;
D. to facilitate the evaluation and development of tasks;
E. serve as a project schedule;
F. allow consultation after the developed project;
G. to instigate the power of project decision;
H. force the academic to use the information of the problematization in the other stages of the project.

In view of the defined requirements, four platform possibilities have been developed as possible solutions (see Fig. 4):

1. Explanatory leaflet to fill in: a leaflet that presents the analyses with brief explanation and indication of tools, 3 support pages to fill in: one with space for project information and list of analyses to select which ones to do (using the leaflet as a support for choice); another with space to insert collected data and synthesis of each analysis performed (can be used as many copies as necessary, depending on how many analyses are selected to do); and finally one that allows you to analyze the syntheses to generate the project requirements, in addition to allowing the ranking of these requirements for later use in alternative selection and final evaluation. Each sheet can be a step to be delivered and validated or evaluated by the subject teacher at the weekly face-to-face meetings.
2. Cards with map: a deck with cards that contains an explanation of the analyses and indication of possible tools; and the map is like a board where the academic includes project data, adjusts the selected analysis cards in the spaces to serve as a guide for its realization, space for filling with the collected data, space for summaries of the analyses and for a list of requirements—which can also be used in other stages of the project. The map can be used as an evaluation for the teacher in face-to-face meetings.

3. Interactive digital platform: site or program that works as a portal for the development of projects, IES, teachers, classes and students are registered, academics enter information from the project received, select the analyses to be performed, fill out the data collected, develop synthesis of each research, generate list of requirements, define the importance of each requirement, include alternatives and confront the requirements and when selecting enter the solution to validate project requirements in their final choices. With validation, registration and feedback from the subject teacher possible in each activity developed, which allows him/her to follow in the development of the project and record its evolution, as well as create a kind of project portfolio.
4. Gamification: make the project process visually similar to the progress of a game where the missions are the stages of the project. The academic will include information about the project as if he were creating the scenario or the character of his game, then he defines what path he will follow when choosing which analysis he will perform, so the academic begins to experience the game, walking the path he defined and filling each analysis with the data collected for the game to develop, he must complete the path by defining a conclusive synthesis of each analysis performed, until he defines the project requirements generated by each synthesis. Thus the academic returns to the game to check the list of requirements in the selection and validation of the chosen solution. The option allows the professor to check deliveries by locking the game progress at each delivery and making the game only continue with the complete and verified steps—evaluations and feedbacks.

The requirements were checked in each possibility developed and the interactive digital platform was chosen to be the alternative used as the most suitable solution, as shown in Fig. 5.

The choice was made due to verification of requirements, but also due to further analysis that encompasses development issues, time, cost x benefit, complexity, adjustments, possible tests, technical availabilities, etc. The beta version is under development and the first tests are scheduled for the second half of 2020, as well as the final adjustments and tests for the official version of the platform. It is possible to notice that besides the requirements and external issues the choice provides several options that make the project more relevant than initially thought, such as:

- blind review'—other IES (or external) teachers evaluating the projects;
- competitions, gymkhanas, competitions at or between IES;
- mapping the types of projects being developed by academics;
- mapping academic interests;
- mapping areas of interest of HEIs or regions or countries or design skills (product, graphic, fashion, service trends);
- mapping research trends, design and detailing used by academics, by IES, by country;
- mapping scholars' thinking;
- academic project database;
- database with history of IES (documentation of activities).

		01	02	03	04
A.	serve as a means of raising academic awareness of the importance of problematization	✓	✓	✓	✓
B.	be intuitive to use	✓	✓	✓	
C.	fit into the study context, but may also cover other realities	✓	✓	✓	
D.	facilitate the evaluation and development of tasks	✓	✓	✓	✓
E.	serve as a project schedule			✓	✓
F.	enable consultation after the project developed	✓	✓	✓	✓
G.	instigate the power of projectual decision-making	✓	✓	✓	✓
H.	forcing the academic to use the information from the problematization in the other stages of the project	✓	✓	✓	✓

Fig. 5 Verification of requirements [9]

4 Final Considerations

The design has undergone significant evolution in the way of design, it is complex to apply all the necessary tools to the project opportunity seeking to equate simultaneously so many factors in the face of the problem in project activity, but everything depends on the context of work [10]. In this sense, the proposal seeks to encourage this clarity of thought in design already at the beginning of the design process by encouraging students in the visible need for change in relation to project thinking. Thus, the study in question presents potential precisely for stimulating critical reasoning and definitions in understanding and defining the problematization of the project opportunity.

The result that is intended to be delivered with the indicated option as a solution, should be visualized as a teaching aid tool. It is known that for the formation of the designer, the project methodology is a central axis, since it underlies the practice of professional performance. It appeared as a discipline between the 50 s and 60 s, but over time the complexity of the subject has increased due to "new technologies, new programs of use and consumption, changes in cognitive paradigms, new social relations, new market structuring, dilution or intensification of references and professional specialties, etc.". [11]. In the contemporary world, it is clear that the knowledge needed by designers is a valuable contribution to innovative and efficient approaches in the field of education [12].

It is not so simple to understand the project activity in the area of design, since the demands of projects today are more dynamic, complex and eager for creativity.

The initial understanding of the project articulates theoretical knowledge and practical application of the activities, besides valuing the capacity to solve problems in a creative way, it requires logical reasoning and consistency in the argumentation. Since it is a challenge for Higher Education Institutions to effect real innovative changes in the context of teachers due to the complexity and inaccuracies of the current panorama. It is urgent the need to change the outdated teaching format where the teacher holds all the knowledge, and provide a space for interaction between the theory and practice of content, allowing future professionals to experience during their academic period what they will exercise after graduation. This, "from the problematization, research and reflection on the lived experiences, that opportunities the development of complex cognitive and social skills" [8], which allows greater absorption of information and protagonism in the learning process. Therefore, a project that intends to foster the understanding of the problematization stage of the design process, its possibilities of use and strategies becomes the starting point for other studies to complement their results with more research proposals, visualizing, for example, other phases of the project method.

Acknowledgements PUDCAD Project developer (leader) and participants.

References

1. Gil AC (2010) How to elaborate research projects. Atlas, São Paulo
2. Pope C, Mays N (1995) Reaching the parts other methods cannot reach; an introduction to qualitative methods in health and health service research. British Med J 311:42
3. Marconi MA, Lakatos EM (2011) Scientific methodology. Atlas, São Paulo
4. Martins VS, Wollf F (2015) Competencies in product design disciplines. Stud Des Maga 23(2):37–58. (Rio de Janeiro)
5. Brasil. CNE/CES n. 0195/03, de 5 de agosto de 2003. https://portal.mec.gov.br/cne/arquivos/pdf/CES_0195.pdf. Last Accessed 10 Mar 2020
6. Cunha CM (2016) Exigência de novas metodologias na pesquisa em educação para expressão de práticas inovadoras. In: Vieira et al (org.) Inovação Pedagógica do Ensino Superior. De Facto Editores, Santo Tirso, Portugal, pp 25–38
7. Yin RK (2005) Estudo de caso: planejamento e métodos, 3rd edn. Bookman, Porto Alegre
8. de Miranda DL, Soares SR (2016) Práticas Pedagógicas Inovadoras na Universidade: Investigando os sentidos atribuídos pelos docentes. In: Vieira et al. (org.) Inovação Pedagógica do Ensino Superior. De Facto Editores p. 13–24, Santo Tirso, Portugal
9. Developed by the Authors
10. de Van Der Linden JCS, de Lacerda AP, de Aguiar JPO (2010) A evolução dos métodos Projetuais. In: Proceedings of the 9th Brazilian Congress on Research and Development in Design. Blucher, São Paulo
11. Lessa WD (2013) Objectives, development and synthesis of the design project: the method awareness. In: Westin D, Coelho LA (org) Study and practice of design methodology in graduate courses. Novas Ideias, Rio de Janeiro
12. Jacinto A, Valença M (2016) Design Thinking na educação e na formação. In: Vieira et al. (org) Inovação Pedagógica do Ensino Superior. De Facto Editores, Santo Tirso, Portugal, pp. 115–128

Playful Spaces and Interfaces

An Exploration of Interactivity and Tangibles in Blended Play Environments

İpek Kay and Mine Özkar

Abstract In this paper, we present a study exploring digital augmentation as an integral part of spatial experience in children's play with physical objects. We introduce a blended play environment, a combination of digital and physical media, for enhancing children's physical activity and play through interaction with tangibles. This play environment called Monnom, a novel digitally-enhanced physical environment, offers body-object interaction where the body frames the scene, controls and improvises the play. The prototype has been assessed in studies with 67 children (4–12 years old) in two different settings, one at a museum and the other at a school. Based on an analysis of existing designs, we highlight different play actions that children may employ, and delineate various resources for meaning making. Digital technologies for play are mostly structured, rule-bound and goal-directed virtual playgrounds. Our study expands these and suggests a set of qualities to think about interaction design for children's play and future research.

Keywords Interactive play environment · Physical activity · Spatial interaction · Design for play

1 Introduction

Recent years saw the development of several play environments for children that integrate interactive technology. Grounded in the constructivist paradigm, new approaches focus on interaction design that incorporates body and space. In the human-computer interaction (HCI) context of playful learning environments, bodily

İ. Kay (✉)
İstanbul Technical University, Istanbul, Turkey
e-mail: kayip@itu.edu.tr

M. Özkar
İstanbul Technical University, Istanbul, Turkey
e-mail: ozkar@itu.edu.tr

interaction has been revitalized and research on evaluating this interaction has highlighted important benefits in enhancing meaning-making, exploration, and collaboration in children's play [1–3]. However, further research is still needed to articulate ways of bringing children back into the places of their daily environments. There is a reciprocal relationship between physical activity and the activity setting [4]. Most digitally-enhanced play environments are based on specific interactive objects and the isolated play to be performed with them [3, 5, 6]. Especially, for indoor play, these environments target a structured form of play that rules and goals are predefined.

To address these shortcomings, our study aims to support children's bodily experiences by integrating the physical and digital environment through intuitive interaction modalities. In a previous study, we presented the theoretical framework for designing digitally-enhanced environments for children's play to support their engagement and active exploration in their everyday places through objects [7]. Based on that framework, this paper presents a scenario to interact with digital environments from within the physical world through unique feedback to children and to invite them to intervene in the flow of their play. The crucial question has been how to use the features of children's surroundings to integrate physical and digital environments.

This paper introduces the design, development, and assessment of the "Monnom" prototype as a digitally-enhanced play environment. The prototype integrates the physical environment and the digital environment into the child's experience in order to enable children to transform a place physically via giving a symbolic meaning to objects around while actively engaging with the daily environments. For this purpose, we present a qualitative study with children playing with Monnom to explore how interaction with digital environments through tangibles affects children's play-action patterns, the creation of their own play space, and social interactions. Below, we analyze four children's experiences as being representative of variations of children's play and activities. The analysis highlights the potentials of blended environments, a combination of digital and physical media. To conclude, we derive a set of qualities to think about interactive design for play and future research. Unless otherwise stated, all images and figures in this article are the first author's own creation.

2 Background

In the context of designing an environment for play, it is important to understand the role of the play environment [8, 9]. Research on designing places for children has shown, there is a direct connection between play and the physical environment. Children's indoor and outdoor play differ physically and socially related to the play actions that happen there [9, 10]. One of the reasons for this difference is that indoor and outdoor settings have different types of equipment and materials [10, 11]. In outdoor settings, natural landscape environments provide a setting for open-ended play with various conditions such as wind, sun-shadow, rain and provide greater space and freedom of movement for children. Thus, children frequently engage in the exploration, manipulation of natural materials, and locomotion. In indoor settings, objects become more important for children's play and children frequently engage in conversations with peers through playing with objects.

Frost [12] describes three different forms of play that are particularly relevant with physical activity and the environment during play: functional play, constructive play and symbolic play. Functional play is play that involves full-body activities such as running or climbing a tree. Constructive play involves building things, such as building a shelter by collecting materials or manipulating parts to build. Symbolic play involves pretend activity which allows children to construct alternative worlds by role-playing. Henniger [13] shows that preschool children prefer constructive play in indoor settings and functional play in outdoor settings due to the different toys and equipment that were available in each setting.

With regards to interactive digital environments for outdoor play, most approaches focus on location-based surface design [6]. On the other hand, for indoor play environments, most digital environments are based on specific interactive objects [2, 3]. For the purpose of this paper, we look for a way of using digital technology to support interaction both with the physical and digital environment. We design a blended play environment called Monnom to support (a) different forms of play, (b) spatial interaction with their surrounding, (c) social interaction. Monnom invites children to interact with the digital environment through using features of the child's surroundings.

3 The Prototype: Monnom

Monnom, a digitally-enhanced physical environment offers body-object interaction where the body frames the scene, controls, and improvises the play. This system does not require the user to wear any physical device. It is able to employ various tracking systems, and thus allows easy integration of nearly any object into the virtual world. Moreover, physical objects are used, not only for haptic interaction, but as controllers, and to drive the interaction with the digital world. Children can use Monnom individually or as a group.

The whole installation consists of colorful objects, a vertical surface where the interactive-digital content is projected, a bounded area where the children can play, a projection, a webcam for collecting data (in front of the screen to perceive children's play with objects), a computer with Monnom software for data transmitting and transforming the interactive digital content (see Fig. 1). Two fixed video cameras record children's activity.

We use vertical surfaces for a display to provide children's own composition in the digital environment synchronously by allowing the reciprocal connection between the digital and physical environments. Children, with their eyes on the two-dimensional display, move around and add objects to the physical space while the system captures size and color information of objects through body movements, analyses and interprets compositions with predefined patterns. The technology inside the system allows children to make their own spatial composition in both physical

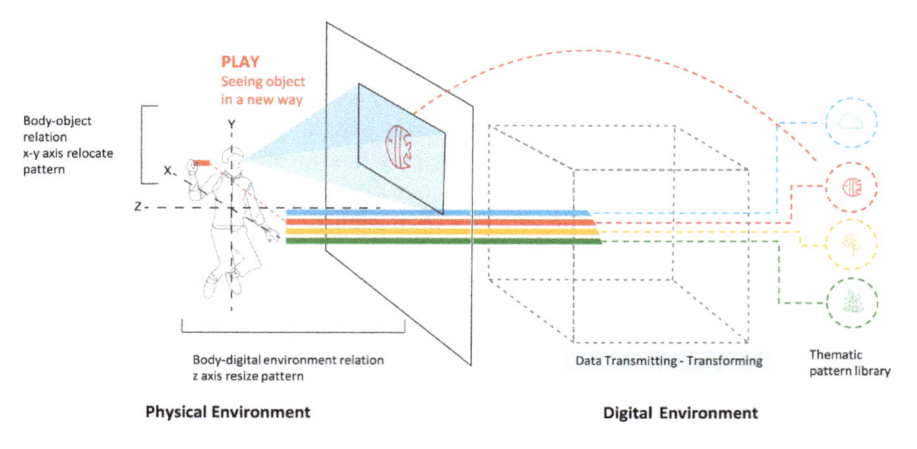

Fig. 1 Technical infrastructure of Monnom

and digital environments, they can resize patterns in the digital world by moving with objects in the physical world.

Here, we report on children's interaction with "Monnom". The present exploration is part of a larger study aimed at evaluating user experience in Monnom. The purpose of the current analysis is to demonstrate how digital augmentation supports children's play through activating objects.

4 Study Setup

We conducted user studies with children in two different settings, one at a museum and one at a school. In order to optimize the installation conditions for Monnom, we first tested its prototype in a multi-purpose room on our campus, Istanbul Technical University, Architecture Faculty and four children played with Monnom. The main goal was to try and decide how we should install our system. We then assessed the prototype in studies with 67 children (4–12 years old) in two different settings. These studies included unique features such as thematic patterns and background images related to the settings at a museum and a school (Fig. 2).

Our study protocol was approved by the Istanbul Technical University Committee On the Use of Humans as Experimental Subjects. For the first study, the museum (Istanbul Modern) made an announcement about the workshop named for two different age groups. Each group was limited to 20 participants. It was an open public event that families could apply to without any precondition. Participants were informed by the museum about the study and permission procedures. 15 children participated in the first group (aged 7–8) whereas 14 children participated in the second group (aged 9–12). For the second study, the school (ITU Vakfı Özel Sedat

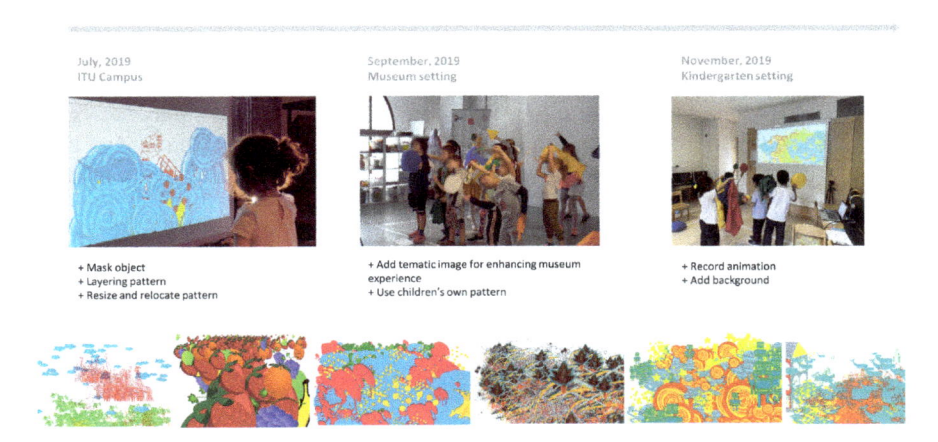

An Exploration of Interactivity and Tangibles … 345

Fig. 2 Research settings and sample outcomes

Üründül Kindergarten) wrote an invitation letter to parents seeking individual permissions. Parents of 38 children (aged 4–5) agreed to have their children participate. They gave written informed consent prior to the start of the study, and on the day of the study, the children assented to participate. All children had the opportunity to play with Monnom for about 10 min.

Children's activities and the digital content that children created were recorded with video cameras. Recorded documents were stored on computers that were password protected and accessible only to the researchers. Each session was digitally filed with the name and date of birth (month-year) of the participating children. For any publication of the work, any visuals and information that could identify the individuals were omitted, e.g. faces of the children in the images and videos were blurred. In research documents, children were identified by age and a letter code rather than by name. Audio recordings were kept only as transcription and confidentially.

5 Data Collection Method

The primary form of data collection was video recording and notes taken based on the play session observations. With reference to this data, we considered how interacting with the digital environment through physical objects influences children's play, spatial interaction with their surrounding and peer communication. In post-study viewing of the videos, any interesting interaction, a special play event or anything notable was noted down and labeled with the time it happened, duration, number of participants, age group and gender of the involved children for each play event. We defined behavioral codes to illustrate patterns related to:

- Play actions
- Spatial interaction (use of space, engagement with object)

346   İ. Kay and M. Özkar

- Peer communication.

Based on the detected patterns, one case study was analyzed with focus on four children's experiences as being representative of diverse children's play activities. We then performed an in-depth transcription by focusing on the behavior of each child during the play session. These transcriptions were performed by annotating data from both the video recordings and verbal interaction.

6 Observations

Here we report our study of one of the nine groups in the school case study. The school prepared a group of 4 or 5 children for each classroom. We designed play patterns in two themes according to the school program in order to create a shared and familiar interest among the children: Autumn and Space (see Figs. 3 and 4). For each theme, we created eight patterns and used four colors. We also created an

Fig. 3 Patterns for the Autumn Theme

Fig. 4 Patterns for the Space Theme

An Exploration of Interactivity and Tangibles … 347

additional theme to provide children a theme out of the school context: Sea (see Fig. 5).

We designed the soft objects, i.e. pillow and blanket, that are familiar to children's daily environments (see Fig. 6). We intentionally made their shape simple for easy physical manipulation. These objects were in four different colors.

The session began with the introduction of Monnom. We made a demo to help the children understand the system. We showed how to change, place and resize patterns in the digital world by playing ourselves with different colored objects and by moving around with them in hand. Then the children decided on the theme, selected the play patterns which we then imported into the software. Afterwards play time started.

The group in the study results we present here consisted of four girls. Three were 4 years old and classmates whereas the fourth was 5 years old. Together, they selected

Fig. 5 Patterns for the Sea Theme

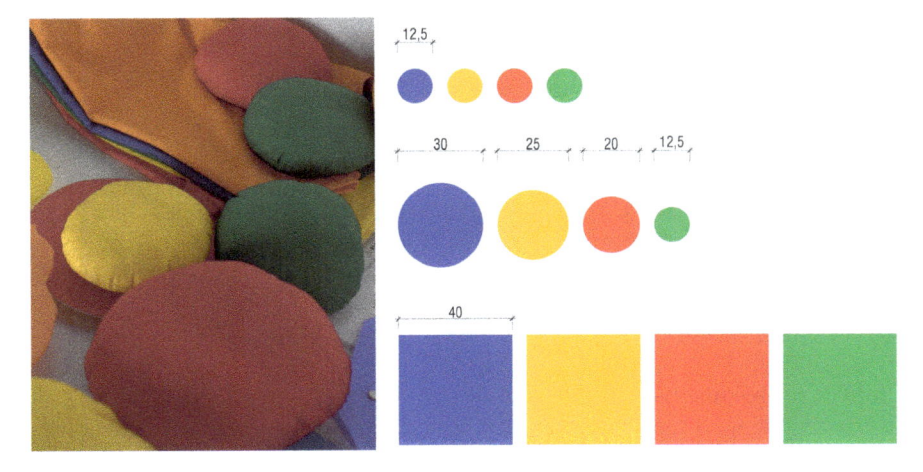

Fig. 6 Objects and their dimensions (cm)

Fig. 7 Patterns that children chose together

autumn as the theme and decided on the patterns (see Fig. 7). They matched the cloud with blue, birds with yellow, the kite with red, and leaves with green.

While the size of the pillow and blanket affected the size of the pattern in the digital environment, children also resized them by coming closer to the camera or stepping back. Each child took on a different role in the session.

Child 1: planner
Once the play session started, the first child C1 quickly picked up objects and built a place on the floor. And then the second and third child participated. They prepared a place together for "sleep" by using pillows and blankets as they should be in the sleeping environment. When their interaction with Monnom started, the first child tried to collect all blue objects. After she picked up the big blue pillow, she made big blue clouds on the screen. With this initial exploration, she began to create patterns with different colored objects. She was not specifically exploring variations in physical movements, but she used her actions to systematically test out cause-and-effect relations until she tried and observed all colors and their patterns. She then went back to her initial location where they made a place on the floor, and she continued to build her place without looking at the screen. After this point, her play pattern mainly focused on collecting all objects, trying to keep them together, and creating her own place via spatial transformation using objects. She also communicated with the second child who participated at some points. She started to give directions to her, e.g. "let's sleep", while observing others' play.

Child 2: player
Child C2 started the play by trying to take the big blue pillow from C1. At this point, the C3 helped them negotiate by bringing the small blue pillow. After trying to create patterns with that object, C2 stopped and observed the screen for the effect of her actions. Later she tried other small pillows. It was difficult to observe the effects of her movement because she always chose small objects. She also observed her peers playing. After trying a couple of times, she participated in C1's play on the floor, and she helped her build a place for their collective play.

Child 3: problem-solver
At the beginning of the play, C3 picked up the blue blanket. At that moment, she realized that the first and second children had a problem sharing a big blue pillow. In order to solve this problem, she found and gave another blue pillow to the second

child. Then she began to create clouds with the blue blanket. After the initial trial, showing a clear understanding of the effects of different colored objects, she began to have a strategic approach. She collected four pillows of the same size but with different colors and created different patterns with them. Instead of focusing on resizing patterns, she focused on creating different patterns on the different places of the screen. Thus, with every new object, she also changed her position.

Child 4: competitor
Child C4 was from a different class and did not speak to the other children during the entire session. She started with the red blanket and physical play activities, such as walking, jumping. When she moved closer to the screen and showed the entire blanket, she created the biggest pattern. She observed that in the front position while jumping, she was able to control her creation on the screen. She also explored the effects of her bodily movements on resizing patterns. After this observation, her activity mainly focused on competition for creating the biggest pattern and exploring variations between different colored objects and their effects on the digital environment.

7 Results

Interacting with the digital environment through tangibles invites children to experience different interaction paths (see Figs. 8 and 9). Children tended towards different actions based on their play patterns and familiarity with one another. For all, the seamless integration of the physical and digital world in Monnom allowed easy moves from a physical environment to a digital environment. With the prototype, the children immediately understood its basic idea—picking up differently colored objects for selecting patterns in the digital environment and resizing and relocating the pattern by moving in the physical space. This simplicity allowed children to make their own

Fig. 8 Children engaging in multiple play patterns during playing with Monnom

Fig. 9 Childrens' creation during the play session

rules. Over time, children seemed to collect objects for creating their own palette and learned to control the size and the location of the pattern as they watched the results of their movements.

In Monnom, the body becomes the vantage point and frames the scene, while the eye controls and improvises the play. We have observed that with feedback from a digital environment, children can fictionalize the meaning of that space by moving around and adding objects to the physical space. For example a child picked the blue object and drew clouds, and she said: "I have so many clouds in my sky" while showing physical surroundings. Then she went to the object box to take a yellow object, she said "let's add birds here" while jumping around pretending to be a bird.

Since the system allows multiple players, children learned different interaction paths observing other actions. They talked about which color produces which pattern on the screen as well as their exploration of different actions with different objects together. In particular, the visibility of actions via the screen in Monnom helped children to acknowledge others' perspectives and encouraged negotiation. This feedback allowed children to influence and react to the behaviour of the system and also observe others' action.

Beside simplicity, feedback and multiple-player approach, Monnom invited children to engage diverse play patterns through dispersed quality. Instead of designing a special interactive object, the system involves multiple objects without requiring any digital equipment. During play, children expand their play beyond the digital interface, and the objects serve as both tools of digitally represented narration and props for physical play. For instance, the first child focused on creating patterns on the screen, later she focused on making a physical place for her play by using the same object.

8 Conclusion

In the context of designing a digitally-enhanced environment for play, it is necessary to ask how we can design conditions to facilitate children's different play patterns while supporting bodily experiences. Our study with Monnom explored different interaction paths children followed us in a blended environment. The broader analysis is ongoing but a few preliminary insights expand the understanding of using digital technologies for play. The current study can provide an initial set of qualities for designing blended play setups: simplicity, feedback, multiple players, dispersed. Furthermore, by documenting the differences in children's interaction paths, the study highlights the importance of designing for diversity by offering affordances that support children's active engagement and exploration. The prototype is responsive only to predefined objects' features. Future work aims to make this blended system accessible directly from children's daily environments and open for children to use their own daily objects instead of determined play objects.

Acknowledgements We would like to thank Istanbul Modern Education Department and ITU Vakfı Özel Sedat Üründül Kindergarten for their support to the study and all the children who participated in them.

References

1. Malinverni L, Ackermann E, Pares N (2016) Experience as an object to think with: from sensing-in-action to making-sense of action in full-body interaction learning environments. In: Proceedings of the TEI'16: 10th international conference on tangible, embedded, and embodied interaction ACM, pp 332–339
2. Boon B, Van Der Net J, Rozendaal M, Stappers PJ, Van Den Heuvel-Eibrink MM (2016) Playscapes: A design perspective on young children's physical play. In: Proceedings of IDC 2016—the 15th international conference on interaction design and children, pp 181–189
3. Van Beukering A, de Valk L, Bekker T (2014) Wobble: supporting social play through an open-ended play environment. In: Creating the difference: proceedings of the Chi Sparks 2014 conference, 3 Apr 2014, The Hague, The Netherlands, pp 91–99
4. Murdoch E, Whitehead M (2010) Physical literacy, fostering the attributes and curriculum planning. In: Whitehead M (ed) Physical literacy: throughout the life-course. Routledge, Abingdon, pp 175–189
5. Seitinger S, Sylvan E, Zuckerman O, Popovic M, Zuckerman O (2006) A new playground experience: going digital? InCHI'06 extended abstracts on Human factors in computing systems, pp 303–308
6. Price S, Rogers Y, Scaife M, Stanton D, Neale H (2003) Using 'tangibles' to promote novel forms of playful learning. Interact Comput 15(2):169–185
7. Kay I, Özkar M (2020) Designing for spatial narration in children's playscapes. A to Z İTÜ J Facul Archit 17(3):155–167
8. Johnson JE, Christie JF, Wardle F (2005) Play, development, and early education. Allyn & Bacon, Boston
9. Pellegrini AD, Perlmutter JC (1989) Classroom contextual effects on children's play. Dev Psychol 25:289–296
10. Swetha Chakravarthi (2009) Preschool teachers' beliefs and practices of outdoor play and outdoor environments. Ph.D. thesis. University of North Carolina at Greensboro
11. Davies MM (1996) Outdoors: an important context for young children's development. Early Child Dev Care 115:37–49
12. Frost JL (1992) Play and playscapes. Delmar Publishers Inc., New York
13. Henniger ML (1985) Preschool children's play behaviours in an indoor and outdoor environment. In: Sunderlin S (ed) Frost J. When children play. MD, Association for Childhood Education International, Wheaton, pp 145–149

A New Data Collection Interface for Dynamic Sign Language Recognition with Leap Motion Sensor

Burçak Demircioğlu Kam and Hatice Köse

Abstract This paper presents a new data collection tool for sign language recognition with *Leap Motion Controller*. The main motivation of this study is to develop assistive technology in order to support hearing-impaired people. This study is a part of *RoboRehab* project where we aim to develop an affectively aware robotic rehabilitation platform to assist hearing-impaired children in hospitals. The tool is cost efficient and has a simple and user-friendly interface design. The study involves a set of 12 dynamic two-handed signs (words) from Turkish Sign Language (TID).

Keywords Sign language · Sign recognition · Leap motion · Data processing · Machine learning · Deep learning · Human–machine interaction · Assistive technology

1 Introduction

The recent developments in technology improves the studies involving assistive technology which supports the vital issues of impaired people such as health, education, communication, and daily activities. Sign language is a visual communication method used by hearing-impaired people, and the developments in assistive technology includes recent successful attempts in sign recognition, technology based L_1/L_n teaching for hearing impaired people, and automatic translation systems from/to sign language. This paper focuses on the data gathering and data processing for the signs in Turkish Sign Language (TID) to be used to train deep learning models which will be used in an effective communication system based on sign language by hearing impaired people. This system will be employed within human–machine/robot interaction interface in the future projects.

B. Demircioğlu Kam (✉) · H. Köse
Istanbul Technical University, Istanbul, Turkey
e-mail: demircioglubu@itu.edu.tr

H. Köse
e-mail: hatice.kose@itu.edu.tr

To make this sign language communication system as natural and easy to use as possible, the system must be compact, mobile and robust. To solve this problem, for this project, a *Leap Motion Controller (LMC)* is used as the input device.

There are several recent studies on sign language recognition using *Leap Motion Controller*. In a study based on American Sign Language, 26 letters of sign alphabet are recognized by k-nearest neighbor (the recognition rate is 72.78%) and support vector machine (*SVM*) approach (recognition rate is 79.83%), using *Leap Motion* [1]. In another study, 2 *Leap Motion Controllers* (*LMC*s) are used and their data is fused together at the feature extraction and classification phases for the recognition of 28 Arabic Alphabet Signs. *Linear Discriminant Analysis (LDA)* classifier is used on the fused features, and 97.7% accuracy is reached. Using the classifier level fusion, 97.1% accuracy is reached. In this study, 2 *LMC*s gave better result than a single one [2]. A real-time recognition system is implemented by jointly calibrating *Leap Motion Controller* with a depth camera (*Kinect*) to increase the recognition success by adding features such as hand contour, and distance of hand samples from the centroid to the *Leap Motion* data. 10 American Sign Language gestures are used for recognition. The data is fed to multi-class *SVM* classifier and one exploiting *Random Forest*. For *SVM* the accuracy reached is 96.5% and for Random Forest 94.7% accuracy is obtained [3]. Three different feature selection methods such as *F-Score*, *Sequential* and *Random Forests* are used in the study. In another study, 28 single-handed-isolated sign gestures of Indian Sign Language and 28 different Latin Language finger-spelling words (air writing) are used for recognition. First, *SVM* classifier is used to differentiate between manual and finger spelling gestures, then two *BLSTM-NN (Bidirectional Long Short-Term Memory Neural Networks)* classifiers are used for the recognition based on sequence-classification and sequence-transcription approaches for manual signs and finger-spelling respectively. In this study the overall accuracy is obtained as 63.57% in real-time [4]. In the study conducted by Kumar, et al., 3-D texts drawn by fingers are recognized. In this study data is gathered as sentences and then word segmentation is done by a heuristic analysis of stroke length between two successive words whose accuracy is obtained as 78.2%. After the segmentation, recognition is done by sequential classifiers. With *Hidden Markov Model (HMM)* classifier, the accuracy is 86.88% and with *Bidirectional Long Short-Term Memory Neural Networks (BLSTM-NNs)* the accuracy is 81.25% [5].

To support the sign recognition studies, especially the approaches based on machine learning methods, big amount of data is required. This need increases especially in cases of *Deep Learning* approaches. Data collection and annotation tools are required for this purpose. Also the interface should be easy and demo videos should be included for the participants and annotators, since they might not be fluent in the sign language, or there might be conflicts due to different sayings, accents of the same sign. Unfortunately, there are a few studies which are specifically on sign language data collection via *Leap Motion Controller* device. In a recent study, a tool is created to collect synchronized data from *Microsoft Kinect 2* and *Leap Motion* sensors. The tool targets multi-media data collection for off-line processing. The data is collected as video and data text tables. The study includes a *C++ framework*, with support for the official *Microsoft Kinect 2* and *Leap Motion APIs* to record, a command-line interface, and a *Matlab GUI* to initiate, inspect, and load *Kinect 2* recordings. The tool gathers 125 data points from *Leap Motion* device representing each joint with two 3D vectors, per hand tracking state, confidence, and left/right indicator [6].

This paper summarizes our current study where we create a tool to be also usable by non-experienced users who are not fluent in sign language or computers, they might be deaf signers and not be able to track very complex instructions. Therefore, the interface is kept as simple as possible, and several precautions are included in the application to make the data as much error proof as possible. As the first precaution, before recording any data the user has to choose the sign explicitly from the list (which is used to label the data automatically after the recording is terminated) and then a video clip is shown to user to make the user more confident about what is expected from her/him. As the second precaution; after user starts the recording, a check for device and service connection is made by the application and the process is halted if any of these connections is not successful. As the last precaution, after the connection checking is done, the application waits for *Leap Motion* to recognized both hands in the sensible area and after this recognition is made the application starts a countdown to enable the user to get ready for the sign simulation. These precautions are added to the application to make the data more consistent and reliable. Also, with these additions the usage of the application does not require any expert supervision during data recordings.

Another important point is that this tool is specifically designed to collect data from *Leap Motion Controller*, and it includes a simple but efficient interface. In the related studies, there are no such kind of *GUI* studies for gathering data from *Leap Motion* even though there are vast amount of studies for other sensors such as *Microsoft Kinect*.

The most striking feature of the current tool is that it is very flexible and easy to be updated for additional features. The tool is configured to collect sign language data, but it is usable to gather any kind of data without the need to do any change in the code. By only changing (adding, deleting, editing) the simulation videos in the gallery folder of the executable file, the tool can be configured to gather another type of data which will also be automatically labelled with the video file name and timestamp.

This tool is also simpler and requires less resources in comparison to other recent *Leap Motion* applications since it does not need additional devices and environments such as *Virtual Reality (VR)* and *Unity*.

2 Methodology

This app is created as a *Windows Form Application* by using *C#* as the coding language. This approach is chosen because it's ease of use for the end user. This means to run the application the user does not need to install any additional thing then the *Leap Motion* device's driver while using a computer with *Windows* operation system.

After the successful installation of the driver the application can be run through the.*exe* file. Additionally, *Windows Media Player* libraries and *NuGet* packages from *Accord.Net Framework* are used. *Windows Media Player* libraries are used to display the video player and the *Accord* libraries are used for getting and displaying the images from the *Webcam*.

For the data connection between *Leap Motion* and the application the *Leap Motion SDK v2* is used. This *SDK* is used rather than the latest *SDK* because the latest *SDK* is especially created for *VR* applications and it is not useful when the *SDK* is used as library outside of the *Unity* application. With the *Leap Motion SDK,* a listener is created as a separate thread then the *GUI* thread of the application, to make *GUI* thread always responsive for the user, to get the data stream from the device.

To make user more informed about the sign which she/he want to simulate, a video player is added to the application. The video player is configured to play the video of the chosen sign from the sign list (at the left pane of the application, can be seen in Fig. 1 automatically. Therefore, with this video player, the aim was to make user absolutely confident about which sign she/he expected to simulate when the specific sign is chosen from the list. This precaution was excessively necessary because of two reasons. The first reason is; there are different signs in the sign language which has the same meanings which could cause a big confusion in the data set if the user simulates a different sign then the intended one. The second reason is; this application has to be efficiently usable for the users which are not experts of the sign language to be able to collect broader data. Therefore, with this prevention the user can be sure which kind of a sign is expected by the application to be simulated. As the result, with these precautions the saved data is made more error proof.

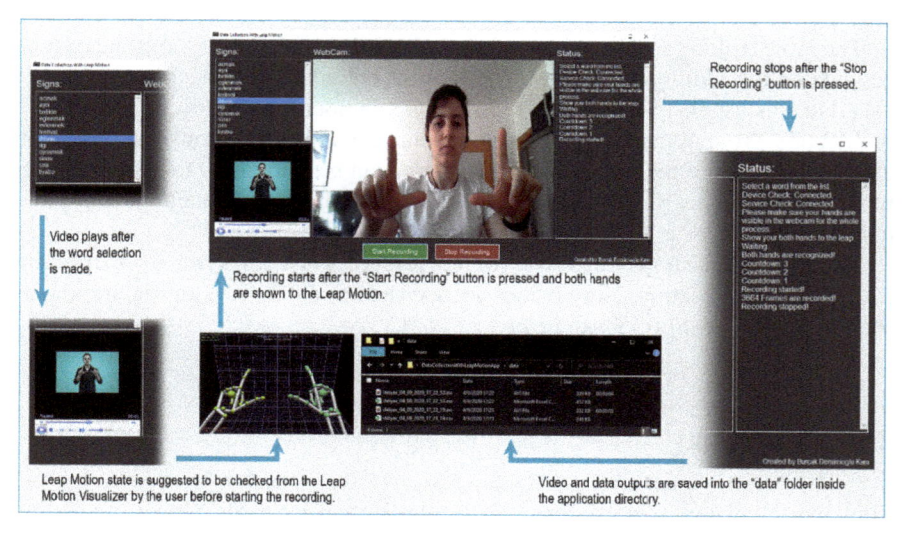

Fig. 1 Workflow of the application. (Figure is create by Burcak Demircioglu Kam)

To keep the data even more accurate, a checking mechanism is created to run after the user presses the "Start Recording" button. With this mechanism the connection status of the *Leap Motion* is monitored. After the validation of the device and service connection, the application waits for the sensor to sense both hands as the initiation step of the sign to be sampled, as it can be seen in the Fig. 2. When the application receives the information of both hands via the listener it starts a countdown for the data recording to make the user informed about the current status of the process and also to make the data cleaner by giving time to the user to get ready for the sign simulation. After recording is started, the frames received, coming from the *Leap Motion* sensor via the listener, are saved into the memory until the user stops the recording and then all the frames in the memory are written into a *.csv* file and labeled with the sign name, which is chosen previously from the list, and the current timestamp. The created file is saved under the data folder in the application directory. This process can be done repeatedly as much as the user wants until she/he explicitly closes the application via windows close button.

The application also captures video from the *Webcam* synchronously to the leap motion data and saves under same data folder. This additional data will be useful as a reference if the *Leap Motion* data has bugs or invalid data points. Therefore while the data is used in a related work, if the user suspects that the data includes some false positive or false negative elements, she/he is able to refer to the video file and investigate what is happened while the data is recorded. Also this *Webcam* video recording and real time playing (Please refer to the application screenshot in the Fig. 1) is expected to raise the users attention, and enable them to detect if they

Fig. 2 A Sample Leap Motion Setting. (Figure is create by Burcak Demircioglu Kam)

are making any mistakes during signing. Using the *Leap Motion Visualizer* will also support the user by displaying the data recorded.

3 Data Collection and Setup

The proposed tool is used to record a set of two-handed dynamic signs from *TID* via *Leap Motion* sensor. The tool can be easily adapted to different sign languages, and additional signs can be uploaded to the system easily. The tool can be used in *Windows* systems as an executable file (*.exe*), and will be adapted to cross-platforms including *Linux/Mac/Android/IOS* in the future.

3.1 Leap Motion Sensor

The *Leap Motion* sensor is a very small and light device that consists of 2 cameras and 3 infrared *LEDs* [7]. By tracking the infrared lights, the device can track the hands for around 120 fps with its *SDK* including the uncompromised math running behind. The device can track roughly 8 cubic feet of the 3D space on itself which gives 135° of field to the user [8]. The *Leap Motion* device is connected to computer via *USB* port, and does not require additional energy supply. The applicants should keep their hands 10–20 cm above the *Leap Motion* sensor which is kept on the desk, between the control computer and the user, in a horizontal position facing upwards. With the *SDK* working on the *Leap Motion* raw data, some positional and directional vectors are gathered frame by frame to be saved as a *.csv* data file that includes a dataset of 178 feature per frame. The tests had an indoor setup, with low, medium and well lighted environments.

3.2 Setup

As a first step, the *Leap Motion* device should be connected to the computer and it should be working. The status of the device could be controlled from the *Visualizer* of the *Leap Motion* controller.

The user should start the application, and to start data collection, has to select a sign from the list on the left side of the application, as seen in Fig. 1. After the sign is chosen, the demonstration video of the expected sign is displayed automatically at the bottom left side of the application screen. These videos are from the formal web site of TID [9].

The user must press the "Start Recording" button, to start recording. After this, the application starts the *Webcam* visualization, checks the connection of the *Leap Motion* and the service software (SDK) in the computer, and then waits for the user to place her/his hands on the sensor. Notice that the user should keep her/his hands within the area covered by the sensors, else the hand information will be out of sensor's limits. After both hands of the user are detected, the recording starts after a count down, just after informing the user by the text "Recording started!" on the status pane (at the right side of the application). Also, for the video reference, the *Webcam* recording starts at the same time with the data recording. The user must press "Stop Recording" button to stop the data collection. When the button is pressed both data and video recording stops, "Recording stopped!" information appears on the status panel and the *Webcam* visualization stops. This process can be repeated continuously, until the close button is pressed to close the application.

3.3 Data Collection

The data and video files will be created in the "data" folder in the same director of the application file. The data and the reference video file will include the sign name, as the label of the data, and the timestamp which is taken at the time the file is created.

In the data file, there are 178 columns (features) and multiple rows corresponding to time frames. The features include various directional and positional vectors for palms and fingers as well as other specific data related to the positions of the limbs such as extended fingers. All the data (except the first row which is used for the column titles) are in 'long' format. The boolean data coming from the device SDK are converted to binary as 0 and 1s in 'long' format, for easier processing. If in a particular frame, any of the hands are not recognized then for that hand none of the data, desired to be collected, is received from the device which causes gaps in the frame. Because these gaps may cause potential problems when the data is used in training purposes, the gaps are filled with 0.

Currently the application is configured to support a selected set of 12 signs of *TID*. All the signs are dynamic (include a sequence of motion, do not consist of a single frame of motion) and include the action of both hands. These signs are chosen by considering the hand shapes forming the signs. The 4 hand shapes that are included in our selection criteria are: *"Asl A Bar"*, *"Asl Y"*, *"L"*, and *"V2"*. These hand shapes were the most successfully recognized shapes in our previous research [10] 11. In this study the aim was to recognize static hand shapes which form the signs in *TID* with *Leap Motion* sensor. The hand shapes used in the current study are presented in Fig. 3. For each of these four hand shapes, three two-handed dynamic signs are chosen arbitrarily from *TID* by using the online dictionary [9].

The selected 12 signs are (in Turkish): *"birlikte"* (together), *"evlenmek"* (to marry), *"sınav"* (examination), *"aynı"* (same), *"eğlenmek"* (to have fun), *"oynamak"* (to play), *"festival"* (festival), *"ihtiyaç"* (need), *"ilgi"* (interest), *"açmak"* (to open), *"sıra"* (row), *"tiyatro"* (theatre). The sign list can be managed easily. To add/remove signs, the related *mp4* videos of sign demos should be configured under the "gallery/double" folder (name of the folder can be modified).

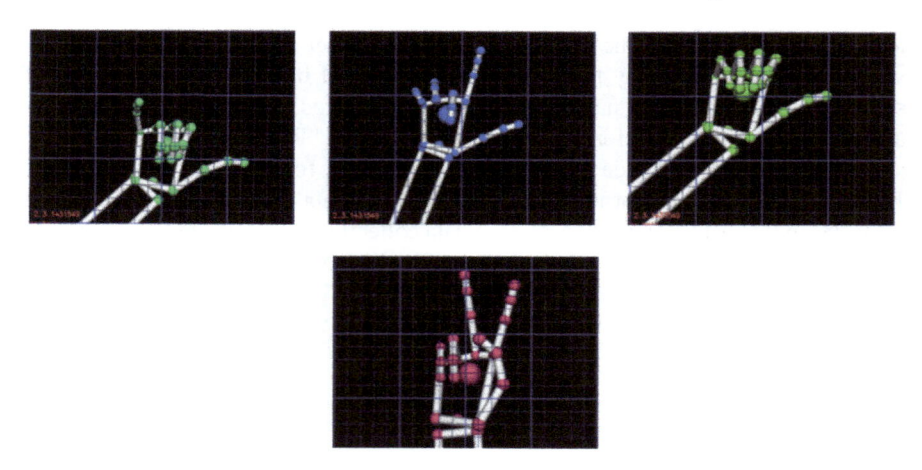

Fig. 3 ASL Y, L, ASL ABar, and V2 Shapes (in order). (Figure is create by Burcak Demircioglu Kam)

4 Conclusion

This paper represents an application which is created to collect and process data coming from *Leap Motion*. For the purpose of the study this application is configured to be used to create a dataset of the 12 dynamic signs (words) in Turkish Sign Language. This project will be extended in the future to be used within a human–robot interaction interface. The collected data is used to train traditional machine learning classifiers like Gaussian Naïve Bayes, Support Vector Machine, K-Nearest Neighbors, Random Forest, Linear Discriminant Analysis and Multilayer Perceptron as well as to train deep learning models like RNN, CNN and LSTM for the recognition of Turkish Sign Language as the follow up of this study. The results of the trainings are very promising to continue with research and to increase the sign amount to cover broader amount of the sign language. To increase the success rate, multiple *Leap Motion Controllers* can be used to detect the differences between complex signs; these *Leap Motion Controllers* can be added to the proposed tool, and the data from multiple sensors can be integrated within the tool for better deep learning models.

Acknowledgements This project is funded under the grant TUBITAK 118E214.

References

1. Chuan C, Regina E, Guardino C (2014) American sign language recognition using leap motion sensor. In: Machine learning and applications 13th international conference 2014. ICMLA, pp 541–544

2. Mohandes M, Aliyu S, Deriche M (2015) Prototype Arabic Sign language recognition using multi-sensor data fusion of two leap motion controllers. In: 2015 IEEE 12th international multi-conference on systems, signals & devices 2015. SSD15
3. Marin G, Dominio F, Zanuttigh (2016) Hand gesture recognition with jointly calibrated Leap Motion and depth sensor. Multimed Tools Appl
4. Kumar P et al (2017) Real-time recognition of sign language gestures and air-writing using leap motion. In: Fifteenth IAPR international conference on machine vision applications. MVA
5. Kumar P et al (2016) Study of text segmentation and recognition using leap motion sensor. IEEE Sen J
6. Kooij J (2016) SenseCap: synchronized data collection with microsoft Kinect2 and Leap-Motion. In: Proceedings of the 24th ACM international conference on multimedia, MM 16. Association for Computing Machinery, Amsterdam, The Netherlands, pp 1218–1221
7. Leap Motion Specs, https://blog.leapmotion.com/%20hardware%20-%20to%20-%20software%20-%20how%20-%20does%20-%20the%20-%20leap%20-%20motion%20-%20controller-work/. Last Accessed 12 July 2018
8. Leap Motion Specs Basic, https://www.leapmotion.com/product/desktop-controller/. Last Accessed 12 July 2018
9. Güncel Türk İşaret Dili Sözlüğü, https://tidsozluk.net/. Last Accessed 04 Aug 2020
10. Demircioğlu B, Bülbül G. Köse H (2016) Turkish sign language recognition with leap motion. In: Signal processing and communications applications conference, SIU. Zonguldak Turkey, pp 589–592
11. Demircioğlu B, Bülbül G, Köse H (2016) Recognition of sign language hand shape primitives with leap motion. In: 7th workshop on the representation and processing of sign languages: corpus mining, language resources and evaluation conference 2016, LREC, vol. 1. 1. Portoroz, Slovenia, pp 47–52

Gamification and e-Learning in Design

A User-Centered Design Research for Gamification Applications

Duygu Koca and Ebru Yücesan

Abstract Today, by taking advantage of game theories and models, gamification techniques are used in order to obtain various gains in areas other than games. This field, which cannot be associated to game, mainly deals with the behavioral components of gaming. Games have been a research subject of design in terms of their physical and virtual environments. With the incorporation of gamification techniques into design processes, the gamification also started to transform the design action besides this physical and fictional similarity. By virtue of gamification, the designer who is a factor in the creation process in game design can be a part of the game dynamics by using the basics of the game. In this process, at which point the designer will take an active role in the gamified design process and how s/he will adapt to these mechanical and dynamic components are the issues to be questioned. To this end, how and with which title the designer will be involved in this process should be questioned in order to apply gamification techniques to design processes. Furthermore, the levels of interest in the game and the game processes will occupy an important place in the development of applications. In this context, the aim of the study is to reveal relationally the mental connection of the designer with the game elements for the gamification application on the design to be designed with the gamification hierarchy asserted by Werbach and Hunter. In order to achieve this goal, literature review regarding the gamification and design areas was performed. In addition, 15 people who have received design education and are professionally interested in design were interviewed. The target population of the study is individuals who have received design education and the sample group was determined as participants who are professionally interested in design. In this process, open-ended questions based on gamification elements were asked to participants. The questions were asked by structured interview technique and the data were evaluated by the content analysis method based on the participants' discourses. At the end of the research process,

---

D. Koca (✉) · E. Yücesan
Hacettepe University, Çankaya 06800, Turkey
e-mail: dygsener@gmail.com

E. Yücesan
e-mail: ebruyucesann@gmail.com

suggestions were given on the use of game elements for gamification applications, which can be applied, to designers.

Keywords Gamification · Gamification in design · Game elements

1 Introduction

Gamification design is subjected and used in many different fields such as education, health, advertising or marketing. Nowadays, gamification practices can be used as a means of socialization and interaction as well as educational purposes. Considering the fact that game culture appeals to large masses makes it easier to apply gamification methods in disciplines other than games. When the studies in existing literature that combine design discipline with gamification examined, it has been seen that the gamification is tried to articulate the department curricula, studio projects and mostly workshops.

According to Schanabel, gamification can be offered as an alternative education method to traditional architectural education. It was not only used as a support but also as a tool for the internalization of knowledge to improve design knowledge [1]. In architectural design courses, gamification has been a problem solving method, in other words a tool that supports creativity. Furthermore it can be considered as an application used to increase motivation towards the course [2]. Considering the role and the effect of gamification in design education through these studies, it is thought that the achievements of gamification applications can be increased by user oriented approaches. Before the gamification application is designed, all the sub-components to be selected for the application should be selected by considering the audience and used for the specified purpose, according to Werbach and Hunter [3]. In this context, it was observed that the quality of the investigated group participating the gamification application has not been examined in the existing literature. In other words, the user profile of this application has not been subjected before. Accordingly, in this framework of this study, it is considered that the user analysis will create a permanent and sustainable experience. In this case, 15 designers were interviewed to conduct the research, and the responses received from the designers were examined by the content analysis method.

Also, with this study, it is aimed that users can better internalize information in gamification applications, manage collective work effectively, and encourage them to work with different disciplines. In order to meet this expectation, firstly the semantic equivalents of game and gamification concepts were studied.

2 The Concept of Game

Game is a very comprehensive phenomenon, which has been included in human life for different purposes throughout the history. In fact, according to Huizinga, playing games can be considered older than human being, when animals are assumed to be playing games [4]. It is quite difficult to clarify the term equivalent of this old and powerful experience because the game is the subject of today's research for many different disciplines. The game is an experience designed for single and multi-user environments in line with specific tasks and purposes, with reference to Kendirli. When it is evaluated in accordance with game typologies, this definition can be shaped [5]. When the act of playing games is questioned, the motivation to play for each individual may contain different goals. Accordingly, games can be designed for various behavioral gains and the purpose of each game may not be for entertainment purposes only.

3 The Concept of Gamification

Although gamification is a game-based approach, it is used for different purposes than game and game design. According to Karimi and Nickpayam, gamification is a different phenomenon that takes the game as reference and mostly is shaped around the game [6]. The concept of gamification can be considered as a utilitarian approach benefited from the game, however, apart from being a game. Designing gamification with a behavior-oriented and acquisition-oriented structure can provide solutions to the various problems of several disciplines. In this case, the reason for the need for gamification should be questioned. According to Kendirli, gamification method can be used to raise awareness against a behavioral situation. This state of awareness may involve drawing attention to the subject and increasing the interest of the subject by creating the solution process against a determined problem [5]. Beside a disciplinary focus, gamification is also used to bring together certain communities. According to Brigham, when gamification is used in education, it can help collective work by bringing together different student communities. It can also create an opportunity for participants to make mistakes and receive feedback from this mistake in a collective environment [7]. The gamification concept, which is used extensively in business environments, can also create positive behavioral changes on individuals. According to Akkemik, gamification methods used in the applications of business circles can improve the relations between the company and the consumer. Companies can make individuals more dependent on themselves, with this use. The needs of consumers such as socialization, individualization and following the current events can be met by gamification [8].

Gamification has a detailed and long process in terms of the design and implementation phases. According to Brigham, gamification may require disadvantages, such as requiring a long research process before application and implying software information when designed digitally [7]. Considering the field of education, gamification and its application process have grounds for different results on the participants individually. According to Gündüz, attention should be paid to the participants' feedbacks to the competitive situation in gamification. Considering the subject, gamification components should be experienced with participants who are interested in games and gamification [9].

3.1 The Gamification and Game Components

Game mechanics and dynamics are the auxiliary elements frequently used in the gamification process. As mentioned in one of the gamification platforms—Bunchball Nitro, these two concepts both complement each other and are interactive among them. Concepts of game mechanics can be used to trigger behaviors and activity can be made interesting with these mechanics. Game dynamics can be used to motivate the gamification process on behalf of the audience [10].

Werbach and Hunter divided the game elements into three different categories in a hierarchical order and included the game components in the gamification process. Dividing gamification to these three phases may increase success in expected results. In this hierarchical order, gamification elements are shown with a pyramid. (Table 1). This pyramid game dynamics can improve the story, the social achievements of the game and the motivation process for the participant. Mechanics can be used to increase the participation of the players in the game. Game components can be seen as elements supported by mechanics and dynamics. The components are defined as elements that interact with the player closely [11] (Fig. 1).

In this hierarchical order asserted by Hunter and Werbach, game dynamics are explained as *constraints, emotions, narrative, progression, relationship*. When the game elements are examined with their subtitles:

Constraints are strategy limitations created within the game. These can be used to prevent a single strategy from winning. Game design can be used to activate *emotions*. Narrative personalizes the game for the participant and can entice the player with story editing. *Progression* defines the participant's self-development process. *Relationship* defines the socialization process in the game [11].

When it comes to game mechanics, they can be considered as factors that ensure the sustainability of the game in terms of usage and participation [12]. According to Werbach and Hunter, game mechanics can be used to activate the game dynamics. Game mechanics can be listed as *challenges, chance, competition, cooperation, feedback, resource acquisition, rewards, transactions, turns, win states* [11]. When the subtitles of mechanics are examined:

Challenges can be a dynamic designed to encourage participation in the game among participants [12]. In this process, time limit, skill level and creativity of the person can be decisive in the task defined as challenge [11]. *Chance* factor can enable the participant to prepare himself for any probability [12], as well as to create

Table 1 Interview questions prepared for the participants

Game elements		
Game dynamics	Game mechanics	Game components
Constrains What are the constraints determined by the designer or user during the design process?	**Chance** What are the elements of chance in solving a successful design problem?	**Avatar** How can a designer customize himself?
Emotions What are the cases that change your mood during the design process?	**Competition** How can the competition environment in design bring benefits for the designer?	**Badges** What might be the way you are rewarded in a design competition?
Narrative How can a narrative be when you imagine yourself as a designer in a fiction?	**Cooperation** Which disciplines can the designer collaborate with most?	**Bossfight** What are the most challenging tasks you encounter in the late stages of design?
Progression What are the bounce situations you experience while developing your skills as a designer?	**Feedback** What topics can be criticized most during the design process?	**Combat** Considering the constriction of limited time in the design process, what are the different constrictions for a designer?
Relationship What could be the place of social relations in the design process?	**Resource acquisition** What are the design tools you use most in the design process?	**Levels** How do you level the design process?
	Rewards What could be the best title or reward the designer can get as a result of the design?	**Quest** What could be the most important task performed in the design process?
		Teams When acting as a team, which disciplines will you interact most in the design process?

Fig. 1 Game Elements
Werbach, Hunter, 2015

Dynamics
are the big-picture aspects of the gamified system that you have to consider and manage but which can never directly enter into the game.

Mechanics
are the basic processes that drive the action forward and generate player engagement.

Components
are the specific instantiations of mechanics and dynamics.

new moves and opportunities for players by reflecting coincidences into the game. *Competition*, on the other hand, may be an element that brings together the different groups and also individuals, where as not having something to be found in every game. The competition can be simply considered as the games with winners and losers [11]. *Cooperation* is effective in finding solutions together for specified tasks. *Feedback* provides information about the level and status of the participant, as well as providing information about the mistakes and the right moves of the participants. *Resource acquisition* can be summarized as collecting items for the tasks in the game. *Rewards* can be considered as badges & points in the game. *Transactions* define the transaction process between players. *Turns* can be used to divide the time equally for the participants, except for video games [11]. *Win states* can be considered as crossing a defined limit [12].

The components in the game elements are the elements that the participants interact directly [12]. Besides being an appearance of the emergence of the game mechanics, they also emerge the dynamics of the game. The game components are defined as *achievement, avatar, badge, boss fights, collection, combat, content unlocking, gifting, point, leaderboard, levels, quest, social graph, teams, virtual goods* [11]. *Achievement* can be seen as accomplishing additional missions that extend the game's time period [12]. *Avatars* are representations reflecting the participant and also can be personalized according to the player's wish [11]. Avatars can be used to improve inner motivation [12]. *Badges* are symbols obtained as a result of achievements [11]. *Boss fights* are the last and difficult task for the player at the peak of the game. *Collections* are collecting items that affect the course of the game or visually satisfy the player [11]. *Combat* is an artificial fight of players or fight with another player [12], so the player can enrich his experiences such as winning and losing. *Content unlocking* can be considered as content that is locked in the game and must be opened to continue. *Gifting* can be seen as an in-game socialization tool within the game. *Point* can be seen as the numerical response given in case of determined behaviors [11]. *Leaderboard* can be a motivation tool that shows the position of participants who care about proving themselves [12]. *Levels* allow players to be divided according to their level of competence. *Quest* is used to create the narrative; and, at the end of the quest, reward can be determined. *Social graph* can show the position of the players and interaction compared to other players. Potential competitors, competitors can be included in this interaction. *Teams* are multi-player groups that come together with similar goals and tasks in the game. *Virtual goods* are the name given to the assets won in the game and are obtained at a certain price [11]. After these entire theoretical infrastructure were examined, the interview process to be held by selecting suitable game components for the participants was designed.

4 User Analysis Research

According to Werbach and Hunter, a comprehensive research on the audience should be done before gamification. As one of the six important levels in gamification, it should be examined who the audiences are and which situations motivate them in general. In this case, what the users think against the act of playing should be analyzed [3]. From this point of view, interviews were made with 15 people who received design education and are professionally interested in design. Questions were prepared on the basis of gamification elements in order to define the role of the designer in gamification fiction. Accordingly, no answer was sought for all subtitles of gamification elements in the interview questions. For the research, elements that make organic bonds between the design process and the design practice were chosen from among the gamification components. Also, it is thought that the unused elements and the designer group cannot synthesize their design knowledge.

In this context, the concepts of game dynamics (constrains, emotion, narrative, progression, relationship), game mechanics (chance, competition, cooperation, feedback, resource acquisition, rewards), game components (avatar, badges, bossfight, combat, levels, quest, teams) are selected. Sub-components other than these concepts were not included in the interview process, considering that they could not give the necessary data on the user profile.

The interview questions prepared for the participants were set up as follows:

4.1 Findings

In this section, the answers given to the questions prepared to read the gamification elements that constitute the general framework of the study within the scope of the design will be explained. When game dynamics are considered, the participants evaluated the design **constraints** through the design of the entire process, project cost, design programs and rhetoric of design knowledge. On the other hand, they saw **emotion** as a changing phenomenon in analyzing the challenging processes of the project, finalizing the design, realizing the design, managing the concept of time, and feedbacks of users. They discussed the **narrative** item through design and improvement constructions based on riddles that they were leading. **Progression** was seen as the stages in which the designer would increase her/his gamification competencies. Participants stated that they developed themselves through creative fields such as observation, art, literature, travel and following technological developments and contemporary designs. **Relationships** were seen as an element that motivates designers, allows brainstorming, improves workflow, and brings the user and designer closer.

As for the game mechanics, the element of **chance** could not be associated with the design process by the participants. When it came to the **competition** element, it was seen that the participants evaluated this element through design competitions. In line with the answers received, they described this concept as a dynamic environment that would make the gamification process exciting and may impassion the designer. About the **cooperation** element, the statements show that participants cooperate in design process with architects, landscape architects, civil engineers, industrial designers, graphic designers, sales specialists, furniture manufacturers, and artists.

They interpreted another mechanical element, **the feedback**, on the topics criticized by the designers. The designers described that they were criticized in terms of color, texture, material, application solutions and user requests at the end of the application. **Resource acquisition** was defined as geometric forms, drawing tools, elements of the structure, production tools. **Rewards**, on the other hand, were evaluated on the design by user satisfaction, self-efficacy and professional competence.

As for the components of the game, the participants were evaluated in terms of **avatar** based on the characteristics of the designer's character, the originality of the design and body language, signature, and color use. Participants made statements about prestigious design awards, financial gain, traveling and vocational training among the ways of awarding the **badges** component. **Bossfight** was defined as the tough final tasks including planning the time and budget for the designers, choosing the right material, application errors. **Combat** was described as space limitations, competencies about equipment in the drawing process, insufficient time in research, limited time, and the persuasion process of the user. They also described that the **levels** could not be explained in a plane that developed from hard to easy. The **quest** was described as the design being applicable, detail solution, communication with the user, personalization of the design, design of the process, presentation, concept studies. In the application process, the design and concept studies were focused on. Finally, for **the team** component, the designers listed the site officers, mechanical engineers, architects, landscape architects, civil engineers, electrical engineers, acoustic specialists, art historians they worked with.

5 Conclusion and Suggestions

The answers of the participants to the questions prepared by intersecting the gamification elements and the design knowledge were analyzed in order to find and to analyze the emotional thoughts, perspectives and attitudes towards the concepts that the designers had during the design process.

Considering the responses of the designers, it is thought that the analysis of these elements differs in the design with gamification parameters. It can be said that there is a difference between the parameters of chance, levels and their reflections on design processes. While the element of chance may be an attractive element for the participant in the gamification process, it is generally seen as an element that does not shape the design action for the designers. In this case, the element of **chance** can be used in the selection of gamification tools that the participants interact with, other than the design action. Considering that the participants fulfill the tasks at certain periods in terms of **levels and progress** in the gamification process, it can be thought that the design has more organic progress processes in line with the data received. In this case, coercive elements can be articulated homogeneously to the process in gamification application for designers. The knowledge of different disciplines can be used to increase the knowledge of the designer for **the progress** sub-component. In addition to all these, the rewarding methods used in gamification processes will also differ according to a design application. In this case, which includes the elements of **badges and rewards**, the designers tended to have the appreciations that fed spirituality rather than material oriented achievements. Methods that develop spirituality rather than material-oriented rewards can be used in the gamification process. Likewise, when interpreting this situation, which includes the gamification element of **emotions**, it can be said that the designers are proud of the feedbacks such as appreciation. In gamification, this situation can be triggered by inner motivations such as professional success recognition. It can be said that the control of limited time, lack of information and negative emotions are triggered. Detailed analysis and time management can be used to overcome negative emotions in order to increase excitement in gamification. Considering the **avatar** gamification component, the answers can be evaluated not only by the physical appearance of the designer but also by her/his perception in the society, personality and competencies. Designers who can be modeled in gamification applications can be used as avatars and their signatures and inspiring words can be added to the avatar feature. When the **constraint** element **and feedbacks** that are evaluated in terms of design studied, it was noticed that the user—customer profile and budget are highly qualified and that shape the process. In order to shape the gamification applications of these elements, limited time, customer and designer relations, application solutions and criteria can be used for design. In challenging situations in the design process, it can be mentioned situations that include **bossfight, combat, quest** elements. **Bossfight** can be interpreted on the basis of last minute changes from the customer, **combat** on the basis of budget management, and **quest**, on the basis of compliance with design procedures and principles, applicability and usability. **Combat** can be considered as project budget and time management within the scope of design constraints. In an alternative **fiction**, such as gamification, it is seen that the designers see their characters in an intrusive and creative position and are in a position to solve the unknown. It is thought that the competition environment may be motivating in the teaching and research processes in application through the **competition** component. In the answers given about **cooperation, relationships and teams**, it is thought that they are interactive with different disciplines that this is motivating, and they can benefit from these elements in practice and theory. In order to develop cooperation, roles can be determined in gamification application through the disciplines of architecture, interior architecture, landscape architecture, and industrial design. Regarding relationships, brainstorms can be added to gamification processes, including the user. Designers can make great use of modular elements in the gamification application environment for **the resource acquisition** element of gamification. The fact that geometric models can be manipulated in the gamification process can be considered appropriate for the design process. In the light of these research and suggestions, gamification studies will be added to the design process. The designer approach of the study in the use and selection of gamification elements will increase the sustainability of the applications.

References

1. Kendirli T (2019) Dijital Oyun Endüstrisi Kavramları ve Terminolojisi Video Game Industry Terminology. Abaküs Kitap Yayın Dağıtım Hizmetleri, İstanbul
2. Aşkın G (2019) Gamification of design process in interior architecture education: who? with whom? where? how? SHS Web Conf 66:1–7. https://doi.org/10.1051/shsconf/20196601040
3. Schnabel MA, Lo TT, Aydin S (2014) Gamification and rule based design strategies in architecture education. In: Design Ed Asia conference 2014. Hong Kong, pp 1–11
4. Karimi K, Nickpayam J (2017) Gamification from the viewpoint of motivational theory. Italian J Sci Eng 1:34–42. https://doi.org/10.28991/esj-2017-01114
5. Huizinga J (2018) Homo Ludens Oyunun Kültür İçindeki Yeri Üzerine Bir İnceleme, 2. basım Alfa Basım Yayım Dağıtım, İstanbul
6. Brigham TJ (2015) An introduction to gamification: adding game elements for engagement. Med Ref Serv Q 34(4):471–480. https://doi.org/10.1080/02763869.2015.1082385
7. Akkemik S (2018) Güncel Tasarım Uygulamalarında Yeni Bir Paradigma. Oyunlaştırma. Stratejik Ve Sosyal Araştırmalar Dergisi 2(2):71–81. https://doi.org/10.30692/sisad.441741
8. Gündüz AY (2020) Dönüştürülmüş Öğrenmenin Çevrimiçi Boyutunu Oyunlaştırmanın Öğretmen Adaylarının Öğrenme Yaşantılarına Etkisi Doktora Tezi. Hacettepe Üniversitesi Eğitim Bilimleri Enstitüsü Ankara, Türkiye https://hdl.handle.net/11655/21695. Accessed 18 June 2020
9. Gamification 101 (2010) An introduction to the use of game dynamics to influence behavior. https://australiandirectmarketingassociation.files.wordpress.com/2011/10/gamification101.pdf. Accessed 18 June 2020
10. Werbach K, Hunter D (2012) For the win: how game thinking can revolutionize your business. Wharton School Press, Philadelphia
11. Berber A (2018) Oyunlaştırma Oynayarak Başarmak. Seçkin Yayıncılık, Ankara
12. Werbach K, Hunter D (2015) The gamification toolkit: dynamics, mechanics, and components for the win. Wharton School Press, Philadelphia. https://books.google.com.tr/books/about/For_the_Win.html?id=abg0SnK3XdMC&redir_esc=y. Accessed 20 June 2020

Asset-Based Extended Reality Model for Distance Learning

Barış Atiker, Ertuğrul Süngü, Kutay Tinç, and A. Burçin Gürbüz

Abstract Distance learning is a phenomenon that comes to the mind especially when it is difficult or impossible for people to come together for educational purposes. It also makes learning independent from the classroom environment. The COVID-19 epidemic, which covers the world in 2020, has led to the approaches of distance learning through new digital technologies and has revealed the need for more effective and efficient education models with interdisciplinary concepts. The fact that distance learning is independent of the classroom environment directly affects the students' interest and interaction in the lesson. In face-to-face learning, the interaction between the teacher and the student has not only cognitive but also emotional and physical factors. Lack of these factors in distance learning has negative consequences, especially in learning and experimenting processes. Many different models and methods have been developed for distance learning so far. These models were mostly provided by adapting traditional methods and educational contents to existing technological tools and unfortunately did not bring an effective solution proposal to the specified problem. Extended Reality (XR) applications, which are considered as an exciting technology today, also offer great opportunities for distance learning. Various models have been proposed to use these technologies in distance learning, which provide ideal tools for both spatial and interpersonal interaction with virtual and augmented reality. In this study, the Asset-Based Extended Reality Model was proposed as an alternative to other models and compared by using quantitative data. The model has three pillars; Assets, Gamification, and Immersion.

B. Atiker (✉) · E. Süngü
Bahcesehir University, Galata 34425, Turkey
e-mail: baris.atiker@comm.bau.edu.tr

E. Süngü
e-mail: sunguertugrul@gmail.com

K. Tinç
Istanbul Technical University, Macka 34367, Turkey
e-mail: tinc@itu.edu.tr

A. B. Gürbüz
Garage ATLAS, Kabatas 34674, Turkey
e-mail: burcin@garageatlas.com

© The Author(s), under exclusive license to Springer Nature Switzerland AG 2021
Ö. Cordan et al. (eds.), *Game + Design Education*, Springer Series in Design and Innovation 13, https://doi.org/10.1007/978-3-030-65060-5_30

Keywords Learning · Distance learning · Online learning · Virtual reality · Mixed reality

1 Introduction

Education is a concept that a person has been involved in throughout his life whether he is aware of it or not. In particular, the ability to improve one's life conditions is directly proportional to the ability to implement the education that one receives. This is where the importance of education comes not only from an individual perspective but also from a social perspective. Equalizing opportunities for all in education is one of the most challenging obstacles to the enlightenment of society.

Education is one of the areas most affected by new technologies in the age of global communication. In particular, the hybridization of different cultures in the field of education by using the same technology reveals new needs. Although it is perceived as irrelevant to each other, distance learning and gamification are undoubtedly at the top of these needs.

Just like Huizinga [15] states in his book Homo Ludens, games present a natural form of teaching. It can be seen that those who started playing digital games while they were young can much more easily adapt to new games whenever they face them, because visuals, audio feedback, user interfaces, and controls generally follow certain kinds of parameters. As such, the concept of "learning while playing" becomes a phenomenon in this context.

The use of digital games in the field of education, on the other hand, is not a new idea, and it seems that it provides a structure that will last for a long time. Before utilizing digital games as digital tools for learning, it should be noted that many different kinds of digital games provide a myriad of varied experiences for teaching as they exist already. The productions categorized as MMORPGs constitute an important place especially in terms of experiencing things with different people and having their own closed economies. In this context, the game World of Warcraft (Blizzard Entertainment, 2004) would be a good example. In this production, which is still experienced today by tens of thousands of people on a single server, players learn the teachings offered to them by the manufacturer in a virtual world that has been created by the producers. This type of game, which inculcates the person in terms of human relations, ethics, economy, and tactics, is one of the best examples for the educational power of digital games that can be offered to those who play them.

In this context, Squire [27] suggests that we can learn 'academic' content through games, including the in-game terminology, a range of strategies, and "the emergent properties of the game as a system." As such, digital games it can be said that digital games help us understand different kinds of topics and emphatically connect with the world they have created and learn about them. According to Gee, all the players learn "empathy for a complex system" [10]. In other words, when we look at it, it can be observed that games have a direct connection with learning on many different

Fig. 1 Bloom's taxonomy cognitive domain [3]

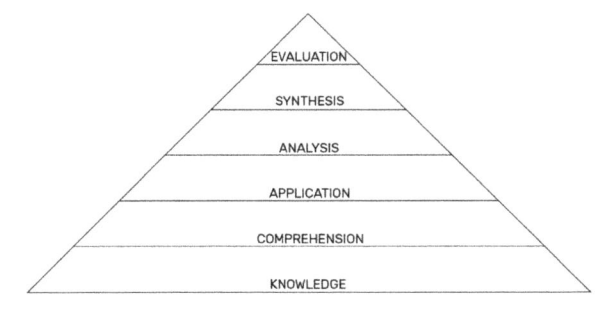

Fig. 2 Bloom's taxonomy effective domain [3]

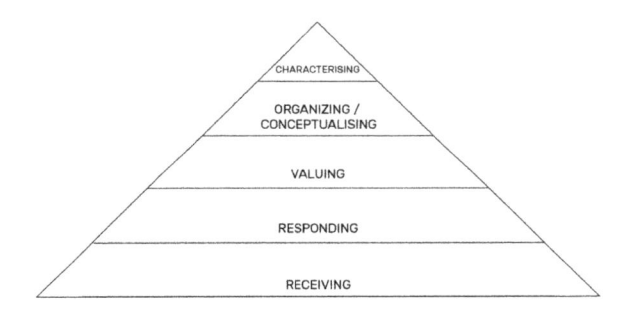

levels. On the topic of learning, the first thing that comes to mind is the classification of learning that Bloom [3] introduced in 1956 (see Fig. 1).

Bloom's proposed pyramidal system provides a methodical structure that is based on the concept of "values" or emotional reactions. As can be seen, the state of "Receiving" lies on the bottom and it takes the first place as the first level. At this point, the Receiver is waiting without having any idea about the experience that they will be encountering soon (see Fig. 2).

Anderson [1], on the other hand, changed the new concept of information that lies in the "Cognitive Domain" idea, which was put forward by Bloom, in a different and more meaningful way. Instead of the four-tier system offered by Bloom, Anderson presented a six-tier system and displaced the already existing steps. Furthermore, if we take this pyramid into account in the context of education and gaming experience, we can create different types of model structures and evaluate these structures through the concepts of emergent technologies such as Virtual Reality, Augmented Reality, and XR (see Fig. 3).

The new structure that emerged as a result of this change, as Matthew Barr [2] emphasizes, offers a more suitable structure for learning with video games. He has classified the points of intersection between learning theories and games as such; Constructivism, Experiential Learning, Social Learning, Scaffolding, Mastery Learning, Surface and Deep Learning, and Gee's Learning Principles. During this classification, the closeness of each topic to the subject of learning while playing or learning through games has been taken into account.

Fig. 3 Anderson and Krathwhol's revision of Bloom's taxonomy [1]

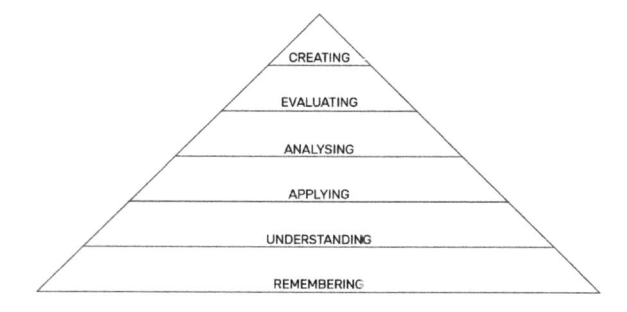

- CREATING
- EVALUATING
- ANALYSING
- APPLYING
- UNDERSTANDING
- REMEMBERING

Constructivism refers to a person's ability to adapt his existing knowledge to new problems and learn through this experience. Experimental Learning is, as the name itself suggests, the structure of finding solutions through the utilization of different ideas. According to Dewey [8], there is a teacher-focused learning style and a learner-focused learning style. He also states that for good educational design, students' place in society should be understood as well. The learning environment will be different as each student's learning experience will be different. At this point, the teacher needs to handle all these factors and adapt to their methodology well [8].

This view of Dewey's, which is still widely accepted even today, is considered to be an important educational model in terms of different experiences that games offer to the players, especially when we examine it through the lens of games. It also affects the mechanics that Kolb [16] emphasizes and should be at the foundations of education, such as thinking, analyzing, doing, and feeling.

Social Learning, on the other hand, emerges as a common learning style that people come together to give form. Based on this learning style, which develops on the common idea space and thoughts of a particular group and subsequently on their common goals; there is a dominant shared practice. Especially MMORPG games, in which thousands of different people experience the game with their avatars on the same server, are great examples of this form of learning and its development.

Scaffolding, on the other hand, is a theory that aims to improve the learning slope with questions that progress with certain questions where the level of the learner is understood and the difficulty of each inquiry increases over time. In terms of game-based learning, the clues and information provided to the player in many games can be exemplified as Scaffolding [31].

Mastery Learning is similar in many ways to Scaffolding. The biggest difference is that it is not possible to switch from one task to another and continue the training with new tasks at each new level. Depending on the content of the game, each new level contains different tasks, goals, and teachings.

Surface and Deep Learning aims to melt two different models in one pot. Especially, as Marton and Säljö [19] mentioned, Deep Learning will enable a subject to develop skills in critical thinking, adaptation, and provide them with the means to develop ethical value and social awareness. Besides, deep learning is associated with the "active" learning offered by the games. In this context, Barr [2] suggests "If video games may offer a means of enhancing graduate attributes then the educational literature would suggest that it is games." Gee's Learning Principle is definitely a must-read resource for the topic of learning with games.

Gee argues that learning, in general, should be active, not passive. In 2007, in his book "What Video Games Have to Teach Us About Learning and Literacy" [11], Gee suggested the idea of 'semiotic domains'. In the book he explained this terminology as such; which actually explains his approach to the education model; "any set of practices that recruits one or more modalities (e.g. oral or written language, images, equations, symbols, sounds, gestures, graphs, artifacts, etc.) to communicate distinctive types of meanings".

When we start to examine the concept of learning with games, these theories would surface, as they are topics of discussion for a long time. What we are focusing on is not the so-called traditional platform of PC but VR and indirectly XR. We think, although the "Bloom's Taxonomy Effective Domain" structure and the pyramid system developed bay Anderson and Krathwohl [1] are effective in their frameworks, this model should change in many ways when it comes to learning with XR.

2 Models for Learning with Extended Reality

Technology undoubtedly facilitates our lives while providing more efficiency with less cognitive effort. Therefore, the use of technology, especially in the field of education, is an exciting subject for everyone. The physical world is blending with virtual content and people are living in an extended space enhanced through digital technology.

With the growing impact of digital content, the experience of learning and teaching in higher education is being changed significantly. (Wang et al. 2015) Emerging VR and AR technologies, for the first time, offers an authentic hyper-immersive learning experience in a technically feasible format for large cohort teaching at a decent price.

The intervention of multiple elements such as 3D models, animation, graphics, and audio display in a technology-integrated learning environment is crucial. The fusion of 3D models, animation, video, and graphics with the addition of text and audio can enhance the understanding of the content.

Salzman [25], describes three promising features of VR for learning: three-dimensional immersion, multiple frames of reference, and multisensory cues. For VR education, Bomsdorf [4] makes a distinction between a digital learning space and a digital learning context. A digital learning space comprises the particular digital exercises undertaken by a learner, where the context refers to a broader set of circumstances through which sense-making and fundamental understanding are formed.

The blurring of boundaries between learning space and context challenges many established theories of learning. The most significant impact of VR on learning may not be about the technology itself at all, but rather the radically different potential configurations of learning space and context that VR tends to promote [26].

2.1 Experiential Learning Model (ELM)

Kolb's [16] experiential learning model (ELM) is a learning way that is about approaching life experiences with a learning attitude. Experiential learning theory draws on the work of prominent 20th-century scholars such as Jean Piaget, William James, John Dewey, Kurt Lewin, Carl Jung, Paulo Freire, Carl Rogers, and others to develop a holistic model of the learning process from the experience.

The experiential learning model (ELM) is a learning way that is about approaching life experiences with a learning attitude (see Fig. 4).

Concrete Experience is doing or having a new experience or situation which is encountered, or a reinterpretation of existing experience.

Reflective Observation of the New Experience is stepping back from the task and reviewing what has been done and experienced.

Abstract Conceptualization is the process of making sense of what has happened and involves interpreting the events and understanding the relationships between them. This gives rise to a new idea or a modification of an existing abstract concept (the person has learned from their experience).

Active Experimentation is using theories to solve problems, make decisions. Here the learner applies their idea(s) to the world around them to see what happens.

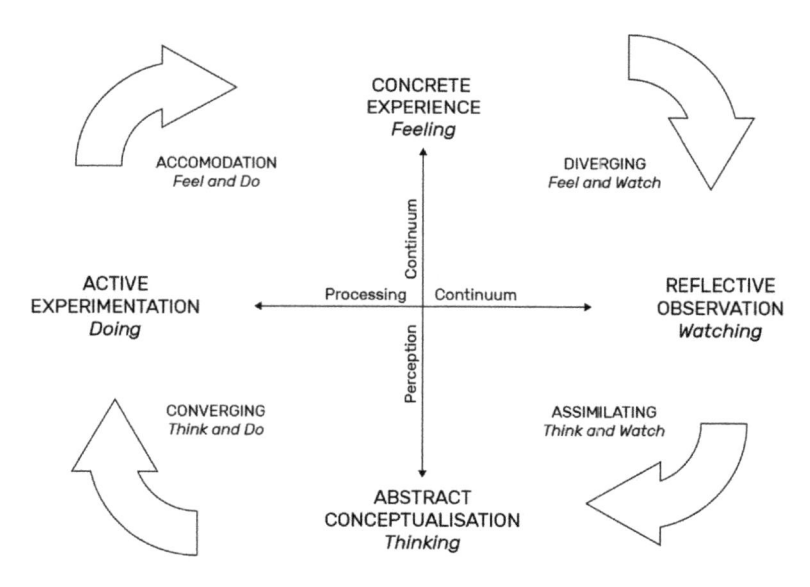

Fig. 4 Kolb's experimental learning model [16]

2.2 Assesment—Pedagogy—Technology Model (APT)

He et al. [14] proposed an English Learning VR Game based on the APT Model. In their research, the APT teaching model contains three aspects: Assessment, Pedagogy, and Technology. Their model is mostly built on the pedagogical aspects of learning while it is supported by technology and assessments (see Fig. 5).

In the pedagogical aspect, the model analyses the students, teaching goals, design of teaching contents, and design of teaching activity. The model also considers the design of both teaching contents and activities, while expressing the teaching key points as tasks and challenges and teaching activities as a roleplaying and game-based task-driven approach.

In the assessment aspect, the model emphasizes both formative and summative assessment where the system offers feedback and help the students to achieve the tasks.

In the technology aspect which covers the equipment and instructions, including the usability of the tools as functional design elements. Interface design elements such as learning cards, real-time feedback, and navigation are crucial elements of a successful learning experience.

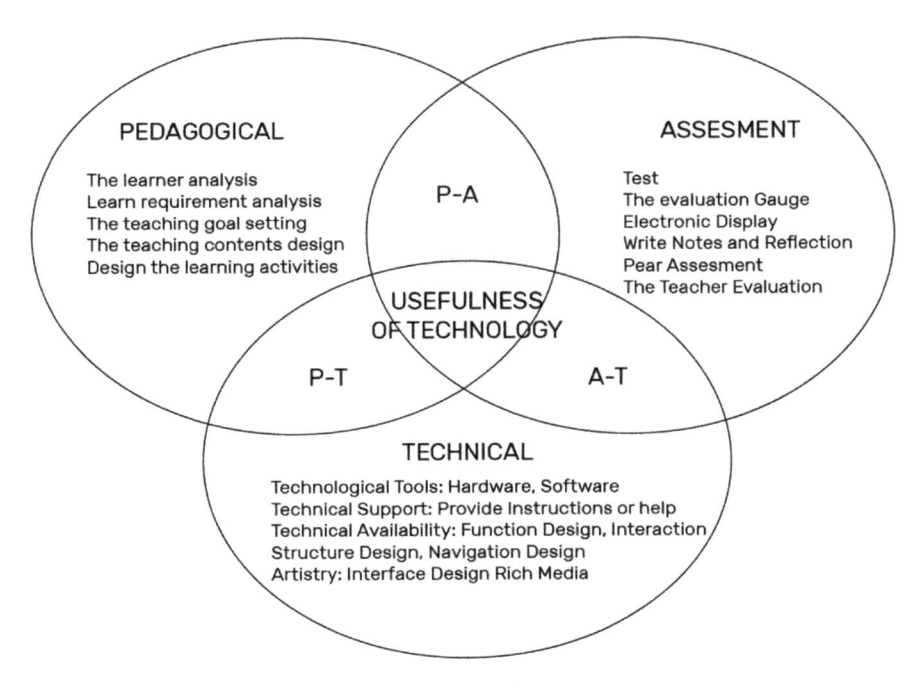

Fig. 5 Assesment—pedagogy—technology model [14]

2.3 Ergonomy—Learning—Hedonic Model (ELH)

This multidimensional model proposed by Pribeanu et al. [22] is depending on the Technology Acceptance Model (TAM) which is developed by Davis [6] who explains user acceptance in terms of perceived ease of use and the perceived usefulness (focusing on extrinsic motivation). TAM model was further extended to include the perceived enjoyment [7].

The conceptual model has three dimensions: perceived ergonomic quality, perceived learning quality, and perceived hedonic quality. And also in return, each dimension has two sub-dimensions (see Fig. 6).

The first concept of the model is the Perceived Ergonomic Quality and it has two facets such as ease of learning how to use (learnability) and ease of use, where learnability refers to the ease of understanding, learning, and remembering how to use an application.

Perceived learning quality has also two facets as Perceived Efficiency which is a distinct construct pointing to a better and faster understanding, and Perceived Usefulness as improvement of knowledge, usefulness for testing of knowledge and support of learning [6].

The third and the last concept of the model is the Perceived Hedonic Quality which also has two facets as Cognitive absorption which is the state of total engagement when the attention is focused on the interaction with the application; and Perceived enjoyment refers to the enjoyable experience with the application [22].

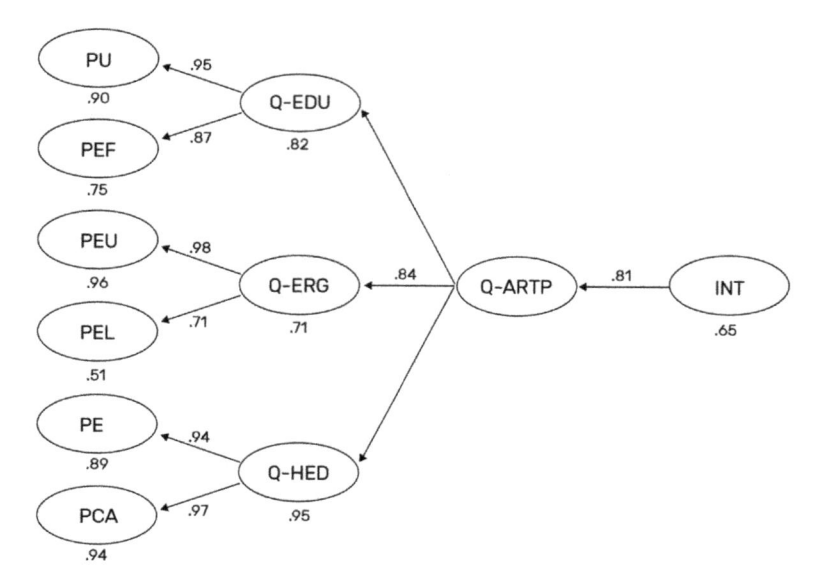

Fig. 6 Ergonomy—learning—Hedonic model

2.4 Interactive Persuasive Learning Model (IPL)

In recent years, there has been vast interest in discovering how computer and information technology influences, motivates, and persuades people to change their behaviors and attitudes. Known as persuasive technology, it promotes an interactive technology that can change a person's attitudes or behaviors [9].

As presented by Zulkifli [33], IPL model is based on three broad categories: interactive media features (layout and consistency, simulation, navigation, and minimal input device), interactive persuasive elements (motivation, experience, cognitive and emotional appeal) and learning outcomes (performance and satisfaction) (see Fig. 7).

In this model, the four interactive media features are the interface (as layout and consistency), the simulation which can be simple 2D or complex virtual 3D, the navigation, and minimum input devices as usability factors.

The effects of Interactive Media features are categorized as motivation, experience, cognitive and emotional appeal for learning activities. Motivation leads to positive performance outcomes; cognitive is understanding the learners thought processes.

Emotional appeal is the aesthetic approach to the design with human emotions, affects, feelings, and mood; and finally, the experience is all about the learning process.

As learning outcomes, Zulkifli [33] puts performance and satisfaction as the end of the learning process. It is about recognizing the changes in knowledge and the feelings after learning with interactive media which may have an impact on persuasion.

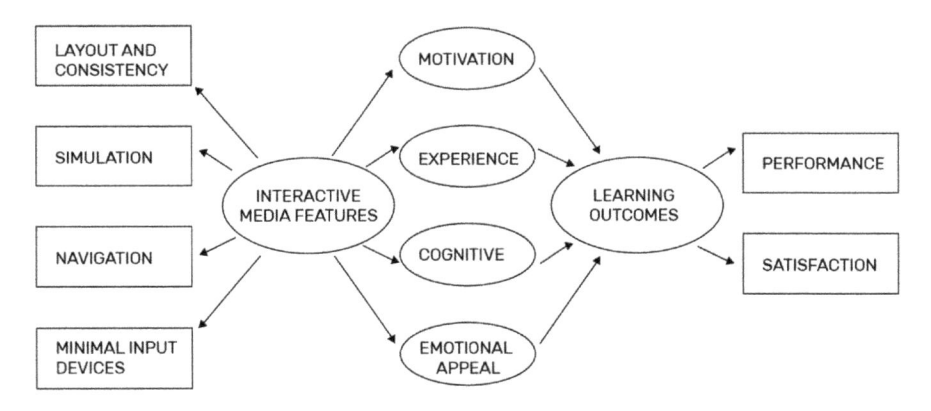

Fig. 7 Interactive persuasive learning model

3 Asset-Based Extended Reality Model Proposal

After examining the different training models applied in the previous section, we searched for a much more efficient model for XR. The main reason for this was that the existing models did not bring enough XR opportunities and advantages to the fore. However, it was an important criterion to include innovations offered by developing technologies within the model.

We set the three pillars of the model as a target for Kolb's learning styles and for a sustainable flow in itself. According to Kolb [16] four learning styles are accommodating, divergent, assimilating, and convergent. Different learning styles would impact learning outcomes. Diverging learners can explore a range of observations and generate many ideas. Assimilating learners transform learning experiences into abstract concepts. Converging learners evaluate and refine ideas and theories for better practical uses. And, accommodating learners conduct hand-on activities [13] (see Fig. 8).

Addressing all of Kolb's learning styles on 3 pillars, the Asset—Gamification—Immersion (AGI) model has been developed to create an efficient and balanced structure, especially in XR applications for educational purposes. The model, which is built under the main headings of Assets, Gamification, and Immersion, also includes Technology, Content, and Experience subtitles in the learning cycle (see Fig. 9).

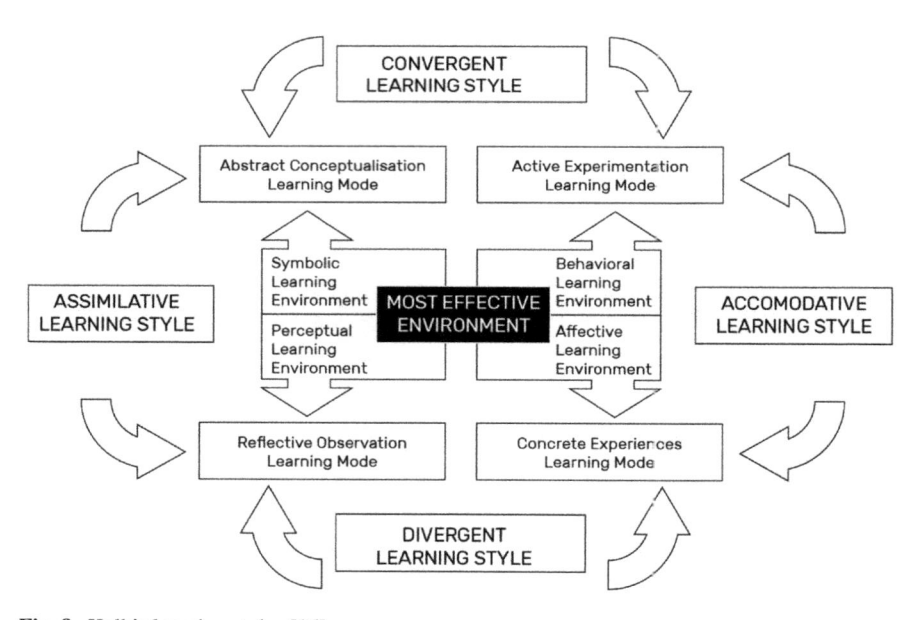

Fig. 8 Kolb's learning styles [16]

Asset-Based Extended Reality Model for Distance Learning 385

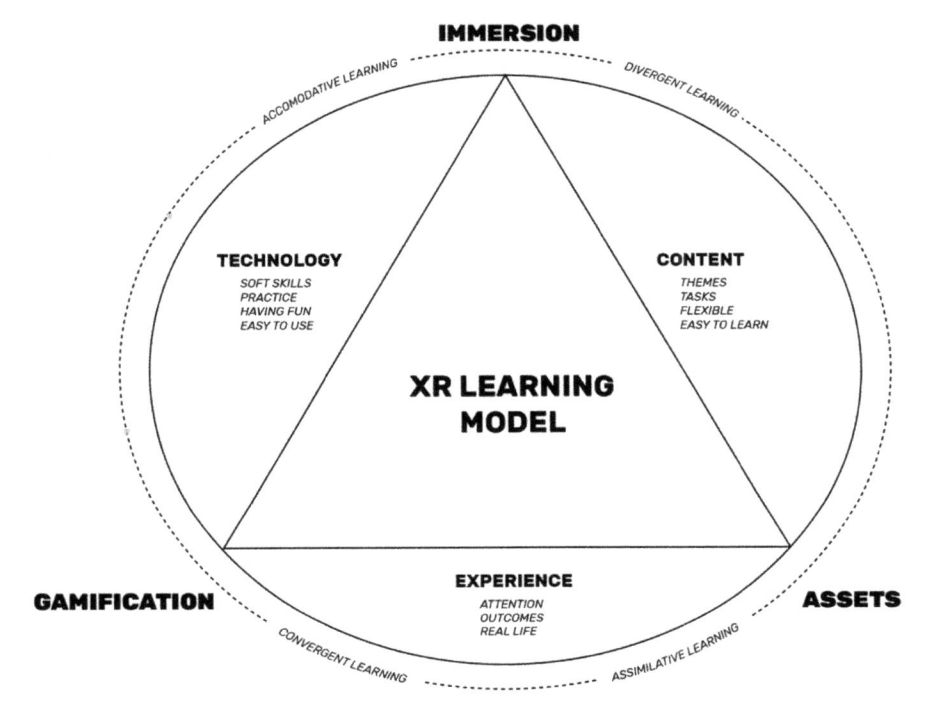

Fig. 9 Assets—Gamification—Immersion XR learning model proposal (Graphic by B. Atiker)

3.1 Assets

Assets are the resources that are used to deliver information for training and development. Learning assets facilitate mental exercise and it varies from passive to active learning processes. In the XR learning model, digital learning assets have transformed from tangible objects such as books and manuals to mobile apps, video streams, and much more. In XR video and audio content is much more dominant than the textual sources.

3.2 Gamification

The reason for using 'Gamification' in education is the element of motivation it provides. Different game mechanics are used to motivating the person about the work they are doing. The most obvious of these mechanics is undoubtedly leveling up. Just like it is in real life, as a person fulfills certain achievements while doing their work and subsequently go into an "upper level" in their career; this is true in the mechanics of gamification itself as well. Motivation is among the important predictors of student academic achievements, which influences the effort and time a student spends engaged in learning [17]. Games are known to increase motivation and different educational models under the guise of "gamification" have seen much support in certain places.

3.3 Immersion

Immersion is usually defined as the degree of involvement with something. Brown and Cairns [5] identified three levels of immersion in games. The first is "engagement," which is when the interest and desire to keep playing is sufficient to justify the time and effort needed to learn how to play the game. The second level is "engrossment," a feeling of emotional attachment that "makes people want to keep playing and can lead to people feeling 'emotionally drained' when they stop playing". The third level is "total immersion," a state in which players are cut off from reality and the game is the only thing that matters.

The relationship of distance learning with students' environment will be more effective with a virtually created or enriched spaces. Immersion takes place right in front of the students' eyes, not just as visual effects but also as cognitive isolation from reality.

3.4 Content

The content area covers all topics and approaches covered by XR Learning Model. Since the XR pieces of training are spread over a very wide area, an interdisciplinary perspective has been developed here. Of course, especially the advantages of XR education over traditional education are highlighted and the issues that cannot be presented in real life in terms of content are evaluated.

Themes
In the next generation of education, it is inevitable to handle more inclusive and experience-based educational content as well as current curricula.

Tasks
Experience-based training brings with it numerous tasks and process management. These tasks and processes provide important data for the measurement of education success and can update the system according to the learning speed of the students.

Flexibility
It is much more possible to create an individual approach and tailored curriculum scopes in education compared to traditional education. In this case, a more flexible content structure can be formed spontaneously according to both the student's learning speed and manual skills.

Easy to Learn
Although lesson content is prepared in different areas, the pedagogical approach is the same in terms of the necessity of preparing the subjects with a specific learning ease scheme.

3.5 Technology

The technology field aims to address and apply all existing XR technologies within the scope of the model. It follows the developments especially in immersive media technologies and keeps itself up-to-date by catching possible opportunities and challenges in-classroom use.

Soft Skills
Education, above all, involves a collaborative social structure. Learning action never means to isolate students from the learning environment and social interaction. So, the inclusion of social and extra-curricular personal skills within the curriculum will bring positive results in terms of the efficiency and impact of education.

Practice
Practice, one of the most basic topics of Experimental Learning, aims to transform students' theoretical knowledge into maximum practice. Especially, the structure that constructs the different stages and processes of the experience with the logic of game mechanics aims to make the student master the subject both theoretically and practically.

Enjoyment
Enjoying while learning is an important factor that increases permanence after learning. It is expected that the content and experience will be prepared in a way to provide maximum pleasure, especially in the process of gamification of educational content.

Easy to Use
Usability is always at the forefront of XR training. The student should be able to play not only the game but also the system easily. When UX is good, user interaction contributes to immersive experiences. When UX is bad, the user interaction with the machine results in frustration and disruption. Properly designed, the graphic user interface of a game should make it easy for learners to interact with the game [32].

3.6 Experience

The most essential criteria to keep the immersive learning experience at the maximum level are the continuity of the learner's interest and the sustainability of the concepts learned. To achieve this, it is necessary to focus on educational content, presentation style, and outcomes. As a result, a process-based assessment should be made to internalize the student's experience, customize it according to their abilities and skills, and ensure that they follow their progress.

Attention
According to Ratey [23] attention is more than just noticing incoming stimuli. It involves several processes including filtering out perceptions, balancing multiple perceptions, and attaching emotional significance to these perceptions.

Outcomes
Learning outcomes are statements that describe the knowledge or skills students should acquire by the end of a particular assignment, class, course, or program, and help students understand why that knowledge and those skills will be useful to them. With XR, it can be easier to get the results of learning outcomes compared to classical education methods. The feedback of the learning experience, especially in the gamification process, supports the visibility of these outcomes.

Real Life Use
One of the most important criteria of the model is also how far the topics learned can be applied in real life. Especially the closeness of simulative training to the real world is of great importance in terms of continuity of experience.

4 Comparison of Learning Models

Analytical Hierarchy Process (AHP), which was proposed by Thomas Saaty in 1980, is an analysis method widely used for multi-criteria decision-making problems [12]. Using AHP, we can compare our alternative models for distance learning concerning the criteria we have chosen to find out the best one that suits our goal.

Many applications of AHP can be found in the literature, from risk assessment of metro systems [18] to material selection for structural applications [21] and even supply chain development in the energy sector [20]. This flexibility and its ease of application make this method a natural choice for our research.

The first step of AHP is to decompose the problem into a hierarchy of criteria. These criteria are then compared to each other, which makes the general analysis easier to apply. The comparison might either be a pair-wise human evaluation of the criteria or use of data previously collected. For n criteria, there will naturally be n^2 comparisons [24].

After the priorities of the criteria are established, each alternative that can fulfill our goal is evaluated for the criteria we have, giving the alternatives weights based on each criterion. Then these scores are multiplied by the criteria weights and summed to end up with a single score for each alternative. The alternative with the greatest score is chosen as the best alternative.

In this study, we have used the AHP methodology to compare education methods as alternatives and used 11 different criteria to score them. The criteria used are:

- A: Having up to date and new course material (textbooks, slides, notes etc.)
- B: Keeping student interest and participation high during class
- C: Having a high number of projects/homework
- D: Imparting soft skills (connectivist education)
- E: Adhering to standard learning outcomes (objectivist education)
- F: Having practice opportunities in the school (Labs/Studios)
- G: Having flexibility (student driven courses)
- H: Having fun during the course
- I: Implementation of course subject in real life
- J: Learning easiness of the subject
- K: Having easy to use course materials.

These criteria, when compared to each other by more than 200 experts, yielded these priorities (Table 1):

Our alternatives were education models already used in the world and the AGI model we are proposing:

- A_1: Asset Based Extended Reality Model (AGI)
- A_2: Experiential Learning Model (ELM)
- A_3: Interactive Persuasive Learning Model (IPL)
- A_4: Assessment Pedagogy Technology Model (APT)
- A_5: Ergonomy Learning Hedonic Quality Model (ELH).

When the alternatives were compared by the experts in education with respect to the criteria we have picked, the weights were found as such (Table 2):

Table 1 Criteria priority weights

Criteria	Priority
A	0.147237
B	0.156576
C	0.047109
D	0.157829
E	0.029911
F	0.156814
G	0.076081
H	0.060143
I	0.092631
J	0.038741
K	0.036928

Table 2 Weights of alternatives

Criteria	A_1 Weight	A_2 Weight	A_3 Weight	A_4 Weight	A_5 Weight
A	0.12	0.07	0.06	0.11	0.10
B	0.14	0.13	0.09	0.10	0.10
C	0.05	0.05	0.06	0.08	0.05
D	0.12	0.11	0.10	0.11	0.10
E	0.04	0.08	0.09	0.10	0.06
F	0.04	0.11	0.07	0.10	0.07
G	0.08	0.09	0.10	0.07	0.09
H	0.12	0.09	0.11	0.10	0.11
I	0.11	0.11	0.12	0.10	0.10
J	0.08	0.08	0.10	0.06	0.10
K	0.08	0.09	0.11	0.10	0.10

Table 3 Alternative scores

Alternative	Score
A_1	0.0994
A_2	0.0970
A_3	0.0878
A_4	0.0951
A_5	0.0938

To calculate the final scores of the alternatives, we sum the products of the multiplication of each criterion's priority weight by its alternative weight (Table 3)

The scores found give us a clear picture for the effectiveness of the learning methods that we have compared in the eyes of the experts. When the methods are ordered from high to low we get:

$$A_1 > A_2 > A_4 > A_6 > A_3$$

This shows that according to the result of the survey we have made, the Asset Based Extended Reality Model we are proposing is ranked better than the other methods used.

5 Conclusion

The most important challenge of new technologies is to adapt them to education systems and get maximum efficiency from them. The main reason for this is those existing systems and those who use these systems do not give up the methods and exercises they are used to easily.

The immersion afforded by effective educational games has implications for the engagement and the learning that students experience. Higher levels of immersion are likely to make students more engaged in their learning, which can then lead to greater learning gains.

Starkey [28], states the current challenge for teachers is to convert established learning theories into new practices that most effectively leverage and engage the upcoming, digitally literate generation.

XR technology is itself still under development, and neither the definition of VR nor the particular implementation of the technology is stable or comprehensive demonstrations of VR today or into the future [29]. According to Wang [30] educators are more likely to focus on technology use rather than thinking about the underlying pedagogical problem. The variety of the educational themes included in XR learning exposes a huge need for content creation based on the virtual simulations. This is both digital assets such as 3D models, animatic, visual effects, simulations, and conceptual assets such as storytelling, navigation, and flow.

With the AGI method, we aimed to show that a system where different disciplines are synthesized together, much more accessible, and sustainable education curricula are created, and the learning experience of the student is made more effective and enjoyable.

References

1. Anderson LW, Krathwohl DR, Airasian PW, Cruikshank KA, Mayer RE, Pintrich PR et al (2001) A taxonomy for learning, teaching, and assessing: a revision of bloom's taxonomy of educational objectives, 1st edn. Pearson, New York
2. Barr M (2019) Graduate skills and game-based learning using video games for employability in higher education. Palgrave Macmillan, Glasgow, UK
3. Bloom BS, Krathwohl DR, Masia BB (eds) (1956) Taxonomy of educational objectives: the classification of educational goals. Longman, New York
4. Bomsdorf B (2005) Adaptation of learning spaces: supporting ubiquitous learning in higher distance education, dagstuhl seminar proceedings 05181. The Challenge of Multimedia, Mobile Computing and Ambient Intelligence
5. Brown E, Cairns P (2014) A grounded investigation of game immersion. In: Proceedings of the conference on human factors in computing systems. ACM, New York, NY, pp 1297–1300
6. Davis FD (1989) Perceived usefulness, perceived ease of use, and user acceptance of information technology. MIS Q 13(3):319–340
7. Davis FD, Bagozzi RP, Warshaw PR (1992) Extrinsic and intrinsic motivation to use computers in the workplace. J Appl Soc Psychol 22(14):1111–1132
8. Dewey J (1938) Experience and education. Macmillan Press, New York

9. Fogg BJ (2003) Persuasive technology Using computers too change what we think and do. Morgan Kaufmann, San Francisco, CA Amsterdam
10. Gee JP (2005) Why video games are good for your soul: pleasure and learning. Common Ground, Melbourne, VIC
11. Gee JP (2007) What video games have to teach us about learning and literacy, 2nd edn. Palgrave Macmillan, New York
12. Haji E, Azmani A, Harzli ME (2017) Using AHP Method for educational and vocational guidance. Int J Inf Technol Comput Sci 9(1):9–17
13. Hsu CHC (199) Learning styles of hospitality students: nature or nurture? Hosp Manage 18:17–30
14. Huang X, He J, Liang Y, Han G, Du J (2018) Design and application of a VR english learning game based on the apt model. In: 2018 seventh international conference of educational innovation through technology (EITT)
15. Huizinga J (1938) Homo Ludens. Penguin Random House LLC, Netherlands
16. Kolb DA (1983) Experiential learning: experience as the source of learning and development, 1st edn. Financial Times/Prentice Hall, Upper Saddle River, NJ
17. Linehan C, Kirman B, Lawson S, Chan G (2011) Practical, appropriate, empirically validated guidelines for designing educational games. In: ACM annual conference on human factors in computing systems. Vancouver, Canada, pp 1979–1988
18. Lyu HM, Zhou WH, Shen SL, Zhou AN (2020) Inundation risk assessment of metro system using AHP and TFN-AHP in Shenzhen. Sustain Cities Soc 56
19. Marton F, Säljö R (1976) On qualitative differences in learning. Outcome and process. British J Educ Psychol 46:4–11
20. Mastrocinque E, Ramírez FJ, Escribano AH, Pham DT (2020) An AHP-based multi-criteria model for sustainable supply chain development in the renewable energy sector. Expert Syst Appl 150
21. Patnaika PK, Swain PTR, Mishraa SK, Purohit A, Biswas S (2020) Composite material selection for structural applications based on AHP-MOORA approach, Mater Today Proc
22. Pribeanu C, Balog A, Iordache DD (2017) Measuring the perceived quality of an AR-based learning application: a multidimensional model. Interact Learn Environ 25(4):482–495
23. Ratey JJ (2001) A user's guide to the brain. Pantheon Books, New York
24. Saaty TL (2008) Relative measurement and its generalization in decision making: why pairwise comparisons are central in mathematics for the measurement of intangible factors—the analytic hierarchy/network process. Review of the Royal Spanish Academy of Sciences, Series A, Mathematics, Madrid
25. Salzman M, Dede C, Loftin R, Chen JA (1998) A model for understanding how virtual reality aids complex conceptual learning. Presence
26. Schwanen TIM, Dijst M, Kwan M-P (2008) ICTs and the decoupling of everyday activities, space and time: introduction. Tijdschrift Voor Economische En Sociale Geografie 99(5):519–527
27. Squire K (2011) Video games and learning: teaching participatory culture in the digital age. Teachers' College Press, New York
28. Starkey L (2011) Evaluating learning in the 21st century: a digital age learning matrix. Technol Pedagogy Educ 20(1):19–39
29. Wang R, Newton S, Lowe R (2015) Experiential learning styles in the age of a virtual surrogate. Int J Arch Res 9(3):93–110
30. Wang TJ (2011) Educating avatars: on virtual worlds and pedagogical intent. Teach Higher Educ 16:617–628
31. Wouters P, van Oostendorp H (2013) A meta-analytic review of the role of instructional support in game-based learning. Comput Educ 60(1):412–425
32. Zin NAM, Jaafar A, Wong SY (2009) Digital game-based learning (DGBL) model and development methodology for teaching history. WSEAS Trans Comput 8(2):
33. Zulkifli AN, Noor NM, Bakar JAA, Mat RC, Ahmad M (2013) A conceptual model of interactive persuasive learning system for elderly to encourage computer-based learning process. Man India 96(1–2):377–386

Exploring Success Criteria of Instructional Video Design in Online Learning Platforms

Atakan Coşkun, Elif Büyükkeçeci, and Gülşen Töre-Yargın

Abstract Today, increasing use of technology and contemporary educational needs make self-regulated ways of multimedia learning highly prevalent. Instructional videos in various fields are provided in Online Learning Platforms (OLPs) as multimedia learning tools. However, despite their effectiveness as educational tools, there are limited studies on design suggestions for OLPs and instructional videos. This paper aims to explore the success criteria of OLPs and instructional videos from their users' perspective to propose design suggestions. For this purpose, we conducted semi-structured interviews to investigate individuals' experiences and opinions about these mediums. Also, eye-tracking technology was employed to evaluate the gaze behaviors of users. Ten users having experience in OLPs participated in the study. The results were categorized under six titles as System Quality, Information Quality, System Delivery, Use, User Satisfaction, and Benefits.

Keywords Instructional videos · Online learning platforms (OLPs) · Eye tracking · The DeLone and McClean IS success model

1 Introduction

Video as a multimedia learning tool has been widely used for instruction and communication over the last two decades in classroom and distance education [1]. The number of OLPs, which use instructional videos as a primary teaching medium, such

---

A. Coşkun
Department of Computer Education and Instructional Technology, Middle East Technical University, Ankara, Turkey
e-mail: atakancoskun45@gmail.com

E. Büyükkeçeci (✉)
Department of Industrial Design, Middle East Technical University, Ankara, Turkey
e-mail: elif.buyukkececi@ieu.edu.tr

G. Töre-Yargın
Department of Industrial Design, METU/BILTIR-UTEST Product Usability Unit, Middle East Technical University, Ankara, Turkey
e-mail: tore@metu.edu.tr

© The Author(s), under exclusive license to Springer Nature Switzerland AG 2021
Ö. Cordan et al. (eds.), *Game + Design Education*, Springer Series in Design and Innovation 13, https://doi.org/10.1007/978-3-030-65060-5_31

as Udemy, Coursera, Lynda, and Khan Academy, have recently increased. Accordingly, many people use such platforms for self-development or as an aid to support their learning process. Despite their widespread use, studies on OLP design and learners' satisfaction with them are limited. E-learners' satisfaction, however, plays a vital role in the success of OLPs [2, 3]. More importantly, researchers do not know the reasons why learners stop taking online courses after the first experience [3, 4].

Differences in educational organizations' and institutions' preferences in using video production styles may cause different learning effects, which has been recognized by researchers. Therefore organizations, institutions, or individuals creating and developing these videos have to make conscious decisions while designing them. However, there is still a lack of guidance about how to design them and lack of knowledge about relevant design principles, which help to increase the satisfaction of individuals who prefer instructional videos with the purpose of self-regulated learning [5]. Considering all these factors, this study aims to propose design guidance related to instructional video design in OLPs by focusing on learners' expectations, satisfaction, and learners' definition of success criteria for these platforms. To do that, the methods, including an interview with a UX curve session [6] and eye-tracking, were employed, and the results were categorized depending on DeLone and McLean's [3, 7] Model of Information Systems Success.

In the following sections, firstly, a brief literature review on online self-learning through videos is introduced by highlighting definitions and significance of instructional videos and OLPs. The review also includes an overview of the success criteria for OLPs. After that, the study's methodology, which includes semi-structured interviews involving a UX curve session and an eye-tracking application, is introduced. Then, the results of the study are presented. Finally, discussions and conclusions are presented as a result of the study.

2 Literature Review

2.1 *Online Learning Through Videos*

In this section, to provide a brief introduction about how online learning is conducted through videos, definitions of instructional videos, and OLPs and their design requirements are briefly discussed.

Instructional Videos. There is a wide range of media through which instructional videos meet their audiences. Woolfit [8], for example, examines instructional videos in three different categories, namely *live lecture capture, screencast,* and *web lectures*. According to Woolfit, in a *live lecture capture,* the topic is covered in front of the students in a classroom where the camera is on. A *screencast* is the video format in which students are given the course through a computer screen, displayed entirely or partially, on which action is narrated synchronically [9]. As Day [10] defines, *web lectures* are "condensed, studio-recorded lectures made available via the web as multimedia presentations that combine video of the lecturer, audio, lecture slides, and a table of contents" (p. xi). In general, there are two screens, including the lecturer and the learning content in web lectures [8]. At this point, screencasts and web lectures seem to be similar. A screencast is kind of a web lecture that usually has only the narration and the presentation on the screen, whereas it possibly has the lecturer as well [11].

There are also suggestions for designing an instructional video in terms of its structure. Length, context, actions, and the number of characters refer to the structural elements [12]. According to Berk's suggestions, first, the video should not last more than three minutes if it is possible to handle the instructional content in this while. Second, everyday language is better to be used to the extent permitted by the aim of the video. Third, actions irrelevant to the aim of the video should be avoided. Finally, again considering the aim, the number of actors in the video should not be excessive. It can be inferred from these statements that unnecessary elements must be avoided to obtain an instructional video suitable for educational purposes. Berk [12] also reminds the emotional effect that videos have on the audience and states. This effect must be determined according to the learners' specifications, educational purpose, and learning outcomes.

Online Learning Platforms (OLPs). There are differences in the meaning of the terms for OLP, e-learning, and distance learning that is used in the field [13]. However, in this paper, we prefer to use the term "Online Learning Platform," also known as Massive Open Online Courses (MOOCs), since online learning is a more inclusive term as it covers both e-learning and web-based learning [14]. Many authors define online learning as a learning experience with technology providing learners with certain features, such as accessibility, connectivity, and flexibility [14]. There are many OLPs in the market, such as Udemy, Coursera, and Lynda, as the leading ones. These platforms have thousands of instructional videos, and each of them has different system designs and features. Udemy is the world's largest marketplace for online learning holding over fifty-five thousand courses, and Udemy teachers are the experts in their field. They can design and produce the course. Besides, learning tools of Udemy contain videos, articles, PowerPoint presentations, audio materials, assessments, and online discussion boards [15].

Lynda, on the other hand, offers six thousand courses, and it includes videos, playlists, notes, and assessments. Like Udemy, the experts in their field can create and manage the course. Coursera works with top universities and organizations, and it holds more than two thousand academic courses. Unlike Lynda and Udemy, teachers are the instructors from top universities and educational organizations around the world, and learners can freely get the course materials like videos. Besides, a large mass of people prefers using MOOCs for learning. For instance, more than 1,900,241 participants who are from 196 countries have applied in at least one course that belongs to Coursera in November 2012 [16]. However, even though a large number of people enroll in the courses in OLPs, there is still a need to improve OLPs when the expectations and needs of the educators or students are considered [17]. In light of this information, the academic world should bring solutions for OLPs' problems while trying to define the reasons to upraise the success of OLPs [16]. As a result, this study aims to understand and explore learners' experiences of MOOCs to propose design guidance for increasing their success levels.

3 Method

The purpose of the study is to investigate learners' experiences, satisfaction, and expectations about instructional video design in OLPs to understand their success criteria and propose design recommendations for such systems. This is a qualitative study in which a two-phased interview was implemented with ten participants. OLPs and instructional videos that are used in different phases of the interviews are shown in Table 1.

The study procedure can be summarized as follows:

Table 1 Screenshots from three videos about 'what UX design is' shown during eye-tracking

Video types
Video 1—Animation—"What is UX?": a digital animation film that includes a speech in the background, synchronized with the flow of images, frequently relying on statistical data (*Source* https://www.youtube.com/watch?v=bsla797t2Vk)
Video 2—Video with instructors' hands—"What is UX design?": a description by a narrator using concrete objects to exemplify the issue; only hands of the narrator is shown (*Source* https://www.youtube.com/watch?v=6uW-7Tj79z4&t=4s)
Video 3—Video with instructors' face—"Don Norman: The term UX.": direct recording of the instructor's face in r which the instructor gives information about the topic (*Source* https://www.youtube.com/watch?v=9BdtGjoIN4E&t=2s)

In this paper, tables and figures are produced by the authors unless otherwise indicated

Phase 1:

(a) Questions about OLPs: Participants' experiences about the OLPs that they used before were questioned.

(b) UX curves about OLPs: A UX curve session was conducted to understand participants' previous experiences with OLPs [6]. UX curve is a pen-and-paper based technique employed to receive information about changes in users' experiences related to a product, a service, or an application. In a UX curve session, participants draw one or more curves and indicate the factors that have caused the rises and falls by considering how and why their experience has changed over time [18].

Phase 2:

(a) Eye tracking while watching instructional videos: At the beginning of the second phase, by showing them three different types of instructional video formats as stimuli, participants' eye movements were recorded by Tobii Pro X2-60 eye tracker that records gaze locations at the rate of 60 Hz. Eye trackers capture eye movements and show us where someone is looking and the sequence of their eye movements [19]. All three videos participants watched were about 'what UX design is' Table 1. The videos were shown to the participants in the same order, as seen in Table 1. The reason for selecting these three videos is that these types of videos are not frequently used in OLPs, and it was considered that providing video formats different than the ones which they have experience with while using OLPs can enrich the conversations about video design.

(b) Questions about the videos: Participants' opinions about the videos and suggestions for instructional video and OLP designs were questioned. Also, they were asked to mention what they like and dislike about each video; we asked them to assign a number, from one to five, according to their satisfaction level.

These two phases were conducted in a single session, which lasted between 25 and 35 min., approximately 5 min. were allocated to videos. Interviews were audio-recorded, aside from having UX curves drawn by the participants and eye tracking data. Recordings were transcribed verbatim, and the transcripts were analyzed by two authors separately in spreadsheets. Then, they were compared with each other. At the last stage, it was rechecked by the third author. The analysis of UX curves and eye tracking results were employed to support the verbal protocol.

Ten individuals who enrolled at least one course from OLPs participated in the study. While selecting the participants, it was considered that participants who have experience in OLPs could provide us more effective and useful information about the design of instructional videos in online learning. Table 2 presents background information about the participants.

4 Findings

Interview results were categorized following the dimensions of the models proposed by by DeLone and McLean [7] and Holsapple and Lee-Post [20] (Appendix 1). Based

Table 2 The background information about the participants

	Gender	Age	Educational background	OLPs experienced
P01	Female	25	Physics	Ted/MIT Open courseware
P02	Female	29	Computer education and instructional technology (CEIT)	Khan Academy/Lynda/Code Academy
P03	Female	25	CEIT	Khan Academy/Ted/Lynda/Yargı Yayınları, Ekol Hoca
P04	Female	35	Computer engineering	Udemy/Coursera/Ted/Lynda
P05	Female	32	CEIT	Udemy/Lynda/Plural Sight/Edx
P06	Male	26	Graphic design	Ted/Plural Sight
P07	Male	26	Chemistry	Code Academy/Edx
P08	Male	29	CEIT	Udemy/Coursera/Khan Academy/Ted/Turkcell Microsoft Academy
P09	Male	24	Civil engineering	Khan Academy/Ted/Anadolu University Online Platform
P10	Male	27	Mining engineering	MIT Open courseware

on these categories and the results of the study, we proposed several design principles related to OLPs and instructional videos (Fig. 1).

Concerning the system quality of OLPs, the participants commented on the ease of use, and they mentioned "simplicity" in terms of interface design; "availability" as they want to find what they are looking for without any help; and "learning path" as an effective way to learn and to use the system quickly (Table 3). Also, some participants talked about feedback in OLPs and instructional videos.

Regarding information quality, three different issues should be considered, including the instructor, video content, and video design. Table 4 briefly overviews the results related to information quality.

Appearance of the instructor can be a critical issue. For the second video showing the instructors' hands without his face, participants told that instructor's tattoo, and t-shirt distracts them (Fig. 2). Eye tracking results also supported this finding by showing that eight participants fixated on tattoo1, and seven participants fixated on tattoo2 (Table 5).

Besides, the presence of the instructor's face in the video (as in the third video) was also perceived as distracting by some of the participants. In contrast, some others found it preferable by considering the instructor's diction and tone of the voice.

Another issue, on which some participants made comments, is video content in which there are three different types of categories consisting of concreteness, examples from daily life, and statistical information (Table 4). Some participants found the second video more understandable because it explains UX by using a banana as a metaphor to make it more concrete and more precise for the learner. Giving such examples from daily life makes them satisfied and supports their learning

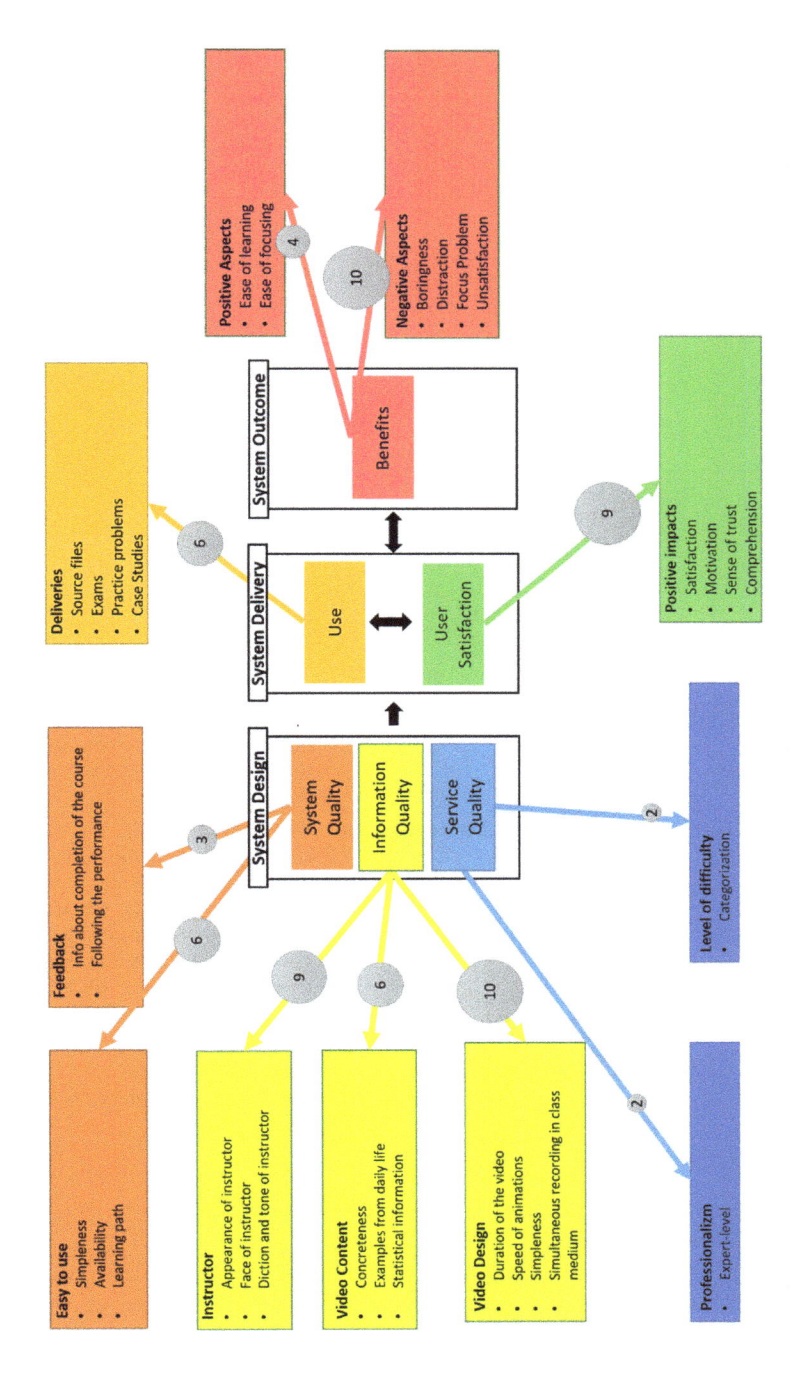

Fig. 1 The proposed design principles (Circles represent the number of respondents who mentioned the OLPs and instructional videos in the interview.)

Table 3 Summary of the results related to system quality of OLPs

	Relevant issues	Explanations and relevant quotations from the interviews
Sub-dimension: Ease of use	Simplicity	Simplicity is a preferable quality of the interface: "Lynda's design is simple. It always makes a better impression. If what I focus on is the learning itself, it is better to be simple. At least you'll find what you're looking for (P05)"
	Availability	Participants give importance to "availability": "It is essential that people can find what they are looking for, the subject that they want to study, without any help (P09)"
	Learning path	Participants stated that the learning path is an effective way to learn and to use the system easily "In Plural Sight, you usually choose a program, and it gives you a learning path depending on that. For example, if I want to learn 3D max, it offers me a learning path for it. [...] It offers you a route map. I like Plural Sight because it's nice to offer you a learning path (P05)"
Sub-dimension: Feedback	Information about completion of the course	Some participants like the content tree giving the feedback. For instance, one of the participants says: "On the left, there is a content tree that is full as we watch them. It was nice to receive such feedback (P03)"
	Following the performance	Participants like the following performance and want to see selected headings and sub-headings as highlighted on the left

process. Moreover, providing statistical information, as being in the first video, can provide confidence for the learner.

Video design was an essential issue for all participants. They do not prefer videos with long durations, and also animation speed was a considerable issue, especially in the first video. For this video, eye tracking results showed that participants' attention is distributed through different parts of the video (see Table 6, Video 1). As opposed to

Table 4 Summary of the results related to information quality of OLPs

	Relevant issues	Explanations and relevant quotations from the interviews
Sub-dimension: Instructor	Appearance of the instructor	In the second video, which shows the instructors' hands without his face, participants told that instructor's tattoo, and t-shirt distracts them "I could not focus. I cannot tell you what a guy is talking about right now; I see a banana, a wrinkled t-shirt, a tattoo (P05)"
	The face of the instructor	In the third video, some participants found the presence of the instructor's face in the video distracting "I think something was missing when the instructor was directly seen to speak. It was face-focused. He was distracting a little bit. That's why I couldn't focus on talking. I spent much more time watching the instructor's face (P01)"
	Diction and tone of the instructor	The diction and tone of the instructor can affect the preference for the presence of the instructor's face in the video "If the tone of the voice is proper, you listen what it is told, but if there is a bifurcation in the speaking, and the tone and diction was not proper, you would be distracted. You focus on how it is told, not what it is told (P05)"
Sub-dimension: Video content	Concreteness	Some participants found the second video more understandable because it explains UX by using a banana as a metaphor to make it more concrete and more explicit for the learner "It is good to show me an example from daily life in learning. The banana we often see helped me to understand the topic (P04)"

(continued)

Table 4 (continued)

	Relevant issues	Explanations and relevant quotations from the interviews
	Examples from daily life	Giving examples from daily life makes them satisfied, and it is helpful for learning "I liked The Khan Academy's style; I mean it appeals to the student. [...] I liked the style of the videos. I mean giving examples from daily life, especially in physics... I loved it (P03)"
	Statistical information	In the first video, there is some statistical information about UX, and two participants stated that statistical information in the video gave confidence to them "The percentages on the video are increasing, they took a lot of caution, they were fine. It is reassuring for me to see the number (P07)"
Sub-dimension: Video design	Duration of the video	The participants stated that they do not like watching the video with a long duration, and they suggested that the videos with a long duration should be divided into five- or ten-minute parts
	Speed of animations	Most participants told that they were distracted and had focus problems due to the speed of the animation in the video that explains UX with animations: " They speak on the screen with their keywords, but the transition of the animation was speedy. It made it a little hard to follow. I missed the icons they put while looking at the article. I missed the articles they put while looking at the icons (P03)"
	Simplicity	Participants expect instructional videos to be plain and simple "In instructional videos, what is told to me must be simple and plain. Redundant words and images distract me (P09)"

(continued)

Table 4 (continued)

	Relevant issues	Explanations and relevant quotations from the interviews
	Simultaneous recording in class medium	A few participants who enrolled in courses at MIT Open Courseware stated that the courses that were recorded at a simultaneous classroom environment were satisfying for them

Fig. 2 Snapshot from video 2

Table 5 Total fixation duration (s)

Participant	Tattoo 1	Tattoo 2
P01	2.02	0.32
P02	–	0.27
P03	0.25	1.07
P04	0.40	0.53
P05	2.55	0.49
P06	0.07	–
P07	0.97	0.72
P08	–	–
P09	1.36	3.41
P10	0.48	–
Average	1.01	0.97
Count	8	7

Table 6 Heatmaps of the three different types of video

Video 1: Animation	Video 2: Video with instructors' hands	Vide 3: Video with instructors' face

this situation, participants expect instructional videos to be more understandable and straightforward. Furthermore, heat maps generated according to the fixation counts, while the participants were watching the videos are illustrated in Table 8.

Furthermore, the simultaneous classroom environment presented in the videos is preferable for the participants, because they can see the classroom environment and hear the questions the students ask, which means they can experience the real classroom environment.

In terms of Service Quality, a few participants want instructional videos to be categorized in accordance with the level of difficulty. Also, participants perceive Lynda and Plural Sight as more professional. They claim that there is a self-controlling mechanism choosing the instructors depending on their expertise level in their field.

In system delivery, some participants stated that they like seeing source files and practicing on them, and these source files help to learn and increase satisfaction. Also, two participants like participating in the exams in OLPs because it creates a challenge and helps to learn the topic. Moreover, a few participants like practicing on the problem that OLPs created.

5 Discussion and Conclusion

The primary aim of the study is to reflect learners' needs and thoughts about OLPs and instructional videos and contribute to the success of OLPs because education is one of the building stones for humanity. Interview results showed that system quality (ease of use, and feedback) and information quality (instructor, video content, and design) are associated with user satisfaction and system outcome. To guide designers, instructional technologists, and developers of OLPs, we tried to create some categorizations depending on the learners' experience.

In OLPs, ease of use is an essential issue for learners because they want to find what they are looking for quickly, which is also suggested by previous research [21, 22]. As a result, techniques like learning paths can be used in OLPs, or such techniques can be developed further. Another vital issue is feedback. OLPs should inform the students about what is going on with the platforms. The participants highlighted that they like seeing the completion percentage of the course or content tree displaying the progress of the learners in OLPs.

The instructor is a significant factor affecting learners' satisfaction and system outcomes. Like the other studies [3, 23], the results show that instructors are significant predictors of e-learner satisfaction. In the current study, instructors' tattoo and a t-shirt can cause a distraction for the learners. Therefore, especially in videos where instructors' hands and gestures are recorded, instructors' outlook should be considered. Also, instructors' faces, diction, and tone are another issue that should be taken into consideration. Regarding video content, in instructional videos, making theoretical subjects concrete and giving learners examples from daily life has the potential to enhance learning and increase user satisfaction. Shortly, there is a significant relationship between user satisfaction and video content [23]. Also, giving statistical information in instructional videos can affect learners' trust in the topic. The other crucial topic is video design, in which the duration of the video is a significant factor for learners. Especially instructional videos with a long duration should be divided into five- or ten-minutes parts. Moreover, the student can be distracted because of the speed of the animation. Besides, OLPs like MIT open courseware that includes the instructional videos with simultaneous recording in the classroom environment can have a positive impact as they present the real classroom environment. Regarding service quality, the learners expect instructional videos to be categorized depending on their difficulty level. Also, learners want to have self-controlling mechanisms, such as allowing learners to choose the instructor, which seems more professional. In system delivery, learners would be satisfied when source files, exams, and case studies are involved in OLPs because some participants highlighted that they create a challenge and allow them to practice what they learn. Moreover, system delivery is vital for the success of e-learning which affects system outcomes such as enhanced learning and academic success [20].

Regarding the limitations of the study, the sample size is limited to ten individuals, which may fail to represent the whole population. However, a small number of the participants in interview-based qualitative research enable the researcher to build a good rapport with the participants, resulting in a more in-depth investigation of the issue [24]. Furthermore, the educational backgrounds of the participants are very similar to each other, which may affect the diversity of the information. Also, in the study, the experience of some participants with OLPs was restricted to a short period. For future studies, this study should be done with more participants who have different backgrounds. The participants who have more experience with OLPs should also be considered.

To sum up, since education is always an essential issue for individuals and countries, research about e-learning plays a vital role in the field of education. Therefore, in this study, we tried to increase and contribute to the success of e-learning by conducting an interview-based qualitative study related to OLPs and instructional videos. By taking the learners' expectations and comments into consideration, we proposed several design principles that will hopefully be useful for professionals who design and develop these systems.

Acknowledgements We would like to thank the participants of the study for their valuable contribution. This study was conducted as part of a graduate course ID531 Methods of User Research given at Middle East Technical University, Department of Industrial Design, during the 2017–2018 Spring Semester.

Appendix 1

The definitions of the proposed principles based on DeLone and McLeans [7] and Holsapple and Lee-Post's [20] definitions

ID	Dimensions	Sub-dimensions	The definitions
1	System quality	Ease of use	reflects the ease of use of the OLP
		Feedback	includes the methods of feedback in OLPs and learners' expectations from OLPs
2	Information quality	Instructor	presents the details related to the instructor, such as the appearance, the diction and tone, the face, and the language in the instructional videos
		Video Design	assesses the instructional video designs in terms of duration, simplicity, speed, etc
		Video Content	evaluates the content of the instructional videos
3	Service quality	Professionalism	means that OLPs examine and assess their instructors in terms of expertise
		Level of difficulty	evaluates OLPs in terms of categorization of the instructional videos such as advance, intermediate, beginner
4	System delivery	Use	gauges what OLPs provide to users, for example, case studies, exams, source files, etc
5	User satisfaction	Positive impacts	reflect positive opinions about OLPs
6	System outcome	Benefits	show the positive and negative aspects of the system outcome

References

1. Whatley J, Ahmad A (2007) Using video to record summary lectures to aid students' revision. Interdisc J Knowl Learning Objects 3:185–196. Retrieved from https://libproxy.boisestate.edu/login?url=https://search.ebscohost.com/login.aspx?direct=true&db=aph&AN=28097597&site=ehost-live
2. DeLone WH, McLean ER (1992) Information systems success: the quest for the dependent variable. Inf Syst Res 3(1):60–95. https://doi.org/10.1287/isre.3.1.60
3. Asoodar M, Vaezi S, Izanloo B (2016) Framework to improve e-learner satisfaction and further strengthen e-learning implementation. Comput Hum Behav 63:704–716. https://doi.org/10.1016/j.chb.2016.05.060

4. Wu J, Tsai RJ, Chen CC, Wu Y (2006) An integrative model to predict the continuance use of electronic learning systems: hints for teaching. Int J E-learning 5(2)
5. Chorianopoulos K (2018) A taxonomy of asynchronous instructional video styles. Int Rev Res Open Distrib Learning 19(1)
6. Kujala S, Roto V, Väänänen-Vainio-Mattila K, Karapanos E, Sinnelä A (2011) UX Curve: a method for evaluating long-term user experience. Interact Comput 23(5):473–483
7. Delone WH, Mclean ER (2003) The DeLone and McLean model of information systems success: a ten-year update. J Manage Inf Syst 19(4):9–30. https://doi.org/10.1080/07421222.2003.11045748
8. Woolfitt Z (2015) The effective use of video in higher education. Lectoraat In: Teaching, learning and technology. Inholland University of Applied Sciences, Rotterdam
9. Udell J (2004) Jonudell.net. Retrieved from https://jonudell.net/udell/2004-11-15-name-that-genre.html
10. Day J (2008) Investigating learning with web lectures. Georgia Institute of Technology
11. Gorissen P, Bruggen JV, Jochems W (2012) Students and recorded lectures: survey on current use and demands for higher education. Res Learning Technol 20(1063519):297–311
12. Berk RA (2009) Multimedia teaching with video clips: TV, movies, YouTube, and mtvU in the college classroom. Int J Technol Teaching Learning 5(1)
13. Moore JL, Dickson-Deane C, Galyen K (2011) E-Learning, online learning, and distance learning environments: are they the same? Internet Higher Educ 14(2):129–135. https://doi.org/10.1016/j.iheduc.2010.10.001
14. Wu XV, Chan YS, Tan KHS, Wang W (2018) A systematic review of online learning programs for nurse preceptors. Nurse Educ Today, 60:11–22. https://doi.org/10.1016/j.nedt.2017.09.010
15. Chen, C (2018) Online learning may be the future of education. We compared 4 platforms that are leading the way. Business Insider, Business Insider, 4 Jan. 2018, www.businessinsider.com/online-learning-platform-comparison-udemy-skillshare-lynda-coursera/
16. Adamopoulos P (2013) What makes a mentor? ICIS 4:125–138. https://doi.org/10.1145/1164394.1164397. Author, F., Author, S.: Title of a proceedings paper. In: Editor, F., Editor, S. (eds.) CONFERENCE 2016, LNCS, vol. 9999, pp. 1–13. Springer, Heidelberg (2016).
17. MOOCs on the Move: How Coursera Is Disrupting The Traditional Classroom. Knowledge@Wharton (2012, November 07). Retrieved from https://knowledge.wharton.upenn.edu/article/moocs-onthe-move-how-coursera-is-disrupting-the%20traditional%20classroom/
18. Balasubramoniam V, Tungatkar N (2013) Study of user experience (UX) and UX evaluation methods. Int J Adv Res Comput Eng Technol (IJARCET) 2(3):1214
19. Ball L, Poole A (2010) Eye tracking in human-computer interaction and usability research: current status and future prospects. Web-Dokumentti. Saatavilla: https://www.Alexpoole.Info/…. Retrieved from https://scholar.google.com/scholar?hl=en&btnG=Search&q=intitle:Eye+Tracking+in+HumanComputer+Interaction+and+Usability+Research+:+Current+Status+and+Future+Prospects#5
20. Holsapple CW, Lee-Post A (2006) Defining, assessing, and promoting e-learning success: an information systems perspective. Decision Sci J Inn Educ 4(1):67–85. https://doi.org/10.1111/j.1540-4609.2006.00102.x. https://doi.org/10.1080/07421222.2003.11045748
21. Davis FD (1989) perceived usefulness, perceived ease of use, and user acceptance of information technology. MIS Q 13(3):319. https://doi.org/10.2307/249008
22. Younis A, Cater-steel A, Soar J (2016) Computers in human behavior determinants of perceived usefulness of e-learning systems. Comput Hum Behav 64:843–858. https://doi.org/10.1016/j.chb.2016.07.065
23. Ozkan S, Koseler R (2009) Multi-dimensional students' evaluation of e-learning systems in the higher education context: an empirical investigation. Comput Educ 53(4):1285–1296. https://doi.org/10.1016/j.compedu.2009.06.011
24. Crouch M, McKenzie H (2006) The logic of small samples in interview-based qualitative research. Soc Sci Inf 45(4):483–499. https://doi.org/10.1177/0539018406069584

Challenges in Synchronous e-Learning in Architectural Education

Meriç Altıntaş Kaptan, Ecem Edis, and Aslıhan Ünlü

Abstract Distance learning is a centuries-old method, from first correspondence courses to educational broadcasting. It eventually evolved into e-learning, where the acquisition of knowledge is managed via electronic media and nowadays, the Internet became the prominent medium for information delivery. The use of internet technology and applications allowed two-way communication between students/audience and lecturer/presenter, either simultaneously, or with a time-lag. Despite its long-standing history, e-learning methods still preserve their novelty in terms of changing the traditional ways of face-to-face learning methods in which both lecturer and audience are considerably much familiar with. In an Erasmus + partnership project titled Re-use of Modernist Buildings (RMB), the use of both synchronous and asynchronous e-learning methods was concerted within the context of a joint master's programme that is planned to be established by the partner universities. Concerning the decision to employ e-learning, some synchronous seminar and lecture sessions were tried and tested both during an RMB project workshop and within other university courses. A survey was conducted after each session in order to understand students' opinions on e-learning in comparison with traditional classroom learning. In this paper, open-ended responses collected through the survey are examined in detail, and comparative analysis of personal opinions and comments in relation to certain Likert scale questions are reported in order to review and discuss participants' perspective on the synchronous e-learning session attended. In this respect, a brief introduction regarding the RMB project and e-learning is provided primarily, followed by the synchronous session cases and evaluation method, and finally, the findings are presented and discussed with examples.

M. Altıntaş Kaptan (✉) · E. Edis
Faculty of Architecture, Department of Architecture, Istanbul Technical University, Istanbul 34367, Turkey
e-mail: altintasme@itu.edu.tr

E. Edis
e-mail: ecem@itu.edu.tr

A. Ünlü
Faculty of Architecture and Design, Department of Architecture, Özyegin University, Istanbul 34794, Turkey
e-mail: aslihan.unlu@ozyegin.edu.tr

© The Author(s), under exclusive license to Springer Nature Switzerland AG 2021
Ö. Cordan et al. (eds.), *Game + Design Education*, Springer Series in Design and Innovation 13, https://doi.org/10.1007/978-3-030-65060-5_32

Keywords Synchronous e-learning · Architectural education · Learning experience · Audience perspective

1 Introduction

Distance learning, a topic of regular interest in today's world, is more than just a mere attempt on taking education to the next level through technology or innovation, but a requisite to meet the ever-increasing demand and overcoming the on-going challenges. The constant need for training, upgrading skills and knowledge to achieve career prospects incite people to participate in various online courses whilst the allure of accessing information without time or location dependent restraints are the main factors of growing interest in such a model of educational delivery. The demand for acquiring knowledge rapidly is being satisfied through the fast supply of online learning like nothing else before. In addition to the flexibility provided to both parties, the digital environment also facilitates a considerable reduction in individual and institutional educational costs [1].

On the other hand, lack of physical and social interaction may result in loss of motivation on the part of recipients. Technology-based transmission constitutes the core of distance education therefore; the modes of communication and interaction are mostly dependent on the medium being used. Facilitating effective modes of communication is an essential feature of remote learning yet the determinant factors in success are based on the means provided by the online platforms or software of choice. The insufficiency or absence of participation may easily prompt the disinterest and detachment of learners. In addition to motivational factors, the self-discipline and time management skills of the students are critical for an effective remote learning experience. Recounting the challenges of distance learning, one must not forget quality issues in regards to services, systems, and content, which are significant measures of online education in overall but equally hard to assure. The instructor's attitude and the selection of methods adopted in educational delivery in accordance with the context and audience have a substantial influence on learners' experience just as with traditional classroom education.

The Re-use of Modernist Buildings (RMB), an Erasmus + partnership project running between 2016 and 2019, aimed to initiate an educational framework for shared definitions, methodologies, and approaches to be implemented in the refurbishment and conversion of the existing 'modern era' building stock [2]. The project's consecutive outcome, the Joint Master Programme on the Re-use of Modernist Buildings, is to be based on a comprehensive and well-balanced curriculum with a particular emphasis on e-learning and adoption of remote teaching formats supporting traditional courses with particular focus on design. Exploring new ways of online teaching strategies in design education, the curricula proposed through the master's programme would facilitate the collaboration of partner universities and international contributions from varying geographic locations. Throughout the project, combinations of on-site events and several e-learning methods have been experienced, especially focusing on synchronous modes. ITU, as a partner university, has implemented several synchronous e-learning seminars, lectures, and design studios with reference to the RMB project within its ongoing face-to-face learning curriculum in order to experiment adoption of certain remote teaching methods. After each session, a survey was distributed to attendees to generate feedback on distance education with the intention of exploring its utilization in architectural education. In this respect, the paper presents and discusses the analysis of the responses provided to the open-ended question of the survey where participants reflect their remarks freely with their own words.

At this point, moving education to digital platforms and adoption of online learning has become an obligation, an educational response to the on-going pandemic crisis. The participation growth in distance learning is at its peak due to the rapid shift towards online platforms for all levels, from primary to tertiary education. Currently, distance learning programmes and online degrees offered are in high demand. By extension, the learners' attitude and perspective have become prominent elements determining the success of digital learning. Nevertheless, the data collected and presented here reflects online learning perspectives and experiences before the pandemic, thus the focus of this study shall be treated independent of the currently offered emergency remote teaching.

2 Methods and Materials

This study is aimed to investigate the assets and deficiencies encountered while utilizing synchronous e-learning methods and to provide an explicit evaluation of the participants' perspective, thereby contribute to the elimination of inconveniences. The main steps adopted in this study were (i) questionnaire design; (ii) execution of distant lectures and data collection; and (iii) assessment of data and theme generation, which are explained briefly in the following subsections.

2.1 Questionnaire Design

The questionnaire had been developed by RMB-ITU team with the contributions of other RMB members and consisted of 10 questions addressing three different contents all of which inquired through multiple-choices, Likert scale questions, or free text boxes (Fig. 1).

The first group of questions includes demographic questions that seek to find age and gender data, and multiple-choice questions designed mainly to identify the characteristics and setting of the distant lecture as well as students' previous experiences.

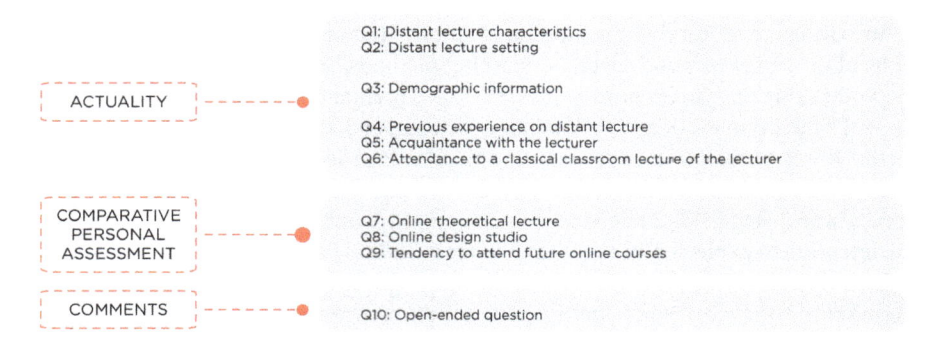

Fig. 1 Questionnaire structure (prepared by authors)

- ACTUALITY
  - Q1: Distant lecture characteristics
  - Q2: Distant lecture setting
  - Q3: Demographic information
  - Q4: Previous experience on distant lecture
  - Q5: Acquaintance with the lecturer
  - Q6: Attendance to a classical classroom lecture of the lecturer
- COMPARATIVE PERSONAL ASSESSMENT
  - Q7: Online theoretical lecture
  - Q8: Online design studio
  - Q9: Tendency to attend future online courses
- COMMENTS
  - Q10: Open-ended question

The second group of questions is Likert scaling questions, in which personal opinions and assessments about the distant learning session attended were being queried in comparison to a traditional classroom lecture. Here, all three questions (Q7, Q8, and Q9) embody sub-member questions related to the assigned theme. Q7 and its sub-member questions deal with a comparison of online theoretical lecture to that of traditional classroom whereas, Q8 addresses the online design studio compared to the typical studio experience. Q9, on the other hand, interrogates the respondents' tendency for a future online course/design studio or programme, based on their previous experience(s). The third group incorporates one open-ended question that aims to unveil further assessment and recommendations regarding the distant lecture attended and acknowledge general impressions on online courses. The unprescribed response format employed in this group is targeted to understand and reveal attendees' assessment in their own words.

2.2 Execution of Distant Lectures and Data Collection

Within the scope of this study, the online learning methods had been experimented with different audience-lecturer pairings; i.e. with different distant lecture settings. A total of seven distant lectures for different courses with varying student populace were held starting from the 2017 to 2018 spring semester until the end of 2019–2020 fall semester, all of which were performed using Adobe Connect. A brief description of distant lecture characteristics is presented at Table 1.

The majority of the distance lectures executed were of undergraduate and graduate level; only one lecture was carried out as part of the students' workshop organized in relation to the RMB project. There were four major content areas (i.e. technology, history, architectural design, restoration/conservation) identified in advance and listed within the questionnaire. However, during the execution of distant lectures, 'technology' was the main subject covered except for one lecture, which was on

Table 1 The features of the distant sessions executed (Eng: English Tr: Turkish) (prepared by authors)

Distant Session #	Semester	Level	Subject	Method	Setting	# of responses to questionnaire	# of responses to Q10	Session language
DS1	17–18 spring	Undergraduate	Technology	Theoretical lecture	s3	13	7	Eng
DS2	17–18 spring	Master's	Technology	Theoretical lecture	s1	14	2	Tr
DS3	18–19 fall	Student workshop	History	Theoretical lecture	s1	36	7	Eng
DS4	18–19 fall	Master's	Technology	Theoretical lecture	s1	10	4	Tr
DS5	18–19 fall	Undergraduate	Technology	Design studio	s5	5	4	Tr
DS6	18–19 spring	Master's	Technology	Theoretical lecture	s1	13	0	Tr
DS7	19–20 fall	Undergraduate	Technology	Theoretical lecture	s3	31	9	Eng

'history'. The lecture content was mainly delivered through the method of 'theoretical lecture', while there was only one lecture that adopted 'design studio' method and no lecture included 'group discussion' or 'debate', which were the methods acknowledged beforehand. Initially, there were five different distant lecture settings identified and intended for use, however, due to the infrastructural and collaborative restrictions, only three of them were implemented up to now. Most of the distant lectures employed the settings of either 'S1' *(Classroom lecture given by a distant lecturer using classroom's data show/projector screen)* or 'S3' *(Distant connection to an online theoretical web lecture)*. Only one lecture used the setting of 'S5' *(Design review using a web based platform with screen sharing feature)*.

The primary data collection method adopted in this study was survey comprising a written set of questions as described in Sect. 3.1. that is aimed to compile quantitative (numerically rated items) and qualitative (open-ended questions) data, while disclosing the attitude of the target audience and their level of satisfaction in regards to the subject. After each online session, the questionnaires were distributed to the attendees to gather comprehensive information on the attended distant lecture. Ultimately, 122 responses were collected through the survey research that reflects participants' experience on the provided e-learning course. The number of respondents to survey does not yield the exact number of distant lecture attendees since the participants filled in the questionnaire voluntarily.

2.3 Assessment of Data and Thematic Analysis

The focus of the study presented here is a deep investigation of qualitative data collected through open-ended question thus; only these responses and their relation to certain circumstances (which were disclosed through some other questions within the survey) will be discussed from here onwards.

Open-ended questions can be very valuable and beneficial as they pose no limitations and provide an opportunity to the participant to address any issue/concern that might not have been involved within the survey form itself. Out of 122 participants, 33 had responded to the open-ended question of the survey; the age and gender distribution of 33 open-ended responses compared to the overall respondents of interest are provided below (Table 2).

Ayres defines 'thematic analysis' as "a data reduction and analysis strategy by which qualitative data are segmented, categorized, summarized, and reconstructed" in the interest of capturing the fundamental notions within [3]. Thematic coding is an essential segment of qualitative data analysis; herein reoccurring patterns and a consolidative model are to be established. Auerbach & Silverstein describe the procedure of 'coding' as a routine mechanical process in which raw text is examined over and over again in order to discover the patterns embedded [4]. It comprises the process of identification, organization, and systematization of raw data to generate key ideas, concepts, and categories from which certain conclusions can be drawn [5]. The reoccurrence of certain ideas and notions within the data set indicates a shared

Challenges in Synchronous e-Learning in Architectural Education 415

Table 2 Distribution of open-ended responses (prepared by authors)

	No. of respondents	Gender			Age	
		Female	Male	Number of no Answer	Range	Mean
		Number/ratio to Total (%)	Number/ratio to Total (%)			
Open-ended question	33	18/54.5	15/45.5	0	19–37	23.5
Survey in general	122	82/67.2	38/31.1	2	19–45	24.0

vision and the point of saturation through which a 'theme' can be derived [6]. The use of similar words and phrases to express the same idea/notion compose 'repeating ideas', and an organized assemble of repeating ideas produce a common 'theme' [4].

The qualitative data collected from the open-ended question has been examined through 'thematic analysis and coding' in order to obtain meaningful comprehension of respondents' perspectives. Primarily, the data (open-ended responses) had been inspected to identify repeating ideas and key concepts to construct themes; for this purpose, each response and statement had been carefully read, re-read, and categorized according to the distinguished labels. The descried themes were then grouped together and classified according to the best possible phrases and expressions to connote the meaning. The collection of recurring ideas into coherent categories makes up the basis of 'coding', the representative 'codes' were further evolved over time, merging and breaking down to diagnose the most frequently occurring themes that exemplify the responses at optimum.

To investigate the possible factors influencing the recurring concerns expressed by respondents, the data that is categorized according to the representative 'themes and codes' were matched with the facts collected under 'actuality' and analyzed in correlation to various variables (e.g. gender, distant lecture characteristics and setting, etc.) that may be related. The outcomes of this analysis are provided in the findings section, in addition to themes and codes determined. Correlations with particular Likert scale questions (i.e. comparative personal assessment) are also sought to understand the respondents' tendencies.

3 Findings and Discussions

3.1 Characteristics of the Open-Ended question's Respondents

The 33 participants who have responded to the open-ended question were between the ages ranging from 19 to 37 years (Mean = 23.5). The ratio of female respondents was more than that of male respondents (i.e. 54.5 and 45.5% respectively). Among these respondents, only two of them revealed a past experience regarding online lectures. The remaining 31 respondents identified themselves as first-time participants in such a distant lecture practice. The four of the distant sessions were run in Turkish, and the remaining three were in English, which is a second language for all respondents. Among 33 respondents, only 30.3% (10 participants) were attended a distant lecture of their native tongue.

3.2 Themes and Codes Extracted from Open-Ended Responses

The open-ended responses collected have been worked on several times; 33 responses were analyzed one after another in order to extract and organize the principal themes, relevant sub-categories, matching statements, and eventually, 62 statements were identified. The statements acquired were grouped repeatedly into coherent categories and assisted in structuring the primary themes in return. The concluding four principal themes designated are as follows: (i) general comments (positive/negative), (ii) assets, (iii) drawbacks, and (iv) suggestions. While constructing these themes (Table 3), the classification procedure as explained below has been followed.

- Statements that include positive or negative subjective judgments but do not specify the qualifications related to conditions, i.e. opinions and statements that express views and tendencies in general terms, but do not establish a cause-effect relationship or provide reason and evidence have been categorized under

Table 3 Themes and codes extracted from open-ended responses (prepared by authors)

	Themes and codes	Exemplary statements
General comments	Positive remark	*"it was a pleasure"*
	Negative remark	*"I would like to have the lecture in classroom face to face"*
	Neutral comparative judgment	*"It was really like the lecturer was in the classroom…"*
Assets	Distance	*"it is good if there is no possibility to meet"*
	Greater productivity/less distractions	*"It made me focus on the screen and follow the slides"*
	Time efficiency	*"Distant lecture was much more comfortable since I did not have to spend my time on the road."*
	Other	*"It can be beneficial if we don't have enough lessons in our Ph.D. programs"*

(continued)

Table 3 (continued)

	Themes and codes	Exemplary statements
Drawbacks	Lack of proper communication/interaction deficiencies	"a contact is needed to maintain attention, ..."
	Distractions/less productivity	"I couldn't concentrate the lecture"
	Time inefficiency	"More time was needed for the topics that could be explained in a shorter time period." (originally in Turkish)
	Technical problems	"I would prefer that the microphone/sound system would be in a better condition, so it would be easier and more fluent to understand the lecture in total"
Suggestions	Lecturing method/preferences	"With a chat box option added, we would be able to participate in the class by writing." (originally in Turkish)
	Technical/technological	"The connection problem due to the internet connection should be solved"

'general comments'. In addition to positive or negative remarks, neutral comparative assessments that do not yield any absolute judgments, i.e. lacking favorable or unfavorable aspects of the subject when compared to other conditions, were also compiled here.

- Statements that comprise subjective evaluations and yet supported by establishing a cause-effect relationship, comparisons, evidence and reasoned judgment statements were gathered under two groups as 'assets' and 'drawbacks' based on the positive and negative meanings they deliver as well as the advantages and disadvantages identified by the respondent.
- Statements based on personal experience and informing how the deficiency can be corrected, without positive or negative subjective judgment, were compiled under the category of 'suggestions'.

In relation to the research concerns and objectives; i.e. identification of the challenges in synchronous education, drawbacks derived from the open-ended responses were grouped into four as follows: lack of proper communication/interaction; distractions/less productivity; time inefficiency; and technical problems. The responses compiled under the sub-category of 'lack of proper communication/interaction' addresses a significant barrier frequently faced in distance education. Whether it is nonverbal gestures and body language of the lecturer or technical delays during the message delivery, the problems related to communication and interaction affect the quality of human contact and beclouds the exchange and transmission of ideas and information among instructors and students. The second sub-category 'distractions/less productivity' reveal rather personal experiences regarding a drop in productivity due to loss of concentration. The causes of attention deficit are not explicitly specified within the responses yet can be interpreted as being caused particularly either by the environmental conditions or methods/settings adopted in the delivery of lectures. There was only one statement concerning 'time inefficiency', yet acknowledged as a substantial sub-category in regards to its counterpart in assets. The 'technical problems' represent the most significant sub-category derived among drawbacks as emphasized by the respondents. The responses collected here mostly refer to the unforeseen equipment, software or Internet connection difficulties, which adversely affect the lecture comprehension in overall.

3.3 Comparative Assessment

Taken by theme category, it is observed that the responses and statements were mostly concentrated on the 'drawbacks' and 'comments' without cause and effect relationship, both with the same ratio (34%), followed by 'assets' (24%). Suggestions, on the other hand, were the least in ratio and constituted 8% of all commentary as given in Table 4. Following the respondents' comments and concerns which refer to more than one issue in general, the counts and ratio calculations provided in Table 4

Table 4 Distribution of responses/statements by thematic groups in relation to gender, distant lecture characteristics and setting (prepared by authors)

		COMMENTS			ANSWERS (with reasoning)								SUGGESTIONS
					assets				drawbacks				
		positive remark	negative remark	neutral comparative judgement	other	distance	greater productivity / less distractions	time efficiency	lack of proper communication / interaction deficiencies	distractions / less productivity	time inefficiency	technical problems	
Female		4	3	2	1	2	5	1	3	3	1	6	5
Male		6	4	2	0	2	3	1	3	3	0	2	0
Total		10	7	4	1	4	8	2	6	6	1	8	5
% (among 62 responses)		16.1	11.3	6.5	1.6	6.5	12.9	3.2	9.7	9.7	1.6	12.9	8.1
LEVEL	undergraduate	6	3	1	0	2	8	2	2	3	1	7	4
	master's	1	1	2	1	2	0	0	1	1	0	0	0
	student workshop	3	3	1	0	0	0	0	3	2	0	1	1
SUBJECT	technology	7	4	3	1	4	8	2	3	4	1	7	4
	history	3	3	1	0	0	0	0	3	2	0	1	1
METHOD	theoretical lecture	10	6	4	1	4	8	2	5	6	0	5	3
	design studio	0	1	0	0	0	0	0	1	0	1	3	2
	discussion	0	0	0	0	0	0	0	0	0	0	0	0
	other	0	0	0	0	0	0	0	0	0	0	0	0
SETTING	S1	4	4	3	1	2	0	0	4	3	0	1	1
	S3	6	2	1	0	2	8	2	1	3	0	4	2
	S5	0	1	0	0	0	0	0	1	0	1	3	2

were based on the number of statements relevant to the thematic category (i.e. 62), instead of the total number of respondents (i.e. 33).

On the basis of themes and codes, it is identified that positive comments are the prominent sub-category with a commentary ratio of 16.1%. It is followed by 'greater productivity/less distraction' in assets (12.9%) and 'technical problems' in drawbacks (12.9%). Data show that negative comments comprise 11.3% of all statements, and 'lack of proper communication/interaction deficiencies' and 'distractions/less productivity' in drawbacks both follow it with a 9.7% commentary ratio. The commentary on the disadvantages regarding distractions and productivity in drawbacks reveals a lower ratio than its positive equivalent in assets. Lastly, 'distance' in advantages, which addresses the benefits of being able to attend a lecture or class activity without being physically present, is yet another significant sub-category among themes with a ratio of 6.5% (Table 4).

The data provided had also been analyzed in regard to the number of respondents who had filled in the open-ended question. However, theme categorization had been altered as the responses given by some respondents were split up and filed under more than one category. Additional groupings were added to this section in order to identify the responses of one solid/consistent idea and others containing more complex opinions. Accordingly, the supplementary groupings of 'more than one category–contradictory', 'more than one category—positive' and 'more than one category—negative' were generated to compile the complex responses. The former comprises respondents whose answers convey both positive and negative messages; for example, a respondent that provides a positive comment yet mentions disadvantages is cataloged here. However, it was identified as an issue to be discussed in more detail and thus, was excluded from the detailed analysis in this study. 'More than one category' sections, either positive or negative, represent the respondents whose answers yield more consistent opinions yet fall under different sub-categories. For example, a respondent that remarks different disadvantages and elicits a negative comment or a suggestion at the same time, was compiled under this category.

The responses of Q10, grouped as described above, then correlated with the answers given to particular Likert type questions (i.e. Q7-a, Q9-a, and Q9-b as given in Table 5) investigating respondents' opinion on the distant lecture attended in comparison, their approach and preferences regarding prospective remote education possibilities in general. The answers to these questions are only analyzed if they represent 'strongly disagree' or 'disagree' reply. The findings of this analysis are provided in Table 6.

Table 5 The questions of Q7-a, Q9-a, and Q9-b (prepared by authors)

Question #	Question type	Question text
Q7-a	Likert scale	Distant lecture was not different from the others in general
Q9-a		If there is any other distant lecture/design studio, I want to attend it
Q9-b		If the same lecture/design studio is given at both classical classroom environment and as distant lecture, I prefer to attend the distant one

Table 6 Grouping of responses in relation to Q7-a and Q9-a and b (based on number of respondents) (prepared by authors)

	total # of respondents	# of respondents who 'strongly disagree' or 'disagree',		
		Q7-a	Q9-a	Q9-b
Comments (positive)	7	1	0	2
Comments (negative)	2	1	2	2
Neutral comparative judgements	1	0	0	0
Positive answers (assets)	3	0	0	0
Negative answers (drawbacks)	1	1	1	1
Contradictory categories	7	4	0	4
More than one category (positive)	4	2	0	0
More than one category (negative)	8	8	2	7
General Sum	33	17	5	16

The relationship between Q10 responses and Q7-a scores indicate a coherent affiliation in general. The respondents who had provided either positive comments or referred to the advantages of the distant lecture were found to answer this question (Q7-a) in favor or indifferent as well. For Q9-a, out of 33 respondents, only five people in total have filled in either 'strongly disagree' or 'disagree', and no contradiction has been detected between the Q10 responses and Q9-a answers since these respondents provided either negative comments or draw attention to drawbacks. For Q9-b, similarly, 14 respondents out of 16, who have filled in any of 'strongly disagree' or 'disagree', responded either adversely or offered contradictory statements to Q10. Although relatively small in number, there were some 'strongly disagree' or 'disagree' responses to both Q7-a and Q9-b, provided by those who had given positive commentary to the open-ended question. This finding might indicate that regardless of the positive statements and advantages addressed about the distant lecture attended, when it comes to a comparison between e-learning and classical ways of education, the participants show a preference towards face-to-face contact with instructors rather than a general adverse attitude towards e-learning. In addition to this, difficulties in communication, technical problems, distractions caused by lack of an efficient classroom environment were the most common negative commentaries and disadvantages provided by the participants who had stated that they do not prefer to attend the distant lecture if both options were available. The data provided in Table 6 were also analyzed on the basis of gender and no remarkable finding was found.

The relationship between lecture setting and characteristics, academic degree, subject, method, and participants' responses were hard to explore via the survey since the different lecture environments offered were not equal in number and hereby, in participant number as well. Even if more comprehensive research is needed, certain conclusions may be deduced from the present data, e.g. 'lack of proper communication/interaction' is referred mostly in relation to S1 ('Classroom lecture given by a distant lecturer using classroom's data show/projector screen') lectures, while S3 settings with 'distant connection to an online theoretical web lecture' are found to enable 'greater productivity/less distraction' as expressed (see Table 4). Nevertheless, the latter is found to be distracting by some respondents as well.

4 Conclusion

This study focused on the identification and assessment of potential challenges in distant education in the field of architecture observed from the standpoint of participants. Different student groups with experiences from different e-learning settings have participated in the survey; a total of 122 responses were collected and among these, 33 responses provided to the open-ended question were investigated in detail through the thematic coding process. This is because open-ended questions prompt participants to give deeper insights in a free-form answer without limiting them by any means, i.e. with a predefined set of possible answers, through the structured survey. The responses submitted are to be very favorable as they can disclose experiences, opinions, or concerns in detail other than anticipated by the researcher.

The findings of this study reveal that the most frequently addressed issues and deficiencies by the respondents in distance education were technical problems, lack of efficient communication and interaction, and personal distractions caused by either ambient conditions or lecturing methods, respectively. Time inefficiency was the least referred shortcoming. The positive equivalent of personal distractions which suggests greater productivity, on the other hand, was a frequently-cited asset overall. In addition to drawbacks, the negative commentary provided by the survey participants uncovers a substantial amount of students yielding a hesitant attitude about distance education. Even the participants who were pleased by the amenities of remote teaching are still in favor of attending face-to-face lectures when compared. The detailed analysis of the survey results and comparative assessments demonstrate the inadequate level of preparedness in regards to the practice of synchronous e-learning, with reference to the quality of services, systems, and technical support. Besides, both on behalf of students and lecturers, the implementation of distance education models requires prerequisite instructions and training in advance for clarifying the limits and possibilities of the method at hand thus; both parties could maximize their benefits.

The distant lectures executed within the scope of this study were mostly theoretical lectures, setting an example model for similar prospective implementations within the RMB curriculum where partner universities from different locations would all come together virtually. In consideration of both positive and negative feedback provided by the participants of this survey, especially once the technical problems are eliminated, the application of e-learning methods in the curriculum of architectural education would be beneficial. At this stage, the 'new normal' necessitates effective development and evolution of the traditional education methods in consideration of new educational models blended with online learning. It is necessary to experiment with new remote methods, especially for architectural/design education where face-to-face learning is essential, and in this context, more elaborated survey studies are needed that target the perspectives of both lecturers and learners in order to reveal the challenges and to work on new education models accordingly.

References

1. UNESCO Webpage, https://en.unesco.org/themes/higher-education/digital. Last accessed 18 May 2020
2. The RMB Homepage, https://www.rmb-eu.com/about/. Last accessed 10 June 2020
3. Ayres L (2008) Thematic coding and analysis. In: Given LM (ed) The sage encyclopedia of qualitative research methods, vol 1–2, pp 867–868. Sage Publications, Inc, Los Angeles, California
4. Auerbach C, Silverstein L (2003) Qualitative data: an introduction to coding and analysis. New York University Press, New York and London
5. Benaquisto L (2008) Codes and coding. In: Given LM (ed) The sage encyclopedia of qualitative research methods, vol 1–2, pp 85–88. Sage Publications, Inc, Los Angeles, California
6. Firmin MW (2008) Themes. In: Given LM (ed) The sage encyclopedia of qualitative research methods, vol 1–2, pp 868–869. Sage Publications, Inc, Los Angeles, California